ERNEST AUGUSTUS, DUKE OF CUMBERLAND
AND KING OF HANOVER

King Ernest Augustus

(*By L. Blanc*, 1841)

ERNEST AVGVSTVS

Duke of Cumberland
and
King of Hanover

by

G. M. Willis

9046
943

ARTHUR BARKER

London

First published 1954

MADE AND PRINTED IN GREAT BRITAIN BY
MORRISON AND GIBB LIMITED, LONDON AND EDINBURGH

PREFATORY NOTE

A BIOGRAPHY of Ernest Augustus must cover so many topics that it is impossible to give each of them adequate treatment in one volume. Considerations of space also required the shortening of the original manuscript of this book by one-fifth. In deciding what had to be sacrificed I gave preference to new material rather than that already to be found in printed works, and though this has caused much background and explanatory detail to be omitted and led to more exclusive concentration upon the subject of the biography, I am sure that this was the proper course to adopt, since his doings and writings shed new light upon so many fields of history.

. . . . . .

I have to acknowledge the gracious permission of Her Majesty the Queen to make use of material from the Royal Archives, Windsor.

Further, I am grateful to the following for allowing access to family papers :

His Royal Highness the Prince of Hanover ;
His Highness Prince Frederick Ferdinand of Schleswig-Holstein-Sonderburg-Gluecksburg, Trustee for the House of Mecklenburg ;
Count von Grote, the Honourable Sir Ernest Scott, K.C.M.G., and Baron von Linsingen-Gestorf ;

and for assistance in many ways :

Sir Owen Morshead, K.C.V.O., D.S.O., M.C., and Miss Mackenzie, M.V.O., of the Royal Archives ; Professor G. Schnath, Dr. Droegereit and Herr Huck of the State Archives, Hanover ; Alois Count von Kielmannsegg ; Mrs. Westland, late of the Control Commission, Germany ; Professor H. Butterfield, Professor A. Aspinall, Rector A. Asche, Dr. Neukirch of the Celle Museum, and, of course, the staffs of the British Museum and Public Record Office.

No acknowledgement implies responsibility.

5

CONTENTS

LIST OF ILLUSTRATIONS

CHAPTER I

BIRTH AND CHILDHOOD

THE circumstances of the birth of Prince Ernest Augustus were as unusual as everything else about his life.

In 1771, Charlotte, George III's demure and domesticated Queen, then twenty-seven years old, had already borne her husband seven children, and when they retired to their summer residence at Richmond Lodge, yet another addition to the Royal nursery was expected. It was not anticipated, therefore, that the Queen would take part in the ceremonies and celebrations of the King's Birthday on the 4th June, for which the Court returned to London.

In the morning there was a brilliant display at St. James's as members of the Nobility and the Diplomatic Corps presented their compliments and at one o'clock the guns at the Tower and in the Park fired the salutes. But when in the afternoon the usual reception was held, everyone was astonished to behold the arrival of the Queen, now in an advanced stage, and she surprised the company again by attending the ball in the evening. Perhaps that gave the impression that the event was not imminent and enabled Ernest Augustus to make his entrance into the world in the blunt and original manner which remained with him throughout life.

After the dancing the Queen retired as usual to her apartments in the Queen's House, as the red-brick palace which the King had recently bought from the Duke of Buckingham was then called. At about five o'clock, on the morning of Wednesday, the 5th June 1771, her labours began and at a quarter to six she was safely delivered of a baby prince. It had all happened so rapidly that none of the officers of state customarily present at a Royal birth, nor the Princess of Wales, had arrived in time, and only Dr. Hunter and two of the Queen's German ladies were present.[1] In the afternoon, couriers left from the King conveying the news to his fellow-monarchs.

At home the Queen's accouchements were regular occurrences, but at least they provided occasions to present compliments to her husband, and on the 13th the Lord Mayor and Corporation of

[1] *Gentlemen's Magazine.*

the City of London expressed their confidence that every increase in the Royal Family would prove an additional safeguard for " the Great Charter of Liberty, which, in consequence of the Glorious and Necessary Revolution, that Illustrious House was chosen to defend " and that it would prove equally a guarantee for their religion—momentous words for the fate of the being still in the cradle.[1]   The next important event in the young Prince's life was his christening, which took place on the 1st July in the Great Council Chamber, with the Archbishop of Canterbury officiating. He was given the names Ernest Augustus, which have a traditional place in the House of Brunswick.[2]

Nothing interfered with the routine of the Court until the death of the King's mother, the Princess Dowager of Wales, on the 8th February 1772. Her palace at Kew had been the scene of the King's own childhood and he decided that it should replace Richmond Lodge as his summer residence. In spring the family moved to Richmond as usual, while the late Princess's palace was being prepared for their reception. On the 14th May 1772 the King and Queen were able to move into their new residence, bringing with them their eight children, ranging from the ten-years-old Prince George to the eleven-months-old Prince Ernest Augustus, and thus began the latter's lifelong association with the village of Kew.[3] When he was an old man, he wrote [4] that " hardly a day passes over that I do not feel melancholy and wretched at being forced to leave my dear old Kew, where, though not born, still, I may say, I was bred, for hardly was life in me, that I was not carried there, and therefore having lived so many years there, both as child, boy and man, I look upon it as if I had literally been bred and born there. . . ."

In the days of his childhood the village consisted of little more than the houses surrounding the Green; behind them on the north side was the River Thames, on the south and west the fashionable residences of the Royal Family and the Nobility, and all round open country. At the lower corner of the Green was the quaint little Queen Anne church, whose beadle had among his many duties that of protecting the flocks and herds grazing on the Green. In the evenings, when it was sunny, the scene was brightened by the servants in their red liveries strolling about or sitting

[1] *Gentlemen's Magazine.*
[2] The sponsors were Prince Ernest of Meckleburg, the Queen's brother, in person, Prince Maurice of Saxe-Gotha, represented by the Lord Chamberlain (Lord Hertford) and the Princess of Hesse-Cassel, represented by the Countess of Egremont.
[3] *Rutton.*   [4] To the Rev. D. Delafosse, 14th June 1844. *van Thal*, p. 297.

under the old trees by the church. This was how Ernest Augustus himself nostalgically described it when often, in his old age far away in Hanover, he would picture himself back there.[1]

The Royal Family lived in the White House, the palace built by the King's father. George III had passed his secluded childhood in its gardens and now he returned there to lead a homely and retired life when he could rest from the heavy duties which his conscientious conception of kingship imposed upon him. Every year the Court moved to Kew in mid-May and remained there until the beginning of November, returning to London for the week in which fell the King's Birthday celebrations.

The King's special interest was farming and here he could indulge in it to his heart's content. He supervised all the details and the routine of the estates, and personally inspected the dairy-horses and cattle-stalls ; the elder Princes, and sometimes guests and visitors, were to be seen helping in the work and learning the farmer's craft. On Thursdays the public was admitted to the Gardens ; the Royal children could be seen at play and the King and Queen frequently came to the windows. On those days the Green was crowded with carriages, and parties also came by water accompanied by musicians, a picture which, immortalised by Handel's music, has remained as a souvenir of the Hanoverian Dynasty. The little Prince was faithful to the tastes of his race, and we read of a party given by his eccentric great-aunt, Princess Amelia, at her house at Gunnersbury, at which " There was also music for Prince Ernest, who, though only two years of age, has a fondness for it very extraordinary in one of that age. The moment he heard it, he danced about the room so ridiculously as made everybody laugh, then laughed so excessively himself as very much diverted the Princess." [2]

The Royal cradles were being filled regularly. The White House was soon too small and the older children had to give up the nursery to make way for the periodic new arrivals. They were allotted the various houses in the Gardens accessory to the King's residence. In 1773 the Prince of Wales and Prince Frederick were given an establishment in the Dutch House,[3] and in 1776 Princes William and Edward were moved to the house on the south side of the Green [4] and Ernest and Augustus, aged five and

---

[1] To the Rev. D. Delafosse, 2nd August 1845. *van Thal*, p. 301.
[2] *Journal of Lady Mary Coke*, 3rd July 1775.
[3] What is now called Kew Palace.
[4] Later known as Cambridge Cottage.

three respectively, to the house next door,[1] accompanied by Mr. Powell, their page, and Miss Sorrel, their lady dresser.[2]

The elder sons associated little with their younger brothers and so Ernest and Augustus, later to be so different from each other in every way, spent this period of their childhood together under the charge of their governor, Mr. Hayes.[3] All their activities were shared, including even that of the rather painful operation of inoculation, which they underwent on the 1st October 1775.[4] When at length Prince Adolphus [5] joined the establishment, having to leave the nursery to make room for Princess Sophia, born in 1777, the staff consisted of the governor, two instructors, two pages,[6] a pages' man, a porter and a watchman, and to cover the expenses the King asked the Prime Minister for an allowance of £3,500 per annum.[7]

Spartan simplicity and stern morality were the keynotes of life at Kew. The children rose early and went from their scattered quarters to breakfast with the strictest punctuality; the elder began their lessons, while the younger were taken out into the Gardens by their nurses and played there until lunch-time. In the afternoon there were more lessons or games, or perhaps some work on the model farm. Once a week the King and Queen, followed by the whole family, paired off according to age, toured the estate. In the evening the children would say good-night to their parents and then return with their attendants to their respective dwellings. From this programme there was hardly a deviation throughout the whole time in which the family was at Kew. These quiet and careless days were the only days of peace which the majority of this remarkable family were ever to know.

But they were already learning the duties of Princes. It is recorded that at the age of eighteen months Prince Ernest saw company after a reception [8] and now they were taken regularly on Thursdays (when the Court was in London) to the drawing-rooms at St. James's, where they received the compliments of the

---

[1] Previously that used by Lord Bute for study, appearing in a notorious scandal print in the *Annual Register* of 1767.

[2] *Rutton,* and *Mrs. Papendiek.*

[3] He had been a captain in the 58th Foot and served in the war in America.

[4] *Annual Register.*   [5] Born 1774.

[6] The two pages were Powell and Brown. The former subsequently became librarian to the Prince of Wales. Brown had been captain of a Lisbon government packet which had suffered shipwreck. Lady Charlotte Finch, in charge of the nursery, recommended him as assistant to Powell. When the latter gave up his post, he became sole page, continued in the service of the Princesses and eventually in that of the King himself.—*Mrs. Papendiek.*

[7] *Letters of George III.*   [8] *Lady Mary Coke,* 1st January 1737

company. From the age of ten they also attended the evening parties, where there were cards and music. The children all received visitors appropriate to their ages and played in the gardens with the sons and daughters of the local residents and retainers. Their birthdays were celebrated in the customary way, though those of Prince Ernest were always somewhat eclipsed by the events of the previous day.

Soon the question arose of tutors. With Augustus and his two elder brothers, Prince Ernest shared instructors in fencing, dancing, writing, drawing and riding, but now was the time for more serious studies. For advice, the King consulted the Reverend John Fisher (afterwards Bishop of Exeter and later of Salisbury), and he was recommended a Dr. William Cookson,[1] with whom he was fully satisfied. The other tutor was the Reverend Thomas Hughes, D.D., Clerk of the Closet to the King and Prebendary of St. Paul's and Westminster Abbey.[2] In their selection George III was obviously influenced by the stress which he laid upon religious instruction. This he considered more important than all other subjects, most of which were in consequence much neglected. " Nothing would please me more than to find that they pursue all subjects with industry and profit," he wrote of his children, " but I regard religious and moral instruction as the most important, because it must be mastered for the world to come as well as for the world of the present." [3] Prince Ernest was very keen and found much pleasure in reading the Bible.[4] In this, again, another of his lifelong characteristics began to show itself in his youth. Of all the sons of George III, he was the only one in whose life religion played a noteworthy part, and certainly it was his religious feeling which led him into his most questionable acts.

Apart from this, the education of the three youngest Princes in earnest seems to have been postponed. There was Latin, in which Ernest was quite outstanding, and they began Greek; German was not yet taught, but French Ernest soon spoke naturally, though

---

[1] An uncle of Wordsworth, subsequently Canon of Windsor. He always treasured the ambition of becoming a Bishop and the King sympathised, but whenever he recommended him for some dignity, the Government replied that another candidate had a prior claim and he died in 1820 with his ambition unfulfilled. He remained in contact with his Royal pupils, and when his son returned from soldiering in India the Duke of Cambridge endeavoured to use his influence towards finding him a post which would enable him to support himself and contribute to his father's peace of mind, but, again, the Government was unable to offer anything.—Add. MSS. and *Farington*.

[2] Grandfather of the author of *Tom Brown's Schooldays*.

[3] Directions for the Princes' instruction, *Frensdorff*.

[4] *Von Malortie*, p. 11.

he could not write it so well; in mathematics, he made progress, but was not keen. Everything else was at this stage very much neglected and when the three brothers went to university, their backwardness, compared with the German students, shocked the professors. Of history, their knowledge was confined to a little of the ancient world and a rather superficial reading of Hume's *History of England*, while of geography they were taught nothing. Ernest was, however, from his earliest days absorbed in the history of his ancestors and proud of being a Guelph. The other part of the curriculum was three hours' walking every day for bodily health.[1]

In all things, Prince Ernest was proficient, provided that his heart was in what he did. It was not that he refused to do unpleasant things, but that all his actions had to accord with his own inclinations and convictions. Thus we can see his character taking shape. He was quite impervious to outside influence and all his qualities, good and bad, were not instilled by instruction but came from within.[2]

Another characteristic now becoming evident, which some would call good and others bad, was his crushing wit and flair for satire. Weaknesses in those about him, including his masters, were to him a source of amusement and this caused no little embarrassment to those concerned. Reproved, he often tried to restrain himself, but soon his wit was pouring forth again.[3] It has brought much blame upon him, but, after all, it was an eighteenth-century mannerism and had he been, say, a Johnson or a Walpole, it would have brought him renown.

In August 1785 the Royal Family paid an unexpected visit to the University of Oxford, and the three young Princes appeared dressed in blue and gold. They stayed the night at Lord Harcourt's, near Nuneham, and Ernest considered it a great compliment that their host had allotted him a room to himself, with a yellow damask bed.[4] The family was growing up and now only Ernest, Augustus and Adolphus remained at home. Already plans were being made for their future.

Many considerations led to the decision that they should study abroad. The choice of Göttingen was a happy political and dynastic idea and it was also believed that there they would receive the best education. The weightiest consideration, however, was the

---

[1] *Frensdorff* and *Von Malortie*, pp. 7, 11.
[2] *Von Malortie*, p. 11.   [3] *Ibid.*, pp. 11–12.
[4] Princess Augusta to Lady Harcourt. *Harcourt Papers.*

distracted state of the family.   A rift had grown up between Ernest's
eldest brother, the Prince of Wales, and his parents.   The Whigs
cultivated it for political purposes, but it was aggravated by the
King's and perhaps even more by the Queen's intransigence.   As
the younger Princes grew up, there was no doubt that the Whigs
would attempt to win them into their camp too.   Besides this,
their protégé, with his debts and love-affairs, would, it was considered, exert a baneful moral influence.   To remove the Princes
well out of their vicinity was the only safeguard.   So, in March
1786, the authorities in Hanover learnt that they were to prepare
to receive the three younger sons of the Elector.

Before their departure the three young Princes were invested
as Knights of the Garter,[1] in order that nothing might be lacking
in their status.   On the 17th June two Hanoverian footmen arrived
in London, and on the 23rd the yacht *Augusta*, under Captain
Maitland, lay off Gravesend ; the next day the Princes' baggage
was sent off from Tower Wharf.   On the 27th the whole family
drove from Windsor for an entertainment which the King gave
in honour of the three Princes, and the following morning they
left their cottage at Kew and set off across the Green for foreign
parts, accompanied by Lord Howe, General Faucet and their
preceptor, Dr. Hughes.[2]

On their arrival at Gravesend the Princes were saluted by the
Tilbury garrison, the yacht, her attendant cutter and the many
spectators in small boats ; then, after dining with members of the
local Nobility, they embarked.[3]

At two o'clock, the *Augusta* was under sail with a fair wind.

---

[1] The investiture was held at St. James's on the 2nd June 1786.
[2] The papers describe him as going to Hanover with his pupils, but if he did so,
there is no trace of what became of him there, for he certainly did not remain.
[3] *Morning Herald* and *Public Advertiser*.

CHAPTER II

GÖTTINGEN [1]

GEORGE III had striven all his life to make himself the typical Englishman, but his reign in England was not outstandingly successful. In Hanover, however, though he had never set foot there, he found steadfast support throughout all his trials, even when he was engaged in wars in which no Hanoverian interests were at stake.[2] The long absence of their Sovereigns had not shaken the loyalty and affection of the Hanoverians.

One of the most patriotic institutions in the Electorate was the university which George II had established in Göttingen. After Rodney's victory at S. Domingo in 1782, the whole city was illuminated in blue and white, and reports reached the King from many sources of the fine spirit of the professors and students there. Jean de Luc, the Queen's Swiss reader, who paid frequent visits to the university, emphasised its high moral tone and the fact that nowhere was religion the subject of mockery. It can be imagined how such reports impressed the King and Queen, now so apprehensive lest their younger sons should come under the sway of the Prince of Wales, Fox and the other young Whigs and profligates. In any case, the Royal House was permanently established in Britain and the memory of its origin in Hanover was becoming increasingly remote. Some fresh link had to be devised to preserve the association with its native land, and so the idea of sending the Princes who were not in the line of succession to study at this renowned and loyal university was adopted as serving two purposes at once.

The first news of the King's decision reached Hanover in March 1786, and on the 18th May it was officially announced to the Electoral Privy Council. The Lord Chamberlain (of Hanover) was directed to order horses and servants, and officers arrived in Göttingen to make the necessary arrangements.

[1] Where not otherwise noticed, this chapter is based upon *Frensdorff*.
[2] Three Hanoverian battalions under Brigadier La Motte underwent the siege of Gibraltar, 1779-83.

For the position of chamberlain to the Princes the King had selected the fifty-year-old Colonel Carl von Malortie. This soldier came from the cadet branch of an ancient house of the Norman Nobility which had left France at the Revocation of the Edict of Nantes and gone into the service of Duke George William of Celle, brother of the first Elector of Hanover. He had served under Duke Ferdinand of Brunswick and particularly distinguished himself at the battle of Minden. He had hardly known domestic life, for he had become a widower after only two years of marriage. His appointment met with universal approval; he was sternly religious, had received a many-sided education and represented just the combination of qualities which the King and Queen wished to see in their children.[1]

His first task was to find accommodation worthy of his charges, and this was made easier for him by the offer of a prominent citizen, the publisher Dieterich, who placed his own house, the finest in the town, at the Elector's disposal. It was stately and spacious with flights of steps leading up to it, and lay at the hub of the life of the university. In the background was the university church of St. Paul and the Library, and the rest of the neighbourhood was occupied by dignified private residences. Behind the house lay the garden and courtyard, and on the north and east sides were narrow thoroughfares.

On the 28th June 1786 the Princes Ernest, Augustus and Adolphus, aged fifteen, thirteen and twelve respectively, left Gravesend on board the yacht *Augusta*. They were accompanied on the journey by Major-General Grenville (A.D.C. to the Duke of York), Captain Vandebutt and several naval officers. After a very rapid and uneventful crossing, the yacht arrived early on the 1st July at the mouth of the Schwinge, the river leading up to the Electorate's port of Stade. At about ten o'clock she docked and the Princes and their suite were received and entertained by Herr von Ende, the principal of the College of Stade.[2]

Frederick, the King's second son, was in Hanover. He had been some five years on the Continent learning the military arts and he was very pleased at the coming of his brothers. He set out the same day, accompanied by the officers who were to form the Princes' suite, von Malortie, von Uslar and von Linsingen. At half-past eleven the next day the party left Stade. The following morning they were in Hanover, and Ernest and Adolphus saw for the first time the city in which so much of their lives was to be spent.

[1] Nachrichten der Familie von Malortie.   [2] *Von Malortie*, p. 9.

Hanover had none of the grandeur of a German Residenzstadt. It was a typical mediæval town of narrow streets winding between tall half-timbered houses and enclosed by walls and towers. Sections of the old moat had recently been filled up to form boulevards which were named after the King and the Duke of York. Most of the time during which Hanover had been a Royal residence the Sovereign had been absent, and the long, tall and unsymmetrical Palace was still almost as it had been when it was converted from the old monastery of the Barefooted Monks in the seventeenth century—a miscellaneous cluster of buildings between the River Leine and the narrow Leinestrasse dominated by the gables of the chapel and with the other tall buildings of the mediæval city jostling up against it. Opposite lay the smaller and more modern Palace where the Prince of Mecklenburg-Strelitz had lived while in the service of his brother-in-law and where his famous daughters were born, and nearby were the mediæval Ducal arsenal and tennis-court and the horse-mill. To the north of the city lay Herren-hausen, as it has been said, like a very sophisticated perruque found unexpectedly upon the head of an old bumpkin. A long avenue led out to the Palace, whose pomp and splendour, like that of Cinderella at midnight, had suddenly vanished one night in 1714. The Elector's absence, however, had the effect of preserving the seventeenth-century character of the gardens, for everywhere else the baroque had been superseded by the English style.

It was in the small horse-shoe-shaped palace of Montbrillant on the Herrenhausen Avenue that the Elector's sons were now making their acquaintance with the city of their forefathers. They stayed several days and were shown the gardens, the fountains and all that was to be seen in Hanover. Ernest displayed a taste predominantly military and appeared daily at the parades. He was also entertained by several generals, including two under whom he was later to serve, von Freytag and von Wallmoden.[1] The Princes and their suite left Hanover on the 6th July and reached Göttingen the same evening. George III had given strict orders that simplicity had to be maintained and anything in the nature of a formal reception was forbidden. Instead, they were greeted on their arrival by their host, Dieterich, with a poem in which he spoke of the honour accorded his humble dwelling by the King. A few days later they were formally matriculated into the university by Professor Less.

[1] *Von Malortie*, pp. 9–10.

The Princes were to conform to all usual university regulations, and immediately after matriculating they had to lay aside their swords, since the carrying of these had recently been forbidden to students. For their usual wear, the King recommended plain blue jackets with, on gala-days only, gold buttonholes. They were distinguished from the other students only by the Stars of the Garter, with which they had been invested before their departure. Their governor had instructions not to allow too great a familiarity with anyone. The Princes were to mix with diligent and well-mannered young people without restricting themselves to those of any particular nationality or displaying any preference, and they were always to be accompanied by von Malortie or one of his staff.

The household was run on military lines and consisted entirely of Hanoverians. George III had wished to send an English clergyman but he was persuaded to place his confidence in Less. By this means it was hoped that the Princes would speedily pick up the tongue. As early as November 1786 the King considered that they had been long enough in Germany to speak German as the language of the household, and if they spoke anything but German at table they were punished.

At the head of the household was Colonel von Malortie. Under him was Captain von Linsingen, a member of one of Hanover's most ancient families. He soon impressed his charges with his efficiency. On the 4th August 1786 a butcher's shop four doors away caught fire in the middle of the night and the flames raged so violently that sparks began to fall on to the roof of the Princes' house. Von Linsingen, " who always has his eyes about him," as Prince Ernest said, quickly summoned some soldiers, who stood on the roof keeping it wet with pails of water. In one minute he had all the plate and papers packed in case it should be necessary to leave the house. The Princes slept until the dog which slept in their room barked at the commotion, " but Adolphus," wrote Ernest, " pretends he was awake but was so frightened as not to be able to speak." The following day they went over the smouldering remains of the two houses, which were totally destroyed.[1]

Next in rank to von Linsingen was Lieutenant von Uslar. He had served with the Hanoverians at Gibraltar and later became senior aide to his youngest charge, Prince Adolphus, in which capacity he fell fighting at Rexpoede in September 1793. Of lesser importance were Lieutenants von Jonquières and von Hanstein, and the only civilian on the staff was George Tatter.

[1] W.A. E. A. to King, 6th August 1786.

Though only the son of a family of Royal gardeners,[1] he had come into prominence through his abilities ; he was still under thirty but had seen much of the world and now he was appointed to help the Princes in their history and geography studies. So much for the notion that scope for talent was denied to the humbler orders in the eighteenth century.

At first there was the language difficulty, for the Princes spoke no German on their arrival and only one of the professors, Lichtenberg, could speak English. An attempt was made to use Latin, but it failed as the English and German pronunciations differed, so eventually French had to be employed until the Princes spoke sufficient German. Lichtenberg[2] taught them mathematics and physics ; he took great pains and illustrated his lectures with experiments. Greek, which they had just commenced, was not to be continued " because," the King said, " the time can be occupied with more necessary things."

The most important subject of instruction was still religion, and this was entrusted to the theologian Gottfried Less. The King had such confidence in him that he forbore sending an English clergyman to look after the spiritual well-being of his sons. Ernest was more and more impressed by the Christian faith[3] and, though this inclination had already existed in him, the teaching of Less probably had no little influence on the course of his life. Much of his letters to the King consisted of description of his progress in his religious studies. " We have just finished the first part of our course in religion," we find him writing. " The second is about Angels, which I find is extremely interesting for it has explained a great number of things which until now I have never understood."[4]

The King was well pleased and expressed his satisfaction to the Bishop of Worcester, an adviser who had meddled much in the affairs of the university and made no favourable impression there. " My accounts from Göttingen of the little colony I have sent there," he wrote, " are very favourable. All seem highly delighted and pleased with those that have the inspection of them. But what pleases me most is the satisfaction they express at the course of theology they have begun with Professor Less."[5] To von Malortie he summed up his son's qualities very accurately.

---

[1] Tatter's father was head gardener at Montbrillant and his grandfather had been appointed to the Orangery at Herrenhausen under George II.

[2] Lichtenberg had acted as the King's link with the university. He had lived in England from 1774 to 1775, visited the King at Windsor and was in regular correspondence with the King and Queen.   [3] *Von Malortie*, p. 11.

[4] W.A.   E. A. to King, 22nd February 1787.   [5] *Jesse*, II, p. 531.

" Ernest," he wrote, " is certainly the most impulsive ; Augustus is the laziest, but has a good heart. Adolphus has much zest and energy in learning and is better led with friendship than by other means."

On the whole the curriculum was varied and the studies certainly not superficial. In his letters we find Ernest drawing up tables of the history of the Empire from Henry I to Henry III, being examined by Heyne on Tacitus, which he considered the most difficult of the classics, and measuring the height of the tower of St. Jacob's Church by trigonometry. As he was studying so much in German, he feared that he might begin to forget his native tongue, and so, besides Goldsmith and Hume, he read regularly the *Spectator* and the *Guardian*.[1] He had lost none of his love for music and took steps to have this included in the curriculum, though apparently already at this age his sight was somewhat defective. " Having an hour to spare and wishing to learn musick," he told his father, " I have prevailed on Malortie to let me have a master which he granted me and I now take lessons on the flute, it being the only instrument that I could play for I am able to be as near the notes as I like." [2]

When they had been at the university a year, the Princes were considered able to attend the lectures ; hitherto their tutors had taught them in private. Now they heard Blumenbach on natural history, a subject which particularly appealed to Ernest. " The more I hear of Blumenbach's lecture," he wrote, " the more I like it, and what rendered it more interesting was that at the time he treated of lions, tigers and leopards, the very beasts were to be seen in life at an inn here in the town." [3] They also heard Martens on international law and the great legal authority of the day, Pütter, on politics, Imperial history, public law and all the other subjects with which Princes were especially concerned. Prince Ernest's feelings can be imagined when he showed them the *Genealogie Ascendente*, a collection of genealogical trees published in Berlin in 1768, and pointed out that among their ancestors, " back into far-away times none is to be found who is not of august rank."

Augustus was already showing different tendencies from his brothers. He was very delicate, and when the King learnt that he was growing fat, he attributed it to laziness and ordered plenty of walking. He was very often ill and could not pass the winters in

[1] W.A. Various letters to King.
[2] *Ibid.*, 11th January 1787.   [3] *Ibid.*, 22nd January 1787.

the cold north ; his brothers envied him for his travels in Switzerland and Italy, where he could indulge his interests to the full. " I suppose Augustus will bring back with him a case full of minerals and stones in which he finds a great deal of amusement," wrote Ernest to the Prince of Wales.[1] " He has already a pretty large collection left behind him sealed up 'till his return. As for me I do not know what amusement there can be in collecting stones, but as the French proverb says, *Chacun à son goût*, and it really is so for Augustus has a taste for stones and prints, the latter of which I have no objection to but however think there are more amusing ways of spending money." Ernest's interests lay in a different direction.

Ernest was born to be a soldier. True, few princes did not receive the baptism of fire, but in his case it was not merely a matter of *noblesse oblige*. From his earliest days he had cherished military ambitions and they had been strengthened since his coming to Göttingen. From there he had visited the armies encamped at Münden, Northeim and across the frontier in Hesse-Cassel, besides meeting and corresponding with some of the most illustrious soldiers of the time.[2] " In my opinion," he wrote to his father in 1789,[3] " a soldier's life is the best and finest in the world." His instructor in military subjects—artillery, fortifications and field surveying—was an officer named Hogreve, who had carried out the country's ordnance survey. When the French Revolution broke out the Prince could say that he was fitting himself for serving his country, for if " I could not show myself to be of service to my country, I should never venture to show my face to anybody." [4]

Meanwhile Ernest's outspokenness and, at times, sarcasm, were still in evidence despite all his efforts to restrain them. His staff was frequently embarrassed and von Malortie often found himself in a difficult position. Ernest's strong will and his governor's sternness were bound to clash eventually. The Colonel, however, displayed great tact, though Ernest, as he used to relate later in life, often treated him very coldly and for a whole year hardly spoke to him. " I thought I knew everything better than my teacher," he commented. " The chick is always more clever than the hen." [5]

" Here do I lead a very happy life," wrote Prince Ernest, with his Germanised word-order,[6] " being in company with a number of

[1] W.A., 2nd January 1789.   [2] *Ibid.* Various letters.
[3] *Ibid.*, 1st October 1789.   [4] *Ibid.*, 22nd October 1789.
[5] *Von Malortie*, pp. 11-12.   [6] W.A., 15th December 1787.

young Noblemen of all countries from the age of seventeen to twenty. Every week have we public concerts, assemblies and balls where nothing but joy reigns." In their house the Princes entertained lavishly in the English style, though nothing was allowed to interfere with the routine of either professors or students. In the summer the students went out into the woods round the town and the Princes participated in all these activities. In September 1787 the university celebrated its fiftieth jubilee with a week of festivities and, for the Princes, an examination.[1] Great sadness was caused by the news of the King's malady in 1788, and on his recovery there were again joyous celebrations. The Princes gave a ball in the traditional German students' style, with plenty of singing in which they themselves joined heartily, while all the students wore on their hats the motto " God Save the King ! " That July the town and country people celebrated with the Princes in the woods at Friedland,[2] south of the city.

By the time that the ceremonies of leave-taking drew nigh, Göttingen had had a hectic and exciting four years. The sojourn of the Princes had conferred great prestige upon the city and, of course, had brought immeasurable material prosperity. Here was no jealousy or hostility towards Princes, none of the " oppression " under which these states were supposed to groan in the eighteenth century. On the contrary, Princes and Nobles were highly desirable entities. Many institutions in Göttingen, including its famous riding-school, had been founded with the object of enticing them, and when, in 1788, Goethe visited Jena with the little sons of the Duke of Saxe-Weimar, the people begged them to stay. " This idea," he wrote to his master, " gives rise to a particular optimism. Everyone thinks of Göttingen, which possesses the English Princes."

Prince Ernest had long ago hinted to his father that he desired to take up a military career, and when he learnt that the Prussian Army was mustering in Silesia he could no longer forbear approaching him directly, for this was the army in which all aspiring officers hoped to receive their training. " What pleasure would it not give me to see it in my power to resemble so many of our ancestors who are renowned in history for their glorious deeds in battle," he wrote.[3] Hopefully he studied Silesia and the Seven Years'

[1] *Jesse*, III, pp. 15–16.
[2] The name means " Land of Peace " and the woods became famous after 1945 as they were used by so many refugees from the Russians to cross the zonal frontier.
[3] W.A., 28th June 1790.

War. For a long time he heard nothing, then at last, in October, von Malortie informed him of the King's plans for his future. He was not to train with the Prussian Army, but with his own Hanoverians, and he was to learn every branch of the service. Though it was not quite what he desired, the Prince was overjoyed that at least he was to become a soldier, and on the 14th October he expressed his gratitude to his father. He would, he said, spend the remaining two months at Göttingen in diligent study under Major Hogreve to fit himself for his profession.[1]

Augustus had already left Göttingen and at four o'clock one January morning of 1791 Ernest and Adolphus set out for Hanover, which they reached late in the afternoon. " I never quitted a town with more regret than I left Göttingen," wrote the elder.[2] " Everybody behaved with so much kindness to me that I should be one of the most ungrateful of men if I was forgetful of all I owe to Göttingen and its professors." Immediately afterwards the two Princes wrote a letter of thanks to the professors of the university, to which Pütter replied on their behalf in terms of devotion. He also wrote a personal letter expressing the view that " The memory of the four-and-a-half years' stay of the Princes and of that time so brilliant for our Georgia Augusta University [3] will certainly remain with posterity." [4]

---

[1] W.A.   [2] *Ibid.*, 11th January 1791.
[3] The University was named after George II, whose style as Elector was George Augustus.
[4] *Von Malortie*, pp. 13–14.

CHAPTER III

CAMPAIGN IN FLANDERS, 1791–93

AFTER a day's journey from Göttingen the two Princes arrived in Hanover, where they were to reside during their military training. Their first days there were not very encouraging. The weather was so inclement that they could not go out of doors and Adolphus contracted chickenpox and had to be isolated.[1]

They lived in the Palace on the Leine and were still under the charge of Colonel von Malortie. The King had implicit confidence in him and without him he would have been nervous of allowing them in a strange city in the company of young officers. He assured him of " how much I rely upon your prudence in a situation so changed with the further stay of my sons in Hanover. All great cities combine much good with much evil and youth is easily drawn to the evil if not guided by the advice of an elder. My sons seem to value you and that will prevent many difficulties." [2]

Field-Marshal von Freytag, Hanover's senior officer, was entrusted with the arrangement of the Princes' military education. After Hogreve's instruction, Prince Ernest was already far advanced, but he had set himself to learn the profession from the very beginning, and before commanding a regiment he wished to gain experience in all branches. First of all, he was to train under Captain von Linsingen of the 9th or Queen's Light Dragoons. The Hanoverian cavalry was quartered out on the countryside and the regiments assembled at certain times of the year to drill and exercise. The 9th trained in the barracks at Isernhagen, a straggling village a few miles from Hanover, and Prince Ernest travelled there three times a week. On the other days he continued his studies with Hogreve, besides still learning modern history with Tatter and keeping his French in trim with a M. Fleury.[3]

His exact status is not clear. According to the State Calendars and the lists of officers in the Hanoverian War Office, he received no commission until the 23rd March 1792, when he became a

---

[1] W.A., 11th January 1791. [2] *Von Malortie*, Appendix, p. 22.
[3] W.A., 11th February 1791.

colonel, though acting as captain.[1] Von Malortie, however, gives the date of his commission as the 17th March 1790, and it was on the 17th March 1840 that he celebrated his military jubilee. This must refer, therefore, to the military training which he received while still at Göttingen. Until 1792, it seems, he was merely a pupil attached to the various regiments.

The Prince used to leave for Isernhagen at nine and return at three o'clock ; he began the day then by riding with the dragoons, then exercising with them as a trooper and, at the end of the afternoon, he would command a party of eight or ten men as an officer. He was a better horseman than anyone in the regiment and was able to regard its riding with a critical eye. After only a month, von Linsingen considered him sufficiently advanced to exercise a small division in the riding-house, and at the end of the second, von Freytag gave him a place with the cavalry as captain.[2] These two officers took great interest in their pupil and, the Prince told the King, they treated him as if he were their own son. " I must own," he wrote, " never did a man take greater pains to teach another one something than Captain de Linsingen does with me." [3]

In June 1791 von Freytag appointed Major von Drechsel of the Footguards to train the Prince in infantry-work. This did not appeal so much to him, and it is easy to see that his turbulent and independent character suited him more to the rôle of a cavalryman than to the slower, soberer and more co-ordinated tasks of foot-soldier. He told his father that though he wished to learn in all branches, when this training was complete, " I hope Your Majesty will be so gracious and permit my remaining in the cavalry, and in the Queen's Regiment of Light Dragoons." [4] In October and November he began studying artillery, under a Captain Brown, and they more than once visited the foundry in Hanover to see the cannon being bored and polished.

The Prince now participated fully in the social life of the capital. He was introduced into the Billiard Club, to which most of the Nobility belonged,[5] and we find for the first time his fondness for the fairer sex showing itself. Apparently, he had many adventures in this field and he used to keep his brother Augustus, far away in Italy, informed of all that took place. " About the galavanting (?) affairs," he wrote, " here passes very little. Ompteda the tall

---

[1] Staatskalender and H.A. Des. 4le. xix. 6 and 7.
[2] W.A., 11th February 1791.   [3] Ibid., 11th March 1791.
[4] Ibid., 1st July 1791.   [5] Von Malortie, Appendix VII.

lieutenant is paying his addresses to Mad. de Arden, a very disagreeable and ugly little woman. Your friend Mad. de Wangenheim
has lost both her lovers. . . ." [1]

Of course this did not please his governor. It was the same
story with all George III's children—they were not allowed to
grow up. This treatment must have given rise to the situation in
which the Prince hardly spoke to the Colonel for a year, for he
wrote to Augustus, " Malortie and I are quite quarrell'd, we never
see one another but at table at dinner, for sup I never do. I am
mostly civil to him but otherwise we seldom ever talk together.
Linsingen is a good but very hot fellow ; I own I love him though
he has used me ill, and cannot be so with him as formerly, altogether
I am friendly and civil to all. . . . All my endeavours are to be a
good officer. You cannot but approve my conduct when you
come to consider that as Captain of Light Cavalry I refused to be
treated as a schoolboy, and to show what I am I never appear but
in uniform or a green frock which all officers are permitted to
wear, otherwise I have no other clothes." [2]

That his son was such a zealous and satisfactory officer should
have been enough for the King. However, he still permitted him
only the allowance which he had made for him on coming to
Germany at the age of fifteen, fourteen louis a month. The result
was that, like many young officers, he ran into debt and, the next
thing, was in the hands of a money-lender. This was a twenty-
eight-years-old riding-instructor from Göttingen. With the Prince
in his power he thought that he could safely issue cheques in his
name. [3] His victim tried to escape from his clutches by leaving
Hanover and so chose the moment to renew his requests to be
allowed to train with the Prussian cavalry, something which he
had always desired.

On the 26th July 1791 the Prince wrote to his father, [4] " For
certain reasons which my respect for Your Majesty prevents my
explaining any further, I wish to quit Hanover where, agreeable
as my stay there has been 'till now, it would hinder me from
employing my time to advantage. . . . Be so gracious dearest
father, listen to the entreaties of your son, let me accomplish myself
in a service which has the general reputation of being the best and
only school in which a young man who really has love for the
military profession can perfect himself. . . . I beg and entreat
Your Majesty that you will permit my quitting Hanover as soon

---

[1] W.A. To Prince Augustus 1791.   [2] *Ibid.* To Prince Augustus 1791.
[3] H.A., K.G. Hann. 9. Sec. Dom. III.   [4] W.A.

as possible and that I may enter the Prussian cavalry. Have the goodness to answer my letter soon, for with the greatest anxiety do I await your commands." The King had never understood the troubles of his family, and attributing his son's request to youthful restlessness, he refused it. The Prince dutifully resigned himself to his fate. He had not been prompted by such motives, he protested, " but many circumstances that determined my wish that could only be very tedious in a letter . . . but several reasons concurring to persuade me that a removal from Hanover would remove also some hindrances that have hindered since some time my improvement, the fault of which, I will not deny, lies partly in myself." The forger was eventually traced and apprehended and the whole story came out during the investigations which followed. He was not only Ernest's but also Augustus's creditor.[1] Thus the King's misguided strictness had the opposite result from that which he had intended.

Prince Ernest was, however, sustained by the prospect of active service. In May 1792,[2] before going into camp in soaking rain at Lüneburg, he wrote to his father that " The war on the Continent appearing now to be sure, I cannot help expressing my earnest desire of making a campaign and thereby enlarging my knowledge in the art of war. I should be very happy if Your Majesty would be so gracious and permit my serving as a volunteer with the Prussian army which is just marched." The next month he was allowed by von Freytag to spend a fortnight at Salzwedel (just across the frontier in Prussia) to see the Prussian troops as they passed through ; he was very much impressed, but thought that, upon closer inspection, the cavalry rode " abominably." [3]

The political situation was now so threatening that von Freytag began to organise a protective cordon on the frontier of the Electorate. Prince Ernest was still not sure whether he would be allowed to accompany his regiment, in which he was now colonel, should it be ordered to this duty. He begged the Field-Marshal and the King that he should, " for I think it would have been *shameful* for me who have now almost been two years with the Regiment, just to quit it as it was going to be employed against the enemy. As a Christian and a citizen, I should hope that it may not be necessary to march, but as a soldier I wish most earnestly that we may get orders to march . . . for I am doubly obliged as soldier and as son to defend my father's dominions, and I hope on

[1] H.A., K.G. Hann 9.   Sec. Dom. II.
[2] W.A.   [3] *Ibid.*, 17th June 1792.

every occasion that our regiment marches, you will permit my accompanying it, for the fellows know that I am vastly attached to them." [1] In November this permission was given. [2]

War broke out and the Hanoverian Army was taken into British pay, as the King thought that it should serve with his other troops rather than with the Imperial armies. [3] Prince Ernest's regiment, with three other cavalry, two infantry regiments and some artillery, was to form part of the Auxiliary Corps, as it was tactfully called. " All I wish," he wrote in his eagerness, " is that we were already in Holland, and that those murderers had received a complete drubbing." [4] According to the Prince's letter, they were to march on the 15th March 1793, [5] but according to von Malortie's biography, on the 13th. The Prince took leave of his friends in Hanover. " It will be for me," he wrote, " a very dis-agreeable moment when I take leave of Malortie, who has been with me almost seven years, and has taken the same care of me as if I had been his son." [6] The evening before the departure, he held a farewell reception and concert in the Concert Room of the Palace, then he joined his dragoons. The regiment, resplendent in its blue, white and red uniforms with gold lacing, its Royal Colonel at its head, left the barracks at Isernhagen and marched through the old streets of Hanover, entering by the Stone Gate, and out of the city through the Calenberg Gate. [7]

Most of the route lay across territory of the ecclesiastical posses-sions of the House until it reached Bentheim on the Dutch frontier on the 20th. There the last formalities and dispositions for active service took place, and the King's commissioner, Major Gunn, assembled the Hanoverian troops on the 2nd April, administered the oath to the King of England and took them into English pay. At the same time, it was ordered that the 9th and 10th Cavalry were to be employed on light service, that is to say, as skirmishers and outposts, a service which was after Prince Ernest's own heart. The Allied armies were faced by only a rabble, and the history of the world might have been happier had there been a competent general among them that April. They lay idle waiting for the reinforcements which their commander supposed to be necessary, and the French drew their corps of 30,000 men into an entrenched

---

[1] W.A., 2nd November 1792.   [2] *Ibid.*, 27th November 1792.
[3] The Hanoverian Army would otherwise have been obliged to contribute a con-tingent to the Imperial Armies.
[4] W.A., 7th February 1793.   [5] *Ibid.*, 1st March, 1793.
[6] *Ibid.*, 1st March 1793. Von Malortie died in Hanover on the 4th April 1798.
[7] *Von Malortie*, pp. 16–17.

camp at Famars, just south of Valenciennes. It was at this point
that the Hanoverian troops became engaged.[1]

Prince Ernest and his regiment marched into Tournai on the
29th and 30th April 1793, and he at once became the cause of a
violent quarrel among his superiors. The Duke of York had set
up his headquarters in the town, though for several days he had
been without a garrison. On the arrival of the Hanoverian troops
of his army, they came under the subordinate command of von
Freytag, the seventy-two-years-old veteran of the Seven Years'
War and supervisor of the Princes' military education. He took
his orders from the Duke loyally, but, of course, friction was bound
to arise. Already on the 8th April he had been in disagreement
with the British and Dutch generals at their conference in Antwerp.
The Duke of York was delighted that Prince Ernest should be
among the troops now coming under his command, for he had
not seen him for so long and he felt acutely the lack of warmth
existing among his staff. He ordered the Light Dragoons to be
quartered in the town and had a table of forty covers laid to welcome
him and entertain the generals and officers, including the Hanoverians, von Freytag and von dem Bussche. Having seen to this,
he rode out in the afternoon to survey the field of Fontenoy where
his unfortunate great-uncle had sustained defeat forty-eight years
before. From the outposts he learnt that the enemy was advancing,
so he ordered the Light Dragoons, who were still on the march
to Tournai, to make haste. The French proceeded no farther,
however, and he ordered the troops into their quarters. In the
meantime von Freytag, who had been in disagreement with the
quartering of troops in the town, ordered them to cantonments
outside, and Prince Ernest, much puzzled at all this countermand-
ing, had to accompany his regiment. The Duke of York had
been looking forward with eagerness to meeting his brother, and
on his return was extremely angry. Von Freytag and von
dem Bussche did not appear at table and now the Duke was
gravely offended, though they explained that they had had to go
to the walls to supervise the occupation of the town, as it had
been several days without a garrison.

The atmosphere did not improve. On the 1st and 3rd May the
British and Hanoverian troops formed a camp at Orcq, just west

---

[1] For details of the opening of the campaign see *Von Sichart* and *Fortescue*, IV (i),
cap. iv. and v. The Hanoverian corps marched from Bentheim through Overyssel
and Geldern to Emmerich, where it crossed the Rhine, crossed the Maas at Grave
and then proceeded through Antwerp to Tournai.

of Tournai, and on the 2nd, the French attacked the outposts at Rumes, to the south-west of the town. In the morning the Duke of York had ridden out on reconnaissance. He had acquainted the Field-Marshal of his intention, and when, on his return, he learnt of the attack, he hurried to him, expecting to find him in his quarters. However, he and von dem Bussche had also ridden out on reconnaissance despite the Duke's notice. The angry Duke ordered out the Light Dragoons and hurried off to Rumes, but von Freytag had previously given instructions that the regiments were not to leave their station. The officers were now in a dilemma and the troops did not depart until the Duke's orders had been repeated, when they were too late. Owing to their tardiness, only one cannon was taken, instead of the five which had been expected. The Duke of York was exasperated and again Prince Ernest had the misfortune to become involved, for the Field-Marshal excused himself on the grounds that he had wished to demonstrate to him how a reconnaissance should be carried out and that he had not thought that the Duke's absence would prevent his doing so.[1]

But Prince Ernest had been in action. As he was riding with von Freytag they met an Imperial officer, who told them that a party of the French were approaching. " I embraced with the greatest eagerness an opportunity of sharing in the sport," he told his family, as he wrote home about it the next day.[2] During the next few weeks, every two days each officer of his regiment was on duty at the outposts, bivouacking. " For four weeks I have been in no sheets," the Prince reported.[3] " All the bed that I have consisted of straw on which I lay a bearskin covering of my horse, and wrapped myself up in my cloak, and no man can possibly sleep better." On the evening of the 9th, the Prince's piquet was attacked and he drove the enemy back until he had to halt " for the rascals go into houses and fire from windows." [4]

Though personal relations between the Duke of York and the Hanoverians were strained, these disputes did not affect the conduct of the campaign, and as a single unit the Anglo-Hanoverian army broke camp at Orcq on the 19th May and joined the combined Allied army, whose commander, the Prince of Coburg, now considered himself strong enough to take the offensive. His intention was to invest Valenciennes, but preliminary to this it was necessary to drive the French from their camp at Famars, just to the south, and so the troops for this attack were to move up from their encampments. The Duke of York's army, marching via Baisieux,

[1] This episode is described in *Von Sichart*.   [2] W.A.   [3] *Ibid.*   [4] *Ibid.*

where it camped, arrived at Sebourg on the night of the 22nd. The attack was planned for the morrow. After an all-day battle, the French withdrew in the night and the main army was moved up to invest Valenciennes.[1] Famars thus lay in the path of a possible French relieving army coming via Querenaing and the Hanoverian corps remained there to safeguard the rear, with the Light Dragoons spread out as outposts around it. There was still no relaxation for the men, but at least they could forage, and on the night of the 6th June Prince Ernest led his regiment in a very bold and well-calculated raid at the village of Aspre, taking thirty cartloads of corn. In this way the cavalrymen made themselves independent of the bungling commissariat. In these little actions Prince Ernest soon became at home and began to show his recklessness even after such a short time in the field. The duties of the light cavalry were particularly hazardous and in a few days he gained experience which might have required months of campaigning in another arm. On the 21st June a French force far superior in numbers fell upon Querenaing but was repulsed by the Hanoverians, and on the 4th July, they were strengthened and pushed forward to Monchaux.[2]

The siege of Valenciennes, which was the principal operation, was proceeding well, but Prince Ernest was so far from the headquarters that he could not see what was happening. He therefore begged the Duke of York to let him remain attached to his suite until after the fall of the town, and this he did. The Prince watched the batteries open the bombardment and fire break out in several parts of the town, and that day, the 18th June, he wrote his first letter, since the opening of the campaign, to his eldest brother, the Prince of Wales.[3] " If only you were here ! " he concluded. After the fall of the city he was present when the garrison of Condé, to the north, laid down its arms, then he returned to his post at Monchaux.

The main French army was now concentrated at Cæsar's Camp, to the south of Bouchain. To attack this was the next task—the last which the Duke of York's army was to undertake in concert with the Allies—and the assault was planned for the 7th August. It was a swelteringly hot day and the march was very wearying. At Avesnes-le-Sec the Hanoverian column ran into the enemy outposts ; Prince Ernest's men, light cavalry and well in the van, had to engage a force far superior in numbers—some fifty horsemen—and were soon in grave danger. The Prince suddenly saw

[1] *Fortesque*, IV. (1), pp. 108-111.   [2] *Von Sichart*.   [3] W.A.

Prince Ernest Augustus at the age of nineteen

(*Artist unknown*)

Ernest Augustus as a young man

(*Artist and exact date unknown*)

Princess Frederica in her youth

(*Artist uncertain*)

that his little party had been cut off and surrounded. The choice
seemed to be between death and an ignominious captivity.   In
the latter event he could not have expected much mercy from the
murderers of Louis XVI, certainly not the treatment hitherto
accorded prisoners-of-war. Even more catastrophic would have
been the political consequences of a Prince of the Blood's becoming
hostage of the sansculottes.

So the little band fought back desperately. Prince Ernest was
thrown to the ground, and as he lay there with the hostile horsemen milling round him, his devoted dragoons, including their
sergeant, Beyerstorff, Corporal Freytag and Trooper Harjehausen,
shielded him with their bodies. His clothes were torn to tatters
by sabre-cuts ; one blade struck him on the right side of the head
and gashed it open. Certainly the whole party would have perished
had not some other cavalry galloped up and saved the situation.
The Prince had taken one prisoner with his own hands and " To
save my own life I saw myself necessitated to take the life of a
French chasseur." [1]

When the attackers arrived, the French had evacuated Cæsar's
Camp and so ended the last of the concerted actions which, if
followed up, would have led the Allies to Paris. We cannot go
into the details of the political necessity of capturing Dunkirk.
Suffice it to say that this was the task now set for the Duke of
York by the Ministers at home, and so the armies divided.

The 9th August 1793, following the actions round Cæsar's
Camp, was set aside as a day of rest before the march on to the
positions for the investment of Dunkirk. The plan was that the
corps immediately under the Duke's command should effect the
actual reduction of the city while von Freytag's Hanoverians
formed an army of observation, or protective cordon, round the
south of the besieging army, as at Valenciennes, distributed along
the Yser opposite the French camps round Cassel. Before the
Duke's corps was in position, the Hanoverians were to attack on
the 21st. At two in the morning Prince Ernest and his regiment
broke camp and crossed the Yser at Rousbrugge as planned, taking
the enemy by surprise and advancing to the Maison Blanche. The
Prince had to remain one and a half hours under concentrated
cannon fire, unable to move forward, but though grapeshot fell all
about him, he was not hurt. The next morning the enemy was
attacked and driven from Esquelbecque and Wormhoudt. At

[1] W.A., 9th August 1793 ; *Von Malortie*, pp. 17–18 ; Aus Hannover's militärischer
Vergangenheit.

E.A.—2

six o'clock in the evening, however, he made an attack upon
Esquelbecque with four thousand men, which was only repulsed
after much bloodshed. General Fabri sent Prince Ernest with a
reinforcement of grenadiers, and " such a smart and infernal fire
I never met with before. . . . In the moment of the affair I did
not feel but on riding early the next morning and seeing the spilt
blood my heart bled." [1] On the 25th he was engaged in another
attack upon Wormhoudt, and on the 2nd September the advance-
guard under Fabri was posted there.

But von Freytag was well aware of the dangers of his position,
for thirty thousand hostile troops under Houchard were concentrated against him. When at length they opened their attack, on
the 6th September, and he learnt that both ends of his long chain
of posts were being assailed by numerically superior forces, he had
to order an immediate withdrawal to Houdschotte through Rexpoede. Through ignorance of the latest French moves resulting
from the death of a despatch-bearer, the movement became dis-
ordered, the Hanoverian column was ambushed in that village,
and von Freytag and Prince Adolphus were taken prisoner for a
short time. Prince Ernest had under his command his own regiment and a squadron of the 7th Light Dragoons, and he was always
with the rearguard. It was, he said, impossible to describe the
scenes which he witnessed during the retreat, and only the bravery
of his men was their salvation, but he was proud to have
brought the troops under his command to safety. In a wood near
Houdschotte the enemy could have surrounded them.[2] Von
Wallmoden's [3] corps encamped at Bulscamp, near Furnes, until
the 10th September, when it joined the Duke of York's (which had
arrived the day before) at Furnes. The operations against Dunkirk
had been a complete failure.[4]

From the middle of September the Duke of York's army was
entrusted with the defence of Flanders on a front extending from
the coast at Nieuport to Cysoing, and Prince Ernest was stationed
at Campfie. On the 27th October he led two squadrons in a
charge, killing 120 of the enemy—" Never did I see such havoc
and chopping." [5] However, he now had leisure and he felt what
had not mattered much while he had been continuously engaged

---

[1] W.A., 26th August 1793.
[2] Ibid., 10th September 1793.
[3] Von Wallmoden (the reputed son of George II) succeeded von Freytag in command
when the latter was recaptured wounded.
[4] For the siege of Dunkirk see Von Sichart and Fortesque, IV (i), pp. 122–132.
[5] W.A., 29th October 1793.

—the meagreness of his allowance. It would have been very ungracious had the King refused to consent to an increase, nor did he.[1] Apparently, then, he recognised that after eight months continuously in the field, his son was grown up. But, as will be seen, this increase was only to be the sugaring of a bitter pill.

[1] W.A., 10th and 29th October 1793.

CHAPTER IV

ESTRANGEMENT FROM THE KING

THE conclusion of the campaign of 1793 was a mile-stone in the life of Ernest Augustus. Thereafter, he hardly knew peace or happiness. The event which marked this change in his fortunes was seemingly a trifle—his transfer to the Heavy Cavalry.

In November the campaign was already drawing to a close and the armies were taking up winter quarters. There were only small skirmishes and the time was spent in replenishing and preparing for the next year's fighting. The Hanoverians were in cantonments round Tournai and the King sent them new and warmer coats for the winter. Prince Ernest was now able to relax and participate in the social activities, the dinners, balls and theatre-parties, which the officers of the staff and garrison patronised in Tournai and the neighbourhood. At them he met the wives and guests of the English officers and it is from one of these, Lady Harcourt, that we have the first impressions of his nature from an English viewpoint.

" He is excessively liked here," she wrote,[1] " but would not do in England ; he talks too much, and I am sure he would not bear the life of Windsor three days. He is a true Hussar ; but open, lively and very good-natured." She met him frequently in the social life of Tournai and he came regularly to the evening parties which she gave to the British, Hanoverian, French Emigré and Austrian officers. " The Prince," she wrote,[2] " is beloved, and thought a good officer. . . . The more I see of Prince Ernest the more I like him. In good hands, he might be made a charming young man. I never knew a better temper or a kinder heart."

Like a " true Hussar " (though this description was not quite correct militarily) and a son of George III, he could not resist the attractions of the other sex and, through his recklessness and naiveté, Lady Harcourt found herself in extremely embarrassing circumstances. " He carried me yesterday," she wrote from Tournai on the 24th November,[3] " to a convent in the country,

<hr />

[1] *Harcourt Papers.*   [2] *Ibid.*   [3] *Ibid.*

where he was quartered for a week last summer. I had some difficulty in endeavouring to make him behave well. He would kiss the Abbess, and talk nonsense to all the poor nuns. I know a thousand traits of the goodness of his heart, but I fear he is too wild for England."

At the beginning of this November occurred the event which was to disgust and embitter the Prince and alter the course of his life for many years. He had been very happy in his regiment ; all the officers were his friends and he was deeply attached to his second-in-command, Major von Linsingen, his old instructor. But now he was transferred to the command of the Second Cavalry, a totally different arm of the service. Exactly why this was done is not clear, but Lady Harcourt gives a clue. The King, she wrote,[1] " has given him a regiment, but he is sorry to quit that of the Light Dragoons, in which he has served five [sic] years. He loves the officers of it like brothers. His own regiment is Heavy Dragoons, which is a service he hates ; but it is safer, and probably the King and the Duke of York have made this arrangement to prevent his being killed or taken, as his spirit and courage make him expose himself wherever he can."

The Prince wrote to the King on the 8th November to express his thanks, but these were purely formal, for he added, " I must own I am very sorry being put out of that career in which I was brought up." [2] On the 25th he went to Menin to prepare for his departure from the regiment. " There is not a more honourable, a more distinguished, and what is more, a more gentlemanlike corps of officers, and the idea of soon being obliged to quit them makes my heart bleed." [3] His new regiment was stationed in Bruges and there his A.D.C., Lieutenant von Ramdohr, found him some comfortable quarters.[4] He took up the command early in January 1794, commending von Linsingen to his father.[5]

The men were engaged upon the repair of their clothing, saddlery and equipment in preparation for the field again, and the Prince had to begin by clearing up the accounts, for he found the internal order of the regiment chaotic and, as he described it, great disharmony reigning. It was the most violent of contrasts to his late regiment. He decided that his only hope lay in a personal appeal to his father. On the 22nd January 1794 he wrote requesting fourteen days' leave. " My desire of embracing my parents is very great . . . as it is now near nine years since I have

[1] Harcourt Papers.   [2] W.A.   [3] Ibid., 26th November 1793.
[4] Ibid., 10th December 1793.   [5] Ibid., 6th January 1795.

not seen my family " [*sic*], he said.[1] He was now in the habit of confiding all his troubles to his brother, the Prince of Wales, and he wrote to him of his unhappiness a few days later. " I am damned to enter into the Heavy Cavalry, a service I am not made for and which I hate. I have written to His Majesty for a fortnight's furlough in order to have it in my power to speak with him." [2]

He received a reply from his father early in February. His request was refused and no reason was given. " My hopes of coming over to England and of seeing my father are vanished," he told his brother.[3] " It is impossible for a father to write a more affectionate letter, but at the same time I see clearly I am born to be the most unhappy of men ; all my projects, all my desires I see generally fail ; it is hard that I should be the only one of the whole family who has not been at home in nine years, but my complaints help nothing ; *tout est pour le mieux dans ce monde*."

It is difficult to explain why the King should have acted in this manner. Perhaps he was aware of the close friendship between the brothers and feared that the younger would join the Whigs, and, in general, the conspiracy against him. The Prince himself was very apprehensive and he told his brother that " Perhaps may it [*sic*] turn out my greatest misfortune that His Majesty has not thought proper to consent to my coming over ; for as he has not seen me since nine years, it is as if he never knew me, and his not knowing me may be of great mischief to me as things may happen." [4]

He was still endeavouring to introduce some order into the affairs of the regiment, hampered by the incompetence of his major, when it received orders to break up winter quarters and march to the environs of Rouselaere on the 23rd February to meet an unexpected attack. Hurriedly the Prince organised his troops, which was not easy as half of the clothing and saddlery was still in the hands of tradesmen for repair, and they left at six o'clock on the morning of the day appointed. They were then quartered in cantonments successively at Zonnebeke and Rhorlegen. The Prince was still hoping little by little to perfect the regiment and restore harmony, for his predecessor " let everything go as it would." [5] But he found some comfort in the prospect of once more being quartered in familiar surroundings.

On the 24th March [6] he wrote to his brother from Rhorlegen, " I am under orders for marching to Tournai, which is for me one

---

[1] W.A., 21st January 1794.   [2] *Ibid*.., 25th January 1794.
[3] *Ibid*, 4th February 1794.   [4] *Ibid*., 12th February 1794.
[5] *Ibid*., 25th February and 24th March 1794.   [6] *Ibid*.

of the pleasantest garrisons, as I know almost all the pretty girls in the town, which will make up for the *ennuyant* time that I have passed since my quitting Bruges. . . . To tell you the truth, I am sick of war. From the bottom of my soul I am a soldier, and by honour I know nothing else, one can know but one thing well, and I flatter myself I give myself trouble enough ; but when one does not serve willingly, that is no service ; in my former regiment when I was but a Lieutenant-Colonel I was the happiest of men, I was in a society of gentlemen, many young noblemen, altogether the Ninth was the finest in His Majesty's service ; and now to be put in a Heavy Cuirassier regiment, where, first of all, all the officers are most of them blackguards, where the greatest disharmony, what the most disagreeable thing is reigns,[1] all that by God breaks my heart. . . . I intend as soon as this campaign is over to quit unless His Majesty gives me the Ninth Regiment which will be vacant. . . . If anybody else gets the regiment, I should break my heart. . . . I am only very very happy to hear from everybody that you dear brother are *my friend*, remain so, and I shall be very lucky ; for as far as I hear, I am afraid I have some enemies t'other side of the water, God knows what I have done to make them so. *Mais helas, il parait je suis né sous une étoile malheureuse* —better times come, *remain only my friend* and then I am sure."

Tournai was still the centre of social life. There were now four of the Princes with the army, the Duke of York, Princes Ernest, Adolphus and William (of Gloucester), and Lady Harcourt gives us glimpses of them at parties and in the theatre. In April the campaign was resumed. Clairfait, the commander of the Hanoverian cavalry, had concentrated most of his squadrons at Marquain, west of Tournai, and on the 19th he rode out thence on a reconnaissance towards Lille and the French camp at Flers. Prince Ernest accompanied him with his regiment and they came under fire. They drove back the French posts as far as the fortifications of the village of Hellemes, but fierce artillery fire prevented a further advance. Clairfait and the Prince were riding together about twenty yards in front of their ninety men, headed by Major von Einem, when a ball from a howitzer passed just between them and shattered the Major's leg. He died a few hours later. Twenty-four men had been wounded.[2] On the 24th, at Villers-en-Cauchies, Prince Ernest led his regiment in a cavalry skirmish, during which it bore heavy losses.

[1] The Prince has here put a German construction into his English.
[2] *Harcourt Papers.*

The army was now drawn up round Tournai and there a fierce battle developed on the 10th May. Prince Ernest had charge of two squadrons and a battalion, which were ordered to strengthen the outposts. He and his men were forgotten by the commanders and almost surrounded. Cannon-balls rained among them and the horse of the orderly following him was killed. The Prince's hand let his bridle fall and he said to his aide that he was wounded. He believed at first that a small ball had struck him, but then he thought that he had been mistaken and that nothing was wrong until some unpleasant symptoms began to show themselves. What had happened was that the blast of the ball which had fallen behind had injured his left arm and, though this did not become apparent until much later, his left eye.[1] In his despatch,[2] von dem Bussche said, " The Princes Ernest and Adolphus have distinguished themselves by the coolness hereditary in their august house. The first has also received a slight contusion in the arm—probably from the blast of a cannon-ball." The day after the battle the Prince wrote home that " Although I have been in a most horrid fire for some hours, yet I have been tolerably lucky, I have got a small contusion on my left arm." [3]

Soon the wound began to show itself as serious and the Prince had to leave the regiment and go back to Tournai. " My arm," he reported, " is as stiff as if it were dead, except the fingers, which I cannot straighten, and my elbow, which pains me much." He could not even hold a fork.[4] All the time, he knew that his men were still engaged out on the field and his spirits sank very low. The surgeons told him that it would be some time before the wound would heal.[5] On the 15th the Emperor arrived and the Prince was presented to him " like a cripple," with his arm in a sling.[6] For one of his exuberance it was unbearable to feel an invalid at a time like this. " God knows what it will do," he commented when his elbow was set in plaster. Leeches were applied.[7] On the 29th the surgeons agreed that, instead of improving, the wound was worsening.[8] The Prince was on the verge of despair. " I am still as Your Majesty will see obliged to remain here in an inactivity which grieves me all the more, as 'till now I have prospect of cure," he informed his father at the beginning of June, " I have tried every possible means, rubbing

[1] W.A. To Prince of Wales, 11th May 1794.   [2] *Von Sichart.*
[3] W.A. To Prince of Wales, 11th May 1794.
[4] *Ibid.*, 13th May 1794.   [5] *Ibid.*, 15th May 1794.
[6] *Ibid.* To Prince of Wales, 15th May 1794.
[7] *Ibid.*, 27th and 29th May and 3rd June 1794.   [8] *Ibid.*, 29th May 1794.

in opodeldock,[1] applying leeches, and by blistering my arm, but all alas without any effect. I am in the horridest state possible, and Heaven knows when I shall be cured." [2]

When he and his cousin, Prince William, visited Lady Harcourt in Tournai, she shared his pessimism. "I fear Prince Ernest's arm is a bad business," she wrote.[3] "The wind of the ball is often worse than a wound, as it deadens all the flesh; it is much swollen, is in a sling, and he has hardly any feeling in it, or use of it. He has an excellent heart; I wish him to go to England, but not to stay there long." Astonishingly, she adds, "I find General Harcourt, being in the left wing, which only marches to appear to cover Lille, will be absent but a few hours. Prince Ernest will go, lame as he is; think of the danger of riding with one arm in a sling, increased as it is by his not seeing ten yards before him."

At last the King gave his wounded son leave to return and convalesce, though, it was feared, too late. After all these years, he would be with his family again and, above all, he would see his elder brother with whom he had, through their letters, become more and more intimate. On Friday night, the 30th June 1794, after an absence one week short of eight years, he arrived in London.

There were two Courts in England—that of the King and Queen and their daughters, who were still strictly under parental control, at Windsor and Kew, where life differed little from in the old days, and the Prince of Wales's more elegant rival Court at Carlton House and Brighton. The brothers George and Ernest were both in difficulties. The Prince of Wales was about to marry his cousin, Caroline of Brunswick, and this gave rise to many delicate negotiations in which Prince Ernest played a large part. It was he who induced Mrs. Fitzherbert to agree to break off relations with his brother.[4] On his side the Prince of Wales was exerting his influence to obtain an establishment—that is, an independent status and income, which was so badly needed—for his brother.

However, Prince Ernest had to join the Court at Windsor and participate in its activities. In June he went with the King and Queen and his sisters for a four-day visit to Portsmouth. They inspected the Fleet, launched a man-of-war and ran aground in the Royal Barge off Cowes for five hours. Otherwise these months were passed at Kew or Windsor. On Sundays the family attended worship in St. George's Chapel; the days consisted of "airings"

---

[1] Balsam ointment.   [2] W.A., 3rd June 1794.
[3] *Harcourt Papers.*   [4] W.A.

E.A.—2*

round Frogmore and the neighbouring countryside, dinner in the
Queen's apartments and the walk on the Terrace in the evenings.
One day the Royal Family went up the river in the Royal Barge
from Windsor to the Earl of Inchiquin's at Clifden, where dinner
was served under the shade of the trees in the garden. It was all
very peaceful, and Prince Ernest could not have had a more idyllic
rest from fighting the revolutionary armies across the Channel,
but what he desired most was to be with his brother, the Prince
of Wales. They had so much to discuss and decide and, perhaps
for this reason, any intimacy between them was prevented as much
as possible. On the 24th July he wrote,[1] " It is exactly as if I
poor devil were intended never to have a moment's pleasure, only
think, all my fine prospects of coming and seeing you dear brother
at Brighton are at once vanished ; *notre très cher père* thinks sea-
bathing will comfort him in his old days, and therefore Weymouth
is to be visited . . . but I must go on in the old humdrum manner,
to-day, to-morrow and evermore."

On Friday, the 15th August, the Royal Family—Prince Ernest,
his parents and his sisters—arrived in Weymouth and there they
diverted themselves sailing in the Channel, or at the theatre, where
they saw a performance of *She Stoops to Conquer*, and in walking
along the Esplanade in public in the evenings. It was thought
that the French might attempt a descent upon Weymouth to carry
off the Royal Family and for that reason numerous frigates were
standing by and there was a large military camp in the vicinity.[2]

Prince Ernest was thoroughly disgruntled. This sort of life
did not suit him, as Lady Harcourt had foreseen. His physical
sufferings did not make him any happier. In August, *The Times*
reported that " Prince Ernest is drawing plans of different fortifications, but is much interrupted from weakness of sight. His
Royal Highness continues lame in his left arm through the wound
he received on the Continent." By the 30th, it was reported that
he had lost the sight of one eye. Altogether, he was very bitter.
One day there was an alarm when some ships were mistaken for
the French and he was interrupted in the middle of writing a letter
to his brother. When he resumed, he commented that " I for my
own part could not refrain from laughing when I was told of the
French coming, being convinced the idea of landing at that time
of night was ridiculous." [3]

[1] W.A., 24th July 1794.
[2] Contemporary journals and Court Circulars, especially the *St. James's Chronicle*.
[3] W.A., 14th September 1794.

However, he could not be kept from the Prince of Wales for ever. On the 27th September the Court returned from Weymouth and in the first week of October he took up residence with him at Carlton House. It was then that he carried out so many important and secret personal missions for his brother. But it was then, and possibly for that reason, that he was ordered to return to the army, having been promoted to the rank of major-general on the 18th August. "I am almost broken-hearted at going away," he told his brother, "but don't think *I am afraid* ; no, Ernest is no coward ; however, I am very sorry." [1] His feelings about returning to the campaign were very different from those with which he had originally set out for it.

On the 25th October he and his two brothers went to Windsor and he took farewell of the family in the midst of the celebrations of the anniversary of the King's accession. He was too overwhelmed to speak to the Prince of Wales as he left with William in the evening, and from Sittingbourne, on the journey, he wrote a letter of farewell explaining, "My heart was too full last night to say anything to you, not that I felt less." [2] From Sittingbourne he went straight to his port of embarkation, Margate, accompanied still by the Duke of Clarence. They arrived the next day and breakfasted with the unhappy Mrs. Fitzherbert. She received them very civilly, making no allusion to the recent painful events, and lent them her phaeton. They also visited the Duchess of Rutland and dined with Lord Cholmondeley. The wind had become favourable for the first time in three days, and Prince Ernest was about to go on board his ship when Admiral Payton sent instructions to Captain Patterson, her captain, to sail at once without the Prince as three French frigates had yesterday run out of Dunkirk and were cruising in the vicinity. [3] There was now no ship available, and on the 28th the Prince suggested that he should sail from Dover, "but as a soldier I remain at my post till further orders." He was eventually told to sail from Dover. [4]

Everything was in keeping with the unhappy atmosphere of his journey. The crossing was rough and the Prince was "dead sick." He arrived at Helvoitsluys late at night on the 30th October and wrote to his brother a letter betraying the deepest depression and concluding, "Excuse this horrid scrawl but I am in an infernal alc house, rather like Catharine's Wheel at Colebrook. God were

---

[1] W.A., 9th October 1794.   [2] *Ibid.*, 25th October 1794.
[3] *Ibid.*, 26th October 1794.   [4] *Ibid.*, 28th October 1794.

I back in old England ! " [1] The next day he went on to the Hague.
He had dinner with the Princess of Orange and left immediately
afterwards for the army as a great attack was shortly to be made
" and you know I would not remain absent, my first entry will be
in fire, perhaps an opportunity may offer itself for me to distinguish myself, and I'll try to render myself worthy of the *red coat*
I have now on." [2] On the 3rd November, at eight o'clock in the
evening, he arrived at the Headquarters at Arnhem. " My reception was *civil*," he told his brother, " but not such as you dearest
brother would give me." [3] The very next day he was plunged
into action.

The armies were in a critical position along the north bank of
the Waal and in the first week of November the French had begun
to menace their position by erecting batteries at Looi, a little
above Nijmegen. The only way to maintain the line was by their
demolition. To accomplish this, von Wallmoden planned a sortie
of British and Dutch infantry and Hanoverian cavalry ; a squadron
of the Second Regiment was detailed for service with the latter.
Major-General or no, Prince Ernest accompanied them and
astonished the world with his most celebrated exploit.

On the 4th November the force advanced. The infantry
jumped into the French trenches without firing a shot and put
those of their occupants who remained to the bayonet ; the batteries
were destroyed and their fire checked for some days. Prince Ernest
was leading his regiment when he encountered hostile horsemen
and, in defending himself, broke his sabre. Seeing this, a French
dragoon engaged him and aimed fierce blows at his head. The
Prince parried them with the stump of his blade and swung his
arm round the man's body, then he tore him from his saddle and
carried him, no doubt somewhat stunned and bewildered, back to
the British lines a prisoner ! [4]

But despite his brilliant exploits on the field, Prince Ernest was
subjected in camp to continuous humiliation. Its object is not
clear, or whether indeed it was intentional or merely a chain of
unhappy coincidences. The climax was reached on the 23rd
November. Prince Ernest was proud of his military experience
and of the confidence which his commanders, the Prince of Coburg,
Count Clairfait and von dem Bussche had reposed in him. " Now

---

[1] W.A., 30th October 1794.   [2] *Ibid.*, 1st November 1794.
[3] *Ibid.*, 4th November 1794,
[4] *Von Malortie*, pp. 18, 19. This is one of the few events of the Prince's youth
which is generally known, though it is not clear from which source, since von Malortie
has certainly never been read in England.

on my return here to the army I was yesterday [22nd November] told by the Duke [of York] I should join my regiment and take command of it ; as colonel I commanded 3000 men, now as major-general having sacrificed health and everything for the good of my country to be put back to the command of a regiment, when three younger major-generals have brigades and corps is a thing by God I cannot bear ; I had yesterday a very—[?] conversation with the Duke and told him if he absolutely ordered my return to my regiment, a thing uncustomary for a major-general, I should— [?] to put it out of his power to say I have disobeyed orders, but that immediately on joining the regiment I should throw up my commission and retire. For this was an affront and dishonour to me." Bitterly he wished that he were wounded and he appealed to the Prince of Wales to obtain for him a commission in the British Army.[1]

"Only try and get me over to be there at the marriage," he wrote.[2] If all these humiliations were inspired by the King, they were certainly calculated to drive the Prince into the hands of his enemies. But never once did he, like some of his brothers, translate his personal grievances into political opposition, though the Whigs would have been eager to exploit them and become his champion.

Adolphus, at least, was pleased to see him. They met as their regiments were erecting huts for the winter. "I was rendered very happy by the arrival of Ernest," he wrote. "I found him very well ; but his sight is grown very bad, and in my opinion much worse than when he went over to England."[3]

All remained quiet until the end of the month. The Hano-verians were quartered between the Nijmegen-Arnhem road and the Pannerden Canal and Prince Ernest was with the Headquarters at Arnhem. The right bank of the Waal offered ideal winter-quarters, and considering the campaign over, the Duke of York left for England, leaving von Wallmoden in command.[4] The French were also badly in need of winter-quarters, but now a certain Dutchman who wished to revenge himself upon his own country for some private grievances prevailed upon the French Government to order Moreau to cross the Waal. On the 11th December he attacked. The Allied army desperately needed to

---

[1] W.A. To Prince of Wales, 24th November 1794.
[2] *Ibid.* To Prince of Wales, 11th November 1794.
[3] *Harcourt Papers.*
[4] He could only issue orders to British troops through General Harcourt.

go into cantonments, for the cold was severe and sickness rising ; Prince Ernest was suffering from rheumatism and his brother Adolphus was ill.[1]   Only a thaw would enable the army to maintain its position.   The weather improved and so it was believed that the present line would be defensible.

Hopes were dashed on the night of the 14th January 1795.   The wind blew fiercely and in the morning the ice was thicker than ever.   Late in the evening, therefore, von Wallmoden ordered the withdrawal of the army behind the Yssel.   Prince Ernest commanded the rearguard of one of the columns in many skirmishes. The conditions of the army were now frightful.   There were eighteen degrees of frost.   Men were frozen as they slept, or lost limbs ; the very water in their eyes froze, their hair was stiff and they were covered with icicles.   To make matters worse, bread and forage were short, for the district was so bleak and barren that it hardly fed its own inhabitants.[2]

To have maintained discipline under such conditions was a great triumph for von Wallmoden.   He knew already that soon a retreat would be necessary right out of Holland, across the Ems to the lands of Osnabrück and he prepared accordingly.   The march began on the 28th January across miles of snow- and frost-covered heath with never a tree or house in sight.   In the first days of February the army crossed the Ems and the Hanoverians took up quarters in the neighbourhood of Münster.   " Your army is destroyed," wrote von Wallmoden to the Duke of York.[3]

From Münster, Prince Ernest wrote to the Prince of Wales on the 19th and appealed to him to speak to Pitt, as his return to England depended so much upon his receiving an establishment.[4] He also told the King of all the hardships and of the pains which he suffered from rheumatism and " a putrid fever." [5]   But at least, the hell of the winter was past.   All, British and Hanoverian, were gratified to be in Germany, where the inhabitants behaved towards them with great kindness and friendship, in contrast to the hostility of the Dutch.   The relief of the British troops at being among Germans and the impression made by Osnabrück are well described by Lady Harcourt.

On the 22nd, British troops began to withdraw altogether from the campaign.   There was some bitterness at this, but Prussia was

[1] W.A., 27th November 1794.
[2] For details of the campaign and retreat see *Von Sichart* ; *Fortescue* IV (i), pp. 315–322, and the *Harcourt Papers*.   [3] *Von Sichart*.
[4] W.A.   To Prince of Wales, 19th February 1795.
[5] *Ibid*.   To King, 28th February and 8th March 1795.

also finding its continuance impossible. Much against his will, King Frederick William II found himself obliged to negotiate for neutrality. Hanover was defenceless, with no army left in a fighting condition, and abandoned by the British Government. It was the story of Kloster Zeven over again. After a very difficult struggle with himself, George III, in order to preserve his Hanoverian dominions and spare them the horrors of war, decided to separate his interests as King and Elector and agree to the inclusion of Hanover within the neutral zone to be protected by a Prussian cordon.[1]

Throughout this time, while with the army behind the Ems in East Frisia, the Second Cavalry was cantonned in the village of Rhaude and Prince Ernest's spirits sank to just about their lowest ebb. " I am now here in quarters in the most abominable, the most wretched country I ever was in in my whole life," he wrote on the 24th April.[2] " Not a tree to be seen, six miles from my quarters, and one risks to [sic] break one's neck every time one rides out, as there is nothing but bogs all round this country." He was still tormented by rheumatism, he said. For five weeks he lived with the local pastor, and fifty years later he remembered the unhappy time which he had spent there and made a presentation to the church of an inscribed silver communion-cup.[3]

On the 26th May, Prince Ernest, commanding a brigade, left East Frisia and went into cantonments in the contiguous provinces of Münster and Diepholz. Hanover was now behind the Prussian cordon and the Prince's regiment was quartered at Goldenstedt, south of Wildeshausen. On the 21st and 22nd it went into camp and he was ordered to place himself under the divisional commander, Major-General von Wangenheim. This was his brother Edward's former governor, who had not been a soldier for twelve years. " I am now a mere *nothing*," he wrote. " I own were it not out of attachment for my regiment, which would lose by it, I would send in my resignation to-morrow." [4]

The climax of his despair was reached when he realised that the sight of his left eye was now rapidly failing. On the 27th September [5] he wrote to his father and pleaded to be allowed to return and consult Dr. Wathen Phipps. " I am in the horrid apprehension of losing it," he said. There was no reply.[6]

---

[1] *G. S. Ford.*   [2] W.A., 24th April 1795.   [3] *Von Malortie*, p. 19.
[4] W.A. To Prince of Wales, 28th August 1795.   [5] *Ibid.*
[6] *Ibid.* To Prince of Wales, 11th December 1795.

On the 10th November the Prince's brigade moved from Goldenstedt to the district round Hameln (Hamelin) and from his headquarters in the Pied Piper's city he was able to visit Hanover at last. Having put his regimental affairs in order, he arrived there on the 9th December and consulted the oculists Lampe and Richter, from Göttingen. Both gave their opinion that he was suffering from a cataract and that the eye had to be operated upon, but, they said, a period of observation would have to precede the operation, so that the surgeon might choose the right moment for it. Von Wallmoden agreed that he should return home for this, so he immediately wrote a renewed appeal to his father, pleading that he had lost the eye in serving him. . . . " I therefore most humbly entreat Your Majesty to permit me to return home directly as it is of the greatest importance to my recovery." [1] At the same time, on the 11th, he wrote to his brother,[2] asking him to exert all his influence and he indicated the measures which, in his desperation, he was now driven to consider.

" Is it not hard," he wrote, " to have lost the use of an eye in doing my duty and exposing myself for my country, and not to have got as yet an answer from His Majesty though I have written four times for leave to return to my country? . . . Now I am determined if I don't get an answer from His Majesty to return without leave, for I have already sacrificed enough, and will not sacrifice my eye for any whim of others. My intention is to retire to Kew and live quietly there till I am recovered."

His brother Adolphus added his pleas. He wrote to the King on Christmas Eve that he felt it his duty to report that Ernest suffered acutely from his arm and his eye. Richter, he said, was too old and shaky to be entrusted with the operation and the Prince should be allowed to return immediately.[3]

Eventually, in the first days of 1796, the King yielded to these entreaties, to which those of his own brother, the Duke of Gloucester, had been added, and granted permission for his son to return. The Prince was eager to leave the cold climate at once, but he did not leave before he had settled all the affairs of his regiment and that needed three weeks.[4] It is not clear when the regiment returned to Hanover. Von Malortie writes that it left the field for Hanover, with the Prince, on the 29th November

---

[1] W.A., 11th December 1795.
[2] Ibid. To Prince of Wales, 11th December 1795.
[3] Ibid. Prince Adolphus to King, 24th December 1795.
[4] Ibid. To King, 6th January 1796 ; to Prince of Wales, 9th February 1796.

1795, that he led it through the streets of the city, then rode up to the Palace quite alone, dismounted before the arch of the monastery-wing and went unnoticed to his room. On the 11th December, as has been seen, the Prince wrote that he had arrived in the city two days before on a private visit.

After paying a visit to the Duke of Brunswick with Prince Adolphus, he left on the 2nd February 1796 for England.

CHAPTER V

1796–1802

WHEN Prince Ernest Augustus returned to England with so many grievances against his father, his most obvious course to obtain redress was to join the Whigs and the opposition. There he would have found willing support, for there is one privilege which even the wildest of democrats never fails to accord Royalty. Every class of society has its black sheep, its unsuccessful and unpopular members who are eyed askance by their fellows, but when they are persons of high rank, they have a source of redress not open to lesser mortals—they can allow themselves to be adopted and championed by the democrats as victims of Court reaction. But Prince Ernest scorned such a revenge. Consistency and principle were to be the most conspicuous features of his character, and so his family troubles were not now reflected in his political conduct.

He arrived at Carlton House at a late hour on the 15th February 1796, and the next day went with his brother to join the rest of the family at Windsor. Now they were alarmed at the state of his health. . . . " His left eye is shockingly sunk," the Prince of Wales wrote to the Queen, " and has an amazing film grown right over it," while a newspaper reported that " Prince Ernest is much afflicted with an inflammation in his eye."

As he had planned, he put himself under the care of the oculist, Dr. Wathen Phipps, and lived quietly in the house on Kew Green which he had occupied with his brothers before going to Göttingen.[1] He also had some apartments at St. James's, but these were so lacking in facilities that his food had to be prepared in a neighbouring coffee-house until he requested permission to have it dressed in the Royal Kitchen. Though he dined regularly at Buckingham House when in town, on the whole, he lived apart from the King's Court, with the Prince of Wales. Once again he became the bearer of despatches to Mrs. Fitzherbert, for whom his unhappy brother was now pining. To his sisters, he was the hero

[1] In 1806, the King settled the house and its grounds upon him finally.—W.A. King to Lord Eldon, 6th August 1806.

50

and veteran of the wars. Miss Burney wrote to her father on the 10th July 1796 that the Princesses had been speaking of their brothers.

" Yes," cried Princess Augusta, " and I am afraid I have bored her to death ; but when I once begin upon my poor brothers, I can never stop without telling all our little bits of glory." She then outstayed the Princess Royal to tell me that, when she was at Plymouth, at church, she saw so many officers' wives, and sisters, and mothers, helping their maimed husbands, or brothers, or sons, that she could not forbear whispering to the Queen, " Mamma, how lucky it is that Ernest is just come so seasonably with that wound in his face ! I should have been quite shocked else, not to have had one little bit of glory among ourselves!" [1]

These four years formed an interlude in the Prince's life. He had not been entrusted with any part in political or national affairs by his father, and as he took none against him he remained in retirement unknown to the public at large. His opinions were now, however, fully developed and they were not to change in one detail during the rest of his eighty years' life. External influence had no part in their shaping and his varied experiences had served only to strengthen them.

The most important factor in Prince Ernest's life was religion, but nothing would have made him religious had he not been so inclined from the outset. The only influence which outside teaching exerted was upon his belief in precise points of theology, almost in the realm of intellect, and it was here that the damage was done. As has been seen, religion was the first care of the King and Queen in the instruction of their children and it had been one of the weightiest considerations in the selection of Göttingen for the studies of the Princes, but the greatest influence in that of its aspects which was to play such a part in Prince Ernest's life lay not so much in the hands of his preceptors as in the world outside the Court.

At the Prince's birth the House of Brunswick had ruled in Britain for over fifty-six years, years during which no opportunity had been lost of impressing upon its members the fact that they did not rule by the Grace of God but had been called upon merely to exclude the Catholic Stewarts. Even in his address of congratulation to the King upon the Prince's birth, the Lord Mayor had not omitted the usual reference to the defence of Protestantism, and, in the eyes of Liberals and Parliamentarians, this was the raison d'être of the House in England. Catholicism, on the other hand, represented what would to-day be termed " Reaction," and

[1] Fanny Burney, V, p. 280.

it was doubt as to the zeal of the Tories in the Protestant cause which had led to their exclusion from government until the reign of George III. Even then, the surest way to raise a riot and set mobs sacking and burning was, as Lord George Gordon knew,[1] to allege Romish influence in Government circles.

What a revolution was to take place between the eighteenth century and the days when those who had preached war against Popery since before 1689 were suddenly to discover in their own Test Act a supple rod with which to belabour the Tory Government as it carried on the Whig " Glorious Revolution " policy ! This explains the conflict of religious and political policies to which Prince Ernest, as the rest of his party, fell victim. He had been brought up in the Whig Ultra-Protestant school which taught that his duty and that of his House was to ensure the continuance of the Protestant supremacy ; now he saw the Whigs turning upon their beliefs and policies in a manner which belied their sincerity in all that they had done since 1689 and could only be ascribed to lust for votes and power. Naturally, he felt the deepest disgust. As an Ultra-Protestant Tory, he was the heir of the " Glorious Revolution " Whigs, and it cannot be emphasised too strongly that, in religious affairs, his policy was *Whig*.

Of course, Ultra-Protestantism had not been taught to him by his divinity-masters as a Whig precaution against the Divine Right. He learnt that the Catholic Church was wicked—we find him writing home in 1788 that the course of religion and history was very interesting " and shows how the Catholic Bishops and monks are become so rich, by their turning the money intended for the Saints to their own private persons." [2] Mass and other Roman rites, he was taught, were blasphemous. However much, then, he found himself on the side of the Catholics in politics, they were still blasphemers to him for their doctrines.

In temporal politics, on the other hand, Prince Ernest was in advance of his contemporaries. Since the extinction of Jacobitism, party politics in England did not represent a clash of ideals but of families and oligarchies ; in George III's reign they had become almost a personal rivalry between the King and the great aristocratic houses. When the Prince of Wales attached himself to the latter, it meant nothing more than that he had a personal grievance

---

[1] Prince Ernest would well remember the Gordon Riots, when he and the other children were hustled out of London through smouldering and deserted streets where the dust had not settled, to Kew ; from the windows there they could watch the fires in the town, where their father had remained.

[2] W.A., 7th May 1788.

against his parents, and so it was only to be expected that his brother would now follow his example. But when Prince Ernest returned to England he saw that more was at stake than family feuds and conceived politics as a battle of fundamental principles from the very beginning. His experiences on the Continent had given him occasion to witness the real nature of the application of the doctrines which the dandies and sybarites of the Whigs preached in the luxury and comfort of club or salon without ever having seen a revolutionary in the flesh. No doubt his ideals did not differ essentially from those of his brothers who, after flirting at one time or another with the Whigs, finally showed themselves with one exception to be Tory ; but with him, there was not the same vacillation and influence of fashionable trends or personal rivalries.

Prince Ernest's enforced inactivity must have been very galling to him, and even now, though supposed to be convalescing, he could not keep out of danger. One day he rescued an " unfortunate desponding suicide " from the Thames and resuscitated him, an act for which the Royal Humane Society unanimously voted the award of its medallion. On the 2nd July 1798 a deputation, including the principal founders of the Society in 1774, Dr. Lettson and Dr. Hawes, waited upon him at St. James's to make the presentation, and thenceforth he took a great interest in the Society's work and arranged for its annual service, which he attended, to be held in Kew Church. He also paid for the subsequent care and treatment of the person whom he had saved.[1]

In August 1797 the King granted the Prince an annual allowance of three thousand pounds,[2] but this, as the latter soon discovered, betokened no diminution of his jealousy. In January 1798 he learnt that the death of the Hanoverian Commander-in-Chief, Field-Marshal von Freytag, was believed to be imminent. As he knew that von Wallmoden would be the successor and he recollected the humiliations to which he had been subjected by that officer three years before, the Prince decided to seize that moment to resign his commission in the Hanoverian service, " as I should be sorry to appear to do anything personal, and for many reasons I cannot possibly serve under General Wallmoden." At the same time, soldiering was to him the very breath of life and he could not give up the profession. He therefore approached his father with the request that he should be given a rank in the British

[1] *Annual Register* ; Transactions of the Royal Humane Society. With acknowledgments to Colonel G. W. M. Grover, O.B.E., Secretary of the R.H.S.
[2] W.A., 23rd August 1797.

Army.[1] The King made no reply, so he asked him again on the 14th April.[2]

Allow me to address myself to Your Majesty and throw myself on your goodness. Consider for one moment how great must be my anxiety to serve at this crisis, when the whole nation is arming, and even Your Majesty in person intends to come forward, a time in which it behoves every man to assist in the defence of Great Britain. I have again offered my services to the Commander-in-Chief, who answered me by letter *that it would do me more harm than good*, the mentioning the subject to you, alluding to the step which I had taken in quitting the Hanoverian service. Y.M., highly tenacious of your own honour, if you consider this business, must feel, that I should have forfeited *mine*, had I continued in the Hanoverian service, contrary to my solemn and public declaration [3] of never serving under General Wallmoden, who had personally ill-treated me. It would be presumption in me to suppose that I have less enemies than other men and there would not have been wanting those to have represented my conduct, if not in a dishonourable light, at least, as inconsistent in making such declarations without foundation.

Otherwise indifferent to the opinions of men, there was one thing which Prince Ernest feared from them, the possibility that they might think him inconsistent or a coward. He pleaded with the Duke of York for a brevet rank. The 13th Light Dragoons, he said, would shortly return from the West Indies and he desired, if the King would allow it, to become their Colonel-Commandant and reorganise them; he would be quite content to leave the emoluments to the Colonel, General Craiggs. It was always dangerous to thwart this Prince when he was determined upon something and he was not prepared to compromise upon his honour in this case. He therefore told his father that he would not press his request if it would be detrimental to the service, " but should you be determined to refuse this humble request, I will then, Sir, go into the Yeomanry as a private. By that means I shall show my anxiety in a glorious cause, in which I have already served, and by so doing shall prove my zeal and readiness to come forward in defence of my King and country."

Still there was no reply. The Prince broke off all relations with the King and did not speak to him.[4] Certainly, the provocation had been almost wanton, and the Prince demonstrated his feelings in another way. " I went to the Drawing Room, and had

---

[1] W.A., 16th January 1797.   [2] *Ibid.*
[3] Of this declaration there is no trace to be found now in either England or Hanover.
[4] W.A., 14th May 1798.

a fine civilian Court dress made, and I will never forget his [the King's] astonishment as I stepped into the Drawing Room in this costume. I only wore it once, but my father saw that I was determined and not long afterwards I received an English post, but I will never forget my nausea and horror as I saw this cursed dress on my body, so that I almost wept when I saw myself in it." [1] After exactly a month, the Prince decided to make a fresh approach. " Permit me, Sir, to repeat," he wrote, " that I do not solicit Y.M. for any particular rank, but to be *employed* in any military situation. . . . But as I have received no answer to my first letter, I have not thought it respectful to Y.M. to *act*, or to appear in your presence." He emphasised that he could never wish to do anything contrary to his father's wishes, " yet it is highly necessary for the sake of my character to prove my anxiety to assist in the defence of the country." He would therefore join the Yeomanry as a private " and thereby save my being looked upon as an enemy to my country in not sharing the impending danger thereof." [2]

The King realised that the matter could no longer be ignored. Angry, he decided the very next day to appoint his son to the rank of lieutenant-general—in the Hanoverian service.

Prince Ernest certainly conducted himself the more creditably throughout this episode. He wrote to the King the next day expressing his regret that he had incurred his displeasure and protested that his motives were those of honour. " But, Sir," he concluded, " the situation of affairs both here and all over the continent is such that it becomes my duty to bury *all my personal feelings*, and *hard as my fate may be* in compliance with Y.M. wishes and commands, with gratitude and respect to bow to your pleasure and accept the rank of a Lieutenant-General in your Electoral service." [3]

He was commissioned as lieutenant-general of the Hanoverian Army on the 18th May 1798, though developments on the Continent prevented his ever being employed in such a capacity. All that he desired now was the *rank* of a British lieutenant-general, without necessarily being employed as one. [4] At last, after much trouble and frustration, this wish was granted on the 7th July 1799, and his British commission was ante-dated to coincide with that in the Electoral service.

[1] S.A. To Grand Duke of Mecklenburg-Strelitz, 18th May 1848. E. A. said that he knew how terrible it was not to appear in uniform, " for in the year 1797 I had quarrelled with my blessed father, as he wanted to send me back to Germany and that I should serve again under Field-Marshal Wallmoden, who had so hellishly maltreated me in the campaign that I swore never again to serve under him and demanded my release."
[2] W.A., 14th May 1798.   [3] *Ibid.*, 16th May 1798.   [4] *Ibid.*, 7th July 1799.

The King probably felt some shame at his high-handed action. Certainly, he did no more to provoke his son and now at last he accorded him the privileges to which he was entitled. As Prince Ernest was already twenty-seven years of age, this recognition was somewhat belated. Together with his brother Edward, he was raised to the rank of a Royal Duke, with a seat in the House of Lords and a separate income and establishment.[1] On the 27th April 1799 the patent appeared announcing his elevation to the Peerage as Duke of Cumberland and Teviotdale and Earl of Armagh, and on his birthday he was appointed a Privy Councillor. His new dignity, however, boded ill, for there was something unfortunate about the title of Cumberland.

Perhaps the King had deduced wrongly from his younger son's friendship with the Prince of Wales that he had joined the political opposition. To have withstood such temptation and such provocation for so long was no mean proof of his loyalty, and now that the King at last recognised his mistake he made ample amends in the confidence which he reposed in him. Within a year father and son had swung from one extreme to another in their relationship and the Duke of Cumberland thus became a member of both the rival Courts.

His political début was not a spectacular one. On the 23rd May 1800 the House of Lords listened to his maiden speech. It was on the subject of a Bill designed to discourage adultery by preventing the marriage of guilty parties of a divorce. He opposed the measure on the grounds that the existing law was severe enough upon the woman, whose situation was one calling for pity rather than punishment.

It was extreme cruelty to deprive a misguided woman of future marriage and the common comforts of life, but it was not only meant by this bill to reduce her to the most abject state of misery, but to take from her whatever nominal rank she hitherto enjoyed. As to the prevention of the crime by the law now intended, he could not conceive it possible, and there were so few men inclined to marry the women they had seduced, that it would be cruel of all hardships to deprive the females even of this last hope.

Chivalry was not unusual in those days and so this was hardly calculated to arouse much interest in the Duke of Cumberland as a political figure.

---

[1] The Duke's total income thus amounted to £21,000. This remained unchanged throughout his whole life, apart from a conditional grant of £6000 in 1825, which, as will be seen, he hardly ever drew.

The King, however, had now gained complete confidence in his son and nothing better illustrated the change which had taken place in their relationships during 1799 and 1800 than their close association during the crisis which followed Pitt's resignation. At the beginning of 1801 the Prime Minister had brought forward his proposal to remove the disabilities of the Catholics. The King felt that in giving his assent he would be breaking his Coronation Oath, and as neither of them could persuade himself to yield, he reluctantly accepted his Minister's resignation on the 5th February. He was making a stand for the old Whig principles.

Naturally, the Duke of Cumberland warmly sympathised with his father in this matter, so the latter entrusted him with the task of conveying his proposals for a new ministry to Addington, the Speaker of the House of Commons. The Duke is not mentioned in Pellew's *Life of Addington*, nor in other political records of the time, and it is possible that his communications were all verbal, but many years later, as King of Hanover, he touched upon this episode in a letter to a friend. In discussing another topic, he mentioned, in fixing the date of his father's mentioning it to him . . . " about the time that the late Mr. Pitt resigned office, and which brought me into that very close connection with my father, as I was the person whom he employed to make the first overture to Addington, the Speaker of the House of Commons . . ." [1] From his part in its formation, the Duke took a somewhat proprietary interest in this Administration, as is shown by an incident which took place in the Lords on the 2nd June 1803. Lord Boringdon had just made a remark which seemed to reflect upon the origin of the Government. The Duke of Cumberland was soon on his feet.

He did not rise to discuss the question before the House. He was induced to rise merely from an expression which had fallen from a Noble Lord, who had said that he disapproved of the mode in which the present Administration came into office. What the Noble Lord intended by the mode, he really could not say, but he had never known a set of men come into office in a more honourable manner.

Addington took office, but the strain on the poor King had been too great. In the middle of February his mind gave way. Again Dr. Willis took charge and at first he would allow no one to see his patient who might upset him. For this reason the only members of the family who were allowed access were the Queen and the Duke of Cumberland. The Prince of Wales was not

[1] *Jesse*, I, p. 365.

admitted, and resented this deeply. For the first time there was bad blood between the brothers and the Duke of Cumberland was not finding it easy to remain on good terms in both camps. Not until after their father's recovery did they see each other again. Another result of the King's illness was the Duke of Cumberland's unequivocal demonstration of his political alignment, if any were needed. During his father's incapacity he assumed the rôle of guardian of his prerogatives, and severely condemned the Lord Chancellor for commissioning Dr. Willis to obtain his signature for a number of papers when no one else was allowed to be present.[1]

One consequence of the Duke of Cumberland's reconciliation with the King was the resumption of his military career, and in the branch to which he was always the most attached, the light cavalry. In March 1801 the King offered him the colonelcy of the 27th Light Dragoons, with the option of exchanging into the 15th when possible.[2] Lord Dorchester, the Colonel of the senior regiment, was agreeable to this, and so on the 18th March 1801 the Duke was gazetted Colonel of the 15th Light Dragoons. This post was not then an honorary or complimentary one—certainly, not where the Duke of Cumberland was concerned. The Commanding Officer submitted all matters for his approval and he interested himself in the smallest details of the life of the regiment and the men ; there were fresh examples of his care and consideration for those under his command and especially for old soldiers in distress.[3]

The Duke frequently visited his regiment and took over the command personally. It was stationed in the West Country and during his travels there he was soon widely known and respected and became freeman of several boroughs. There were always civic receptions, and in Worcester he took the opportunity of a visit to inspect the pottery where the renowned china was made.[4] In June he commanded his regiment, escorting the King and Queen during their State visit to Southampton and prolonged his stay after their departure. " Southampton has been greatly enlivened since the Duke of Cumberland has taken up residence here," reported the correspondent of *The Times*. " His Royal Highness has the band every evening for an hour and a half before his windows in Vincent's Walk." But his military activities were soon to be of a more serious nature.

[1] *Rose*, I, p. 330.   [2] W.A., 29th March 1801.
[3] *Wylly*. The Duke discovered that the second man to enlist in the regiment when it was raised in 1759, William Ovitts, was in the workhouse, and he made him a pension out of his own purse. Ovitts was still alive in 1827, in his nineties.
[4] *The Times*, 2nd October 1802.

CHAPTER VI

THE DUKE OF CUMBERLAND AND HOME DEFENCE

IN the first months of 1803 war clouds were looming upon the horizon. The Duke of Cumberland, who had seen enough of war and revolution on the Continent not to desire to be spectator of a similar drama in the land of his birth, gave all defensive preparations his keenest support, and upon this subject he could bring to bear the full weight of his military experience across the Channel. In the House of Lords he made his second speech during the discussion of the Militia Bill, which he vigorously supported.

War broke out again on the 18th May and the next day the King sent down a message to Parliament appealing to all to do their duty in defending their country. The Duke of Cumberland was one of the first to answer the call. He went to the Commander-in-Chief the same day and offered his services without remuneration.[1] A few days later he seconded the address which Pelham had moved on the subject of the war and relations with France, and it was this speech which finally announced his political principles and so proved to be the real opening of his political career.

It will be recollected that peace had been signed at Amiens the previous year, much to the joy of Fox and the advanced or Jacobinical Whigs, but now the Duke pointed out what had happened to liberty in France, the cynosure of these liberty-lovers. It is well worthy of note, then, that the Duke of Cumberland's first political speech was one in defence of liberty. It immediately branded him as a Tory reactionary.

Which of the nations of Europe is it that he [Napoleon] has not subdued or endeavoured to subdue, and place in the rank of obsequious vassal-nations, whose happiness and very existence depended upon his smiles or frowns ?

Where is Holland now, which for a century maintained by its industry a most respectable rank among European nations ? That nation is now trampled down by his legions, who, to add insult to their injuries, call themselves allies. Where is the free, the virtuous and the gallant Swiss

---

[1] W.A., 19th May 1803.

nation ? For centuries, they too, in the bosom of peace, had cultivated the virtues, the sciences and the useful arts. They had not meddled in the strife of nations. They had always preserved the strictest and most honourable neutrality. But the destroyer came, and swept away the produce of the industry of ages, and what was dearer to them than their wealth, their independence and ancient liberties ? Where is Italy now— Italy, which for ages has not lifted its head among contending empires, but whose ambition has merely been to call back into civilised Europe the monuments of ancient arts, sciences and tastes of the early ages of Greece, refined by every improvement of modern times ? Where now are those unoffending countries ? They all lie at the proud feet of France, to endure either the anger or the clemency of their conquerors !

How is France herself situated ? After the millions of lives that she has lost in the late sanguinary war, after that waste of treasure which has ruined her subjects and exhausted her finances, what is it that she has gained ? We were told that this was a war of liberty ! What liberty has she gained ? Personal liberty has been violated in France without limits—exile, deportation and Guiana are the consequences of giving any offence to the Consular Government. It is there in vain to appeal to laws against higher authority, and as for that liberty which is the pride of our constitution, the liberty of the press, it is there unknown. It may, then, well be asked of the French people, what was the object of the Revolution, and the war which followed it, or what is it that they have gained by it ?

But when we turn our eyes from the scene which so many other nations present, and look at our own country, we cannot avoid seeing with satisfaction a country where, under a constitution which our ancestors and we have approved of and flourished under, the liberty of the subject has been secured, the nation's trade unsubdued, and perfectly ready and prepared to defend its honour and its rights against any enemy who may provoke war. . . .

They [the French Government] had ventured, in speaking of this country, to say, " England is no longer able, single-handed, to contend with France ! " Insolent and unfounded as this declaration was, it appeared that they had formed so erroneous an opinion of the spirit and resources of the country as to believe it true, and had actually conducted themselves with respect to this country upon that persuasion. . . . When did France make this discovery, or when did Great Britain forfeit the rank and estimation that she has hitherto held among other nations ? But the French Government were not content with endeavouring to regulate at their own discretion, or rather, at their own caprice, the affairs of all other countries. They wished much to be allowed to introduce their own theories, their impracticable systems and destructive innovations into the constitutions and laws of this country. . . .

But His Majesty's Government and the British nation were too sensible of the blessings that they derived from the constitution, the laws, the privileges of our ancestors, to surrender them at the menace or at the bidding of any foreign power, and, least of all, to a power which, when nominally at peace with us, acted with all the rancour and hostility of an ancient and inveterate enemy.

If this war should be of any long continuance, the consequence of defeat would be the overthrowing of our Altars, the destruction of our Nobility, the degradation of the country, the extinction of the national honour and the loss of that character which has hitherto made the people of this country respected among the nations, whereas if we should prosecute it with all that vigour with which our former wars were carried on, there would be no doubt of the same success. We should convince the world that we had not degenerated from the patriotic spirit of our ancestors, and we should teach France that there is still in Europe a powerful and unconquered nation, which, just and moderate in its own conduct, will not bear insult or injustice from any other nation, and is always prepared to defend its own dignity and to oppose unjust ambition, aggrandisement and encroachment.

The tightening up of defensive arrangements which followed the declaration of war again found the Duke of Cumberland anxiously studying all problems and urging the utmost effort and sacrifice from all. Of the Army Reserve Bill, he said that " he was confident that every man who had the feelings of a Briton, and who was devoted to his country and loyal to his King, would give the principle of it his unqualified approbation. The horror and indignation excited by the insults and aggressions of the First Consul were so sensibly felt by the country that he was certain, had the Administration proposed to raise one hundred thousand men instead of fifty thousand, the measure would have been most heartily concurred in." When the General Defence Bill came up for debate, he declared that " There was hardly a man in the country who was not inspired or animated with the most ardent desire to resist that enemy who had threatened to destroy our liberties and independence."

The Duke's offer of service was accepted with alacrity and he was appointed to the command of the Severn District. This had its headquarters in Bristol and comprised Worcestershire, Gloucestershire, Herefordshire, Monmouthshire and South Wales. It was officially described as follows.

This may be considered as a district not exposed to immediate danger —the troops stationed in it are but few, the country is not extensive. The volunteers amount to 1786 cavalry and 8918 infantry, and ought to contribute fully to the general defence.[1]

This report certainly gives a totally erroneous impression, for it was the one district of the Kingdom in which enemy troops had

[1] W.O., 30/65/28.

made a landing. Six years previously a force had landed at Fishguard, apparently with Bristol as its objective, but after being defeated by the local gentry in the Yeomanry it mistook the red cloaks of some women—for the Welsh costume was not a museum-piece then—for approaching regular troops and surrendered.

The Duke of Cumberland took up his new command on the 19th August 1803. He was enthusiastically received by the inhabitants and civic authorities of Bristol,[1] but he devoted himself immediately to his military duties. On his arrival he found among his forces a corps of volunteer infantry, 1470 strong, which should have been a great asset but was worthless as its members would only serve inside the city of Bristol! The very next day he saw a deputation and expressed his regret that, considering the state of the country, they should limit their services in this way. They would go wherever it pleased the Duke to order them, they assured him, but he declined to issue orders to them. They must volunteer, he said, and they did to a man.[2]

More urgent was the problem of the coastal defences. As the officer responsible for the city, Major-General Garth, reported, the Avon and the Severn were entirely unguarded and offered ideal points of disembarkation for invading forces within only five miles of the second-largest and wealthiest city of the Kingdom.[3] The Duke lost no time in making a personal inspection. On the 19th, before anyone had had an opportunity to welcome him to his new command, he went down to the river with his staff and Major Kestermann, the commanding Royal Engineer of the District, and decided that gunboats should be stationed in the Avon, between the islands of Flat and Steep Holm.[4]

The following day, the 20th, the Freedom of the City was conferred upon the Duke and he sat down to a sumptuous dinner with the Mayor and Corporation in the Merchants' Hall.[5] The remaining period of his presence in the district was marked by many brilliant social functions in Hot Wells, the fashionable quarter of Bristol; several balls were held under his patronage, in which he himself "appeared in high spirits"[6] and danced till the early morning, and he also arranged concerts, "where he joined in many charming glees."[7]

[1] *The Times*, 24th August 1803.   [2] W.A., 19th August 1803.
[3] W.O. 30/57, Garth to Duke of Cumberland, 9th August 1803.
[4] *Ibid*. 30/57, Duke of Cumberland to Commander-in-Chief, 22nd August 1803.
[5] *The Times*, 24th August 1803.   [6] *Ibid*. 20th September 1803.
[7] *Ibid*., 18th October 1803.

On the 3rd September 1803 the Duke of Cumberland received from his brother, the Commander-in-Chief, the offer of the command of the South-Western District. It had become vacant through the promotion of its commander and the Duke accepted eagerly.[1] The 16th October was his last Sunday in Bristol and he and his staff attended a special service in the Cathedral. Afterwards he proceeded to Queen's Square, where an impressive array of Militia and Volunteers of all arms was drawn up for his inspection. He walked along the front of the line as the regimental bands played " God Save the King." When he had completed his inspection, the officers of the various regiments formed a circle round him in the middle of the Square and Colonel Baillie delivered a " very handsome and energetic address," expressing the thanks of the Royal Bristol Volunteer Infantry for his great condescension and marked attention towards them. The Duke replied appreciatively, and as he left the Square he was cheered by all the troops and a great crowd of spectators. He had been thoroughly popular during his stay in Bristol and had become known to everyone personally. The next day was that appointed for his departure.[2]

The Duke of Cumberland would here liked to have been given the command of the King's German Legion. Hanover had been erroneously regarded by Napoleon as a British outpost on the Continent and he had declared war upon the Electorate. Its Ministers had appealed in vain for aid in London and the young Duke of Cambridge had also sought help unsuccessfully in Berlin. George III put his English interests first and only the two " Hanoverian " Dukes, the Dukes of Cumberland and Cambridge, stood out vigorously for the country. The defenceless Electorate was overrun by French troops,[3] but many of its soldiers succeeded in escaping to England despite great hardships and the risk of retaliation upon their families. They were grouped together into the Legion to continue serving under their Sovereign. They were *not* mercenaries. The Duke of Cumberland would gladly have rejoined his old war-comrades but the King had made other arrangements and he could not be spared from his duties in home defence.

His new command could be considered as a promotion. It consisted of Hampshire, Wiltshire and Dorset, and included the vital areas of Portsmouth, Gosport and Weymouth. It was not so remote as the Severn and, as the Court moved to Weymouth in

---

[1] W.A., 3rd September 1803. [2] *The Times*, 20th October 1803.
[3] See *G. S. Ford.*

the summer, the Duke would be able to combine military and social activities with ease. The headquarters were at Winchester and there he took up residence.

Immediately upon his arrival he set to work to bring the defences up to his exacting standard. First of all he went to inspect the coastline and fortifications round Portland, Brownsea Island and Weymouth, and he ordered the erection of two batteries by the latter city (at Weymouth Old Castle and Jordan Hill).[1] With Captain Landmann, his Engineer Officer, he continued the inspection of the Dorset coast. He found the stretch between Christchurch and North Haven very favourable for an enemy landing. A mobile force with light artillery and troops on the cliff above the beach were the only remedy, he reported, but there were not enough available in the district for such duties, so it is fortunate that the enemy made no attempt.[2]

In Winchester the Duke again displayed his power of inspiring other men with his own zeal. He was reviewing the Twyford Yeomanry on St. Katharine's Hill and had expressed his satisfaction with all their evolutions. But they had not yet charged, he said, and he would like to see them do so. Sir Harry Mildmay, their commander, very respectfully pointed out that it had been raining continuously for the last twenty-four hours and the ground, besides being very steep, was therefore slippery, and he begged His Royal Highness not to press the order. His men were willing to do their best, he said, but as each provided his own horse, they could not be judged by the standards of the regular cavalry, and if they attempted to charge down the hill, at least half of their number would be injured.

But the Duke knew better. He never ordered men to do what he would not do himself, he said, then he turned to his staff and, saying loudly, " You will follow me, gentlemen," spurred his horse and galloped off at full speed down the hill, with his staff following. The slope seemed very dangerous and Sir. T. Dyer, not a particularly accomplished equestrian, " wore a rueful countenance," but they reached the bottom without mishap and scrambled back to the starting-place.

" Now, Sir Harry," said the Duke, raising his field-glasses, " let your trumpeter sound the charge." The order was given. The men galloped down the hill and then returned safe and sound.

---

[1] W.O. 75/154, Duke to Quartermaster-General, 20th November 1803; Landmann.
[2] Ibid.

The Duke advanced to their commander. " Well, Sir Harry," he said, " you have now a far more favourable opinion of the efficiency of your corps than you ever before entertained of them ? " Sir Harry bowed and confessed that he was indeed gratified to find his corps more efficient than he had believed. As they rode down the hill, the men showed their pride, and it was with some difficulty that they were constrained to follow the roads and not gallop home across country.[1]

In the summer of 1804 the Court moved as usual to Weymouth for the bathing and sailing season. Among the troops there were some from the King's unhappy Electorate, and one of the visitors to the resort described in a letter how the King " saw all the troops pass before him, and in particular the Hanoverian Horse—very fine troops indeed, as I am told, for I did not see them—in honour of them, he mounted a very spirited Hanoverian charger, which he rode and exercised as if he had been a man of thirty and *certainly* galloped as hard." [2]

This year the Duke was able to participate fully in the Court life at the seaside. Before joining the King on the Esplanade, he and all the military and civil officers of the Court dined together, and to ensure that they did not parade either too early or too late, a servant was posted at the door of the house. As soon as the King appeared on the Esplanade, he ran to report it to the dining-room ; the Duke and his officers rose and, without even drinking the wine which they may have been in the act of pouring out, hurried outside.[3]

But the Duke's activities were not purely social. Weymouth was in his command and he was responsible for its defence like that of any other coastal town, but the presence of the King threw an added burden upon his shoulders. It was well conceivable that the French might attempt a landing and, with one swoop, carry off the Royal Family with the entire Court and many of the most distinguished soldiers and sailors. The town was quite inadequately fortified and so six frigates always lay in the roadstead and a military force was encamped nearby, but when the Duke of Cumberland assumed responsibility he did not consider this a sufficient defence. He decided that this was a case for that recent innovation, the martello tower. To-day these buildings round our coasts appear so forlorn that they seem to have been abandoned a thousand

---

[1] *Landmann.*
[2] Ricketts and Jervis Correspondence, Add. MSS. 30,007.
[3] *Landmann.*

years, but they were very carefully sited. The Duke sent for
Landmann, who agreed that one should be erected on the Look-
Out.[1]

The Duke returned to Winchester towards the end of September
and, after a short visit to the New Forest with the rest of the
family, resumed his routine activities. He also continued to speak
as a soldier in the House of Lords. Early in 1805 two matters
concerning the army came up for discussion, the Additional Forces
Act on the 15th February, when he defended the Government
against various charges of " trepanning " recruits into the regular
army, and the Mutiny Bill on the 15th March, for altering some of
the military procedure. The Duke protested vigorously against
this last measure. It implied, he said, that there had been complaints against the present long-standing system. By shackling
the officer's discretionary power, the Bill would make for greater
severity, since this power had always been inclined towards lenity.

As usual, in July the Court moved to Weymouth. This year
it was fuller and gayer than ever. The Duke of Cumberland had
a special rôle, for he commanded personally the large camp which
was gathered there during the visit. Von Linsingen's brigade of
cavalry and Captain Hartmann's battery of horse-artillery were
encamped by the neighbouring village of Radipole and in the
barracks of Weymouth itself. On the 8th July the Duke's own
15th Light Dragoons joined the camp at Radipole from Salisbury.
Some infantry and horse-artillery were also encamped by the sea-
shore and a few companies of rifles near the Look-Out Battery.
The number of troops in camp about Weymouth is assessed vari-
ously between eight and eleven thousand.

The Honourable Amelia Murray, in her *Recollections*, gives us a
vivid picture of Weymouth in the days when it enjoyed Royal
favour. " But Weymouth was a gay place in those days—two
Royal yachts and three frigates in the bay ; a picturesque camp of
sharpshooters on the ' Look-Out ' ; Hanoverian cavalry careering
on the sand, and singing their fine musical choruses as they passed
along the road ; an infantry regiment, with its lively band ; beautiful
girls and charming children thronging the Esplanade ; the King,
Queen and Royal Family walking about among their subjects ;
balls, plays, reviews. . . ."

The camp was broken up after the departure of the Royal
visitors at the end of September, and with it the Duke's days of
soldiering in England came to an end, though he continued as

[1] *Landmann.*

colonel of the 15th, and there were reports that he was to accompany the expedition to the Weser in November. Politics suddenly submerged all other issues in his life.

In any case, he had been suffering all the time from the disorder in his left eye, though it is not clear when it became, as it did, a total loss. He was under the care of Dr. Phipps, an experienced specialist, who had also worked hard among the poorer classes. Often, he told his distinguished patient, he had operated successfully for cataract and had then seen his patient lose his eye subsequently for lack of after-care. What was needed, according to his ideas, was a hospital for such cases. With the growth of industrialism and overcrowding in towns, these complaints were becoming more menacing than formerly. The Duke listened attentively to all these proposals. All that was needed for the success of his project, Phipps told him, was that the Royal Family should subscribe and become patrons of the hospital, then funds would be raised in a very short time. A plan was therefore drawn up, which the Duke sent to the King, adding, " My own sufferings with my eyes make me the more desirous to assist in alleviating those of my fellow-creatures who are not, like myself, blessed with the means of attempting to preserve one of the greatest and most precious gifts of the Almighty—*Sight*." [1]

[1] W.A., 12th December 1804.

CHAPTER VII

1805–10

THROUGHOUT 1805 the country was still living under the umbrella of Pitt's Government and the Duke of Cumberland could devote himself to his military and other duties with an untroubled mind. There were, however, clouds upon the horizon and one of these was the problem of the Roman Catholics of Ireland who, despite the Act of Union, could not sit in Parliament or hold other important offices of State. In 1805 they presented a very reasonable petition to Parliament, and it was on this occasion that the Duke of Cumberland for the first time openly championed the Ultra-Protestant cause. He spoke in the House of Lords on the 10th May and advised its rejection.

. . . When I reflect on what were the circumstances which brought our family to the Throne and when I consider what is the object of the petition on your table, it is impossible for me to remain totally silent. With respect to the circumstances which brought our family to the British Throne, Your Lordships well know that they originated in the Revolution. The great object of that Revolution was to secure the religion and liberation of these realms. These objects were confirmed by the Act of Settlement, by the Declaration of Rights and by the Oath of Supremacy and Abjuration and by the succession to the Crown in the Protestant line. To maintain and uphold all these, our family was called to the Throne, and whatever can militate with these principles to the remotest degree, it is my bounden duty as a member of that family and as a member of Your Lordship's House, to resist.

He then adduced historical arguments to demonstrate that the admission of Catholics to the offices in question would militate with the principles to defend which his family had been called to England.

Far be it from me, my Lords, to shackle or fetter the consciences of any man, but equally far be it from me to pull down by rank innovation any of the venerable pillars of the Constitution. All that can be given consistently with reason and conscience, I am prompt to give. But the Constitution I cannot, *dare not*, WILL NOT give. I must uphold and support, with the best effort of my nature, the establishment in Church and State, as the great step by which the House of Brunswick ascended that Throne.

The most striking thing about this speech is its utter Whiggery.
It was just the sort of speech which had been delivered upon every
occasion for the last century.   Everything is there—the Glorious
Revolution, the Constitution, the denial of Divine Right, the
" summoning of the House of Brunswick. . . ." It would,
indeed, be difficult to understand that this was the speech of an
Ultra-Tory and Monarchist without appreciating the way in which
it had been instilled into the members of family that the only
reason for its presence in England was the defence of the principles
of 1689.   The Duke of Cumberland was a man imbued with a
high sense of duty, and this was the " bounden duty " imposed
upon his House ; he was a Legitimist and only these principles
legitimised his House upon the Throne.

By this speech the Duke had announced himself as the champion of the Ultra-Protestants, and it was not long before associations and institutions were asking for his patronage, particularly
those identified with the present system in Ireland.   His uncle, the
Duke of Gloucester, who had been Chancellor of the University
of Dublin since 1771, died on the 25th August 1805, and in
December he was elected in his place.   On 13th February 1806 a
deputation from the University waited upon him at his apartments at
St. James's with the appointment.

On the 23rd January 1806 Pitt died, and the shield which had
preserved the political security of the country was swept away.
As the Duke of Cumberland followed the coffin to Westminster
Abbey on the 22nd February, he had reached a turning-point in
his life.   Henceforward he devoted himself almost entirely to
politics.   The safety of the political system which he and the King
had favoured, and which Pitt had preserved, was shattered.   There
was no strong man to fill the gap, and a patched-up coalition
dominated by Fox and others of Pitt's opponents who favoured
Catholic Emancipation came into office as the Ministry of All the
Talents.   Of course, the Duke's political alignment in the House
was completely changed and he became for the first time one of
the leaders of the Opposition to the Government.   His hostility
was increased through the Whig impeachment of Dundas, Viscount
Melville, on a charge of having misused Admiralty funds.   The
trial was designed to discredit the late Ministry, and all the Princes
followed the proceedings with close interest.   Their voting showed
their political sympathies ; the Dukes of York, Cumberland and
Cambridge voted on the whole for acquittal, and the Dukes of
Clarence, Kent and Sussex for a verdict of guilty.

The Duke of Cumberland's opposition to the Government became finally apparent on the 3rd April 1806, when the propriety of Lord Ellenborough's having a seat in the Cabinet was under discussion in the Lords.[1] It seems that the Duke sat between the leaders of the Opposition, Lords Hawkesbury [2] and Mulgrave, and marked his approbation of the Opposition by cheers and gestures.[3]

On the 2nd March the Duke's Whig brother, the Duke of Sussex, told their old tutor, Dr. Hughes, that the Duke of Cumberland had decidedly joined the Opposition and that " he was a d——d fool for doing so." [4] There was also a coolness now in the relations between the Duke of Cumberland and the Prince of Wales. On the 19th March, Farington wrote that the Duke of Cambridge was the King's favourite son, " but he also occasionally visits the Prince of Wales—which the Duke of Cumberland does not " [5]—for the ministerial changes had had their repercussions in the life of the Royal Family.

Since 1714 the private life of the English Court was unique in the domination exercised over it by the fortunes of the two political parties. This eclipsed all personal and family issues and the most important things about a Prince or a Princess was whether he or she was a Whig or a Tory. It has been seen how the Prince of Wales was adopted by the Opposition and had become its figurehead through his estrangement from his father. The Duke of Cumberland, although similarly estranged and badly treated by the King, had not altered his politics ; he had remained on the side of the King, but he had also become the most attached personal friend of his brother. When, however, a reconciliation took place with his father, it became increasingly difficult to remain on both sides at once, and finally, when Fox and the Whigs came into office, they could permit it no longer that their patron should be on intimate terms with his Tory brother. It was sought to destroy this fraternal love by whispering stories about the Duke of Cumberland into his brother's ears.

Late at night on the 18th April 1806 the Duke received a letter from the Prince of Wales announcing his determination to break off all personal relations. It began with some reference to an alleged want of respect at the Lord Mayor's Dinner which had been reported to him and which the Duke absolutely denied, adding in parenthesis, " I wished you had mentioned the circumstances." But this was a mere trifle ; we can reconstruct the

---

[1] Lord Ellenborough was Lord Chief Justice.   [2] Afterwards Lord Liverpool.
[3] *Farington Diaries*, III, p. 158.   [4] *Ibid.*, III, p. 170.   [5] *Ibid.*, III, p. 167.

contents of the Prince's letter from the reply which the Duke of Cumberland sent off from St. James's immediately.

" The last part of your letter," he wrote, " contains a charge that I think too *serious* not to answer very fully, as I cannot but consider it as an attack upon my honour and character, unjust on your part either to believe or to state without making me acquainted with the *author*, vizt. ' that I have studiously and invidiously attempted to do you mischief in a quarter to which I have had means of access, and wherein I have mis-stated and misrepresented you.' *This I most solemnly and unequivocally deny* and wonder that Y.R.H. with the penetration that belongs to you did not draw a natural conclusion from such a misrepresentation that the person who could be sufficiently malignant to have made such a report to you could have been capable of inventing it ; and Y.R.H. will find that that person will never come forward to put you in the right by proving so unhandsome an accusation of myself. I have no fears of what people assert *secretly* while my conscience tells me that I act with integrity, which is every man's best security." [1]

The next evening, at Windsor, the Duke received his brother's answer and replied immediately, " Sir, I have at this moment received Your Royal Highness's letter and am sorry that mine to you has not had the desired effect. Having already sufficiently explained myself, Sir, Your Royal Highness's obedient servant. . . ." [2] With this note their friendship came to an end, a friendship which had at one time been so close and affectionate. Nothing could better illustrate the way in which the Royal Family were the victims of scheming politicians. According to Farington, the Prince of Wales now forbade his daughter to speak to the Duke of Cumberland when she saw him and he also ignored Lord Thomond, whom he met in company, for being a friend of the Duke and inviting him to dinner.[3]

We see the gathering storm which the Whigs were preparing for the Duke of Cumberland. Soon the next stage was reached— scandal and slander. Perhaps the first instance of this was reported by Lady Bessborough.[4] There had been a mutiny in the Duke's regiment, she wrote eagerly, and the Scots Greys had had to march against it. Officers had thrown up their commissions and refused to serve under him as his severity was not to be endured. " It is whispered " that he had lifted his cane to several of his officers.

[1] W.A., 18th April 1806.   [2] *Ibid.*, 19th April 1806.
[3] *Farington Diaries*, IV, p. 191.
[4] To Lord Granville Leveson Gower, 24th April 1806. *Private Correspondence.*

Of this alleged mutiny not a trace has come down to us. It is mentioned in the histories of neither of the Duke's regiment nor of the Greys and " It is whispered " seems to sum up the whole matter. The report that he had been angry and demanded the resignation of Lord Hinton as his militia was in such a sad state may have had a little more foundation, but no facts have come to light, and it was not until four years later, with the Foskett affair, that the slanderous nature of the stories of the Duke of Cumberland and his dealings with his officers was revealed to the world.

It was inevitable, of course, that the changed situation between the Prince of Wales and the Duke of Cumberland should involve the Princess of Wales. The marriage had, of course, been a failure, and the Prince, hearing of his wife's indiscretions, was anxious to divorce her. The King still favoured his niece (as he did until his disappearance from politics), and the Duke of Cumberland now had both personal and political reasons for following his lead. In October, after the death of her father from wounds received at the battle of Jena, he visited her several times and the King sent very kind messages to her.

Now, of course, the whole domestic quarrel resolved itself into politics. The Prince of Wales naturally received the sympathy and assistance of those who expected so much from him, the Whigs. The Princess therefore allied herself with the Tories, including the Duke of Cumberland, Lord Eldon and Perceval. " The present Ministers," she wrote to her brother,[1] " are in no way my friends. They are Jacobins and persons recognised as traitors to the constitution and their country. They therefore want to remove me from the King so that he will remain in their claws for a number of years. The feeble nerves of the King and his incapability of seeing their object put him so completely in the power of that infernal sect. Happily Mr. Fox has just left us for Hell—he died a few days ago—and it is to be hoped that the others will join him soon. . . . I have found many friends here ; all the Ministers of the time of my friend Mr. *Pitt* are absolutely devoted to me and the dear Duke of Cumberland acts only as a true brother to me. It is he who has shown me such attention during this terrible crisis. . . . I feel exactly as you do, dearest brother, on the subject of hopes of reconciliation, but alas ! the Ministers will not listen to reason about it."

[1] M.A. Princess Caroline to her brother, the Duke of Brunswick, 20th September 1806 and 30th January 1807.

How the situation was to reverse itself! When the Whigs found that the Prince of Wales would not serve their purposes, they were to champion his wife as an injured woman in order to spite him. But the Duke of Cumberland and his friends were guided by principles, and as soon as they saw that in championing the Princess for party reasons they were acting contrary to those principles, they corrected themselves. It happened in this way.

In May 1806 the Prince of Wales informed his friends, the Whig Ministers, of certain behaviour on the part of his wife. As a result, they instituted the " Delicate Investigation " and prevented her appearance at Court. The Tories then demanded the lifting of the ban, and Perceval, with the approval of Lord Eldon, compiled a book of evidence in the Princess's favour which would be published unless the Whigs yielded.[1] The Duke of Cumberland was, of course, a party to the project, and it was through him that it was dropped. Lady Hester Stanhope describes what happened.

One day the Duke came to her and said breezily, " Well, Lady Hester, it will all be out to-morrow. We have printed it, and to-morrow it will all be out." She asked him what he meant and he told her. " I, for my part, don't like the business at all," she said. " I have too much respect for Royalty to desire to see it made a subject for Grub Street songs." " The Duke turned as if in thought," she said later, " and I saw the same idea struck him, for after a moment's pause, he resumed his position and answered, ' You are quite right, Lady Hester. By God! You are quite right. But what am I to do? We have gone too far. What am I to do? ' ' Why, I think,' rejoined I, ' the best thing you can do is to go and ask Lord Eldon.' So off he packs, and I fancy Mr. Perceval, Lord Eldon and he talked it over, and decided on quashing the business." [2] It was as a result of this realisation that Lord Eldon hastened to Windsor to urge upon the King the undesirability of the publication of the book.

Just at that time (March 1807) the Ministry of All the Talents came to an end. The Duke of Cumberland had no part in its fall, but the hurried departure of Lord Eldon and Lord Hawkesbury for Windsor aroused the suspicions of the Whigs. It was alleged that a ring of secret advisers with whom the King communicated through the Duke of Cumberland had turned him against the

---

[1] " My friends and lawyers have advised me to make public the whole history of this cruel accusation and the persecutions of my enemies."—*Ibidem*.

[2] *Lady Hester Stanhope*, I, pp. 305–6.

E.A.—3*

Cabinet and that their two leaders had been summoned to engineer its dismissal and arrange the formation of a new one. On a subsequent occasion Lord Howick [1] repeated this story in the Lords, and it then became known that Eldon's visit to Windsor had been a coincidence and that he had informed the Cabinet of his intention and purpose beforehand.

The narrow escape by which they had avoided having a government sympathetic to the Catholic claims alarmed the protagonists of the Protestant supremacy in Ireland, and the Duke of Cumberland became the bearer of numerous petitions to the Lords against a relaxation of the present law. The peak of his leadership of the Ultra-Protestant cause was reached in 1807 when he was elected Grand Master of the Orange Lodges, the organisation which aimed at securing the Protestant supremacy in Ireland. That he was acting injudiciously there can be no doubt, but he was only playing his part sincerely according to the terms upon which his family had been set upon the Throne in 1714; he declared his views and fought quite openly, but it became the fashion to ascribe everything to his machinations. He was, for example, involved in the trouble over Maynooth Seminary, where Roman Catholic priests were trained. The Government had made a smaller grant than usual towards it and a member of the Commons accused him of interference, but the Chancellor of the Exchequer denied that he had held any communication with him upon the subject whatsoever.

The Duke of Cumberland was thrown very much into the company of the inner circles of the Tories and there he found his most intimate and lifelong friend, Lord Eldon. This distinguished Lord Chancellor was a fellow-champion of Conservative and Ultra-Protestant ideas; he came of humble stock—his father had been a well-to-do coal merchant of Newcastle—but his rise was no accident, nor was his genius isolated, for his brother became another celebrated lawyer, Lord Stowell. The Duke spent the first two days of October 1808 at Encombe, his seat in Dorsetshire, and his host wrote a lively description of the visit in a letter.

The Duke arrived on a Saturday, and on the morrow all the local inhabitants gathered at the church in the hope of seeing him. However, it rained so hard that they had to be disappointed. When the rain stopped in the afternoon, the Duke and his host went out walking, splashing through the puddles and wet grass to see the countryside; occasional gleams of sunshine broke through the

[1] Afterwards Lord Grey.

clouds which capped the hills. The evenings they spent in conversation. The Duke left on Monday, and the family walked with him to the bottom of Kingston Hill, where Fanny, the ten-year-old daughter, who was " much smitten," " got an embrace, and we have had some difficulty to get her to allow her face to be washed since, lest she lose the impression." [1]

All this time, of course, the campaign of slander against the Duke of Cumberland was mounting in an effort to drive him from politics. Farington writes on the 3rd May 1809, " Lord Oxford was at Eywood in Hertfordshire when Lady Oxford informed him of the infamous reports respecting Her Ladyship and the Duke of Cumberland. He was more apprehensive of the opinion of the people in the country than of those in London, and to show he was not affected by the calumnies he remained at Eywood longer than he intended."

The Duke's close preoccupation with politics had prevented his devoting much of his time to the army, but he did not lose his interest in his regiment and the supervision and regulation of its affairs. In 1807, in accordance with military fashion, it became a regiment of Hussars. Among other changes, all ranks were ordered to grow moustaches, but this proved rather difficult for the officers, and so, according to orders, " His Royal Highness the Duke of Cumberland directs that until further orders officers will discontinue to wear moustachios, it being difficult to preserve uniformity in this respect from the frequent leaves of absence granted, when they are usually cut off." The Duke resisted for as long as possible the general order that Hussars' locks should be cut short and only gave the command reluctantly many months later. His very precise ideas with regard to uniform are illustrated by the order of the lieutenant-colonel in which he said that he had " obtained from His Royal Highness the Duke of Cumberland a pattern boot and spur, hat and feather, which are now Adjutant's possession and to which the officers will immediately conform. H.R.H. has likewise expressed his directions that no part of the *shirt* or *chitterlings* [2] should be visible either above or beneath the *stock*." [3] [4]

The Duke also took command of the regiment personally from August to September 1807, and again in the first months of 1808, when it was in barracks at Woodbridge in Suffolk. He then exercised it several times a week on Rushmere Heath, and commanded it during a grand review there by his brother, the Duke of York,

---

[1] *Twiss*, II, pp. 64–5.   [2] The ruff or frill forming the collar to the shirt.
[3] The stiff band or cravat.   [4] *Wylly*.

and entertained the officers in an Ipswich coffee-house.[1] At the end of July 1808 the Duke of Cumberland requested to be sent with the cavalry then embarking for the Continent,[2] but, it seems, he was no longer regarded as eligible for such commands, though he had been promoted to the rank of general in 1808 (ante-dated to 1803).

Even the Duke of Cumberland's conduct of the routine affairs of his regiment was dragged into politics. Anyone with a grievance against him, however questionable, could be assured of a welcome among his political enemies, and so a discontented officer of the regiment, a Captain Foskett, conceived the idea of petitioning Parliament against his Colonel. Of course, he found ready champions, and on the 18th April 1810 Mr. Lyttelton brought his petition before the Commons. The Captain's complaints were that the Duke had prevented his promotion and advanced a junior officer ahead of him, had not granted him his regular leaves and had not sent him abroad with the regiment. Many members immediately pointed out that if it became the practice for officers to petition Parliament against their superiors, no discipline could be maintained, and several facts came to light which revealed Foskett's failings as an officer. His troop, declared one member, was in such a bad state of discipline that it would be necessary to disband it. He had also, as second, committed a breach of the duelling code for which he deserved to be hanged on the spot, said another. He had been treated with " unprecedented lenity, forbearance and moderation." But the Duke's enemies set about bringing him into disrepute upon issues quite irrelevant to the petition. Whitbread, who could always be relied upon to attack him whenever the opportunity presented itself, had, he said, made inquiries which revealed that the Duke's was the only regiment in the whole army in which the officially-abolished punishment of picketing [3] was still inflicted, so severe was its Colonel. But another member, Sir James Pulteney, declared that " upon subsequent inquiry he had ascertained that fewer punishments and a less number of courts-martial had taken place during the period of His Royal Highness's having the command than during the same length of time under any former Commanding Officer." The matter was finally raised at the Duke's own request on the 7th June, and so weak was the case that it was dismissed without a division.

---

[1] *Suffolk Gazette.*   [2] W.A., 30th July 1808.
[3] Picketing was the punishment where the offender had to stand with one foot upon a tapered staff.

CHAPTER VIII

ATTEMPTED ASSASSINATION [1]

ON the afternoon of the 31st May 1810 the Duke of Cumberland dined at Greenwich with the officers of the Hospital,
of which he was a Governor, and returned to St. James's, where,
attended by his favourite valet, Sellis, he changed for the Concert
of Ancient Music in the Hanover Square Rooms in aid of
the Royal Society of Musicians, of which he was a keen patron.
He returned from the concert at about midnight and was attended
by his other valet, Neale. When his master was in bed, the man
locked the door which led to the State Apartments and put the
light behind a screen. He then went to his own room, that of the
valet on duty, which was separated by an ante-room, and the
Duke, wearing his thickly-wadded nightcap, was soon asleep in
his four-poster bed.

At about half-past two he was violently awakened, and hearing,
as he described it, in the stage between sleeping and waking, a
hissing noise, he thought that a bat had found its way into the
room and was fluttering about the head of the bed. Then he
immediately received two fierce blows from a razor-edged blade
and was fully awake. One had passed right through the thick
wadding of his night-cap and would have gone deeper had it not
already encountered the curtain hanging from the top of the bed.
He instinctively felt for the bell-cord, usually over the head of the
bed but now displaced, and could not leave by the other side of
the bed, for it was in an alcove against the wall. He still had no
idea of the nature of the attack that was being made upon him,
but he leapt up, raising his hand to ward off the rain of blows, and
another almost carried off his fingers. His sight was not good
and all that he could see was the flashing of a sabre. Blood was
pouring from all parts of his body ; it flew eight feet high on to
the wall, sprinkling the portrait of Pichegru and others in large
drops. The blade was so sharp that, when he had tried to seize

---

[1] Where not otherwise noticed, this chapter is from the Place Papers in the British
Museum and the *Minute Detail*. This work, said by Place to be very accurate, contains
the depositions of the witnesses.

it and his attacker had drawn it through his hands, it had cut
through the flesh between the thumb and forefinger. The tendons
and sinews of his right hand and the joint of his left wrist were
torn and he had received in these few seconds altogether three
wounds on the neck, one on the head, five on the right hand, one
on the left arm and another on the left wrist. He quickly jumped
from the bed, not knowing how many assassins were in the
room, and made for that of his valet. As he opened the door into
the passage, a last lunge was made at him, striking his thigh and
taking a large piece out of the door. " Neale, Neale, I am
murdered ! " he called.

Neale jumped out of bed and met his master at the door. The
assassins were still in the room, said the Duke. Neale seized a
poker and ran into the Duke's room. He immediately perceived
that the door into the Yellow Room, which he had locked before
retiring, was wide open and, hurrying to it, struck his foot against
the Duke's regimental sabre, covered with blood, lying in the
doorway. The Duke, whom he had helped into a chair, said that
it was dangerous ; they must rouse the servants and warn the
guard to watch all the entrances of the apartments, so together
they went down the stairs to the office of the porter, Benjamin
Smith. " His Royal Highness is murdered ! " called Neale, and
the man looked up to see the gruesome sight of the Duke, " all
over blood," being helped down the stairs. He armed himself
with his sword, roused the servants, directed the sentries to stop
all persons and fastened the outer doors and area door. They
then went upstairs again, meeting Mrs. Neale, who was the Duke's
housekeeper, and Matthew Graslin, his German servant.

Mrs. Neale had risen at the first alarm and called Graslin, who
had armed himself with two pistols. The Duke told them to find
the other servants and, in particular, his favourite valet, Sellis, for
whom he was becoming anxious. Mrs. Neale, the porter and
Graslin went for Sellis, and Neale helped the Duke, now faint
from loss of blood, back into bed. Sellis's door was locked and
they received no answer, though the porter banged with the hilt
of his sword, so they presumed that he was not sleeping there that
night and returned to the Duke. The Duke asked Neale to find
out where the assassin might be concealed and he began by looking
in the closets at the end of the bed. Inside one he found the
scabbard, a pair of slippers marked in ink " J. Sellis," a water-
bottle and a shaded lantern, and saw that someone had been
sitting on the linen and bed-cushions, which were stored there.

Mrs. Neale had meanwhile despatched two footmen for Sir Henry Halford and Mr. Everard Home, the surgeon, but the Duke was still worried about Sellis. When Mrs. Neale and the porter had returned and reported that he was not in his room, Graslin had gone to find him in his apartments elsewhere in the Palace, but he did not know the way. He returned, and Mrs. Neale sent the porter, who was told by one of Sellis's children that her father was sleeping at the Duke's.

The Duke was now very anxious, so Mrs. Neale and the porter made to go to his room by another way, which she, as house-keeper, knew—through the State Apartments. But they found the Yellow Room locked on the inside, which it had never been before. They therefore went through the Ballroom and Armoury, now convinced that something was amiss, and as, with some trepidation, they approached the door of Sellis's room, there came from within a gurgling sound and one as of trickling water, accompanied by a groan. Terrified, they fled, or, as they put it, " returned for assistance," for the door was slightly ajar and they believed that the murderers were now setting about Sellis. This was what the porter said, but Mrs. Neale said that he looked in and cried, " Good God ! Mr. Sellis has cut his throat ! "

In the hall they met Sergeant Creighton with four or five men of the Coldstream Guards, who had now arrived from the guard-room. The porter showed them to Sellis's room, trembling, and, as they approached it, he hesitated. One of the Guardsmen took the candle from him and they went down the three narrow steps into the room.

Sellis lay on his bed, his throat cut from ear to ear, so that his head was almost severed from his body. The blood was frothing and flowing all over the body and the bed ; in fact, from neck to waist, the man was a mass of blood. A razor with a white handle lay on the floor about two feet away. Sellis was clad in shirt and pantaloons, which were fastened neatly round the legs. It was clear, then, that he had not been to bed, but had been cut short in the act of hastily divesting himself ; elsewhere in the room there was a basin of water discoloured with blood.

Home, the surgeon, had now arrived and found the Duke in a critical condition. So terrible were his wounds that in his right temple, the pulsations of the brain could clearly be seen. Home also later examined Sellis and pronounced him to be dead, clearly having cut his throat while sitting on the bed and fallen back into the position in which he had been found ; death would have been almost instantaneous and there was no question of a struggle, or that he had been murdered. There was no blood where the bed was covered by the body, but everywhere else, and the necktie had been removed after an unsuccessful attempt to cut through it; the razor lay on the floor where it had fallen from the dead man's hand and on the chair by the bedside was his coat, sprinkled with the Duke's blood.

By now, word had reached Carlton House, and the Prince of Wales, accompanied by the Duke of Sussex,[1] had arrived. This Duke began to investigate the events of the night and instructed Neale to go through Sellis's pockets. As he approached his late fellow-valet, Neale lifted his arm and said, " God forgive you; you dug a pit for others and have fallen into it yourself ! " He found in his right breeches pocket the key of the baise door across the gallery. There was now no doubt as to what had happened.

Of course, the news was also public now and by dawn a large crowd had gathered round the Palace. Straw was laid in Cleveland Row and the vicinity so that the noise might not disturb the Duke. As soon as he learnt that his brother was out of danger, the Prince of Wales hurried to Windsor to inform and reassure the Royal Family, who decided to return to London. At eight o'clock a bulletin was issued, announcing that " His Royal Highness's wounds are not immediately dangerous, and he is as well as can be expected under the circumstances of the case," signed by Home. At ten o'clock in the morning Mr. John Reade, the coroner and principal magistrate of Bow Street, arrived and began to take depositions. The whole sequence of events became clear.

Sellis had apartments with his family elsewhere in the Palace, besides the room in the Duke's. The previous day he had told the other servants that the Duke was going to Windsor in the morning and that he was therefore to sleep in the Duke's apartments. Sarah Varley, one of the housemaids, gave evidence that she was in the housemaids' room with Margaret Jones at about ten o'clock last night when Sellis had asked her to put sheets on the bed. Margaret had answered " Very well, sir," and he had left. This had been done and one of the maids had seen him about to undress; he had said good-night and shut his door. He had, however, merely changed into a different suit of clothes for the evil night's work. Thomas Strickland, the under-butler who

---

[1] The news had reached Brook's nearby, and Sheridan, who was there, had notified the Duke of Sussex.

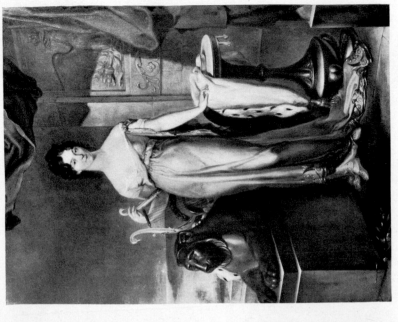

The Duke of Cumberland as Colonel of the 15th Hussars, about 1815

(*Artist unknown*)

The Duchess of Cumberland at the time of her marriage

(*Artist unknown*)

had brought the Duke's late-night drink, had seen him in the Duke's rooms. As he was his valet, that was not remarkable, but he had given him such an extraordinary smile that he had intended to mention it to the servant with whom he shared a room.

Sellis had then, obviously, hidden himself in the closet at the foot of the bed, as was shown by his marked slippers and the shaded lantern, which Sarah Varley said was his. The Duke had gone to bed, and Neale, the valet on duty, had locked the door to the Yellow Room and the State Apartments. Sellis intended then to murder the Duke and hurry, via the Yellow Room, to his own room, wash his hands and obliterate any other traces, and go to bed. In the morning the Duke would be found and suspicion would fall upon Neale, which was, as we shall see, the whole object of the dastardly crime. Had he, in the Corsican manner, used a knife, he would have easily and safely despatched his master with one blow, but he was too frightened of the Duke to approach him so closely, even when he was asleep ; he knew the Duke's great strength and resilience. So he had taken refuge behind the head of the bed and used the sabre, a weapon which could be wielded well out of reach of the victim, and which he had recently sharpened. The first blow, however, had lost much of its force in striking the tassels round the bed and fallen obliquely, even so, cutting through the Duke's thickly-wadded night-cap and deep into his head—otherwise it would have split his skull in two.

As soon as he had realised that the Duke was not to be murdered, Sellis had fled via the Yellow Room, gone to his own room, washed his hands and taken off his bloodstained coat. The porter had knocked and gone, but then he heard footsteps coming to the other door, something which could only mean that a search was being made for him—that he was found out. In this way it was the Duke's anxiety for him which led to his death, for, panicking at what he thought was his discovery, he had cut his throat as Mrs. Neale and the porter arrived.

Many of the Duke's friends were now arriving, besides his brothers. Captain Bloomfield arrived after eleven and found the Duke in bed, his head bound up, with blood everywhere, on the doors and walls and covering the bed. Wathen Waller, the physician, also hurried to the Duke, who asked him to have the room cleared, told him of the state in which he was and entreated him not to leave him. It was now, several hours after the event, that the nervous reaction set in. At Waller's earnest request, it was decided to move the Duke to Carlton House that evening.

The Coroner to the Household was a Mr. Samuel Thomas Adams, and it was laid down by Statute 23 Henry 8 that the jury for such an inquest should consist of twelve Yeoman Officers of the King's Household. It is often attributed to the Coroner's perspicacity that, knowing that rumours would be spread about the Duke of Cumberland, he chose a jury from sources known to be impervious to Court influence. This is writing history after the event. Anti-Royal juries did not concern themselves with justice and facts so much as politics, as several cases prove, and that not all the Duke's enemies would have behaved as Place did on this occasion is borne out by their attitude towards him, including that of Sir Francis Burdett, who denounced him as a hireling of the Court and betrayer of the movement. Had he or many others been chosen, one could hardly call it perspicacity upon Adam's part, but downright stupidity, if not malice.

As has been seen, he sent summonses to many unlikely persons living within the area of Charing Cross,[1] mostly tradesmen. One of these was the notorious Radical, Francis Place, a men's tailor. As soon as he received notification, he suspected that the Court would try to suppress something, and, anxious not to lose such an opportunity, he decided to make himself master of the law of inquests. He therefore went to a barrister friend, who told him, among other things, that a jury had to consist of twelve but might be expanded to twenty-four persons and that the doors must be open. He then hurried on to the Palace, but, having lost much time thereby, he found a jury of twelve already assembled. From his newly-acquired legal knowledge he insisted that more than the minimum should be sworn in and he himself became foreman, convinced that something would now come to light that would finally crush the Duke of Cumberland. "It is my belief," he wrote later, "that every one of the men who served on the inquest was prejudiced against the Duke." He insisted also that reporters should be present.

The inquest began between three and four in the afternoon and lasted until ten o'clock in the evening. The body was examined as it was. The jurors lined up outside the one entrance, went down the three steps into the room one by one, examined the body and left by the other door. Only one was unable to do this, a butcher who turned sick at its resemblance to his own work. They were then asked if they wished to see the Duke, but they

---

[1] This, as Place notes, was of doubtful legality, for these streets only belonged to the " Verge " of the Court at the time of the existence of Whitehall Palace, which was burnt down in 1679.

agreed that it was unnecessary and returned a unanimous verdict upon Sellis of *felo de se*.[1]

We come now to discuss the motive of the crime. Joseph Sellis, who was a Corsican and his master's favourite, was, it is evident, a cross between a scoundrel and a homicidal maniac. The most obvious supposition, that he had a grievance against the Duke, was quite ruled out. It became abundantly clear that the madman had conceived a bitter jealousy of his fellow-valet, Neale, to appease which he was prepared to sacrifice his master. Mrs. Neale said that he was very obstinate and would not bear contradiction or accept that he was ever at fault; he lived to himself and was distant towards the other servants. To him, as to all of them, the Duke had displayed great affection. He insisted upon always being accompanied by him when travelling, and the man had then conceived a violent jealousy of the valets of the Dukes of Sussex and Cambridge who travelled inside their masters' carriages, but only a week or ten days ago Sellis complained of the cold and the Duke had told him to ride inside with himself. On saying that he felt unwell, he had been sent to bed by the Duke instead of having to sit up for him, which was his duty every third night. During the last four or five years, the Duke had had quarters found for his wife and children in the Palace and had had a permit obtained for him that he might have a key to the pair of green baise doors across the gallery separating the Duke's from the Queen's public rooms, always locked (the only other servant with a key being Mrs. Neale), so that he could join his family without going out of doors. He had also made an allowance of coal and candles to him. At the birth of his youngest child about three months ago, the Duke and Princess Augusta had stood sponsors by proxy; the Queen made a present of two pieces of muslin and the Princess

---

[1] Of course, the verdict was a great disappointment to the Whigs and Radicals. Place said that after the inquest, Colonel Wardle, who had attacked the Duke of York a few years previously, "called upon me. He said everybody was dissatisfied with the verdict and that Sir Francis Burdett was among the number. That it was reported, I was in the pay of Government and had procured the verdict improperly." He then gives a glimpse behind the scenes where the Duke's enemies laid their campaigns against him. He told Wardle that the Coroner's clerk would, if he so desired, come and give details of how the verdict was reached, to satisfy him that everything had been properly conducted. Wardle said that he would be obliged and Place intended to send for the clerk the next day. In the meantime, however, Wardle went to Clifford, Burdett's Radical lawyer, and told him that if he would call upon Place unannounced at the hour, he would find him and the Coroner's clerk preparing between them an account of the inquest. Clifford was indignant and immediately informed Place, who gives his opinion of the man. "Of all the dirty rascals I had ever met with," he writes, "I had never before met one to equal Wardle. . . . I never saw Wardle again, though up to this time he was frequently coming to me always when he found himself in extremities."

of another, besides making many other gifts for the baptism. All this Sellis rewarded with the complaint that Mrs. Neale was the Duke's housekeeper and his own wife had no appointment.

Mary Ann, the widow of Sellis, gave evidence that she had always thought her husband grateful to the Duke. He was in no way in straitened circumstances; that very morning, a tailor had delivered some new clothes for him; he was not in debt. They had been receiving presents for two years from Princess Elizabeth, and the very night, when her husband had told her that the Duke was going to Windsor the next day and that he was to sleep with him, she had been making up the muslin and other things for the birthday of one of their children. He had asked her to roast the veal for the next day. About two years ago, she said, her husband had quarrelled about Neale and had said that he was leaving, but she had pleaded with him to stay with the Duke, pointing out all the advantages, the rooms, the allowances and favours that they received. Sellis's maid, Ann Hill, was also a witness.

Another servant who gave evidence was Antonio Panzero, valet to the Duke of Sussex. Sellis had said that, but for his wife, he would leave as Neale was making his life intolerable; he received all the Duke's clothing and perquisites, he claimed. On the 22nd May, walking in the Park at Windsor, he had said that it was through Neale that he was so unhappy and that Neale robbed his master. The Duke had spoken sharply to him (Sellis) and he would be better treated if Neale were not there.

Sellis tried to turn the Duke against his fellow-servant and had written to Captain Stephenson, the Duke's equerry, accusing Neale of dishonesty and theft, saying that since the Duke had forgiven him he no longer wished to remain in his service; Neale over-charged his master, buying soap, for example, at eighteenpence and saying that it had cost two shillings; he recommended that he should be transported for seven years, though even that would be mild, a life sentence being more what was deserved. He spoke of "the mortification of having to live and act in the same room with a man I have convicted as a rogue and with whom no human is able to live upon friendly terms. . . . Should His Royal Highness wish me to proceed with these discoveries, it will be found that the dishonesty of this man has no bounds. . . ." From the evidence which he had gathered, the Duke must realise "that this man is as great a villain as ever existed." Of course, his accusations were found to be baseless, yet the Duke still retained and favoured him.

Still more evil was the man's past. He had associated with a notorious French Jacobin and then became valet to a Mr. Church, who had gone to America in 1797. He had remained a Jacobin, cursing all those whom he imagined better than himself, whether it was the King and Royal Family—he boasted of having thrown a stone at their carriage as they went to Parliament—or his fellows—such as Neale—shocking and offending the rest of the servants. He also cursed the Almighty, which effectually disposes of the theory, sometimes advanced, that he was a Catholic and had been provoked by the Duke's hostility to his religion. After one and a half years, he had robbed his master. All the servants knew of his guilt, but there was not sufficient proof to convict him before the New York magistrates. Mr. Church's chest had been broken open and a large sum of money taken. A hammer exactly fitting the marks on the chest was found in Sellis's possession, and Mr. Church then recollected waking suddenly as he was sleeping after dinner and seeing Sellis start back and close the door. Curiously enough, Mr. Church had also treated him with forbearance and a complete absence of vindictiveness. He had dismissed him, of course, but paid him liberally and sent him back to England. He then, according to Rose, went to Piedmont, where Lord Mount Edgcumbe met and engaged him. The Duke of Cumberland took a liking to him, for he was an efficient servant, and asked his master if he might engage him.

That was his life history as it emerged from the evidence of three former servants of Mr. Church, now in London. One of them, Sarah Wilson, described him as a " very morose, malicious man, and very inveterate against this country." Another, Martha Perkins, when she had learnt that he was in the Duke's service, thought him an " improper man to live in the Royal Family," but, as he was now married, she thought that perhaps his manners and character had altered and so she had no wish to injure him. The third, Robert Lutman, formerly Mr. Church's groom, was astonished " that such a rascal as Sellis could get to live with the Duke of Cumberland." The Duke himself was mystified as to the motive, and when he showed his chamberlain the scene of the attempt thirty-three years later, he told him that he regretted that Sellis had taken his own life as it had drawn a deep veil of mystery over the whole episode. Certainly this was a case in which the Duke's usually accurate judgment of character was at fault.

The Prince of Wales and Duke of York visited their brother during the day, and at about nine, when it was dusk and the inquest was concluding its work, he was moved to Carlton House. With great difficulty he was transferred to the chair, and Wathen Waller walked beside it the whole way. The Duke then went to bed, his nerves in a terrible state. The slightest sound caused him excruciating agony. The Prince of Wales had to take off his shoes or slippers before approaching his brother's bed, and Waller said that if he accidentally touched the bedclothes he cried out with agony and could not bear the scratching of his pen, so he had to write in another room.[1] The Duke himself described these two incidents to von Malortie, thirty-three years later.

In all, the Duke was in agony for between six and eight weeks. Fortunately, he was surrounded with devoted attendants. Waller remained with him all the time and slept in the adjacent room every night until the 4th August, when the Duke went to Windsor. The Prince was a true brother and assisted in dressing his wounds. He was moved to tears by the Duke's suffering and fainted away on one occasion. This was, indeed, the first stage in the reconciliation and life-long love between them; it certainly paved the way for the events of the next two years.

The Royal Family had returned to London on receiving the news, and on the 2nd June the Queen and the Princesses Augusta, Elizabeth and Sophia came from the Queen's House and remained with him for three hours. The next day the bulletin stated that " His Royal Highness the Duke of Cumberland's wound in his head has been dressed for the first time. Though deep and large, it puts on as favourable an appearance as could be expected."

Inquirers after the Duke were allowed into his apartments, which were in exactly the same state as on the morning after the outrage; dried blood was on the walls and pictures, while the same bedclothes were made up on the bed. The idea was to prove that the Court was not keeping anything secret and to show the correctness of the verdict at the inquest. But, of course, it was not only genuine inquirers after the Duke who availed themselves of this facility and an end was soon put to the abuse.

On the 7th, as has been seen, the Duke asked that the Foskett affair should be finally settled, saying that he did not wish to take advantage of his injuries. The regiment was genuinely affected by its Colonel's misfortune and expressed its solicitude. On the 13th, the Duke had a visit from his old tutor, Dr. Cookson, who described it later to Farington. " Dr. Cookson said he had been with the Duke of Cumberland and sat with him some time," we read in his Diary. " He found him in a very nervous state, supposed to be

---

[1] From Waller's evidence at the trial of Philips. *Von Malortie* (p. 24).

owing to the very large quantities of laudanum which he takes, without which he has no rest. He suffers much pain and is much afflicted with spasms. One of the servants at Carlton House, where the Duke now is, told Dr. Cookson that the Prince of Wales is much affected by the Duke's illness, ' the more so,' he added, ' than either his mother or his sisters appear to be.' He went on and said, ' Whenever any of the Prince's family are indisposed he feels for them.' "

No human being could have undergone a crueler trial. For upwards of a month the Duke lay in agony, and it was the opinion of the doctors that only his iron constitution enabled him to survive. It was reported in *The Times* that on the 2nd July he was operated upon and one of the wounds in his head was opened and a piece of fractured skull, one inch by a quarter, removed. Certainly a new disfigurement was added to those which he had received in the Netherlands.[1]

On the 15th, however, the Duke was able to walk for a while in the gardens of Carlton House, and after the 17th no bulletin was issued. On the 20th he took an airing for the first time in a carriage with the Dukes of Kent, Sussex and Cambridge. At noon the King arrived at the Queen's House from Windsor and the Duke of Cumberland alighted to greet him. He was clad in a great-coat, with both arms in slings, and he had not the use of either hand ; his head was bound with black silk and he also wore a black silk cap. He was pale " but not so much reduced as might have been expected." On the afternoon of the 22nd, for the first time since that night, the Duke, accompanied by the Prince of Wales, visited his apartments at St. James's, which had been locked up and were in exactly the same state as then. He went through the suite and spent some time in the bedroom, then he drove in an open landau to the Royal Mews at Pimlico, where he talked for a long time with the lieutenant-colonel and officers of his regiment, which was about to march to Hounslow Barracks. He was very pale, his head bound and hands muffled, and still could not bear his left arm to be touched.[2] After two of these months' convalescence, he went to Windsor on the 4th August.

His attempted murder marks another stage in the Duke of Cumberland's life. It was certainly an unfortunate coincidence that the most bitterly attacked of the Princes should have been the

[1] Years later, when Ernest Augustus was King of Hanover, he picked up his chaplain's little daughter, who ran away in fright, saying that he had " a hole in his his head."—*Wilkinson*.   [2] *The Times*.

victim, for, as has been seen, his unpopularity was quite unrelated to Sellis's motives. It was a godsend to his enemies. Here was an opportunity such as they never could have imagined in their wildest dreams, and for the rest of his life in England new " authentic " versions of Sellis's " murder " appeared at regular intervals, in which the Duke was portrayed as its instigator in order to hide all manner of unmentionable crimes and immoralities. From now on " Duke of Cumberland stories " were on a completely different level of foulness ; looking back, the old tales of his raising his cane to an officer or blocking Captain Foskett's promotion must have seemed absurdly weak and amateurish— henceforth it was to be rape, incest and unnatural obscenities.

At the time, the Duke was overwhelmed with expressions of sympathy. In many places, foreign servants were manhandled by the others as a result and there was a burst of anti-Italian feeling, which found expression in the *Morning Post*. Faced with the testimony of Place and his Radicals, of the Duke's visible injuries and the opening of his rooms to inspection, there was not much opportunity for slanderous stories. But as the memory of these facts grew remoter and the Duke's unpopularity greater, people were more and more prepared to believe everything about him. Indeed, the Sellis campaign did not reach its peak until twenty-three years later, when the Duke was forced to take action, as will be seen.

The first libels appeared in 1812, in the *Independent Whig*, written by one White, a notorious blackmailer.[1] The Duke prosecuted him, and in March 1813 the case was heard before Lord Ellenborough. White was found guilty and sentenced to fifteen months' imprisonment and a fine of two hundred pounds.[2] But such prosecutions were of no use, for, in trying to stem the flood of abuse and obscene slander that was let loose upon him, the Duke might as well have ordered the sea to recede in the manner of King Canute.

---

[1] We are again indebted to Place for a description of this man. He apparently made a practice of obtaining introductions to prominent men and then used to prey upon them. His system was to publish a few hints to give the impression that he knew something the publication of which his victim would do well to prevent. He was thus frequently able to blackmail without possessing any secrets whatsoever, " and," wrote Place, " the money he was said to have obtained was incredible. I however knew three cases in which he obtained considerable sums, in one of these three cases he obtained £300 in one sum." The unpopular Duke of Cumberland seemed to be ideally suited to become another victim, so White wrote in his paper that " Proof is at hand ! " that he had murdered Sellis. He misjudged his man this time, however.

[2] Through having libelled the Duke of Cumberland, this blackmailer became a hero and subscriptions were raised in certain circles to maintain him in a state of luxury during his sentence, a practice allowed in prisons in those days.

CHAPTER IX

1810–13

THE years following the attempted assassination of the Duke of Cumberland saw a train of events which at last straightened out the entangled personal and political relationships in the Royal Family. In 1810 there was a Tory Government in office under Perceval, and this, of course, enjoyed the blessings of the Duke of Cumberland. But he alone among the Princes avowed his Toryism. The loyalties of the others were still determined by the dead family feuds of the days of Fox, and the Prince of Wales was still regarded as the man who would put the Whigs into power as soon as he was able. A deep rift, therefore, still separated the two brothers.

In November the King's favourite daughter, Princess Amelia, died after heart-rending sufferings. At the last scene the poor father broke down and lost his reason. The family was plunged into grief and the country mourned. But in one quarter it was an occasion for rejoicing. For the Whigs, it seemed, " the day " had come. A regent was necessary and he would be their patron, the Prince of Wales. Soon they would be distributing the offices and spoils among themselves. The dismissal of the Cabinet was hourly awaited.

To reverse every policy of the preceding reign would have been sufficiently deplorable had the Prince succeeded to the Throne, but as it was, he was only exercising the prerogatives on behalf of his father who, in theory at least, might at any time re-assume them. It was clear that if he were to make that use of the Royal power, some check would have to be imposed and the person best qualified to represent the interests of the King was the Queen. The Government therefore proposed that she should be associated in the regency and, in particular, the prerogative in such irrevocable acts as the bestowal of peerages was to be withheld from the Prince. The Prince, of course, protested, and he was supported by his Whig brothers.

In the disagreements which followed, the parties appeared to exchange rôles. The hypocritical Whigs appeared as ultra-royalists fighting the Government which was seeking to deprive the representative of the Crown of its prerogatives, and the Government's action, though actually consistent and in the interests of the Crown, seemed to be antagonistic towards it. What course, then, was the Duke of Cumberland to take ? His was never ambiguous. At all costs, he decided, the prerogative of the Crown had to be upheld. In his case there was none of the intrigue which characterised the squabbling of the parties. All the Princes [1] assembled at Carlton House on the 19th December 1810, and drew up a memorandum [2] for the Prime Minister protesting against the Ministerial proposals and declaring them to be unconstitutional.

The Duke of Cumberland was carrying his consistency to the point of quixotism. To uphold his principles he was joining those who had always been his bitterest enemies and separating himself from his dearest friends. He felt this deeply and wrote to Eldon and Perceval of his profound sorrow at being obliged to differ from them. [3] There is no doubt that tension between the Duke and his brother was high. On the last day of October the Prince of Wales had told Colonel H. N. Willis, " The Duke of Cumberland will sit the evening with us, but remember, though we are on terms of civility together, you are not to suppose there exists any cordial union between us " [4]—so the Duke could not, as some say, have been induced to subscribe to this protest in the confidence that the Prince would not call the Whigs. However, the Prince was mature enough not to be guided in the government of the Kingdom merely by memories of the boon-companions of his youth. He did not open the coffers of state to the Whigs, nor did he dispense the offices and honours for which they had hungered so long.

Of course, these events did not increase the Duke of Cumberland's popularity in those narrow circles which arrogate to themselves the right to be styled " public opinion." They gave an added spur to the increasing campaign of abuse and slander against him. The latest cry was one which can always be relied upon to call forth a response in the hearts of Englishmen—that of the sinister foreigner. Farington reports that he had attempted to put a Hanoverian into his regiment over the heads of the other officers, who forced him to desist by threatening to resign collectively. " Baron Geramb and other German officers are much encouraged

---

[1] The Prince Regent and the Dukes of York, Clarence, Kent, Cumberland, Sussex, Cambridge and Gloucester.
[2] Given in Twiss's *Eldon*, Walpole's *Perceval* and Jesse's *George III*.
[3] See his letter to Eldon (*Twiss*, II, p. 137), and Perceval (*Walpole*, II, p. 174).
[4] Jesse's *George III*, III, p. 555.

by the Duke and his brothers, which is supposed to be owing to
their being more obsequious than the British officers." [1]   Again,
this incident is nowhere mentioned in histories of the 15th Hussars
and no such name or title as Baron Geramb exists in Hanover;
the slur upon British officers (for " obsequious " here merely means
reliable) can be ignored. [2]

There was, perhaps, some fire behind the smoke, for a quarrel
about a German officer is mentioned in another place.   No doubt
this occurred during the Duke's visit with the Prince Regent and
his brothers to the Hanoverians at Ipswich and Woodbridge in
September 1811.   The Prince was on his way to Sudbourne Hall,
the seat of the Marquess of Hertford, and there were many festivities and military reviews as he passed through and returned.   The
entire garrisons were inspected on Rushmere Heath, including the
King's German Legion under the command of the Duke's old
instructor, now Lieutenant-General von Linsingen.   Afterwards
the latter was riding with the Duke and his staff along St. Matthew's
Street, just outside the barracks, when three men, indignantly
described in the local paper as " three men (not inhabitants of this
town)," tried to force their way through the party with their gig.
One shaft struck the Duke's knee and the other so wounded von
Linsingen's horse that death resulted the next day.   It was his
favourite charger and he was greatly distressed, but he would with
his magnanimity have suffered the rascals to go unpunished.   Not
so the Duke and his officers, who seized them and took them
before the magistrates, where they were fined. [3]

Though they were seen together in public, there was no intercourse between the Prince Regent and the Duke of Cumberland.
Princess Charlotte, the former's rebellious young daughter, saw
this dissension with satisfaction. [4]   " He spoke of the Duke of
Cumberland as *we could wish*," she wrote, [5] " and assured me he
never told him anything ; said that he was very happy at the idea
of so soon getting into Carlton House, by which means he could
avoid his being *constantly* with him. . . ."   Later in the month of
November the quarrel reached its climax.

[1] *Farington Diaries*, VII, p. 74.
[2] See his views on the promotion of officers in *Wylly*.   When in the Hanoverian
Army he had once been refused permission to appoint an English officer as his
A.D.C. (W.A.).
[3] *Ipswich Journal*.
[4] After the separation of the Prince and Princess of Wales the latter, aided by the
Whigs, had made great efforts to detach Princess Charlotte from her father.   The young
Princess resented the restraint to which she was subjected.
[5] *The Letters of Princess Charlotte*, p. 12.

The Prince Regent was staying with the Duke of York at his house, Oatlands. There was a ball and he tripped while dancing and hurt his foot; he immediately went to bed and, according to one account, insisted upon taking laudanum. The Duke of Cumberland, who was not inclined to be tolerant of what he considered trifles, might well have been sceptical of all this, and Lady Bessborough wrote to Lord Granville Leveson Gower that " The Prince has quarrelled with the Duke of Cumberland from hearing of his saying everywhere that his brother's illness was *higher* than the foot, and that a blister on the head might be more efficacious than a poultice on the ankle." [1] Mr. Fremantle, who had reported this incident to the Marquess of Buckingham, had written on the 28th November, " The Duke of Cumberland is going about saying it is all sham, and that he could get up and would be perfectly well if he pleased." [2]

This coincided with the beginnings of a Ministerial crisis. Lord Wellesley,[3] the Foreign Minister, had for some time been estranged from Perceval, and as the Cabinet was split between the two, it was obvious that one of them would have to go. On the 2nd December Mr. Fremantle wrote that the indisposition at Oatlands was a very fortunate occurrence for Wellesley ; the Duke of Cumberland, who, of course, supported Perceval, had been scarcely admitted there, while the Regent's host, the Duke of York, had taken his side. On the 18th he wrote that " The Prince has no explanation with him [the Duke of Cumberland], but has determined never to see him alone ; and now, when he calls, the Prince always keeps somebody in the room." [4]

In this political situation is to be found the key to the motive for starting the quarrel, for it seems that the Duke had never made the offending remarks at all. No one would ever give the name of the person or persons to whom he had said them. On the 14th December Princess Charlotte wrote to her friend,[5] " I saw Bloomfield yesterday and I *pumped* him all I could, and he told me that he came up one evening to town from Oatlands with the Duke of Cumberland and that he *never had* passed so *unpleasant* a journey in all his life, as he was *vociferating oaths* against the *person* (whoever it was) that *could* set afoot such a *lie* against the Prince, declared that if he could discover the person he would *destroy him* with his

[1] *Private Correspondence* of Lord G. Leveson Gower.
[2] Buckingham's *Memoirs of the Court of the Regency*, I, p. 145.
[3] Brother of the Duke of Wellington.
[4] Buckingham's *Memoirs of the Court of the Regency*, I, p. 162.
[5] *The Letters of Princess Charlotte*, p. 18.

own hands, used the most solemn oaths to declare *his innocence*, in short worked himself up into a sort of frenzy that Bloomfield said he hardly knew what he would do next, as there were firearms in the carriage—and this conduct the whole way up to town." " Poor unfortunate man," said Bloomfield of the Duke's increasing isolation. " Who could ever wish to be him or have anything to do with him ? "

But the Duke of Cumberland was not the man to let such an intrigue continue unchecked, and here Lady Bessborough resumes the story, writing on the 31st,[1] " The Prince had intimated to the Duke of Cumberland that to avoid the appearance of a quarrel, he would speak to him in public or before a third person, but never alone. The Duke of Cumberland came to town, drove directly to Carlton House, begged Lord Yarmouth to help him, who carried him to the Prince's room, and in defiance of his orders, left them together. The consequence was a reconciliation which began with high words, such that their voices were heard in the ante-rooms quite close to the stairs."

So the friendship between the brothers was restored, never again to be interrupted. The fact that it had come to an end as the Whigs came into office and reached the peak of their power and was resumed just as their hold over the Prince was broken, shows that its interruption could only be ascribed to their influence and intrigue and illustrates the tragic way in which the Royal Family was their victim.

The immediate result of the reconciliation was the defeat of the Wellesley faction. Mr. Fremantle noted that it was no longer the Whig Princes and Wellesley himself who surrounded the Regent, but the Duke of Cumberland and, very often, Lord Eldon. Wellesley resigned early in 1812. Perceval remained Prime Minister, largely through the Duke, if the deductions of these chroniclers are correct.

The new fraternal relationship soon bore even greater political fruit. On the 11th May 1812 a madman shot Perceval dead in the lobby of the House of Commons. Now was the opportunity for the other wing of the late Government, the Wellesley group, and the Regent was obliged against his own wishes to authorise him to form a Cabinet. He failed, and other Whigs and Whig-Tories were as unsuccessful. Lord Liverpool [2] formed a Tory Administration on the 8th, and the Duke of Cumberland seems to

---

[1] *Private Correspondence* of Lord G. Leveson Gower.
[2] Formerly Lord Hawkesbury, leader of the Perceval-Tories.

have had some share in this outcome. Romilly claims that Eldon had never shown the slightest apprehension of resigning his office ; he had " been every day closeted with the Duke of Cumberland and, during several days in the term, the Court has been entirely shut up, while His Lordship was employed in some way never known to the suitors of his Court or to the public. We have even had the Duke of Cumberland coming down to Westminster Hall, and sending for the Chancellor out of Court." [1] That the Duke of Cumberland *did* play an important part in these proceedings is borne out by a chance reference in a letter of his, dated 10th May 1814, in which he tells the Prince Regent, " You know I have served you and can be trusted in ticklish affairs. To-morrow's event that took place in 1812 will call to your recollection that *I* am worthy of trust and can be depended upon." [2]

All this gave the Duke's enemies the more reason for wishing him out of the way. Slander and vituperation were the chief weapons employed to this end, and early in 1813 he was involved in a clash with the Commons.

The Duke, it appears, was one of the four trustees of the late Sir J. L. Johnston, who had come into the possession of Sir W. Pulteney's property in Weymouth. On the 26th February it was moved that irregularities had taken place in the voting arrangements for the borough ; freeholds had been split so that more persons might vote as freeholders, and this was a situation which could only be remedied by legislation. The citizens of Weymouth indignantly drew up a petition begging the House not to interfere with the city's independence and pointing out that the proposed measure would concentrate all power in the hands of from thirty to forty men. It was on the 1st April that the Duke of Cumberland's name was mentioned in the discussion for the first time, when Whig members accused him of having had possession of the writ for the election and having promised to obtain a place for one elector. Alderman Atkin of Weymouth pointed out that the Duke had been entrusted with the writ " for the convenience of the election and [it] had been forwarded with all possible despatch." The Duke did not condescend to say a word to the allegations, and the affair was to have a curious sequel thirty years later.

The Duke, who drew all attacks unflinchingly upon himself, was becoming a somewhat embarrassing champion for the Government and his influence was now of little service to it. He realised this and turned himself, now that Lord Liverpool's Government

---

[1] *Romilly*, II, p. 261.   [2] W.A.

was firmly in the saddle, from home to foreign affairs. He had never lost interest in the prosecution of the war against Napoleon, though he had been unable to serve as soldier against him. He decided that if the War Office would not give him a command, he would go to the Continent and obtain one for himself.

He envisaged a long absence and began to break up his London establishment with the sale of his sixteen horses for 1303 guineas and the disposal of his wines by auction. This latter event was attended by a somewhat humorous, if, for the Duke, unfortunate circumstance. The occasion was one of some novelty and drew a crowd of at least three hundred, mostly from the aristocracy, to Robin's Rooms, where it took place. The Duke's good taste was well known and everyone was asking, unaware of his intended departure, why he should have determined to sell his wines. The idea arose that he would not have done so had they been good, and this had a marked effect on the bidding.

The Duke left on the 28th April. He quitted his apartments at St. James's at about one o'clock and walked to Carlton House to take leave of the Prince Regent. Among other things, his brother enjoined him, if he should at last enter Hanover, to put on the sword, knot and sash of a Hanoverian lieutenant-general. An hour later his four servants who were to accompany him arrived at Carlton House in his travelling-carriage. On his orders, it had been prepared the night before for vicissitudes with a new patent " Anti-Attrition Composition " in the axle-boxes, enabling it to go over a thousand miles without overhaul. The servants collected the luggage and set off on the journey, while the saddle-horses were to follow on the morrow. The Duke emerged soon after three o'clock and set out in his open barouche for the East Coast, accompanied by his A.D.C., Captain Poten. He was wearing a green morocco travelling-cap in the Russian style, lined and ornamented with gold lace and buttons.

Owing to the poor roads and the darkness of the night he did not reach Ipswich until midnight. He alighted at the house which von Linsingen had built for himself there, but did not go to bed. He waited up until five o'clock in the morning and then set off again for Yarmouth. On the way he stopped to write a message of affection to his brother to catch the post at Lowestoft during the morning.[1]

At Yarmouth he alighted at the Nelson Inn and stayed over the week-end, attending in the Chapel on Sunday, 2nd May. On

[1] W.A., 29th April 1813.

Monday, before he departed, the local paper reported that " His Royal Highness expressed himself much satisfied with the attention and accommodation offered him at the Nelson Inn." The Duke wrote a long letter of farewell to his brother. " Being just on the point of embarking," he said, " I must write to you two lines to bid you farewell and hope that you are convinced whether present or absent you have only to command my services in any way that may be of use to you, for though I say it still I must maintain you have not one more faithfully attached to your honour and interest than myself. God bless you and do not forget your affectionate . . ." [1]

On the 3rd May the wind was at last favourable. The Duke embarked with his suite at ten o'clock in the morning upon the frigate *Nymph* and was borne out on to the stormy North Sea.

[1] W.A., 2nd May, 1813.

CHAPTER X

THE LIBERATION OF HANOVER

AT the end of April 1813 the coalition which was to drive Napoleon from Germany was taking shape. Prussia and Austria had come to an understanding with Russia and their alliance was joined by the newly-created Prince Royal of Sweden, Bernadotte. On the 1st April Swedish troops landed in Pomerania and Napoleon's former marshal was tempted to play the part of deliverer of North Germany.

The liberation of Hanover from her ten years of French rule did not seem far distant. Count von Wallmoden, the son of the Field-Marshal of the 1790's, who, after many years in Austrian service, had been persuaded by the Prince Regent to take over the command of the Hanoverians in Russian service (the rest of the Hanoverian Army formed the King's German Legion), had arrived in Hamburg in April. The plan of operations, however, was left to Bernadotte, and since his principal desire was to wrest Norway from Denmark, the Hanoverians who had enthusiastically thronged to join the army for the liberation of their country were very disappointed indeed. Prussia desired an extension of territory in the north—she had already once tasted an annexation of the Electorate [1] —and it was also feared that the Emperor Alexander, the leader of the coalition, might offer Hanover to Bernadotte. The necessity of taking possession of the country without loss of time was therefore clear, and with so much to be done the Duke of Cumberland felt certain that he could contribute. He would, he thought, find a command under one of the allies and finally secure the continental possessions of his House. " I cannot describe to you," he wrote to his brother,[2] " how I long to get into activity, and if by my feeble means I can in any way succeed in recovering Hanover for you it will be the proudest day of my life."

The Duke therefore requested Sir Charles Stewart (half-brother of the Foreign Secretary, Lord Castlereagh), who had arrived as British Ambassador at the Allied Headquarters earlier in the month,

---

[1] Prussia had occupied Hanover as agent of the French in 1801.
[2] W.A.* To Prince Regent, 7th June 1813.

to make inquiries. As a result, Sir Charles reported that the presence of British officers at Headquarters was definitely not desired ; the Emperor of Russia was not favourably disposed towards the idea. But when his letter arrived in London, the Duke had already departed.[1]

The *Nymph* was having a stormy passage battling against contrary winds, and the Duke [2] was relieved when she arrived off Heligoland on the 7th May. She was in great danger from Danish gun-boats and the enemy's possession of Cuxhaven and Stade made it hazardous to attempt to reach Hamburg, so the Duke decided to go on to the next safe port, Gothenborg, in Sweden.[3] There he arrived on the 13th and set off the next day across southern Sweden. On the Baltic coast he took the packet-boat to Stralsund, in Swedish Pomerania, where he disembarked at four o'clock on the morning of the 19th, after a very disagreeable thirty-six-hour passage.[4] His carriages were landed and he intended to start for Strelitz immediately, but as he was waiting at the captain's while horses were found, an officer arrived from the Prince Royal, Bernadotte. The Prince had learnt of his arrival at Gothenborg and wished him to be escorted to his headquarters, he said ; a house had been prepared for him as the roads were still not safe. The Duke decided to accept the offer and stay the night and entered the waiting carriage.

A guard of honour was drawn up at the house and soon after the Duke's arrival the Prince Royal himself appeared with hosts of officers and officials. He was very pleased to meet the Duke, for he was trying to establish his position among the legitimate Royalty, while the Duke was favourably impressed and commented, with the hostility of the times to all things French, " Nothing could be more polite than he is, and much less of the Frenchman than anyone could suppose." The Prince began to talk about the war and future plans, but there the Duke had to interrupt him, remembering the Prince Regent's strict injunction (no doubt inspired by the Cabinet) not to discuss politics. He felt his humiliation deeply, commenting in describing the interview to his brother, " I hope *this* answer will satisfy you." That night, the Duke had dinner with his host and some seventy guests.[4] On the 21st May he left for Strelitz, strongly advised by the British envoy to Sweden,

---

[1] Castlereagh's *Correspondence*, 27th April, 1813.
[2] The Duke's suite consisted of Captain Poten (his A.D.C.), Captain Howard Wyse, Lieutenant Dawkings and his private secretary, Mr. F. Watson. The *Nymph* was commanded by Captain Hancock.
[3] W.A., 10th May 1813.   [4] *Ibid.,** 20th May 1813.

Mr. Thornton, always to remain within reach of the Royal Navy.[1]

The little Duchy of Mecklenburg-Strelitz was the homeland of his mother and her two brothers lived in the tiny capital among the lakes and woods of the Baltic coastland. Prince Ernest, the Duke's bachelor godfather, was a very sick man and the whole family, like the rest of the population, was suffering great poverty and distress from the French occupation. But so great was the enthusiasm in all classes that when the Duke arrived there was a report that he was raising an army and peasants crowded round his doors to enlist. The sons of the reigning Duke Charles, the Duke of Cumberland's cousins, were actually engaged in organising a military force, and Prince George, the younger, had sold the greater part of his plate to raise a hussar regiment. Also at home was another of the Duke's cousins, a Princess whose life, in its uninterrupted frustrations and misfortunes, had much in common with his own.

.   .   .   .

In the years preceding the French Revolution the Duke of Mecklenburg-Strelitz had entered his brother-in-law's service and become military commander in Hanover. While he was stationed there, three daughters were born to him, who were to become celebrated throughout Europe for their beauty and abilities— Theresia, who married the Prince of Thurn and Taxis; Louise, the Queen of Prussia, who inspired the resistance of her people to the invader, and Frederica.

Princess Frederica, or Friedrike Caroline Alexandrine, was born on the 2nd March 1778 at Hanover and baptised there in the Garrison Church. She and her sister Louise spent their early childhood in the Altes Palais on the Leinstrasse, though in summer they lived in a little wooden pavilion on the city wall, amidst the trees and streams. All her early associations were thus with Hanover.

As if to prepare the furrows into which so much unhappiness was to be sown (as one writer put it), the infant Princess was soon acquainted with grief. When she was four years old her mother died in childbed. Her father, pained at the scenes of his married happiness, moved out to Herrenhausen, but he soon saw the need for a mother for his six children. Still true to his wife, he could only consider her sister, and so it was she who became stepmother

---

[1] Castlereagh's *Correspondence*, 28th May, 1813.

of her nephew and nieces. After only a year she gave birth to a
son and the same fate overtook her as her sister. Completely
broken, the sorrowing father left Hanover and Hanoverian service
and settled down in Darmstadt, where his children were cared for
by their grandmother, the Landgravine.

When Princess Frederica was ten years old, two of her sisters
were already married, Charlotte to the Duke of Saxe-Hildburg-
hausen and Theresia to the Prince of Thurn and Taxis. The latter
came of one of the most important families of the old Empire, and
through this relationship she and her other sister, Louise, were
often in the Imperial City of Frankfurt. There they saw the Holy
Roman Empire in the glory of its last days at the coronations of
two Emperors in 1790 and 1792. There they also made the intimate acquaintance of a local patrician family which later became
famous, the Goethes. In the courtyard of their house they played
with pump and water, and when they were found out by one of the
ladies of the Court, mother Goethe endeavoured to hold her back
by words and finally locked her in to prevent her interfering with
" the innocent pleasure which is not allowed them anywhere else."

After these visits to Frankfurt the children stayed some time
with their elder sister in Hildburghausen, deep in the Thuringian
forests, until the spring of 1793. War had then broken out and
French troops had advanced and seized Frankfurt, but in December
1792 Prussian troops recaptured the city by storm and their King
made it his headquarters. With him were his two soldier-sons.
The children were about to return from Hildburghausen to Darmstadt when the Landgrave asked their grandmother to travel by
way of Frankfurt and introduce them to the King.[1]

" When I first saw the two angels, at the entrance to the
Comedy," wrote the impressionable King in a letter,[2] " I was so
struck by their beauty that I was quite overcome when their grandmother presented them to me." He wished only that his sons
should meet them and fall in love, and he begged their grandmother not to continue the journey that evening. They were
introduced at a ball, and all happened as the King had hoped.
A double betrothal was celebrated on the 24th April 1793, in
Darmstadt. The King and his sons came straight from the field
and after the ceremony the Princes returned there. Prince Frederick
Ludwig, Frederica's soldier-fiancé, was distinguished for his
courage and on one occasion he narrowly escaped being roasted to
death in a blazing hut.

[1] *Königin Luise*.   [2] Stanhope's *Mystic on the Prussian Throne*, p. 338.

In the camp at Bodenheim, the headquarters of the army besieging Mainz, the young brides visited their betrothed. Goethe was with the army and he has described the impression which they made upon him. " Last night," he wrote in his diary on the 29th May 1793, " a charming picture was presented for us, and for me in particular. The Mecklenburg Princesses had dined with His Majesty the King at the headquarters at Bodenheim and afterwards they visited the camp. I fastened myself up in my tent and could observe from there the distinguished company perfectly as it strolled about right in front of me. And in the midst of this tumult of war one could really take the two young ladies for apparitions from Heaven. I will never forget the impression which they made."

In December the Princes returned to Berlin from the front and on the 22nd their brides made their ceremonial entry into the capital. It was a day of public rejoicing and of demonstrations which defied all description ; the populace was entranced by the two young Princesses who had been won for it. The marriages took place in the Royal Palace, that of the Crown Prince and Princess Louise on Christmas Eve, that of Prince Frederick Ludwig and her sister on the 26th December. The first was held as a Court function and so displeased the King that at the second the public was admitted and the crowd was so great that he could hardly force his way through it to the altar.

After a happy married life of three years and one day, during which time he had born to him two sons and a daughter, the young Prince died after a few days of sudden illness in his brother's palace on the 28th December 1796, and Princess Frederica was left a widow at the age of eighteen. She was naturally of a somewhat melancholy disposition and life had used her hard. During her marriage she had experienced the pain of separation as she remained in Sans Souci while her husband fought with the armies in Poland and the East.[1] Now, while she still mourned him, one of her infant sons followed him to the grave and she was overcome by the fear that negligence on her part had been responsible.[2]

There was no lack of admirers of the sad and tearful young Princess and one of them was her own cousin, Prince Adolphus. He had stayed in Germany after the end of the campaign in 1795 and so come into contact with Prussian society, now that the two states formed a neutral bloc. He fell deeply in love with his cousin

[1] S.A. Many letters.   [2] S.A. To her father, 7th March 1798.

and offered her his hand. She accepted. She was not infatuated, but she thought that by this means she might find happiness.[1] Together, they made plans for the future, and when they were apart they maintained a frequent correspondence. But when the Prince informed his father and, through Dundas, asked his permission to marry, he was told not to mention the matter again until peace was made—which might have been (and was in fact) years to come.[2] Once more the King was behaving arbitrarily and inviting the hostility of one of his children. Naturally, the Princess would have considered the whole engagement as more or less " off."

So young and so beautiful, and in such a state of despair, she was not left free of temptation ; she could not lead a conventual life and was often in the company of other young men. One of these was a friend of her youth, Prince Frederick of Solms-Braunfels, a house which still ruled over a small territory in the Rhineland. He himself, eight years her senior, not handsome, but well built and of very confident manners, had served in the Dutch Army and was now with a Prussian Guards regiment in Potsdam. There he met her and their relations became very intimate. Late in 1798 the young Princess, in great alarm, found that she was expecting his child. She went to her doctor, Browne, but he held himself bound by his oath to apprise the Royal Family of the facts. First the Queen, the Princess's sister, was informed and she told the King. They hurriedly arranged for a secret marriage, which took place on the 7th January 1799, before two witnesses. On the evening of 10th, the Princess took leave of the King and set off from Berlin as quietly as possible to join her husband at Ansbach, where he was now stationed with the Hussars. There their child was born and baptised on the 30th March.[3]

When their plans had been indefinitely postponed, the Princess had continued to write to her cousin, still in terms of warmth, until the affair with Prince Frederick began about July 1798. Then their correspondence had, perforce, to cool off, and Prince Adolphus assumed that her feelings towards him had altered. On the 11th January 1799 he learnt, most probably from the Hanoverian envoy at Berlin, von Ompteda, that she had been secretly married. He informed the King,[4] but, too affected to be able to write to the

---

[1] S.A. To her father, 28th January 1798.

[2] W.A. Prince Adolphus to the King, 12th January 1799.

[3] H.A. Cal. Br. Preussen 239. Reports of von Ompteda, 8th January and 2nd April 1799.

[4] W.A. Prince Adolphus to the King, 18th May 1799.

Prince of Wales about it himself, he gave a full account of the affair to him through—a strange turn of fate—his brother Ernest.[1] That he afterwards understood and forgave the Princess is obvious from the friendship and steadfastness which he displayed towards her when she was ostracised by the rest of the family.

Princess Frederica's marriage with the Prince of Solms was not very successful, though three sons, born in 1801, 1807 and 1812, sprang from it. The Prince, who occupied himself mostly with hunting and wine, was tired of life, and after seven years she found him quite a different man from the one whom she had married.[2] Nevertheless, against the advice of her father and many of her friends, she determined to remain with him, though her life had become one of misery, and she found her only solace in religion and her children. " Happiness," she wrote to one of her most intimate friends, " is not destined for your poor friend in this life. . . . My fate for the last fifteen years has been more or less to be misunderstood or persecuted—I regard it as a long trial from above, to which there will be, I hope, an end." [3] At last, she succeeded in arranging a return to her father and family at Strelitz. Early in 1810 she and her husband moved there from Berlin, but still she was not to find happiness. As she talked with her old friends after supper upon their arrival, her husband loudly demanded, " Am I supposed to spend *every* day like this ? Every day of my life ? " All the time he complained of his boredom, of his small pension and the fact that he had no grounds for hunting. " If you are happy," he once said to her, " I am not, God knows ! " " Just think ! " she wrote to her friend, " to hear that from a man for whom I have sacrificed *everything* ! It is clearer to me than ever that one cannot make a heavier, but at the same time, easier, sacrifice than virtue and all which is good and proper. I must bleed for that my whole life long, for the wound which I have done myself will *never* heal." [4]

As the tide of war turned and everyone in the little capital rejoiced at successive victories, the Prince introduced discord by always taking the part of the French.[5] Eventually, in April 1813, they separated and he left, apparently for the waters at Töplitz, in Bohemia. Though shuddering at the expense, the Princess, her father and the whole Court were relieved to be rid of him.[5] A

[1] W.A. Prince Adolphus to the Prince of Wales, 27th March 1799.
[2] M.A. To Countess von Bruehl, 3rd May 1814.
[3] *Ibid.* To Countess von Bruehl, 1809.
[4] S.A. Princess Frederica to Frau von Berg, 22nd January 1810.
[5] *Ibid.* Princess Frederica to Frau von Berg, 25th April 1813.

week or two later there was great excitement in the little Court as a British Prince, the Duke of Cumberland, arrived. He set eyes on his cousin for the first time in his life on the 20th May 1813. " That moment," he wrote to her twenty-three years later,[1] " is as alive in my memory as if it were yesterday. I see you at the head of the staircase, *you*, the old grandmamma and the ladies, and then [*à cette heure*] there was a serenade from the musicians in the flower-garden under my windows. What a superb night, and one caught the scent of the flowers. . . . I can say with the greatest truth that that was the most beautiful and happiest moment of my life."

The Duke of Cumberland fell in love with his cousin immediately and the more that he observed her the more his conviction was strengthened that she was the woman destined to bring him happiness. To his brother he wrote merely, " La cousine Solms is charming but also very sickly, and like her sister most determined in her antipathy to everything French,"[2] but already, he had determined to marry her as soon as she could free herself. After her life of grief and unhappiness, she could not believe that this would ever materialise. " Sometimes," she wrote, " I believe that I am *dreaming* when I think of all which that great *yes* means. In spite of that, I look upon it as very unsure and unlikely. God alone knows, Whom I begged to guide me and be my inspiration, and yet I am still asking myself all the time, what will become of it ? The dear and loyal Duke merits all your esteem ; he is excellent, and if this succeeds and I still do not become happy, it will be a sign that God does not intend that I should be happy down here. The Duke is an angel to me, and I willingly attach myself to him and his fate, only wishing for his glory and his happiness as my own. God help me ! Without him there is nothing on earth or in Heaven ! "[3]

Meanwhile, the Duke had set about obtaining for himself a military command. He wrote to his brother of the enthusiasm which he found everywhere, of the offers which he had received to join him in a venture to free Hanover and of how necessary it was that a member of the family should take over the leadership. He therefore suggested that he should himself form a Hanoverian

[1] G.A. Duke to his wife, 20th May 1836.
[2] W.A.* To Prince Regent, 26th May 1813.
[3] S.A. To Frau von Berg, 6th July 1813.

corps (with what rebuff we will see),[1] and in the meantime wrote
to the King of Prussia and the Emperor of Russia requesting permission to join their combined army ; if they refused, he intended
to offer himself to the Prince Royal of Sweden, whom he regarded
as a sincere friend of the cause.[2]

In reply to his letter the King of Prussia wrote that he would
be very happy to see him at Headquarters. The Emperor, however, said that " He could not then receive him, but that he would
let him know when he could." The Duke was very much offended.
He considered that he had as much right to be courteously treated
as Bernadotte, especially as he was of equal birth with the Emperor,
and he let this be known, " as I find it is necessary to make these
Russians feel that we Englishmen do not feel ourselves inferior to
them in any respect." [3]

The Duke remained at Strelitz for a month continuing his
efforts to join the Allied armies. He intended first to go to their
headquarters at Reichenbach, in Silesia. If, however, he was not
successful in finding a command, he told his brother, " rather
than show myself in England without having served, I will join
some new corps as a *volunteer* and at least prove myself worthy of
being a descendant of the Gwelfs, for to return without seeing a
shot fired I should consider an eternal disgrace." He implored his
brother to write to one of the Sovereigns on his behalf, requesting
some post—" I care not what it is, all I want is to have an opportunity of showing the world that I am not living on the fat of the
earth without doing something for it. Perhaps when the levies in
Hanover are formed you will then allow me to resume my situation
as senior lieutenant-general of cavalry, which patent I still possess
signed by His Majesty 1796 and which I never resigned, and which
he desired me *not* to do." [4]

There can be no doubt that his brother would willingly have
agreed to this. But the Cabinet, though it had perhaps been glad
to have him out of the country as he had become an embarrassment,
was now fearful of the effects of his determined character upon the
delicate balance of the coalition. " Wallmoden and the Duke
would not go on well together," Sir Charles Stewart wrote to the
Lord Castlereagh,[5] " and I think the latter is best kept out of this
undertaking." " You must try to reconcile the Sovereigns at

---

[1] W.A.* To Prince Regent, 7th and 18th June 1813.
[2] *Ibid.** To Prince Regent, 26th May and 18th June 1813.
[3] *Ibid.** To Prince Regent, 7th June and 6th August 181
[4] *Ibid.** To Prince Regent, 18th June 1813.
[5] F.O. 64/88, 10th July 1813.

E.A.—4*

Headquarters to let him witness as a volunteer what is going on," replied Castlereagh. " He cannot have a command." [1] He also wrote to Lord Cathcart on the matter. " Command is, I conceive, out of the question," he said. " To see service as a volunteer is all that can be looked to ; and, as there might become risk of the Duke's being entangled in some *tracasserie* if he shall attach him-self to the northern corps, in which Hanover and Wallmoden would make an additional difficulty, I wish you and my brother would facilitate his being permitted to witness the Russian and Prussian operations in preference." [1] So the Duke was only to be allowed to watch the soldiers, like a schoolboy. Nor was he to be permitted to raise a corps of his own. For this, money was the excuse.

The Prince Regent had shown Castlereagh the letter in which he suggested the formation of a Hanoverian corps, and the Foreign Minister wrote to the Duke personally to explain the limited funds which were available to the Government for these operations.[2] " It is a painful part of my duty at this moment, Sir, to damp in any degree the glorious spirit of enterprise which animates the Continent, more especially when it is disposed to show itself under a Prince of our own Royal Family," he wrote, " but . . . Your Royal Highness will easily appreciate the utter impracticability with such limited means of giving existence to a corps the com-mand of which should be in any manner suitable to Your Royal Highness's exalted military rank and station. . . . I can fully enter into the disappointment so honourably felt and avowed by Your Royal Highness at not finding a proper field as yet open to your personal exertion." He promised to communicate with Stewart and Cathcart ; what he wrote to them we have seen.

The Duke's only hope now was for a command through a direct approach to one of the Allied Sovereigns, and hearing that the King of Prussia had arrived at Charlottenburg, he posted off to Berlin on the 17th July. He could not see him until the 22nd (as the King shut himself up and saw no one on the anniversary of the death of his Queen Louise), but then he found him very kind and friendly. In the Duke's opinion, however, he seemed to acknowledge himself as subordinate to Russia, for he said that at present he himself was only a visitor at Headquarters, but that he would mention the Duke's wishes to the Emperor.[3]

[1] Castlereagh's *Correspondence*, 14th July, 1813.
[2] F.O. 34/5, 13th July 1813.
[3] W.A.* To Prince Regent, 22nd September 1813.

Peace reigned temporarily through the Armistice of Plaeswitz, much to the disgust of the impatient Duke. Castlereagh was now endeavouring to secure his return and he had an influential seconder in Count von Münster,[1] the Minister who now occupied a position of confidence with the Regent in Hanoverian affairs and who feared that the Duke was about to poach upon his preserves. He therefore wrote to him that his absence gave his enemies an opportunity to abuse him at home. The Duke, however, could not see the logic of that. " As for enemies," he wrote, " everybody has some. Mine at any rate cannot injure here, and you knew when in England I did not care for them. *Mens conscia recti* carries one through many difficulties." He pointed out that he had left home and comfort to suffer privation, expense and humiliation and he could not return " at a moment when there is an appearance of hostilities recommencing, I should in such a case indeed be abused by everyone. . . . Upon my soul I had much rather that the first cannon ball should destroy me than quit the Continent *now*. . . . Feeling as I do our evident desire to uphold our family name, to secure our national interests and to aid by every effort in my power your dignity and the support of your Government, I feel I have availed myself of an opportunity that seemed to be presented to one of the House of Brunswick to manifest his zeal for the great cause of Europe. . . ." Though indifferent to the insults and jeers of his enemies, the Duke did not wish to be thought a coward.[2]

The time passed quietly, though the Duke longed " to hear the first cannon shot." [2] At last the moment came when he had to take farewell of the Princess whom he loved and leave for the uncertainties of the field. He had been waiting for Sir Charles Stewart and on his arrival he set out with him for the Allied Headquarters at Reichenbach.[3] He intended to visit the King of Prussia in accordance with his cordial invitation. Late at night on the 15th–16th August he and Sir Charles arrived at the King's Headquarters at Landeck, to the south in a salient of Silesia. Sir George Jackson, the British Ambassador to Prussia, who had been

---

[1] Count von Münster (1766–1839) had studied at Göttingen and had in 1793 been entrusted by the King with persuading his son Augustus to return from Rome, where he had contracted an illegal marriage. The Prince liked him and asked him to accompany him on another visit to Rome, where he spent five years. The King had now gained such confidence in him that when he decided to send a Hanoverian Ambassador to Russia, he selected him for the post. So began his great part in European diplomacy. He eventually became the King's adviser upon everything associated with Hanover and much else.

[2] W.A.* To Prince Regent, 6th August 1813.

[3] In Silesia.

hoping for a long night, had to welcome them and sup with them.[1]
The next day they dined with the King, then Sir Charles hurried
on to Prague to make arrangements for the Duke to follow and
join the Allied Army in Bohemia. He arrived on the morning of
the 18th and immediately applied for passports for the Duke to
proceed to the Emperor of Russia's Headquarters. These Metter-
mich granted without hesitation and they were despatched to the
Duke by courier. The Duke spent a few days enjoying the social
life of Prague [2] and then set out for Headquarters, which had now
been advanced to Töplitz.[3]

He arrived on the 28th August, as the French under Vandamme
were counter-attacking the sorely-pressed Russians and Prussians
under the Russian General Ostermann. Hungry and tired, this
column was moving back along the Pirna road through the rain
and pitch blackness at the very moment that the Duke arrived at
Töplitz. He immediately hurried forward through the hills and
became involved in some skirmishing at Pleissig and Pirna. " His
Royal Highness the Duke of Cumberland arrived at Töplitz on the
28th," wrote Sir Charles, " at the moment the enemy were making
their impression in that quarter. His Royal Highness ran considerable risk of being taken, but repaired immediately to the field
of battle and assisted in the operations through this and the following days, with all that ardour, true personal courage and ability that
are proverbially the attributes of the Royal Family of England." [4]

Ostermann fought rearguard actions at Peterswald and Nollendorf, as the Russians and Prussians endeavoured to gather forces
to meet the advancing French. On the 29th August he took up
a position at Culm, and turned to face the French. The Duke of
Cumberland was with the army, rejoicing once again to be on the
field after fifteen years of craving to serve again. The battle began
in the middle of the morning and was very hotly contested ; the
front swayed backwards and forwards, but Ostermann's forces
were so greatly outnumbered and already so famished and exhausted
that there could have been no doubt of its outcome. On the
30th, however, the main weight of the Allied forces was thrown
against the enemy's flank and rear and he was annihilated. This
battle was decisive and the advance to Leipzig had begun. As to
the Duke of Cumberland's part in it, little is known. As he was

[1] *Bath Archives,* 16th August, 1813.
[2] W.A.* To Prince Regent, 23rd August 1813 ; F.O. 64/89, Stewart to Castlereagh,
18th August 1813.
[3] *Bath Archives,* 25th August, 1813.   [4] *Londonderry.*

only a visitor with the army and held no military position, he was not noticed in the accounts of the battle. That he had been very closely involved in the fighting is, however, beyond doubt ; C. E. von Malortie says that he displayed his usual " spirit and fire " ; Sir George Jackson wrote that he was at Zekista intending to join the King at Headquarters when he was almost captured,[1] and the Duke himself, in his account to his brother that day, began by writing that he was safe " and not in Bony's hands as reported, but very nearly *his*." [2]

After the battle of Culm, the Duke joined the Allied Headquarters at Töplitz beneath the hills just inside Bohemia. There was, of course, the usual social life of an army's headquarters, though as soon as the army began to advance, things were different. The Duke of Cumberland found it intolerable, for the Emperor of Russia, the dominating personality, was for some reason very cold towards him, and the King of Prussia, though a loyal friend, was too weak of will to be much of a support. The Duke was also humiliated by his position with the armies and the rebuffs which he had met in every direction in trying to serve in some capacity. He only remained for the chance of seeing some action and, ultimately, of liberating Hanover. He saw all the reviews and, whenever possible, joined in some of the fighting. On the 5th September he was present at a small skirmish and joined Major-General von Ziethen's outposts on the 8th.[3]

He arrived at Pirna early in the morning just in time to see an attack launched. Napoleon had intended to make the place his headquarters for that night and the Duke was able to partake of a " precious good dinner " which had been prepared for him. While he and the party were dining, news came that the French were advancing again in force. The commander, Prince von Wittgenstein, gave orders for the other divisions to advance against them and " we sat quietly on until then." When he thought it advisable, the commander ordered the horses and the whole party, including the Duke of Cumberland, mounted and rode out of the town along the road towards Dresden. They observed, however, that the French attack was succeeding. Von Wittgenstein ordered a division of Russian Grenadiers to support, but it was three miles in the rear and too late. During obstinate fighting, Pirna was held for the evening, but in the night the Allies had to fall back upon Gottleuba. Throughout the next two days the Duke

---

[1] *Bath Archives.*   [2] W.A. To Prince Regent, 30th August 1813.
[3] *Ibid.** 13th September 1813.

remained with the troops, as they were continuously attacked and their outposts were forced back as far as Culm.[1] All this he attributed to lack of co-ordination among the contingents forming the Allied Army, and to the inefficiency of the commissariat, which resulted in a shortage of fodder. He told his brother of the conditions on the 20th September.

"I have hardly been able to get anything myself to eat," he wrote, "and the poor soldiers who are constantly laying out a bivouac in the wet have nothing but bread this whole week. I am afraid we shall lose a great number of men by the dysentery. What do you think, Wittgenstein has lost in killed and wounded since the 8th when we had the affair at Pirna no less than 10,000 men, so this must prove to you we have had fighting enough, but in spite of all that, we are still *all* in the same position, and every day longer we stay here, every day our days must increase here. Our horses have no hay or oats, so exhausted is this whole country. . . ." Upon the Austrians, the Duke bestowed great praise, saying that they were doing all possible.[2]

On the 17th September the Duke was once again engaged at the outposts, where he had been since the 8th. It was at an abattis which had been built at the entrance to a wood on the road leading up the mountains to Nollendorf. Early in the morning, as was customary, a trumpeter was sent out to inquire after an officer captured by the French the day before. An answer was promised, and the Duke arrived just as the major commanding the post was told that it was ready and an officer and a drummer were detailed to receive it. The officer, however, perceived that some French cavalry and an infantry section were drawn up on the other side of the abattis with no trumpeter. The drummer beat and the officer called to them; then "this rascal," as the Duke described the French officer, ordered his men to fire, opening the battle. For two hours the Prussians fought "like lions" and, having twice exhausted their ammunition, had to retire. The French brought six cannon to bear "with which they regaled us nobly," while all the time the infantry were closely engaged, "and for two hours there was a fire of the Devil himself, shot, shell and grenade whizzing among us. I saw one poor fellow knocked down and a groom with a led horse had his arm shot off by the same ball. The moment that spectacle began, everyone of the Cossacks who attended Wittgenstein, near 200, took to their heels and the devil a one did I see again till we got to Culm," five

[1] W.A.* 13th September 1813.   [2] *Ibid.** 20th September 1813.

miles in the rear, where the troops took up their positions. Fortunately, it was raining in torrents and there was thick fog, so
von Ziethen, commanding the advance-guard, ordered an attack
with the bayonet and drove the enemy back to the abattis, where
he had to halt as night fell. The next day the field was covered
with corpses. All this could have been avoided, wrote the Duke,
if the Russians had advanced in support when ordered.[1]

On the 19th September the Duke returned to the Headquarters
at Töplitz, not entirely fitting in with the social arrangements of
those who had not been out on the field. " I dined at Lord
Cathcart's when we were kept waiting six hours for the Duke of
Cumberland," wrote Sir George Jackson.[2] " When His Royal
Highness at last arrived, it appeared he had been amusing himself
at the outposts, and that he had dined elsewhere though expected
here. He graciously bade us wait no longer ; but we had already
waited so long that, for the most part, our appetites were as little
improved as the dinner by the delay."

The Duke did not intend to stay at the Headquarters for long.
He had two reasons for leaving the Allied Army. His humiliating
position as a " volunteer " and the hostility of the Emperor had
become unbearable for a man of his pride. But now what he had
been waiting for was in sight—the recovery of Hanover. The
army which was moving in that direction was that of the Hanoverians themselves under von Wallmoden, and it now stood at
Ratzeburg on the Mecklenburg frontier between Lübeck and the
Elbe. The Duke decided, therefore, to go to Strelitz, where he
could await developments and at the same time rejoin his relatives.
He had written to his cousin, Frederica, all the time that he was
in the field. " The Duke's letters," she wrote,[3] " are truly divine
and you could not believe how they attach me to him. . . . Oh
God, Oh God ! ! ! ! How I was blinded, and how can I thank
God that He has sent to me an angel to save me. If only it were
all over ! I believe I will die before it happens ! God protect
him ! I cannot describe my anxiety ! " Even her prospect of joy
was tinged with melancholy. " Yes," she wrote to her friend,[4]
" if God grants it to me, I hope to be happy in the autumn of my
days as much as I have been unhappy in the spring and the summer.
I do not think of my winter, for you know that I believe Death
will be an obstacle to that."

---

[1] W.A.* 20th September 1813.   [2] Bath Archives.
[3] S.A. To Frau von Berg, 20th September 1813.
[4] Ibid. To Frau von Berg, 2nd August 1813.

In the little lanes on the outskirts of the tiny capital they rode or drove together and sometimes they made the pilgrimage to Hohenzieritz, the Duke of Mecklenburg's seat in the country, where Queen Louise had died on her last visit to her family. Then, suddenly, the poor Princess saw all her dreams threatened, at the moment when their realisation had seemed assured. To her faithful friend whom she called " the truest of the true," Frau von Berg,[1] she poured out her heart.

" You will never be able to guess the object of this letter," she wrote.[2] " It is a question of conscience of a very delicate and unæsthetic nature, but I cannot solve it alone. The other day, my niece, the *Duke* and myself were together and the topic of conversation was the unhappy marriage of the Prince Royal of Württemberg and his wife. Charlotte said that he seemed to have a quite peculiar distaste for his wife. ' But why, is she *dégoûtante* ? '— ' Not at all, she is not pretty, but well-built.'—' Perhaps she has bad teeth ? '—' Yes,' replied Charlotte.—' Ah, then that's it,' said the Duke. ' I, for example, can not go near a woman with bad teeth.' After this declaration of distaste for bad teeth, I want to know if it is my duty to confess to the Duke before we inform our father that I have several false teeth. This is like a weight on my heart, between the desire to confess to him, so that I will have nothing on my conscience towards him, and the *dread* that he will conceive a distaste for me *without admitting it to me*, while abiding firmly by his resolve to marry me. . . ." for she did not want to be able to say that she should have told him before matters were so advanced. " So I do not know what to do." She could only feel encouraged that he had told her a few days before, " I will get on your nerves eventually, for I will never leave you."

What the Princess resolved we do not know, but, at any rate, the Duke of Cumberland was too much in love with her to be discouraged by some artificial teeth.

· · · · · · ·

The Duke of Cumberland arrived at Strelitz at the beginning of October 1813. " I feel myself much more comfortable at being nearer my own countrymen than where I was before," he told his brother, " for certainly the life and situation of a volunteer at H.Q. is of all others the most vile." As usual, his movements

---

[1] Frau Caroline von Berg, née von Haesler, had been with the sisters from childhood and was one of Queen Louise's Ladies-in-Waiting. She came to England with the Duchess, and died in 1826.   [2] S.A. To Frau von Berg, 1st October 1813.

were eyed with disapproval officially. Sir C. Stewart wrote to Castle-reagh of his fears of what would happen if he and von Wallmoden came together, and Bernadotte, who was afraid that the Duke might forestall him in the capture of Hanover, hinted that embarrass-ments would arise if that happened. But the Duke was not to be deterred, for it was with just that in mind that he had come to the Continent.[1]

" I think the time fast approaching that I can hail you with the good news of the recovery of your dominions upon the Continent which to *me* I acknowledge will be the happiest of my life," he wrote, in broaching the subject to his brother, " and when that day is arrived then I shall forget *all* the unhappy and uncomfortable time I have passed since I left home." He would not stand in the way of anyone else whom his brother might have in mind for this task, but " I must say from having lived so many years in Hanover I think I may be of use, and you must be aware that in the actual situation of things *one of your own family* ought to be there." The unfortunate Prince, however, was very hesitant in making this request. His enemies, he knew, had rejoiced at the humiliations to which he had been subjected and he did not wish them to have an additional cause for exultation. He begged his brother to reply in his own hand as " I wish *not* this to be *public* that I have made an offer you have not accepted."

At last, matters could be delayed no longer. On the 30th the Duke joined von Wallmoden at Dömitz on the Elbe [2] and sum-moned this officer and the two former Ministers von der Decken and von Bremer to a conference. The French army lay at Cassel and many places in the Electorate were still occupied. They resolved, therefore, to act speedily to forestall Bernadotte in the occupation of Hanover, for it was not to the Duke's liking that his house should be presented with its hereditary possessions through the grace of one not even born a Prince. The Prince Regent's proclamation had not yet arrived, so the Duke and the Ministers took it upon themselves to draw up a provisional an-nouncement.[3] At the same time, to set an example in creating a defence force for the Electorate, the Duke signed a declaration that he would personally donate one thousand pounds towards its formation,[4] explaining to his brother, " I trust this will equally

---

[1] The account of the liberation of Hanover is from the Duke's letters to the Prince Regent (W.A.*), unless otherwise specified.

[2] *Londonderry.*   [3] H.A. Des. 92 XLI, Nr. 82, p. 78.

[4] H.A. Des. 92 XLI, Nr. 82, p. 80.

meet with your approbation and I feel as a Prince of the House I owe *this* to that country."

It was a very bold venture. There were only four hundred friendly troops in the Electorate, while four thousand French troops lay in the neighbourhood. The little band which was to take possession of the country set off on the 3rd November 1813, the two Ministers going first. As he was stepping into his carriage, the Duke received a message from Sir Charles Stewart attempting to dissuade him from the undertaking, but the Duke considered his honour at stake now, as " the only member of the family then on the Continent and on the very confines of Hanover."

The Duke of Cumberland entered the city of Hanover at eleven o'clock on the morning of the 4th November 1813, accompanied by Count von Kielmannsegg,[1] whose green-coated Jäger, the only troops which they had at their disposal, formed the escort.[2] As he was dressed in his English Hussar uniform, not everyone at first realised who he was, but when his presence was known, the Hanoverians went mad with joy, bells pealed and cannon thundered. Only a few days before, the French had been in occupation and now here was the son of their Sovereign.

The Duke alighted at the Altes Palais, the house facing the Royal Palace across the narrow Leinestrasse and hemmed in by the tall half-timbered houses, and there he was received and presented with a garland and a poem by some twenty young ladies of the Nobility and the citizens. He accepted the tokens very graciously and then the Mayor made a short speech and all the assembled City Councillors, officials and ladies of rank were presented to him. From time to time he went on to the balcony to acknowledge the wild cheering. All the time the band was playing under the windows and included in its programme several English folk-songs. At noon, the Duke took the salute from the balcony as thousands of armed citizens on foot and horseback marched past, colours flying, with the band of the Kielmannsegg Jäger.

In the evening the town was illuminated; even the poorest inhabitant participated and hardly a window contained no light. Everywhere there were spectacular transparencies, legends, flowers and triumphal arches. The Duke, escorted by mounted citizens, drove through the narrow winding streets and cheering crowds.

---

[1] Count von Kielmannsegg had arrived from England with von Wallmoden and had raised his regiment, principally from foresters. His first reconnaissance parties had entered the capital a week before.

[2] The description of the Duke's entry into the city is from *Pockwitz* and other contemporary sources.

The horses were taken from his carriage and it was drawn by
thirty citizens to von der Decken's house, where he had tea, and
then back again.   The next day the Duke attended a service of
reconsecration in the Chapel of the Royal Palace, which had been
closed during the last year.

On the 6th the Prince Royal of Sweden arrived, not, thanks to
the Duke, as liberator, but as a distinguished visitor.   The Duke
rode out to meet him and was magnanimous enough to recognise
the services of his arms and to compliment him as the restorer of
the country.   He led him through the city at the head of the troops.
The Prince took up residence at Montbrillant, just beyond the
city limits, where he remained until his departure on the 16th.
Their relations became cordial and they frequently invited each
other to dinner.

The Duke of Cumberland found the family properties in a
very sad state.   Everything in the Palace was destroyed by the
vandalism of the late occupiers, who had used it as a barracks.
" I went over the whole of it and it drew tears from my eyes to
behold such a wretched appearance of a place where I had passed
so many happy days."

The Duke lost no time in reporting upon the state of the
Electorate and the measures which he considered most urgent.
First, with an eye to the military situation of Europe, he considered
it vital that there should be a Hanoverian Army.   No time ought
to be lost, he said, in view of the efforts which the French would
make to recover their losses and also if the fine spirit which showed
itself everywhere were not to go to waste.   Whoever was to have
the command, if it were not to be himself, should come without
delay, he said, and he recommended how the army should be
organised in order to have thirty thousand men.   As he had
promised, the Duke set the lead in building up the new army by
himself contributing one thousand pounds towards the raising of
a hussar regiment of volunteers, which, he intended, should
become a *corps d'élite*.   However, beyond this donation he had no
more association with it.[1]

These were the Duke's efforts for Hanover.   His sole object
was " the consideration of the welfare of the country and maintenance of it for you and our family, recollecting that this soil is

[1] This is clear from a letter which he later wrote to his brother thanking him for
allowing " that regiment of Hussars now at Hanover " to bear his name.   He also
complained of his embarrassment, as it was raised under his personal influence and he
then had to leave, with the result that it was still in March 1814 incomplete and
untrained.

that from which we sprang and therefore must be dear to us all." It must be remembered that there was no prospect of Hanover's ever being *his*. He had four elder brothers and devotion to the Regent, the House and its subjects was his only motive. He was certainly not unreasonable in expecting the governorship or command, for no other Prince had devoted himself so assiduously to the task of reorganising life and government in Hanover. It had been completely forgotten, a part of Jerome Bonaparte's " Kingdom of Westphalia," when he had set off alone and unsupported, even with official disapproval, for the insecurity of the warring Continent. He had traversed Europe, risked his life on its battlefields and endured nothing but misery and humiliation—all that he might reclaim Hanover for its Sovereign. The only other Prince who could be considered for an appointment there was the Duke of Cambridge and he had expressed his unwillingness to return to the Continent. However, the Duke of Cumberland urged unselfishly, if his brother were to be chosen, he should come without delay. In the meantime the enthusiasm for the Duke of Cumberland did not diminish. The city was in celebration all the time. Deputations came to him from all quarters, including one from the people of Hildesheim, which had just been added to the Electorate. " I invited them to dinner when your health was drunk with enthusiasm," he reported. " Some of them stayed till half-past twelve at night and I thought I should never get the house clear of them."

It is hardly necessary to say that the Duke of Cumberland's hopes were to be disappointed. There were his usual enemies, and the Cabinet would naturally have opposed his appointment (though it was subsequently to regret this bitterly). The main influence against him, however, seems to have been that of Count von Münster. The Elector ruled through him and his chancellory in London and all reins were concentrated in his hands. The appointment of a Governor on the spot would have rendered the system unworkable unless that Governor adapted himself to his ideas. That the Duke of Cumberland most certainly would not do. The Minister preferred therefore his more tractable younger brother, the Duke of Cambridge, and the Prince Regent was left with no other choice.

He knew what a crushing blow this would be to his brother and sought to soften it as much as was in his power. He therefore chose Captain Bloomfield, his equerry, to go to Hanover personally to explain the necessity for the appointment. He also promoted his brother to the rank of Field-Marshal in the British Army and ordered a richly-ornamented sword which the officer was to deliver.

At midday on the 9th December 1813 Captain Bloomfield drove to the Duke's residence. The Duke was thunderstruck at seeing him. His first thoughts were of his brother and he inquired anxiously of his health. Then the Captain judged the moment favourable to tell him of the subject of his mission. " The communication was received with fresh expressions of attachment though accompanied with a burst of tears and evident distress and mortification," he reported. The Captain pointed out that it would not be pleasant for him to remain while a younger brother was placed in supreme authority, and the Duke, moved by the Regent's tact, decided to leave immediately. He was completely overwhelmed by this final blow, but his affection for his brother was in no way lessened and even in this unhappy episode he found cause for gratitude. His brother's kindness in sending Bloomfield, whom he knew he could ill spare, " I feel to the bottom of my soul and perfectly calms all the disappointment that must necessarily arise to an ambitious mind as mine at being superseded ; excuse the word, for I feel I ought not to use it, but I cannot disguise to you my feelings. . . . It is a proof that you felt for *me* and to a mind borne down with grief and misery as mine has been for these last *six* months it feels your kindness doublefold. . . . I am fully convinced from all that has passed between Bloomfield and myself that *you* felt *most forcibly* the *unpleasant task* you had to perform and that nothing but necessity compelled you to it, as your heart is too kind willingly to hurt the feelings of any man, still less those of a brother to whom you have always shown such *particular* kindness."

He could not, however, resist giving expression to his bitter disappointment. " Ever since I landed at Stralsund," he wrote, " my constant object has been to seize the first favourable opportunity that might present itself to promote your interests in *this country* and I had ever in view in coming over to the Continent a desire to prove to *this country* and to Germany in general that the Brunswick family was not *callous* to the sufferings of their countrymen. . . . I am convinced that all this must upon reflection, and did, strike your mind, and that you must have had very cogent reasons to have induced you to allow an elder brother who had been for eight months active in your service to be superseded by his younger brother who has been living quietly at home and particularly as it is well known his disinclination to come here. You will excuse my having dwelt so long upon this, but I think it fair to you, and to myself, to disburthen my heart to you upon this subject which must be so galling to a mind actuated by enthusiasm as mine was, and feeling myself at this moment so popular with all ranks." He felt no jealousy towards his younger brother and assured him that he would always help or give advice to him whenever he desired it. The Duke of Cambridge's conduct had been thoroughly brotherly and honourable, he said.

It only remained to leave Hanover. And here another of those little tricks of injustice has turned what should have been to his credit to a reproach to the Duke of Cumberland. His departure without waiting to welcome his brother has been given by the history-books as a proof of his pique and wounded feelings. But it has been seen from Bloomfield's account that this was not his own idea. When the Duke of Cambridge was at Cuxhaven, on his way, he wrote, " I trust though that Bloomfield will by this time have arrived and that he will have persuaded Ernest to leave Hanover before I get there." Preparations for the reception of the new Governor-General on the 19th were eagerly commenced.

On the evening of the 14th December the Duke of Cumberland left the city virtually unnoticed by a route which afforded no view of the preparations for the reception, the triumphal arches decorated with lamps among firs and laurels, and the inscription, " To the Long-Awaited, from the City of Hanover." His feelings can be imagined when he thought of his entry the month before. On the 19th, bands, trumpets, bells, cannon, cries of " Long live the King, the Prince Regent, the Duke of Cambridge, all the Royal Family ! " and crowds of peasants on foot and on horseback along the whole way to the city greeted the Duke of Cambridge and Count von Münster, in a carriage pulled by enthusiastic draymen. Yet it should really have been the lot of that broken-hearted Prince to whom was due the safe recovery of the country, but who had been, in effect, ordered out of it.

CHAPTER XI

ENGAGEMENT AND MARRIAGE

THERE was only one place to which the Duke of Cumberland could go, Strelitz, and so he wrote [1] to his uncle asking if he might come to him. He had to leave Hanover before the arrival of his brother, he said, and he did not know what to do, " *car je suis chassé de chez moi.*"

So he was again with the Princess whom he loved. Her husband had now come to the conclusion that no marriage could exist under the circumstances and agreed to a separation and divorce,[2] but they intended to remain upon the friendliest terms. " He himself," she wrote to her brother-in-law,[3] " wishes to finish the matter properly, so that it will also appear to the world as the result of a voluntary and mutual agreement." She begged her brother-in-law not to hurt her husband by reproaching him, or letting him think that the failure of the marriage was his fault.[4] Everyone was pleased at the decision. The King of Prussia told the Princess that she would continue to enjoy her Prussian income so long as she was unmarried, and her aunt and prospective mother-in-law wrote of her satisfaction at the intended divorce.[5]

In the meantime the Duke of Cumberland did not think it proper to remain at Strelitz and decided to take up residence either at Berlin or Stuttgart, where his sister Charlotte, who was married to the King of Württemberg, lived. The prospect should have pleased her, for she had not seen him since her departure in 1797

[1] S.A. Duke of Cumberland to Duke Charles of Mecklenburg-Strelitz, 9th December 1813.

[2] Rothert says that he gave his assent on the 20th November 1813, but gives no source.

[3] M.A. Princess Frederica to the Prince of Solms-Braunfels.

[4] She was later of great service to the House of Braunfels, which had been mediatised and whose lands had been given by Napoleon to the Duke of Nassau. The Prince complained of financial oppression under his new master and asked his sister-in-law to place the matter before the King of Prussia. This she did and was able to report a successful outcome.—M.A.

[5] S.A. Queen Charlotte to Duke Charles, 28th February 1814. " My niece has just informed me of her divorce. God grant that she may recover peace of mind and re-establish her health. Look after her, dear brother, it is a duty to your children and your country and for the satisfaction of—*Charlotte.*"

and had only very recently been once again in communication with
her family after the separation caused by war and politics. But,
quite unknown to him, she cherished a violent dislike for her
brother—why, it cannot be said, unless it were through her humiliating situation as an ally of Napoleon during the late war.[1] Now
she did everything in her power to avert a visit from him. She
wrote to the Queen, the Prince Regent, the Duke of Strelitz and,
finally, her brother himself, attempting by various excuses to be
spared his presence.[2] She became more and more violent in her
letters home and was soon heaping insult and abuse upon him and
also upon Princess Frederica ; she dreaded, she said,[3] " that Ernest
will forget what he owes to the Prince Regent and will obstinately
persist in a marriage which must be a source of pain to the whole
family "—at a time when, as will be seen, no match would have
given greater pleasure to the Prince Regent and the family.

The Prince was indignant at his sister's attitude, for the Duke
had been hurt enough without the family's taking part against him.
Ernest, he explained, had not definitely said that he was going to
Stuttgart, and a visit would certainly not be from desire on his
part, but merely from a feeling of the absolute necessity, now that
he was on the Continent, of visiting a sister whom he had not seen
and with whom he had had no communication for years.[4] So the
Duke did not visit Stuttgart, nor did he ever see his sister again.

The Duke of Cumberland decided to reside in Berlin, but he
remained in Strelitz for the celebration of Princess Frederica's
birthday on the 2nd March. During this time his uncle and godfather, Prince Ernest, succumbed to his long illness and the Duke
followed the coffin in the cortège. " The Duke of Cumberland,"
wrote the Princess,[5] " behaved as a true relative throughout the
illness of his poor uncle. He was there every day and hardly left
him when he was so bad, tending him like a servant."

The Duke had visited Berlin before the end of 1813 and made
arrangements to rent the Duchess of Curland's house on the
thoroughfare Unter den Linden, the house formerly inhabited by
von Trenck, the ill-fated lover of Frederick the Great's sister.[6]

[1] Württemberg had been a member of the Confederation of the Rhine.
[2] W.A.* Queen of England to Prince Regent, 8th January 1814 ; S.A. Queen of
Württemberg to Duke Charles of Strelitz, 10th January 1814.
[3] W.A.* Queen of Württemberg to Sir Thomas Tyrwhitt, 10th and 11th January
1814.
[4] W.A.* Prince Regent to Queen Charlotte, 22nd January 1814.
[5] M.A. Princess Frederica to Countess von Bruehl, 6th February 1814.
[6] 1726–94, an adventurous Nobleman who met his end under the guillotine in
Paris, where he happened to be staying when the revolution broke out.

He moved in on the 12th March and was soon participating fully in the social life of the Prussian capital, so far as there was any at that time of year and with the fighting just finished. He spent most of the evenings at Princess Radziwill's, where all the distinguished foreigners assembled, or, when operettas were being performed, at the theatre, as he found the orchestra there very good. He also carried out various commissions for the Prince Regent and sent him, among other things, specimen helmets, sabres and prints of Prussian military fashions. He could not cease expressing his admiration for Prussia's tremendous war effort.[1]

In May reports reached the Duke which reopened a wound that had never really healed. The Duke of Cambridge was not happy in his new office, which, indeed, he had accepted with reluctance.[2] The Duke of Cumberland was well aware of his younger brother's feelings. On the 10th May he took up his pen to beg of the Prince Regent " in case what I hear is true to think of me. . . . I hope you will not pass me over again but at least give me an opportunity of serving you there, where I flatter myself I may be of some use, at least if you give me your confidence. . . . You know I am the last man to push myself forward upon an improper occasion but surely you cannot take it amiss my doing so *now* in case Adolphus does not choose to return. I really and truly *love* the Continent and mean to settle myself eventually here, therefore should prefer much to settle *there* where I might be of use to you, and you know I have served you and can be trusted in ticklish affairs." [3]   Of course, nothing came of these requests.

Events were following each other quickly. As the war was drawing to a close and the Hanoverian affair disposed of again, the Duke's whole position was suddenly altered by the death of the Prince of Solms-Braunfels on the 13th April 1814. He had a stroke while at Schlawentschütz, in Silesia, and the Prince of Hohenlohe-Ingelfingen, who lived there and arranged for his burial with full military honours at nearby Cosel, informed Princess Frederica who, in turn, notified her brother-in-law.[4]   She was genuinely affected, but found comfort in the reflection that it was a release for him " as he has left a life which had become a burden for him as for the rest of the world." [5]   But now the Duke had to declare his intentions.

---

[1] W.A.*   Duke to Prince Regent, several letters.
[2] For confirmation of this, see W.A.*   Duke of Cambridge to Prince Regent.
[3] W.A.*
[4] M.A.   Princess Frederica to Prince of Solms-Braunfels, 24th April 1814.
[5] S.A.   Princess Frederica to Frau von Berg, 3rd May 1814.

The Prince Regent, who had only heard of these developments through gossip, made the first move by writing to his cousin, Prince Charles, to inquire what was the state of affairs between the Princess and his brother. Either he should propose to her or see her no more, he said, and if he chose the former course, he, the Prince Regent, would have no objection and the Duke could place his confidence in him. Prince Charles went to Potsdam on the night of the 21st July, where his brother, Prince George, and the Duke of Cumberland went to meet him. After some minutes of conversation the Prince said to his cousin that he had to talk to him seriously upon a subject in which the character of a near relative of his was concerned. "If you mean your sister," replied the Duke at once, "I will save you the trouble for it is my intention to propose to her the moment she returns to Mecklenburg. Nothing had prevented my doing this before but the particular situation in which she had been placed, the divorce having, thank God, been *prevented* by the death of the Prince." The Duke's cousin was delighted to hear this, and told him of the Prince Regent's letter.[1]

Two days later, on the 23rd July 1814, the Duke of Cumberland wrote to Princess Frederica [2] offering his hand to her, addressing her as " *Ma très chère et bien-aimée cousine.*"

I am well aware of the difficulties in addressing this letter to you, as it is upon a subject about which I would a thousand times rather have spoken to you by word of mouth, but I have just learned from George that your return [3] has been deferred until the 8th August, and for the reasons that you will now read, I can wait no longer.

You cannot doubt, dear and truly-beloved cousin, that the happiness of having been so much in your company has heightened the esteem and affection which I feel towards you, and from the time that I have been able to look upon you as free, this esteem and affection has become a more tender feeling. So permit me, my darling, to offer my hand to you. I do so with more confidence, as we have known one another for more than a year, and so you should know sufficient of my character and way of life. If I am fortunate enough to succeed in my prayer, I will be the happiest of men, and my goal will always be to make you happy and imitate that happy union of the dear Angel [4] and the good and honourable King.[5] I would not have dared to speak upon this

---

[1] This account of the interview is from W.A.* Duke of Cumberland to Prince Regent.
[2] G.A.   [3] She was taking the waters at Rehburg.
[4] The Princess's sister, the late Queen Louise of Prussia, whose memory she ever treasured.
[5] The King of Prussia.

subject so soon had I not been obliged to do so by the absolute necessity of sending your answer to my brother immediately, since he must communicate it to Parliament so that the necessary arrangements can be made, and unfortunately Parliament will be prorogued at the end of August, so I beg you to send me a reply as quickly as possible.

You know me, it is for you alone to judge. Forgive me for this reason if I have not waited long enough before addressing myself to you, but time presses so. I have already informed the Prince of my intention, and I can assure you that *he* will be charmed to receive you as his sister-in-law. Your reply, dearest truly-beloved, will decide my fate, whether I am to be the happiest or most miserable of men. I have asked the Regent to inform my mother. The moment that you receive this you can send it to Papa, to whom I have written, and then, in the name of God, be so good as to inform the King, as he must give his consent as soon as possible if no time is to be lost, for every hour is precious. Let me repeat to you once more, my dear, that your answer will render me the happiest or most miserable of men.

Of course, the Princess accepted, but she had some misgiving as to what was to become of her children.[1] On the evening of the 30th, the Duke received her reply and, the next day, wrote to calm her anxiety upon this score.

My God, have I not declared to you that the constant and continuous wish of my heart will be to make you the happiest of women and that every proposal which you make will be for me a *law*, and I could not have supposed for a single instant that a woman so perfect as you, who, without compliment or flattery, have always seemed to me the *model mother*, would wish to separate herself from her children. No, no, the great God is witness that such an idea has never entered my head, on the contrary, you know that I love them so much already, and in accepting my hand, you can be assured that as *your husband* I will become *their father*.

He also called her question one " that must, if it is possible, increase my love and respect for you." [2] The children were, indeed, already impatient to call the Duke " father." [3] The Princess, however, could not believe that happiness was at long last to be hers.

" Even when one feels so happy," she wrote to her friend,[3] " it is impossible that the joy is not dampened by all that one has learned and experienced. However natural my joy, my feelings are not as unrestrained as those of a young being, who still has her life before her. When one has read a book and has come to the last chapter, one is aware that it is all a whole. That is how

[1] W.A.   [2] G.A.
[3] S.A. Princess Frederica to Frau von Berg, 28th August 1814.

it is with me. You know that I believe that there are not many pages left for me to read now."

The Duke immediately informed the Prince Regent of the Princess's acceptance, explaining the reasons for his delay in proposing to her. " I do not deny to you," he wrote,[1] " that I have loved her very long but after an acquaintance of more than a year when I have examined and watched her whole conduct, she appears to me *so perfect* that I have no doubt of being the happiest man with her, and I am certain that her manners are such that they will captivate you and the rest of the family." He asked the Prince to inform their mother, " who must be happy to receive her own brother's daughter as *her own*, and I know that both the Princess and the Duke lay great stress on her good opinion and friendship." Indeed, they had stipulated her approval as a condition of the marriage taking place.[2]

The King of Prussia had given his consent and now the Duke asked his brother for his, on behalf of the King of England. This the Prince Regent signified at Carlton House on the 15th August 1814. Poten, the Duke's aide, arrived with the announcement on the 22nd,[3] conveying also a letter from the Queen with her most " fervent and sincere " good wishes and congratulations which though " not the most eloquent, flow nevertheless from the heart." [4] Overjoyed, the Duke waited the following morning upon the King of Prussia, who cherished great affection for the Princess, both as wife of his brother and sister of his wife. He was delighted at the news and tears came to his eyes when he spoke of her. After his audience, the Duke saw the Prussian Chancellor, von Hardenberg, and asked him to find all the papers and precedents for the wedding, for the King insisted that the bride should be married as a Princess of his House. He then visited all the members of the Royal Family and they dined with him. At eleven o'clock in the evening he left Berlin, travelled through the night and arrived at Strelitz at eight in the morning. The next day, the 26th, the Duke of Cumberland and the Princess were formally betrothed, exchanging rings before the whole assembled Court.[5]

On the 8th September the Duke received the desired papers from von Hardenberg and wrote of them the same day to his

[1] W.A.* Duke of Cumberland to Prince Regent, 23rd July 1814.
[2] *Ibid.* Duke of Cumberland to Queen Charlotte, 19th December 1815.
[3] This date from S.A. Duke to Prince George. Cf. W.A.* (To Prince Regent) which gives the 23rd.
[4] *Ibid.** Queen to Duke of Cumberland, 15th August 1814.
[5] *Ibid.** Duke to Prince Regent, 3rd September 1814.

brother. He and his bride wished to do everything correctly and nothing which might meet with disapproval in England, he said, and though by German law the Princess could marry after nine months of widowhood, he would like the Lord Chancellor's (Lord Eldon's) views as to the English law upon the subject. Von Hardenberg also suggested, he said, that the Prince Regent should send an official document embodying his consent to the King of Prussia. If the Prince and the Chancellor agreed, they would then marry on the 14th January 1815, hurry to England for a few months and have the marriage recelebrated according to Anglican rites, then return and live partly in Berlin, where they were already seeking a house, and partly in Strelitz. At last, each hoped to settle down to peace and happiness.

But they had reckoned without one factor, the malice and hostility of those who were the arbiters of the Duke's marriage through their hold on his purse-strings. Parliament could interfere in the most personal aspects of the lives of members of the Royal Family, and as it was, the whole question of whether the Duke would be allowed to support a wife and family rested upon the caprice and personal feelings of the M.P.s.

Perhaps this accounted for the Prince Regent's delay, for already at the beginning of October the Duke wrote that he was impatiently awaiting the return of his courier, Morand.[1] On the 10th, the Queen wrote to her brother the letter, since become famous, expressing her joy at the coming marriage and containing some advice upon English manners and etiquette for him to give to his daughter.[2]

On the 27th December the Prince Regent sent to the Prime Minister, Lord Liverpool, one of the Duke's letters, with instructions that the Cabinet was to assemble as soon as possible to tender its advice to him. Apparently its members did not take a very sanguine view of the Duke's prospects in Parliament; more time passed and the Duke had still heard nothing in reply to his letter. The new year opened. The Duke was exasperated. " Now, my Lord," he wrote to his friend, Lord Chancellor Eldon, on the 24th January 1815,[3] " it is exactly *four weeks* this day that Lord Liverpool received His Royal Highness's *orders* to deliberate upon *my letter*, and to *this hour* I have heard *nothing* further on the subject.

---

[1] W.A.* Duke to Prince Regent, 6th October 1814.
[2] Liverpool Papers, Add. MSS. 38261 f. 274. Given in *Fitzgerald*, II, pp. 254–55, also various contemporary newspapers (*vide infra*).
[3] Encombe Archives, Duke to Lord Eldon, 24th January 1815.

No one can have shown more *patience* or forbearance than I have done, but *surely* I have *now* a *right* to complain *bitterly* of Lord Liverpool for not obeying the Prince's orders, especially as the Prince who possesses so eminently the feelings of the gentleman felt *immediately* the *very awkward* and *unpleasant situation* I was placed in by *not* receiving any answer to my letter written the 8*th September* of last year."

When he had still heard nothing on the 4th March, the Duke became really alarmed. " Certainly the state of suspense I have been in now so long has worried me dreadfully and made me wretchedly bilious," he wrote.[1] " Two complete months have now elapsed and no tidings have I heard. What makes me now the more *uneasy* and *desirous* for an answer is that the year is fast approaching of the widowhood, which is completed the 12th April, and *then* as a man of honour I shall be placed in a most shocking state if I have not the answer from England. For God Almighty's sake then, do insist on Lord Liverpool's making his arrangements."

But this month the situation was changed by the return of Bonaparte, which brought about a resurgence of anger and military feeling in the Duke's breast.[2] As one would expect, he was again clamouring for a command. Now, he said, there was a Hanoverian Army, and he still held the commission of lieutenant-general in it, one which had, indeed, been forced upon him against his will. However, he told his brother, " rather than not serve I am willing to *go in any rank* you may choose however *subordinate*, for here 'tis not *rank* I *thirst* after, but I feel when every Monarch and every Prince is going again to offer his services, that my *character* must *suffer* if I remain idle." [2] Afraid of a rebuff, the Duke mentioned his request to no one until his stepdaughter-to-be wrote to her mother, " Now, of course, the Duke of Cumberland will also have to go, or will he be able to remain out of it ? " The Duke was in despair at his humiliation. " Unless I serve this campaign," he said,[2] " I can never show *my face again*, for it would be a most disgraceful thing if in *our family alone* there should not be at least *one member* who serves this campaign. Rather than not go I am ready to serve as Colonel with the Hussar Regiment I raised during my stay in Hanover." It must have been regretted that this last request was not granted. The regiment still consisted of raw untrained troops, but had the Duke been at Waterloo to lead it its story might have been a different one. Its colonel fled, was

---

[1] W.A.* Duke to Prince Regent, 4th March 1815.
[2] *Ibid.* * Duke to Prince Regent, 1st April 1815.

sentenced to death for cowardice, then reprieved and cashiered, the regiment was disbanded and so the Duke's thousand pounds was wasted.[1]

Though the Duke's petitions for a command received no better hearing than they had done two years before, he could still proceed with the rest of his plans, for on the 12th April the Princess's year of mourning was over and, at long last, on the 9th May 1815, he was able to greet his courier, Morand, coming up the stairs with the necessary documents from the Prince Regent.[2] He immediately arranged for the marriage to be solemnised, and on the 29th May 1815 the ceremony took place.[3]

The Court gathered at the Palace of Neu Strelitz, where the Grand Chamberlain announced that the bride and bridegroom had been solemnly affianced last year, the Duke of Mecklenburg himself having exchanged the rings. The guests then proceeded to the quaint old town church, which was splendidly decorated for the occasion. They included two Englishmen, Mr. F. Watson, the Duke's private secretary, and Sir George Jackson, the Ambassador in Berlin, whom the Duke had requested to act as witness on behalf of his brother. All the pews had been removed from the nave and the floor was covered with a rich carpet ; opposite the altar and under the organ was an estrade covered with red cloth, on which armchairs were arranged in a semi-circle for the Royalties present. When everyone else was assembled, the Royal guests arrived in a procession of carriages escorted by Mecklenburg Hussars. It was between six and seven in the evening. The Duke of Cumberland, in the uniform of a British Field-Marshal, and Pastor Glaser were already waiting when, the company ranged into two lines, the Reigning Duke brought in his very handsome daughter and led her to the altar. The ceremony was performed and then the couple received the congratulations of all present. The old Duke gave a fine supper and the Duke of Cumberland retired for the first time as a husband.

A few days later the Duke and Duchess left for Berlin, where they arrived in the evening. The King was at a party given by Princess William, but he went to welcome them and the rest of the family followed. They were given the Frederick II Room in the

---

[1] For an English account of this episode see *Cotton*, p. 91 ; for a German account, *Rothert*, II, p. 538.

[2] S.A. Duke of Cumberland to Prince George of Strelitz, 2nd May 1815.

[3] The description of the marriage ceremony is from Sir George Jackson's Diary in the *Bath Archives*, his official reports (F.O.) and von Ompteda's official report (H.A. K.G. Hann. 9 Domestica 184c.).

Palace, where Sir George Jackson again waited upon the Duke, and the King appointed one of his Lords-in-Waiting, Count von Yorcke, to attend the Duchess. On the 7th June there was a grand lunch at Charlottenburg, then the Duke set out alone for England to make the preliminary arrangements for taking his wife there.

.   .   .   .

While the Duke of Cumberland and his bride were being married far away in Neu Strelitz, back in England the blow had already fallen. There the Duke's enemies hunted him down in all that he did, and when he announced that he intended to marry, they determined to frustrate his hopes for personal happiness. Their opportunity lay in the family dissensions which they were so skilful in sowing and exploiting.

The Duchess was most vulnerable in her marriage to the Prince of Solms, but in the isolated state of the country at that time, within a few days of Waterloo and the reopening of free communications with the Continent after more than twenty years, no one had the slightest knowledge of the intricacies of the lives of the various German Courts so many years ago. One member of the Royal Family, however, had lived all those years of chaos and disintegration in Germany, the Duke of Cumberland's sister, the Queen of Württemberg. Her country had been on Bonaparte's side and she had had no communication with her family, who still recognised her only as Duchess of Württemberg. The war over, however, she wrote home and was again admitted to the family circle, but her first deeds were not consonant with a renewed family affection. It has been seen how, for no apparent reason, having had no personal or written intercourse with him, she had conceived a violent hatred for her brother, and it has also been seen how she spoke of a non-existent family displeasure at his intended marriage. The fact that he had at her wish gone out of her life did not satisfy her. She wrote to England relating stories of her sister-in-law's long-forgotten past. These were kept in reserve, for the Duke's enemies did not wish to prevent the marriage taking place, but to involve him in the universal discredit as a result of it and cause renewed dissension in the Royal Family.[1]

[1] S.A. Duchess to her brother, Grand Duke George, 18th October 1816, and 27th October 1828 (they had both learned of the part played by her sister-in-law from different sources) ; W.A. Duke to Queen, 19th December 1815.

As the Duchess had stipulated the Queen's approval as a condition of her acceptance, this was a necessary precaution. When,
therefore, the last courier had left for Germany towards the end
of April, after the *ten months* during which the Duke's intended
marriage had been known at Court and in public and no one had
offered any objection to it, these details were communicated to the
Queen and she announced to the Prince Regent that she would
not receive her daughter-in-law at Court.

The Prince Regent hoped to arrange matters amicably and he
did not disturb his newly-wed brother with the news. The Queen
presumed that he had forbidden him to bring his wife to England,
and when she heard that she might be coming, she took it to be
in defiance of his express orders and formally declared, in a letter
to the Regent dated the 27th May, that she would refuse to receive
her daughter-in-law since, " as he [the Duke] is known to be very
decided in his character, I fear we may be surprised with such a
visit when we least expect it." [1]

The Prince Regent sent for Lord Liverpool and went with him
to Windsor. He begged her to see whether justice had been done
to the Duchess before adopting such a course and he left under the
impression that she was going to follow his advice.[2] On the 6th
June she spoke to him at the Ascot Races and learned that he had
not mentioned the matter to his brother. She therefore had to
write to him herself and this she did on the 13th, when it was too
late to reach him before his departure from Berlin, so she gave
the letter to his equerry, Colonel Thornton, to deliver to him upon
his arrival in this country.

" You are aware of the grounds upon which I was induced to
decline receiving the Princess of Wales," she wrote,[3] " and it is
with regret that I must inform you that the publicity in this country
of the circumstances of my niece's breaking off a former engagement with the Duke of Cambridge and the unfavourable impression
which the knowledge of these circumstances had made here, place
me under the disagreeable necessity of refusing to receive her. . . .
Such being the case, I cannot but rejoice that she does not accompany you to England. . . ." Of course, the facts were false—
despite the " publicity," she had not learned of the " circumstances " during sixteen years, nor until the last moment before
the marriage.

---

[1] W.A.* Queen to Prince Regent, 27th May 1815.
[2] S.A. Duchess to her father, 3rd May 1815.
[3] W.A.* Queen to Duke of Cumberland, 13th June 1815.

On Saturday morning, the 17th June 1815, the Duke of Cumberland disembarked and learned for the first time of " the cabal which was raised against me." He might have known that he would not be permitted to enjoy conjugal happiness any more than any other. Flabbergasted, he decided to go straight to his brother. He stopped his carriage in St. James's Park and walked through the Gardens to Carlton House. He showed the Queen's letter to his brother and they discussed it until late at night and again the next morning.

The Prince Regent hurried straight to his mother at Windsor and told her that he was sure that she wished to take the letter back, but he had forgotten to bring it with him. She was quite unmoved. " All that I regret," he said afterwards,[1] " is not having taken the letter with me to tear before her eyes and so annul it." The Prime Minister, Lord Liverpool, also endeavoured to persuade her to withdraw her letter, but she was unrelenting.[2]

It was therefore a matter of some embarrassment to go to Parliament for the customary grant upon the marriage of a son of the King. Parliament always enjoyed washing the Royal Family's dirty linen in public, but there was no reason to believe that this family quarrel had become public property, since only the parties concerned, their confidential advisers and the Prime Minister were involved. Formerly, there would have been no occasion for this anxiety, as the Crown had its own lands and revenues, but these the King had given up to the State, in return for which the State was to provide adequate revenues as they became necessary.

On the 28th June 1815 the Prince Regent's message announcing the marriage and requesting the grant was read to the two Houses of Parliament. The Lords agreed to it as a formality, and as such, Lord Castlereagh described it to the Lower House. But the very first speakers soon showed that it was not to be so and those following all advanced various objections. It remained for Mr. H. C. Bennet,[3] however, to bring the debate down to the unprecedently vulgar level at which it remained with a personal attack on the Duke. " As to the person on whose behalf this proposition was made," he said, " he would plainly state that whatever respect he felt for the rest of the Royal Family, that respect did not extend to the Duke of Cumberland. His Royal Highness was, perhaps,

---

[1] S.A. Duchess to Grand Duke Charles, 3rd May 1816, relating the Prince Regent's description of these events to her.

[2] W.A.* Account of the interview, 24th June 1815.

[3] Son of the fourth Earl of Tankerville.

the only member of the Royal Family that could come to the House and make a request of this nature, which he could stand forward and refuse. . . . He would put it to the Noble Lord, whether the concurrent testimony of every individual in the country did not bear him out in asserting that, of all the branches of the Royal Family, the Duke of Cumberland was the one to whom the public feeling would be least inclined to grant any pecuniary boon ? No person could go into society of any kind without hearing this opinion supported."

Then he showed the trump card of the opposition, the Queen's refusal to receive the Duchess. " He would ask of the Noble Lord whether a marriage between the Princess of Solms and another member of the Royal Family had not been projected, which intended marriage, in consequence of certain circumstances, had been broken off? Did not the Queen express herself strongly about it ? " So the political opposition knew of the Queen's refusal after all ! How, one may ask, was it so well-informed of this development at Court ? It casts a new light upon the matter and proves its nature as a sordid plot or conspiracy by the Duke's political enemies. But any coarseness so far was eclipsed by Mr. Bennet's peroration—" For himself, he had no hesitation in saying that the union was an improper one, however much the parties might be suited to each other from their habits and morals ! "

It may be asked, who made the Honourable Member judge of the Duke's—or any other man's—marriage ? Were the Members themselves subject to any marital or moral test and would all of them have passed one ? Talk of sexual morality on the part of the Whigs and Radicals was the most audacious hypocrisy, for those circles in which it was the most lax were just those which inclined most towards the new politics, as the slightest acquaintance with the times will serve to confirm.

From now on the Opposition devoted itself to the Queen's refusal to receive the Duchess—as if her refusal deterred them from championing the cause of the Princess of Wales. The Duke's marriage, said a Mr. Wynn, was one of which the Royal Family was ashamed. " Would the Noble Lord now stand forward and move an address of congratulation to the Queen on the marriage of the Duke of Cumberland ? Would he venture to offer such an insult to the House and to the country ? " Parliament's idea of what a Royal marriage should be was set forth in his next question— " Was it a marriage likely to be serviceable to the political interests of the country ? "—followed by more hypocrisy—" Was it a marriage likely to be serviceable to the domestic virtues in this country ? " In fact, the coarser and more hypocritical the speech, the more cheers that it received. It was as if for the occasion the conventions which govern living in civilised society and which the M.P.s found so irksome were in abeyance and they took the fullest advantage of such a rare opportunity to unbridle their tongues ; they were striking at the man whom they feared through a defenceless woman who had never crossed their paths and with whom none of them had ever had any personal contact, and if she had expected to find in the politics of her new land the qualities for which the English gentleman was famous—chivalry and sportsmanship—she had been mistaken. After a protest by Mr. Bathurst [1] that the House should legislate on public and not personal grounds, the vote was taken. Eighty-seven were given for and seventy against, a majority of seventeen for the grant.

The debate was resumed the next day by a Mr. Gordon, who wished to inquire " whether the Duke had, either in his military or senatorial capacity, rendered any services to the country which would entitle him to this additional grant ? "—this of a man who had lost an eye and been disfigured for life in serving his country. As to rumours, which had occupied such a large place in the debate, Mr. Forbes replied that he " had lived long enough in the world to withhold his belief of more than half of what he heard." He did not see why an exception should be made for the marriage of the Duke of Cumberland. Was it not contracted with the Royal Consent ?

The next speaker was the inveterate enemy of the Duke, Tierney, who insisted that the question should be answered, whether the Queen would receive the Duchess. Castlereagh replied that he would not answer questions " calculated to vilify the Royal Family " and that he did not believe that any M.P. had the right to put such a question. Tierney retorted, he must " answer for the satisfaction of the House. . . . In fact, if the House of Commons were not to degrade itself by becoming the mere banker of the Court, it would not agree to a grant of the public money in consequence of this marriage, with regard to which the Ministers dare not call upon it for a vote of approbation." He then made another of the coarse remarks which had characterised the debate. Mr. Forbes believed only half of what he heard, he said, " but surely quite enough would be found to justify the rejection of this motion

[1] Succeeded as fourth Earl Bathurst, 1834.

if only half of what was said of either the lady or gentleman referred
to were to be believed ? ''

The debate closed with an example of the difficulties handi-
capping the Duke's champions against his more licentious and
less-restrained detractors. The vilest insult and abuse imaginable
had been hurled from the House at the Royal Duke and his wife,
but any reflection upon a Member of that House was greeted with
an injured and enraged indignation, as was seen when Bennet
asked Mr. Forbes if he " had meant to apply personally to him the
remark that he had brought disgrace upon himself by those comments which he had felt it his duty to make on a preceding evening
respecting the character of the Duke of Cumberland ? " Of course,
to be disrespectful to Mr. Bennet was outside the rules of the game,
and Mr. Forbes had to disavow any such intention, though he
added that the House would judge whether the expressions of Mr.
Bennet had been Parliamentary.

The motion was voted upon and seventy-four votes were cast
for and sixty-two against—a majority of five less than yesterday.

The debate dragged on to the 30th, when it was opened by
one of the Duke's consistent enemies, Lord Archibald Hamilton,
followed by Sir C. M. Burrell, elaborating upon the Queen's
refusal. The Duke was bravely defended by Mr. Douglas, who
said that the House should ignore rumours—" If they were not
encountered, it was only because they did not appear in a tangible
shape."

One of the most important speeches was that of Edward Bootle-
Wilbraham,[1] who made the now-familiar reference to the absence
of an address of congratulation, saying that " such a deviation,
indeed, warranted a suspicion that those even who supported the
Bill did not think the marriage worthy of approbation. . . . There
could not, it appeared, be any doubt of the fact that the female
part of the Royal Family disapproved of this marriage and their
disapprobation formed a very strong argument against the present
Bill." To this he added that the grant should be given instead,
for some unexplained reason, to the Duke of York. Now, this
man was the brother-in-law of Sir Herbert Taylor, the Queen's
private secretary, who wielded such a power over her, the personal
enemy of the Duke of Cumberland and confidant (and later private
secretary) of his brother, the Duke of York.[2] This man at last
supplies the missing part to the picture of the conspiracy against

[1] Married Mary Elizabeth Taylor, 1796 ; created Baron Skelmersdale, 1828.
[2] The Duke of York took the part of the Queen.

the Duke of Cumberland. His presence in it can certainly be no coincidence and one can only wonder at his lack of finesse in thus revealing his rôle by his speech.[1]

The Duke's fate was certainly sealed and the speech of Hammersley, which gave the House a few fundamental truths, was of no avail, even when he pointed out the constitutional position, in which " the Crown had made a bargain with that House." Upon the vote, the majority sank to eight.

The debate was renewed for the last time on the 3rd July. Sir H. Montgomery said that from what he had heard, he almost fancied himself wicked in having voted for the Bill. " In all the inquiries, however, which he had made upon the subject, he found nothing but loose assertions ; no person knew or could state any crime of which His Royal Highness had been guilty."

The Opposition, however, was determined to drive home the Queen's refusal After Wilberforce had again stressed it, another Member, Protheroe, made an astonishing statement of the grounds upon which the House should legislate—" With respect to the present [N.B.] question, he did not think it necessary that those who opposed the Bill should bring proofs against the character of the Royal Duke. It was competent for the House to exercise its discretion without such a formality " ! The fanaticism of the Duke's enemies was shown by the following speaker, Mr. Ellison, who believed that " the surest way to make the people also honour that House would be to reject this Bill and every measure of a similar tendency," and Mr. Holmes Sumner, who announced that he had come up from the country for the sole purpose of expressing his disapprobation of the marriage. Sir T. Acland brazenly announced the personal grounds upon which he voted, not, he said, because the proposed grant was excessive—if anything, he considered it moderate—but because of the person to whom the Duke was married. Truly, the situation of a Prince of the Blood Royal of England was an unenviable one, subject to humiliation such as no being of the lowest rank had to suffer in his private and family affairs.

When the vote was taken, there was a majority of one against the grant (126–125).[2]

---

[1] Certainly the Duke and Duchess of Cumberland attached great importance to these circumstances.—S.A. Duchess to Grand Duke Charles, 3rd May 1816.

[2] According to Fitzgerald, II, 257–58, this one vote was invalid. Lord Cochrane was under arrest for having started a false rumour to gain on the stocks through speculation. He freed himself, however, and took his seat and voted before the arrival of the officers who came to take him back into custody.

As to the episode as a whole, little comment is necessary. The more one reads these speeches, the more one wonders whether Great Britain was actually a Monarchy. As long as the Crown was a part of the Constitution, it had a *right* to its means of existence, not as charity on the part of the M.P.s, especially as it had surrendered its Domains in return for a Civil List. The grant requested for the Duke was not an exception nor an exorbitant demand upon his behalf but the normal constitutional procedure in the case of a Prince's marriage and that brought about by this contract with Parliament. The enormity of the proceeding needs no elaboration. Certainly, the lesson was not lost upon the Duke of Cumberland.

Parliament had only, according to the theory of parliamentary government, a fiduciary power to apportion the nation's money ; it was not the property of the M.P.s personally to give away as they chose by the yardstick of purely personal likes and dislikes rather than by considerations of State. They were quite unfitted for power and responsibility, and a letter from Bennet, which reveals their puerile attitude towards it and the depths to which human spite can descend, will provide a fitting close to this squalid episode.

" What an age we live in ! " he writes to a friend.[1] " We fare victorious here as you do at Waterloo. Think of our triumph over the Duke of Cumberland. Nothing ever was better done. . . . Cole [a] became factious and announced an opposition, and you see we have thrown out the Bill by one vote. . . . I believe the Queen was our best ally. . . ."

· · · · · · ·

There remained one thing further to be settled. On the 6th July the Privy Council assembled and decided that, though the Duke's marriage in Germany was of full validity, it was desirable for one of such consequence that it should be recelebrated in England. The Duke, therefore, had to bring his wife over to the land in which her name had been so abused and insulted. Exactly a year ago he had been looking for a house between Strelitz and Berlin in anticipation of a quiet married life. Now the future was uncertain and boded ill for his domestic happiness.

With bitter feelings he left England. At seven o'clock on the morning of the 22nd July 1815, from the York Hotel, Dover, where he had arrived twelve hours earlier, he wrote to his brother,[3]

---

[1] Bennet to Greevey, 5th July 1815.—*More Greevey Papers.*
[2] Tierney.   [3] W.A.

" I cannot leave my native shore without once more recalling myself to your recollection and expressing to you my sincerest and most heartfelt gratitude for all your brotherly kindness to me during my stay in England, which, believe me, will never be effaced from my recollection, in short, you ALONE among eleven *brothers* and *sisters* have proved to me that you are really a *brother* and *friend*.   God bless you for it. . . ."   Half an hour later, he boarded the packet and set out on his journey for Calais, through St. Omer, Lille and Brussels, to meet his wife.

CHAPTER XII

BRIEF MARRIED LIFE IN ENGLAND

THE Queen had already written to her brother [1] of her decision not to receive the Duchess of Cumberland. She referred to the circumstances of his daughter's marriage to the Prince of Solms as " having made a great impression here at the time " and being recalled " *vivement*," though she herself had not heard of them until that moment. To her niece, she merely expressed her wishes for her happiness and added, " My son will no doubt inform you of the circumstances which will prevent his establishing himself here." [2] When the Duchess read this, her dream-world was shattered at a blow. She became ill and her father very nearly had a stroke. As soon as he had recovered from the shock he wrote to the King of Prussia demanding his intervention. [3]

The Duke had intended to go to Strelitz, but in consequence of a fractured rib which he had sustained in a recent fall while riding, travelling was so painful for him that he decided to go as far as Frankfurt and send General Wyse to escort his wife thither. [4] On the 26th July she took leave of her father and children and set out for her uncertain fate. [5] She wrote to Frankfurt to say that she could not be there before the end of the month as she was still unwell, and when the Duke received this letter he resolved to drive on as far as he could to meet her. On the 29th they were united again at Seesen, on the frontier between Hanover and Brunswick. [6] The Duchess was accompanied by her brother, Prince George, Wyse and Morand. She was not at all well and the Duke himself had found the going so painful owing to his injuries that he had several times been obliged to slow the pace. They decided, therefore, to stop at Göttingen and send for the Duke of Cambridge,

---

[1] The Queen to Grand Duke Charles, 9th July 1815—Liverpool Papers, Add. MSS. 38261. Strelitz had become a Grand Duchy.
[2] The Queen to the Duchess, 9th July 1815.—*Ibidem* f. 279.
[3] W.A.* Duke of Cumberland to Prince Regent, 3rd August 1815.
[4] S.A. Duke of Cumberland to Grand Duke Charles, 10th July 1815.
[5] *Ibid.* Duchess to her father, 26th July 1816.
[6] W.A.* Duke to Prince Regent.

since he had expressed himself so sympathetically towards them. He arrived on the 1st August and in this town, replete with happy memories of student-days, they—the two brothers, the Duchess and her brother—held a conference. The Duke of Cambridge was " thunderstruck " at the Queen's letters to his brother, and the Duke of Cumberland saw for the first time those to the Duchess and her father. He was shocked beyond measure at the prevarications contained in them, but he made one more attempt at conciliation by a mild and respectful letter to his mother. " I have *now* done all in my power to *bring her round* by *fair* means," he wrote to the Prince Regent, " but at the same time *if I fail in this* I must then for my own character's sake act in a manner very disagreeable to myself but "—and here his wrath exploded—" by the Lord HER letters shall be made publick, and I think she can never be supported after that. I really hate to think on the subject, for my blood boils in my veins. . . . However, I will try *all fair* means first. Dearest brother I rely very much on your persuading her *now*, but if you find she is immovable then tell her to *what* she will drive me." [1]

The Duchess wrote a long letter describing her grief and sadness to the Prince Regent. " Your Royal Highness," she said, " will not be astonished if I say that my heart is broken at the feeling of being dishonoured and covered with shame by the cruel declaration of Her Majesty the Queen," after all her letters expressing affection.[2] Nevertheless, she wrote to the Queen a letter of the deepest respect and in the most conciliatory spirit, and she and her husband decided to wait in Brussels for the Queen's answer. Should it be unfavourable, they would go to see the King of Prussia, who was with the Allied armies in Paris.[3]

They travelled on through Frankfurt, Darmstadt, Homburg, where they passed a day with the old Landgrave, to Mainz, then they spent three lovely days going down the Rhine by water to Cologne and in another three they were in Brussels. There a letter awaited them from the Prince Regent, urging all possible haste in having their marriage recelebrated in England—" The delay of a moment may be most fatal to you and yours." [4]

The Duke and Duchess landed at Dover on the night of the 27th August 1815,[5] and immediately sent off a courier to the Prince Regent. They stayed the night at the port as the Duchess

[1] W.A.* Duke to Prince Regent.   [2] *Ibid.* 3rd August 1815.
[3] *Ibid.** Duke to Prince Regent.
[4] *Ibid.** Prince Regent to Duke, 16th August 1815.
[5] The description of the journey is from S.A. Duchess to her father, 6th and 21st August 1815.

was extremely unwell and nervous, and her nervousness and
" heartbeating " were increased by the conversation which she
heard as a crowd surrounded the carriage during a halt on the way
to London.   One man said to another, " She is very bold indeed." [1]
It was not until half-past ten the next night that they arrived in
St. James's.   The Duke had just shown his wife through the rooms
which formed his apartments when the Prince Regent arrived.
The Duchess was overwhelmed by his kindness and he stayed
while they had supper, conversing until three o'clock in the
morning.[2]   The marriage, he said, had to be recelebrated at once.

    As soon as he had learnt of their landing, he had written to the
Queen and made arrangements for the ceremony to take place on
the morrow.   The Queen and the Princesses, who were completely
under her control, would not be there, of course, but the Prince
Regent insisted upon the Duke of York's presence, despite his
pleas that he would not be able to dress.[3]   The first notifications
of the wedding were sent out on Saturday night, the 28th.   Lord
Chancellor Eldon was already in London and expresses were sent
off to the Archbishop of Canterbury, the Bishop of London and
all other persons whose presence was required.   The following
morning the Lord Chancellor made all arrangements at the Council
Office for the ceremony to take place at Carlton House at half-
past six that evening, Sunday, the 29th August 1815.   It was to
be private, but with some splendour of state.   In the State Rooms,
an altar covered with crimson velvet had been erected beneath
the Throne, the right side of the hall was lined by Yeomen of the
Guard and the left by the Royal servants in full livery.   The guests
began to arrive soon after five, among them the Dukes of York,
Clarence and Kent.   The Duke of York came in a sedan-chair as
he still occasionally experienced great pain in his left arm and was
unable to bear the motions of a carriage.   The ceremony was to be
conducted by the Archbishop, assisted by the Bishop of London
and Mr. Blomberg, Clerk of the Closet.   The description of the
day by the Duchess herself cannot be excelled.   It need only be
added that she wore a white satin robe embroidered in gold and
with a train of about five yards' length, and a tiara and small
diamond crown.[4]

    " Now I will give you a short description of the day," she wrote

---

[1] S.A.   Duchess to her father, 9th January 1815.
[2] *Ibid*.   Duchess to her father, 29th August 1815.
[3] The Duke of York to Sir Herbert Taylor, 28th August 1815—*Taylor Papers*, p. 168.
[4] See descriptions of wedding in journals and *Annua |Register*.

to her father when it was all over.[1] " The morning passed with unending preparations and many visitors whom the Duke brought to me. At six o'clock, the Prince Regent's State Coach with his men in full livery came to collect me. As soon as it arrived, we stepped in immediately, partly to be punctual, partly to avoid the crowds of people which had gathered there and before whom, I confess, I had very great misgivings after the way in which I had been maltreated in Parliament and the newspapers. My joy was therefore not slight when the crowd which was waiting for me gave three cheers as we left.[2] I quietly thanked God, for I am really very shy here for the above reason, as you can easily imagine. When we arrived at Carlton House, the Prince Regent was standing outside and he came and helped me from the carriage. Indoors, he embraced me and introduced his three brothers, the Dukes of York, Clarence and Kent. All three received me very well, although not to compare with the Prince Regent. When the first compliments were over, the Regent said, ' Now, if you will permit, my dear, I will present the Chancellor, the Archbishop of Canterbury, the Bishop of London, the Ministers and my Aides-de-Camp and then the ceremony will take place ! ' He then commanded these above-named to gather round us, the Chancellor came first in his grand costume, carrying the Great Seal in front, then the Archbishop followed, the Bishop, and so on. When he had introduced them all to me and I had spoken to them all, the clergymen (for there were also several others present) placed themselves by the Altar (which was under the dais in the Hall), then the Prince Regent led me into the Hall. The Duke stood by the Altar and the Prince Regent led me to him, so that the Prince Regent had my left hand, which he held throughout the whole ceremony, and the Duke my right, as is the practice everywhere. Not only the Blessing was pronounced, but the whole Marriage Ceremony with all Litanies was held. When it reached the point where the Duke gave me the ring (here only the man gives a ring, not the woman), *he* received the ring first from the hand of the *Regent* and I received it again from the Duke's hand. Each of us had then to repeat loudly the solemn vow, then kneel down and pray with the rest ; the Lord's Prayer was repeated aloud by the whole congregation.

[1] S.A. Duchess to her father, 29th August 1815.
[2] The crowd was waiting to hiss and shout insults. As the Duchess came to the steps, she stopped short and made a very graceful bow to them. Disarmed, they took off their hats and gave three cheers.—Princess Mary to Princess Charlotte, in *The Letters of Princess Charlotte*, p. 205.

" When the ceremony was over, the Prince Regent congratulated me first and embraced me, and so all the Princes, not to forget my dear, dear George.   Afterwards, we had both to sign our names in the Register, then all the witnesses, beginning, of course, with the Prince Regent.   Now we went into the room where we had been first of all, and at seven or half-past seven we dined.   Of the splendour of the table, the services and the food, I can only talk by the way, as it is impossible to describe all these details in writing, but even more often, then, I must mention the Regent's extra-ordinary kindness.   On the first evening after my arrival, he had made me a present of his portrait in enamels, mounted in beautiful large stones, and that in a way which was simply lovable.

" When the meal was well in progress, the Prince Regent asked me if I would not like to change, as I must have found the dress a great weight.   I considered this a courteous command and obeyed, particularly as he added, ' *Je ne vous laisse pas retourner chez vous ma chère, il faut que vous entendiez encore un peu de musique, et nous irons dans mes petits apartements, car la ceremonie est faite.*'   Everything was ready, for to save me the trouble I was to change in Carlton House.   I found everything in order, and also a case containing a necklace and earrings, quite simple, but of the most beautiful lapis lazuli, which the Prince Regent said I was to wear with the *negligée* which I was now putting on in place of the state dress. The next day, Frau von Berg received from him a medallion with his profile on a gold chain.

" After half an hour, I had to let the Prince Regent know when I was ready, then all the gentlemen stood up from the table and the Prince Regent led us into his so-called *petits apartements*, from which we could already hear the music, and which are a real fairy palace.   There we drank coffee.   When the music was over and I thought that we were to take our leave, the Regent said that he would not allow us to withdraw—we had yet to have supper.   He had sent everyone away, even his brothers, and had retained only a small select party between twelve and fourteen persons.   He was so kind that it was once again three o'clock in the morning before we arrived home.

" The next morning, I read everything which I have described in the papers.   Under my window there are still all the time many, many people standing, and although it is not very modest, I must mention for your pleasure, as I know that you are so anxious for me, that when the Duke called me to the window not long ago to satisfy their curiosity and I greeted the people, they all applauded me."

The strain of the day had been too great for the Duchess and a visit to Vauxhall Gardens which they had planned for the morrow had to be cancelled as she felt ill at the last minute.[1] The Duke decided to remove her to the peace and quiet of his cottage on Kew Green the following afternoon. The Duchess was delighted with the house and the celebrated gardens.[2] At last, she had a little peace of mind in the village in which her husband was so much loved and respected, and she wrote to the Prince Regent that she would, to spare him embarrassment, willingly forgo the pleasure of being received by the Queen.

Her brother, Prince George, was not inclined to be so conciliatory. He had already seen the Queen once and made no impression. " I never in my life," wrote Princess Mary,[3] who was not sympathetic to her own brother Ernest, " suffered more or felt so distressed as the poor young man *pleaded* his sister's *cause* with great affection, with such warmth, and in so manly and decided a manner, but never lost either his temper or respect towards the Queen—the sort of adoration he has for his old father, and the sort of love for his sister half killed us all." Exasperated, he wrote a strong letter to his aunt and the very next day, the 1st September, she wrote him a note announcing that she would have nothing more to do with him, nor receive any more communications from him.[4] Her blood boiled at what she called his impudence and in her vindictiveness she wrote to her sons in England, the Duke of Cambridge and the Queen of Württemburg requesting them to adopt a similar attitude should they encounter him. No doubt it was a sign of guilty conscience that she represented herself as the injured one and not her daughter-in-law whom she had so wantonly ruined. She complained of her sinking health and sleepless nights from the affair, and even conceived herself as acting with a certain heroism. " I cannot be accused of acting inconsiderately," she wrote. " Under these circumstances I must repeat that I have felt most *acutely* that I have not experienced the support which I had hoped I should receive in the course of this melancholy transaction.[5]

Though Prince George apologised, the Queen would not relent, and to save embarrassment he was urged by Lord Liverpool and the Prince Regent to leave the country.[6] The idea then arose

[1] *The Times* of the following day.
[2] S.A. Duchess to her father, 29th August 1815.
[3] Letter to Princess Charlotte. Op. cit. p. 205
[4] W.A.* 1st September 1815 ; Liverpool Papers, Add. MSS. 38262 f. 4.
[5] *Ibid*.* Queen to Prince Regent, 4th September 1815.
[6] *Ibid*.* Lord Liverpool to Prince Regent, 2nd September 1815.

that the Duke of Cumberland should do likewise. " For Your
Royal Highness's sake," advised the Prime Minister, " the Duke
of Cumberland ought not to delay his departure from this country.
His Royal Highness can entertain no expectation that the Queen
will relax, and he is only increasing his own embarrassment, as
well as that of every branch of the Royal Family, by remaining in
England." [1] The idea was taken up at once as being, at least, the
simplest way out of the impasse, and the Prince Regent suggested
that Earl Bathurst, one of the Duke of Cumberland's intimate
friends, should be entrusted with approaching him upon the
matter.[2]

Lady Bathurst waited upon the Duchess on the 5th September,
and she delivered a letter from her husband to the Duke, urging
him, for the Duchess's sake, to return to the Continent for the time
being. The Earl pointed out that the Queen's health was not
good and were she to succumb, the Duke's enemies would blame
him. It was expected, he added, that the Duke would go to Paris
and that would provide a reason if one were necessary.[3] To Lord
Bathurst's representations were added those of the Lord Chancellor, Lord Anglesey and Lord Lauderdale, but all to no avail, so
the Prince Regent decided to see his brother himself.[4] The interview took place on the 24th. The Prince explained that while
time might remove all difficulties, by prolonging his stay, the
Duke was committing the country to a course of action from
which it would not afterwards be easy to depart. The Duke
listened in silence most of the time, then he commented that the
money for such a journey was lacking and the Duchess's health
was precarious.[5]

The Duchess's family were also reproaching him for not leaving
the country in disgust. She herself was determined to remain with
him whatever it cost, and, indeed, it was only for her that he was
not leaving the country. As she repeatedly pointed out to her
brother, if they were to leave, it would be tantamount to a recognition of the legitimacy of the Queen's action in not receiving her.[6]

As it was, the most insidious stories were being spread against
the Duchess, and the Duke was soon forced to prove their false-
hood. One story which he had to rebut was that he had married

[1] W.A.* Lord Liverpool to Prince Regent, 2nd September 1815.
[2] *Ibid.* * Bloomfield to Lord Liverpool, 2nd September 1815.
[3] *Ibid.* * Lord Bathurst to Duke of Cumberland, 4th September 1815.
[4] *Ibid.* * Lord Liverpool to Prince Regent, 6th September 1815.
[5] *Ibid.* * Account of interview taken down by Bloomfield, 24th September 1815.
[6] S.A. Duchess to her father, 2nd November 1815.

without the Queen's consent, or that it had been given on the understanding that his wife would not accompany him to England. He was thus forced in defence of his own and his wife's character to show to his friends his mother's letters of those days, but always upon the express promise that no copies were to be made.[1] However, from whatever source it came, the *Morning Chronicle* published on the 7th October an extract from the Queen's letter of approval to her brother following the engagement.[2] The Duke immediately wrote to the Queen to assure her that he had had no part in the publication and she replied at once. There was no need for such an assurance, she said, and she expressed the grief which her course of action was causing her.[3] The Duke was overjoyed at this letter. At last a break in the clouds seemed in sight and he wrote at once to his brother, " I have at this moment received the enclosed letter from our mother, which has done my heart more good than the winning the prize of £50,000. . . . At least with us all our injuries appear to us much soften'd since the receipt of this letter, and whenever the beau moment of reconciliation comes, every misery will disappear before our eyes. Pray find enclosed this jewel." [4]

What made the Queen suddenly write a letter giving this impression to her son is not clear, but, at least, it afforded the Duke an opportunity to prove that it was not his obstinacy, spite or ill-will which caused these family crises and that forgiveness was among his virtues.

On the 19th November he wrote to his mother suggesting that the only means of settling the matter was " an amicable and fair communication between us without the interference of a third person such as ought to take place between a mother and a son who are in their hearts faithfully attached to each other." The Queen replied that she would always see him, without his wife, but would never alter her opinion, so that it would be best to avoid what would be so painful. The Duke repeated, " The only possible means of putting an end to what must give pains to both of us would be that fair and honest pouring out, as it were, our

[1] On how this happened, see W.A.*, the Duke's letter to Lord Lauderdale, 10th November 1815. Proof that the Duke made secrecy a condition is contained in his letters to Sir Robert Wilson, one of those to whom he showed the letters, of the 26th September and 23rd October 1815. Add. MSS. 30113.

[2] This was the letter since become famous, of the 1st October 1814, Add. MSS. 38261 f. 274, printed by Fitzgerald and many times since. The journal then published a contradiction intended to appear as coming from the Queen.

[3] W.A.* Queen to Duke of Cumberland, 18th October 1815.

[4] *Ibid.** Duke to Prince Regent, 8th October 1815.

hearts to each other "; the trouble " after all I firmly believe originates from some misunderstanding. It is impossible that a mother, who has ever been so kind, can at once shut up her heart from all feeling towards a son. . . . Certainly you could not respect or esteem me, if I were capable of submitting to be received myself, and not my wife whom I respect and adore. No, such a conduct on my part would merit my being scouted by all men." The Queen was quite unbending. In that case, she said, " I shall have to lament the existence of an insuperable obstacle to our meeting." The Duke replied that she was being led by her own enemies, " for such those must ever be considered who endeavour to foment and perpetuate a difference between a mother and her children, and who thereby bring into public discussion the concerns of the Royal Family which are of the most private and delicate nature. . . . Being fully convinced that the *secret* informers of yours have *deceived* you, for as truth never shuns light, so would these persons have declared themselves openly. But as you persist to [*sic*] refuse to name the insidious accusers of the Duchess, it is utterly impossible for me to urge more on the subject. . . . Must it not strike you that the sole and entire object of these secret informers was to try to sow the seeds of discord between the Duchess and me, but thank God their vile efforts will prove fruitless, for anything could increase my *love, affection* and *respect* for her, it is my seeing the generous, noble and dignified manner in which she has conducted herself through this cruel and unexampled transaction." [1]

So the Duke and Duchess gave up for the time being the attempts to alter the situation and settled down to as much happiness as they could find in their married life in England.

During the week, they lived at the Duke's apartments at St. James's and spent any days on which they desired peace and quiet at his house of childhood memories on Kew Green. In her letters, the Duchess described the details of their daily life.[2] She always slept so badly in London that she did not rise before eleven ; then the Duke joined her and they had breakfast together, she making the tea. Before lunch, her English master, Mr. North, gave her lessons and afterwards she went out driving. After receiving visits, she changed at seven and the household and guests assembled

---

[1] W.A. Correspondence between the Duke and the Queen, 19th November to 19th December 1815.

[2] M.A. Duchess to Countess von Bruehl, 9th March 1816, and S.A., the Duchess to her brother, Prince George, 27th February 1816.

in " the Duke's pretty library " for dinner. Coffee followed, often lasting until past midnight. On Sundays, the Duke and Duchess attended at the Chapel Royal, which meant merely going across a room and a corridor, and Tuesdays and Fridays she devoted entirely to her corrrespondence with home—a particular source of comfort to her, denied friendship and in a strange country as she was. She thought more and more of her family, and when she went one day to see the sights of London and heard Handel's *Hallelujah* sung in St. Paul's, she was overcome by homesickness, for that was her father's favourite piece.[1] " I would very much like to have sent grandmother and the dear children something," she once wrote to him, " but as I have *no* money, I could not." [2] Sadly she compared her present situation to the high hopes which she had cherished when she became engaged, the prospects of happiness which seemed to lie before her. When one Sunday in chapel she could not restrain a tear, she cut such a pathetic figure that one of the Queen's Ladies-in-Waiting wept even more than she.[2]

So the year closed and on Christmas Day the Duke wrote to his brother, " You will perceive . . . that after all my endeavours to bring this unfortunate business to a conclusion, *I am but where I was.* . . . As it is perfectly clear that the Queen finds herself beat as to argument from the *evasive answers* her *advisers* have prompted her to write, and as I am determined not to enter into a paper war with a *secretary*, I therefore, on the receipt of a letter this evening which I perceived was *not directed* by my mother, but by Taylor, instantly resolved not to open it, but ordered it to be enclosed back to *him* plainly declaring that the subject was of too delicate a nature, and of too deep a concern, for me to communicate with any other person than the Queen herself, or one of the Royal Family. As long as decency was kept up and the Queen copied *his* letters, I was willing *not* to take notice of that." [3] Others besides Taylor, however, were using their influence against the Duke of Cumberland, and in a much wider field.

The Prince Regent had been persuaded that the only solution to all the problems raised by the Queen's actions was the departure of his brother. In particular, he could not afford to estrange the

---

[1] S.A. Duchess to her father, 2nd November 1815.
[2] *Ibid.* Duchess to her father, 7th November 1815.
[3] W.A.* Christmas Day 1815. That the Duke is not wrong in his judgment of Taylor's influence over the Queen is proved by two letters to him of the 26th and 28th June 1816, printed in the *Taylor Papers*, p. 171, in which the Queen asks for his advice as to whether she should reply to one from her son, concluding, " I shall either be silent or write as you think proper."

King of Prussia by the humiliations to which his sister-in-law was being subjected in England. It had been agreed at the Congress of Vienna that that Sovereign should cede Hildesheim and East Frisia to Hanover and such an estrangement could have heavy repercussions. The King had been angered beyond measure and he ordered his ambassador, von Jacobi, not to attend the Queen's receptions. He could not understand why the Prince Regent tolerated her conduct.

A very good solution, therefore, would have been the appointment of the Duke of Cumberland to the Governor-Generalship of Hanover, the post which he had been denied two years before. This would have enabled him to leave with honour, and the idea appealed very much to the Prince Regent. This suggestion, however, brought a new person into the intrigues against the Duke, Count Münster, the Prince Regent's Hanoverian Minister, who resided at Court in London. Again, he exerted all his influence to keep the Duke away from Hanover and away from his Sovereign, for he knew that his days of power and influence were over as soon as the Duke of Cumberland succeeded his younger brother.[1]

On the last day of the year the Prince Regent summoned the Prussian Ambassador, von Jacobi, and Count von Hardenberg, a Hanoverian, to Brighton and asked them to try to persuade his brother to leave the country. The first refused in accordance with his King's policy. The Count agreed to do so only at the Prince's command; he did it against his own conscience, and he was convinced that the Duke would not yield.[2] On the 2nd January 1816, the Count saw the Duke at St. James's and repeated to him the usual arguments in favour of his departure.[3] The Duke was very bitter at the request, remembering how much he had desired to stay on the Continent two years before and how that boon had been denied him.

" I do not like living abroad," he said, " I prefer living here, but if the Prince Regent really is serious in his wish and thinks my departure may accommodate him, then let him only put me in some public situation which may save my character, and I will go, though contrary to my own wishes, but without that I cannot leave the country without being disgraced."

When the Count pointed out that this would be an injustice to

---

[1] S.A. Duchess to her father, 6th February 1816; to her brother 29th July 1816, and infra.

[2] Ibid. Duchess to her father, 2nd January 1816.

[3] The accounts of this interview are from the memorandum in W.A.* and S.A. the Duke to Prince George (his brother-in-law), 9th January 1816.

the Duke of Cambridge, the Duke's anger was roused. He thought of the treatment which he had received at the hands of his family. " Lord ! " he cried. " What, am I *alone* to make a sacrifice ? Have I not been most infamously used, and if I go it is a sacrifice, a very great one, I make for all parties, and it is but fair that all must contribute in part." Afterwards, the Count said to a friend, " If only the Prince Regent would send the Duke of Cumberland to Hanover in place of the Duke of Cambridge, for he *wishes* it really and no one is against it but *Count Münster*." [1]

The Duchess was now disgusted at what she considered the cowardice of the Prince Regent. She could not understand why he did not command that she should be received at his own Court. When he endeavoured to explain to her that the list of guests at the wedding of his daughter, Princess Charlotte,[2] had to be submitted for the Queen's approval, for which reason she was not invited, she exclaimed to him, " Oh, really, sire, you have much cause for complaint; the coal-heaver is *master in his own house*." [3] The Prince Regent, of course, became very embarrassed in her presence and sought to avoid her whenever possible. The Duke once visited him at Carlton House and he sat for five minutes without looking at him or uttering a word, while the Duke also maintained a studied silence (ſchwieg mit fleiß), then he suddenly opened the conversation by asking what distinction was made between the King's *Palais* and his *Schloss* in Berlin.[4]

The Opposition knew, or could guess, that a coolness had sprung up between the two brothers, and in their general desire to injure the Royal Family, they were not slow in the attempt to exploit this breach in a manner which revealed their complete want of principle. Having themselves prevented the Duke's receiving the customary marriage grant, they sought now to ally him to themselves against the Prince Regent. Some Members hinted to him that if he would make a declaration in the Lords, they would lend him their support, and one quite well-meaning friend told von Jacobi that if the Duke would only occasionally see some of the Opposition, all would soon be in order again.[5] The Duke would never modify his principles for personal reasons, however, and he scrupulously avoided politics. At a time when

---

[1] S.A. The Duchess to her father, 6th February 1816.
[2] Prince Charlotte married Prince Leopold of Coburg on the 2nd May 1816.
[3] When the Prince Regent visited her on the 1st May 1816.—S.A. The Duchess to her father, 3rd May 1816.
[4] S.A. Duchess to her father, 9th April 1816.
[5] *Ibid.* Duchess to Prince George, 9th February 1816.

these suggestions were in the air, he deliberately went down to Brighton and spent a day with his brother (1st February 1816) to prove to the world that he was not taking any part against him.[1]

One day there was a party at York House, nearby, and as the Queen, the Princesses and all the guests drove past on their way, the Duchess lay in bed unwell from all her experiences. "I heard them all from my bed as they went by," she wrote, "and the thought that I am so shut out of all family circles did not improve my condition." During the afternoon she sat at the drawing-room window reading and writing as they passed. A crowd gathered below and the Duke said that they would be disappointed if she were to go, so she remained a long time ; two spectators sketched her and many shouted greetings.[2] Another family event emphasised the loneliness of the Cumberlands. The Duke had wished to present his congratulations to his sister Mary upon her marriage to their cousin, the Duke of Gloucester, but this she declined as she followed her mother's line.[3] The Duke of York was also cold towards his sister-in-law. Truly the Duke's enemies had had their vengeance in making him a pariah in his own family.

On the 10th April 1816, however, it seemed as if there were to be a change, for the Prince Regent invited the Duchess to dinner to meet the most prominent ladies of society. He had complained of her coldness towards him and expressed the hope through Lord Anglesey and Lady Stafford that she would now be more friendly. That evening he was at first rather awkward in trying to be polite, but not to overdo it. When dinner was announced, he led her down, the Duke of Cumberland taking Lady Stafford and the Duke of Clarence Princess Lieven, the wife of the Russian Ambassador. The Duchess sat on the Regent's right and he became increasingly friendly throughout the meal, displaying "*petites attentions.*" The Duchess felt at last at ease. She was officially received into London society.

When the ladies had left the table the Duchess went to wash. On her way down again she saw Lady Bathurst and another lady coming out of the salon, leaving Lady Stafford alone. Lady Stafford said that she wished to have a word with her, though she had to hurry as the gentlemen might enter at any moment. She had accepted a commission from Lady Bathurst, she said, to show that she was taking no part against the Prince Regent or the Queen,

---

[1] S.A. Duchess to Prince George, 2nd February 1816.
[2] *Ibid.* To Prince George, 22nd March 1816.
[3] W.A. See D. M. Stuart's *Daughters of George III.*

for if she did that it would cost her her influence. That morning, she continued, the Prince Regent had expressed to Lady Bathurst the hope that as he had given a grand dinner for the Duchess, to which all the first ladies of the kingdom had been invited, she might find it easier to leave the country with honour.

The happiness which had been built up for the Duchess during the evening was shattered. She was indignant that the suggestion had been made even before the dinner was over and she had to make a great effort to retain her self-control. She called in Lady Bathurst and told her why she had to remain, that the dinner might be enough for her honour in England but not upon the Continent if she were to return, and that it was always within the Regent's power to settle the matter by giving her husband a situation on the Continent. The doors then opened and the Prince Regent and the gentlemen entered. Either from his knowing what had been said, or from the wine, which had been very strong, he was quite a changed man and seemed to avoid the Duchess and say little to her. She was standing with Princess Lieven, who was talking of " *un printemps si humide et froid* "; the Prince paused, looked at the Duchess and commented, " *Très froid !* " Though the Duchess only expressed satisfaction with the fine dinner, she left feeling more bitter and humiliated than before.[1]

Only by themselves could the Duke and Duchess find happiness, so they spent the first anniversary of their wedding quietly at Kew, where they sat under the dense lilac bushes which filled the two small gardens attached to the house.[2] But even there fortune was against them and their stay saw the most miserable and humiliating day which the Duchess had so far experienced.

In London they could live almost next door to the Queen and the interruption of their intercourse need not be noticed, but Kew was a little village and there the state of affairs between the Queen and her children could not but be painfully evident to the world at large. For that reason and from respect to the Queen as mother, the Duke authorised Halford to tell her that, if she wished, he and his wife would leave Kew should she go there, and he begged to be warned if that were her intention. On the 4th June the Queen arrived without having given warning, and the idea suddenly occurred to the Duchess that she might have chosen this day, the birthday of the poor old King now dead to the world at Windsor, to effect a reconciliation. But then she remembered what Lady

---

[1] The evening was described by the Duchess to her father in S.A., 14th April 1816.
[2] S.A. Duchess to her father 29th May 1816.

Castlereagh and Lady Bathurst had told her, that even should Heaven bless her marriage, the Queen never would. So she spent the day in suspense between hope and fear, which reached a climax as she watched the departure of the family in their carriages back to town from the window. No call from the Queen came, however, and the Duchess felt humiliated as never before. Despairingly, she wrote to her father of reports that the Duke of Cambridge was giving up the Governor-Generalship of Hanover—" Then I will see you again in Rehburg, dearest father ! Ach ! What bliss [Seeligfeit] ! ! ! !—It is even said that the Duke will be Viceroy— that does not matter ! Only thither, thither [Dahin, dahin] ! That is my wish, then I would come to *you* and see my dear children again. God grant it ! Amen, amen, amen ! ! ! ! " [1]

The Duchess's loneliness was, indeed, becoming unbearable and her position was such as to awaken pity in the hearts of many who dared not show it. One strong-willed person who did was Princess Lieven,[2] and the Marquess of Abercorn extended to her the hospitality of his house, Bentley Priory, near Stanmore.[3] The most unexpected friend whom the Duchess found, however, was the young Princess Charlotte, protégée of the Whigs and Radicals and formerly a hater of her Tory uncle, but now, through her grievances against the Queen, thrown into companionship with the Duchess of Cumberland—another curious comment on the way in which the politicians divided and redivided the Royal Family against itself. To several people she said, " I *dare not* see her, but I am *her friend*, as I have read all the letters and am indignant at the way in which she has been treated." [4] She told the Duke quite frankly that the Prince Regent had formally forbidden her seeing her aunt, and added, " Would to God the old lady [the Queen] were dead ! " [4]

One night in June 1816 the Cumberlands visited Covent Garden. Princess Charlotte entered her box immediately opposite, and as soon as she saw them she threw a kiss and the Duchess responded in the same way. All the time, the Princess focussed her glasses on their box and the Duke visited her in the interval. They spoke for some time and she kissed him and sent through him a book containing the second piece to be performed, a Louis XIV farce. At one point in it, a courtier said to the King,

[1] S.A. Duchess to her father, 7th June 1816.
[2] Princess Lieven to her brother, 30th October 1816.—*Letters* (1901).
[3] In July and August. S.A.
[4] S.A. Duchess to her father, 21st June 1816.

" Her Majesty the Queen is in great passion," and he answered,
" Her Majesty may be damned ! " At this the Princess laughed
loudly and literally clapped her hands above her head, then she
looked at the Duchess through her glasses to see if she had understood and laughed and waved.[1]

In the middle of 1816 the Grand Duke of Mecklenburg-Strelitz
invited his daughter to join him for the waters at Rehburg.[2]
Though she yearned to do so, she could not now for a reason
which she communicated to her friend, Countess von Bruehl.
" I know that you will be interested," she wrote on the 11th July,[3]
" in an event which the dear Duke has desired for a long time and
which, although I am suffering very much, fills me with the dearest
of hopes, as I believe that the Duke's happiness will be increased
by it." The Duke was very anxious for an heir, despite the difficult situation in which they found themselves, for the Duchess
was still living off the appanage which the King of Prussia had
continued provisionally pending her settlement as an English
Princess. She was having to arrange for the disposal of her horses
at home. " Please take over the sale," she wrote to her brother,[4]
" as I need money and receive none here."

The Duchess's one great comfort was in writing home to her
family and looking forward to seeing them again, but in November,
with the news of the death of her father, the Grand Duke, even
this comfort was lessened. He had supported her throughout all
her troubles, and the British Ambassador, Mr. Rose, said of him,
" His rule over his subjects was so paternal that his loss will be
deeply and universally deplored by them." [5] The blow came at a
time when the Duchess was far advanced in pregnancy and very
unwell. In December she spent a week in bed and suffered so
much pain every day that she could not go out alone.[6]

Towards the end of January 1817 the event became imminent.
It was to take place at St. James's and Dr. Clarke was given quarters
there to be always at hand, while Sir Henry Halford visited the
Duchess regularly. The Archbishop of Canterbury and the Bishop
of London remained in town in readiness. They all set off within
a few minutes of receiving the message between nine and ten, on
the morning of the 27th January 1817, that the Duchess was in

---

[1] S.A.   Duchess to her father, 23rd June 1816.
[2] Ibid.   Duchess to her father, 27th June 1816.
[3] M.A.
[4] S.A.   Duchess to her brother Charles, 8th August 1816.
[5] F.O.   Rose's despatch.
[6] S.A.   To her brother George, 13th December 1816.

labour; the Lord Chancellor was late as the carriage went to his house in Bedford Square instead of the court where he was sitting. At about one o'clock the Duchess was delivered of a female child—dead.

It might have seemed that there was to be no end to the trials and griefs of the Cumberlands. The doctors presumed that it was the shock of the Grand Duke's death which had caused the death of the child. It was not until some days afterwards that the Duchess was out of danger. On Sunday night, the 2nd February, the Duke saw his child interred in the vault of the Henry VII Chapel of Westminster Abbey. The Dean of Westminster and the Reverend Mr. Blomberg were witnesses,[1] but as the child was stillborn, there was no service.[2] The Duchess recovered and left her room on the 7th February and on the last day of the month she was able to go out riding.

There was now great sympathy for the Duchess in the land. She was not, as at the time of her marriage, merely a name, but she had endeared herself to everyone by her charm and character. The tide had definitely turned and as early as April 1813, when the Duke was in Greenwich on business as a Governor of the Hospital and she visited the Easter Fair there to buy a few oddments from the stalls for the children at home, she was recognised and greeted enthusiastically by the crowds.[3] Another time, a crowd gathered when she threw some money to two children who sang under her window,[4] and when she visited the English Opera for the first time she was received with loud applause. In the interval, wishing to see more of the theatre, she stood up and took a few steps forward; the applause increased and, each time that she bowed, became still more enthusiastic, so that she was moved to tears. How right the Duke had been in staying in England, she reflected.[5] In the same way, the Queen became more and more unpopular on account of her harsh treatment of her daughter-in-law (not that the Duchess now desired to be received by her).[6] On one occasion, as she was entering her carriage after making a private visit, a crowd had gathered and began to shout, as if arranged, " Why

---

[1] Also present was the Duchess's stepdaughter, the Princess of Solms. Frau von Berg had brought her to England some time previously as the Duchess so desperately desired the company of one of her family.—S.A. Duchess to her father, 12th July 1816.

[2] The child was reburied in St. George's Chapel, Windsor, in 1837. —H.A. K.G. Hann. 9 Domestica 328 and Todesfälle 5.

[3] S.A. To her father, 19th April 1816.

[4] Ibid. To her father, 19th July 1816.

[5] Ibid. To her father, 20th August 1816.

[6] M.A. Duchess to Countess von Bruehl, 11th July 1816.

don't you go and see the Duchess of Cumberland ? She is a very good woman ! " There was a great noise and the windows of the carriage would have been broken had not her coachman driven off in time.[1] Such a distasteful scene was the best proof of the intent and success of the Opposition in discrediting the Royal Family by its intrigue in the family itself.

The Prince Regent could still only wish, therefore, for his brother's withdrawal to avoid all these difficult scenes. His advisers worked to the same end, especially Count Münster. In the presence of the Duke in London and about the Prince Regent, he saw a danger to his exclusive power and influence, and he did all in his power to weaken him and render him innocuous. However, he and the Prince Regent found themselves embarrassed by the King of Prussia's interest in his sister-in-law. His ambassador, von Jacobi, had always taken her part and, on the King's command, absented himself from the Queen's Drawing Rooms. Eventually the withdrawal of ambassadors seemed imminent and Castlereagh begged the Prince Regent to act with caution.[2]

Von Jacobi's successor was a weaker man, Jouffroy. He was completely under the influence of Prince Eszterházy, the Austrian Ambassador, and Neumann, the First Secretary of the Austrian Legation, and through these two accomplices the Prince Regent and Münster worked upon him to recommend to his master that he should let the matter drop and allow his Minister to attend the Queen's functions again. The Duchess therefore begged her brother-in-law to send an envoy specially to deal with this matter and she suggested William von Humboldt; as he was known to be a friend of Münster, however, he would first have to be warned against him, she said.[3] Münster was highly embarrassed and sought to buy him off by saying that 12,000 Thaler from Hanover had been offered to the Duke, but that this was not now necessary as he was shortly to receive an increased allowance from Parliament with his brothers.[4] Another suggestion that the Duke should be given Osnabrück Castle " as he complains that he has no *chez soi* on the Continent " also led to nothing.[5] Count Münster was not anxious to increase his rival's associations with Hanover any more than his intimacy with his master. It was remarkable,

[1] S.A. To her father, 19th July 1816.
[2] W.A.* Lord Castlereagh to Prince Regent, 29th October 1817.
[3] S.A. Duchess to her brother, Grand Duke George, 29th May 1817.
[4] *Vide infra.*
[5] H.A. K.G. 9 Dom. 202. Count von Münster to von Ompteda, the Hanoverian Ambassador in Berlin.

said the Duchess, what a difference there was in the attitude of the
Regent when Münster was present—alone ; he was considerably
more pleasant and friendly towards her.[1]

Through the instigation of Eszterházy, another blow was aimed
at the Cumberlands, again through a member of the family, though
this time from the other side. The last of the three Mecklenburg
sisters famous for their beauty was the Princess of Thurn and
Taxis and her daughter had married Prince Eszterházy when she
was eighteen years old in 1812. Hitherto, the family had resolutely
stood by the Duchess, but now, after the second accouchement of
her daughter, this Princess wrote to the Queen to inform her of
the event. The Duchess was too hurt to be able to talk about it
and left it to her husband to inform her brother of this insult to
him as head of the family, after he had ordered his Minister not to
attend the Queen's functions expressly to show his sentiments.
Even worse, he wrote, he had heard that as soon as they had left
the country, the Princess would come over with her daughter.
" If she comes over to pay her court to the person who has done
all possible to ruin her sister, it seems to me that the whole family
should put her aside and hold no more communication with
her. . . . My blood boils with rage. . . . No, by God, that is too
bad." [2]

When the Duchess had recovered sufficiently after the unhappy
termination of that upon which they had set so many hopes, Halford
advised her to take the waters on the Continent at Spa, and so, at
last, she had the prospect of leaving the land in which she had
suffered so much misery. In June 1817 the Duke decided to leave
as soon as the necessary funds were available and some trouble
which he was having in his regiment was settled.[3]

Although no longer able to take an active part with the 15th
Hussars, the Duke's interest in the regiment had never diminished
and he still examined its affairs down to the smallest details.[4] In
the accounts he found chaos and he told the Commanding Officer,
Colonel Dalrymple, with whom he had already had trouble,[5] of
his profound dissatisfaction ; he went into his grounds in the
utmost detail, to the individual boots and saddles which were

---

[1] S.A.   To Grand Duke George, 1st July 1817.
[2] *Ibid.*   Duchess to her brother, the Grand Duke, 22nd July 1817 ; Duke to the
same, 21st July 1817.
[3] *Ibid.*   Duchess to the Grand Duke, 1st July 1817.
[4] For the many examples of this see Wylly's history of the regiment.
[5] Wylly mentions his bringing an officer into the regiment without the Duke's
knowledge.

deficient in the returns. In July 1816 he wrote to him, " I am
sorry to be under the necessity of remarking that it appears to me
a more unsatisfactory statement and one giving as little information
in point of detail never until now came under my inspection." [1]
In a conversation at Kew, Dalrymple acknowledged that his conduct had been improper and assured the Duke that he would have
no further cause for complaint. In April 1817, however, he denied
that he had said this and the Duke had to call upon the testimony
of Lord Anglesey, who had been present.[2] It was now no longer
a purely regimental concern, for according to the Duchess, the
Duke of York had taken the side of the recalcitrant Colonel and
hoped to prove his brother in the wrong.[3] He did not succeed,
of course, and eventually the regiment received a new commander,
Colonel Thackwell, under whom the greatest harmony reigned.
This was one of the things which prevented the departure of the
Cumberlands for Spa. The other was money, for the Government,
which so desired their departure, refused to aid the impecunious
couple now. Their life was indeed one of paradoxes.[4]

The waters, however, were necessary for the Duchess's health
and those of Tunbridge Wells were recommended as the most
suitable in England. In this spa, so fashionable in the eighteenth
century, they arrived on the 14th August 1817, and they remained
for several weeks, during which it rained almost every day. They
rose at half-past seven and went to the pump-room at nine ; an
hour later they breakfasted ; at half-past twelve they took another
glass of the mineral water, which, the Duchess said, made her
quite giddy. During the afternoon they drove out or rode in the
neighbourhood accompanied by the Duchess's daughter, and
dined at seven. The evening was given over to social activities—
there was, said the Duke, a " right tolerable " comedy there—and
every Tuesday a ball was held.[5] The course was successful and
they went on to Worthing, where the sea-bathing had been recommended to the Duchess. They took up residence at Warwick
House on the 15th October, and there they learnt of the death of
Princess Charlotte.

" Ach ! " exclaimed the Duke to his wife.[6] " So I am despite

---

[1] G.A. The Duke to Dalrymple, 9th July 1816.
[2] *Ibid.* The Duke to Lord Anglesey, 5th April 1817.
[3] S.A. Duchess to Grand Duke, 4th July 1817.
[4] *Ibid.* Duke to Grand Duke, 7th August 1817.
[5] For the stay at Tunbridge see S.A. Duke to Grand Duke, 25th August 1817 ;
Duchess to the same, 21st August 1817.
[6] S.A. Duchess to the Grand Duke, 6th November 1817.

everything happier than poor Leopold, for you are still alive, you have been preserved to me!" On the 8th November he visited the abject widower at Claremont and remained doing his best to console him for two hours ; at the funeral on the 19th, he and his brothers, in long black cloaks, supported him.[1] The Duchess had lost a friend, and she could not help thinking how different her position would be if her child had lived and were now Heir-Presumptive.[2]

When everyone had recovered from the shock of the Princess's death, it was realised that the succession was in danger. Though George III had had thirteen surviving children, not one had an heir and the House was threatened with extinction. The celebrated " Marriage Race " commenced. The first in the line of succession after the married but childless Duke of York was the Duke of Clarence. It was only in the spirit of duty that he applied himself to the problem, for his bachelor existence had been congenial enough to him. However, he insisted with reason, if the country expected something of him, it was only just that it should enable him to meet its wishes. There was also the possibility that the Dukes of Kent and Cambridge would marry, so it was proposed to increase the grant to the Heir by £19,000 per annum and those to the others by £12,000 to enable them to do so. But it would obviously have been impossible that all the other married Princes should have suitably adjusted incomes, while their brother, whose marriage had been approved and enjoyed legally exactly the same status as theirs, should remain treated as a bachelor. He was now nearing the end of his resources, and it was felt that the time was opportune as he had undoubtedly created a favourable impression by his way of living.[3]

On Monday, the 13th April 1818, the Regent's message announcing the intended marriages was read in the House of Commons by Lord Castlereagh and the House agreed to an address of congratulation. But when it came to making the grant, it was another matter, and the proceedings began with a long attack by Brougham,

---

[1] Huish's *Memoir of Princess Charlotte*, p. 548.

[2] S.A. Duchess to Grand Duke, 27th January 1818.

[3] One member of the Government disagreed, Peel, who thought it " infatuated " to believe that Parliament would be more sympathetic to the Duke than in 1815, his " dress and manner having become in the interval ten times more germanised than they were before, and his beard, whiskers and moustachios making a daily increase of their dominion."—His *Papers*, Ed. Parker. This may have been a facetious comment, but we know that so frivolous were M.P.s in granting public money, and so anxious to injure the Duke, that we could hardly be surprised if their disapproval of his style of shaving were to be made a ground for refusing him an income.

mainly at Hanover's expense. On the 15th, the House went into committee and Castlereagh pointed out how it had arisen that the Royal Family had to come and ask for its rightful and legitimate income, and how it would be dishonouring what was, in fact, not only a contract but a principle of the Constitution if it were to refuse. He spoke of " that great change that had been in the former part of the present reign effected in the Constitution of the country, by which it had been thought necessary for the public advantage that all these branches of the revenues which were formerly at the uncontrolled disposal of the Crown should be surrendered into the hands of that House, to be administered for the public benefit—a change which rendered it necessary for the Royal Family to come to Parliament in all the exigencies which might arise, and demand a specific grant from the public to meet these exigencies. The House must feel that in former times this question would not have arisen—the Crown would have made a suitable provision for the different branches of the Royal Family out of the hereditary revenues of the Crown without coming to Parliament for assistance."

The debates which followed were characterised by a bitter hostility towards the Royal Family and, of course, an even bitterer towards the Duke of Cumberland. It is, indeed, difficult to believe in reading them that Britain was still officially and constitutionally a Monarchy. Everyone was dragged through the mud, however moderate and inoffensive he had been, but only the references to the Duke of Cumberland are relevant here.

" Never, perhaps," said one Member, Mr. Protheroe, of the rejection of the Duke's grant in 1815, " had the House so decidedly acquiesced in the universal voice of the people as in the vote which it pronounced upon that occasion," while Holme Sumner again mentioned the M.P.s' hurrying up to town, which seems to have been an obsession with him. " From all parts of the Kingdom, Members hurried to express their opinion and to state what they knew to be the feelings of the country. Never was a question more decidedly settled." Lord Gower raised the voice of a gentleman, a rare event in this assembly, as has been seen. " Her Royal Highness," he said, " had now resided for three years in this country, and he would venture to say without fear of contradiction, she had acquired the respect of all those who had the honour of any intercourse with her ; and he was persuaded from the bottom of his heart that the more Her Royal Highness was known, the more she would be esteemed. Her Royal Highness was indebted to the King of Prussia for her maintenance ever since she had become a British Princess, and he put it to the House whether this was worthy of the pride of England."

Of course, the Duke's enemies did not find it so easy as they had done in 1815, for the assertions which they had made at that time had been disproved by facts alone. Whatever they had said then about the Duchess's morals, they could not deny that she had been the perfect wife and had won golden opinions even from her former detractors—that the "improper" marriage which was to be so detrimental to the morals of the country had become a model of domestic felicity to every couple in the land. Upon this point, indeed, the Duke's enemies realised that they had gone too far and that their words respecting his wife might prove a boomerang, bringing infamy upon themselves. The Duke had married at a late age in life ; he had so many political enemies and had received so many physical injuries that his chances of a long life were not very good. If he died, the Duchess would be destitute in her adopted land, and the Opposition, however low and unscrupulous, hesitated to take the responsibility for that upon its shoulders.

Brougham suggested, therefore, that though he would always vote against the Duke, he would not oppose a grant for the contingency of the Duchess's becoming a widow. He agreed with Earl Gower that her conduct was "altogether unexceptionable. . . . Indeed, it is not necessary to enlarge upon the propriety of her conduct since her arrival in this country." Several Members followed his example. Lord Stanley "could never consent to the motion with regard to the Duke of Cumberland, though he would allow the motion as affecting the Duchess. He certainly felt deeply for the situation of Her Royal Highness, but circumstances would not permit him to extend that feeling to the Royal Duke." The irony was apparent, for in 1815 the Duke had been penalised ostensibly on account of his wife. Now sympathy was being evinced for her as against her husband. Obviously, the Opposition was aware that it had disgraced itself by attacking the Duchess and was doing its best to withdraw from the position which it had taken up without losing face. If we turn back to the 1815 debates, we see that she and her " morals " had been used to confound the whole grant. Now the House was agreeing that it had been wrong, but not conferring what it had withheld in its self-confessed ignorance. Mr. Wrottesley was among those who pointed out that it was illogical now not to make the original grant to the Duke.

However, the voting was 143–136, a majority of seven against the grant ; that to the Duchess should she become a widow was allowed. The proposed grant to the Duke of Clarence had been cut from that of an Heir to that of an ordinary Prince, while that to the youngest brother was, after much acrimonious discussion, approved. Where lay the logic in all this ? The Duke of Cumberland had the strongest case, since he was not merely a *prospective* husband, and that his brothers should have been allowed what was withheld from him showed the arbitrary and personal grounds, the utter caprice, on which Parliament distributed the nation's money, while the tone of the debates in general demonstrated, if nothing else did, its malice and irresponsible unscrupulousness towards the Royal Family. In disgust, the Duke of Clarence went to live in Hanover.

Despite all this, the Duke of Cumberland was not displeased, as he had expected a much greater majority against his grant.[1] The Duchess was determined to decline the offered dower, but he insisted and appealed to her to do so to ease his own mind. As Castlereagh said, she yielded only " to the earnest entreaties, he might say, injunctions, of her Royal husband on this occasion." [2]

It transpired that the first marriage was that of the youngest Prince, who had fallen in love with the daughter of the Landgrave of Hesse-Cassel, his neighbour in Germany. Early in May 1818 they married and he brought her over to England to introduce her to the family. To the Duchess of Cumberland he wrote expressing his deepest regret that he could not bring his wife to her, but, he said, he would be very glad to see her himself and would always introduce his wife to her when they were on the Continent.[3]

" Considering," the Duchess wrote to her brother, " that it is just *he* who is the one member of the family with cause to complain of me, and considering the friendship, respect and sympathy which *he* more than any other member of the family had displayed towards me, I have resolved to see him, for which he *thanked* me with *tears in his eyes*." They spoke together of past events as if they belonged to another age and they arranged to meet again on the 2nd June. The Duke of Cambridge was prevented from keeping the appointment, however, and the Duchess asked him if he would come instead on the 4th. The Duke excused himself, saying that he was

---

[1] S.A. Duchess to Grand Duke, 17th April 1818.
[2] *Ibid.* Duchess to Grand Duke, 17th April 1818. Bathurst and Castlereagh announced this to the House in almost the same words as the Duchess herself used.
[3] *Ibid.* Duchess to the Grand Duke, 29th May 1818.

The King accompanied by his body-gendarme

(*By Krüger*)

Ernest Augustus, Duke of Cumberland, and his son, out riding in civil dress,
about 1830

(*Artist unknown*)

taking his wife that day to Kew to see the village and his cottage, which was on the Green next to his brother's. The Duke and Duchess of Cumberland then acquainted him with their plans, so that he might avoid embarrassment to himself, but he answered that if they went into the Gardens, which backed on to their two houses, he would introduce his wife. So it happened and the two Duchesses embraced.[1]

The Queen was living in the red-brick palace nearby, which she was destined never to leave alive. She was already ill and her life was despaired of when she heard of the meeting between her two daughters-in-law. As the malicious Greville, in the first pages of his *Journal*, describes with relish, she was so enraged that a " spasm " was brought on and it was thought that her end was near. The two Duchesses, however, remained on the best of terms, and when the Landgrave came over to visit his daughter in her adopted land at the end of June, the Duke of Cumberland offered to accommodate him in his library, for the two cottages were very small and in the Duke of Cambridge's the old man had to mount three staircases.[2]

Since Parliament's repeated refusal to grant him the little which his brothers had received on their marriages, it was quite clear that, however long the Duke and his wife were to continue making themselves respected and admired by their way of living, no relief could ever be expected from that quarter and that the Duke's financial difficulties, already becoming impossible to cope with, would thus become worse and worse. But the Duchess's honour had been redeemed, as everyone had recognised—even in Parliament—by their three years' stay, and there was no longer any object in continuing the life in England which brought nothing with it but misery and humiliation, especially as the Duchess was again recommended to take a course of waters on the Continent. Since last year the Duke had been scraping together the money for such a journey. He borrowed £10,000 from Coutts, the banker, for which he had to pay, besides interest, a thousand pounds of the principal back yearly and leave as security his plate, valued at £12,000, and an insurance policy of £4,000 payable at his death. Besides this, he set aside £3,000 yearly to pay off the debts which had been incurred during his stay in England.[3] In this way he was able to fix the date of their departure for July 1818.

[1] S.A. Duchess to the Grand Duke, 4th June 1818.
[2] *Ibid.* Duchess to the Grand Duke, 30th June 1818.
[3] W.A.* Duke of Cumberland to Prince Regent, 25th March 1820.

E.A.—6

The Duchess was overjoyed and the Duke also relished the prospect of peace, security and a normal married life. He was quite excited and looked very well, wrote the Duchess, " but the thought of exiling himself from his homeland for years weighs upon him heavily. It will be particularly painful for him to leave Kew, where he spent the years of his childhood. . . . *Kew alone* I am very sorry to leave. I have become very much attached to it and wish I could take it with me on rollers, just as it is. The poor Duke, however, is really heartbroken . . . leaving thut ihm weh, sehr weh ! " [1]

Not far away the Queen lay dying, while in the Cumberlands' house everyone was busy packing and preparing for the journey. Many people thought that there was some connection between the two happenings and Princess Lieven mentioned this to the Duchess. She and the Duke decided, therefore, to make a last attempt at reconciliation with the Queen before all was irrevocable. They wrote a letter announcing their intended departure and asking for her blessing from her own hands. Having sent this, they felt that they had done their duty and shown their love and respect in giving her an opportunity to make peace with her family before her very imminent dissolution. Her answer came through Princess Augusta : the reasons for her refusal to receive her niece and daughter-in-law were still in force. [2]

On the 7th July 1818, in the evening, the Duke and Duchess left Kew, the Duke sadly. [3] On the evening of the 16th the Prince Regent came to take leave of his brother and sister-in-law. The latter thought that he had such a guilty conscience that he could not look her straight in the eyes. [4] The next day she wrote to her brother from St. James's as the horses were waiting at the door, and, on the 19th, she and her husband were in Calais.

[1] S.A. Duchess to the Grand Duke, 30th June and 7th July 1818.
[2] *Ibid.* Duchess to the Grand Duke, 26th July 1818.
[3] *Ibid.* Duchess to the Grand Duke, 17th July 1818.
[4] *Ibid.* Duchess to the Grand Duke, 26th July 1818.

CHAPTER XIII

1818–28

THE ten years from 1818 to 1828 form a hiatus in the life of the Duke of Cumberland. He was an exile with no part in public affairs and receded from the view of the world. For the only time in his life he enjoyed peace and a normal domestic happiness and so there is little for the historian to record.

On leaving England he took his wife to Spa for the waters and they paid several visits to relatives and friends. In Frankfurt his sister Elizabeth, the Landgravine of Hesse-Homburg, was the first of the family to ignore the ban on his wife and received her with great friendship. They were much happier now on the Continent and on the 12th December 1818 the Duke announced to his brother that the Duchess was in a condition to fulfil his hopes of an heir.[1] He decided that her delivery should take place in Berlin and they moved there towards the end of January 1819, when he had taken a house on the thoroughfare Unter den Linden.[2]

At twenty-past four on Thursday, the 27th May, the British Ambassador in Berlin, Sir George Rose, was informed by the Duke that the Duchess's labour had commenced and he and his Hanoverian colleague hurried to the house. They were placed in a room adjoining that of the confinement, the door was left open and all others allowing access were sealed. At twenty to five a male child was born, which was immediately offered to the Ministers for examination. The day of his son's birth was one of the happiest of the Duke's life. He decided now to settle in Berlin permanently and he leased the house belonging to Frau von Berg, the Duchess's bosom friend and confidante, at the corner of the Wilhelmstrasse and Unter den Linden, at the hub of the world of fashion in the capital. They moved in six weeks after the Prince's birth and the christening took place there according to Anglican rites and in the presence of countless Royalties, including the King of Prussia. The Prince Regent, the King of Prussia, the Prince of Prussia,[3]

---

[1] W.A., 12th December 1818.
[2] F.O. 64/114, report of Sir George Rose; G.A. Agreement for lease of house.
[3] Afterwards King Frederick William IV.

Prince William of Prussia [1] and the Grand Duke of Mecklenburg-Strelitz were among the godparents and the baby was given the name George after his uncle.[2]

During the following years the Duke and Duchess became part of the society of the Prussian capital and their house the scene of some of its principal gatherings. Later, they also had a summer residence at Schönhausen, in the country outside the city. There were always parties at the Palais Cumberland and all members of the aristocracy were to be found there. The Duchess also maintained contacts with the literary world. She corresponded with Goethe, who sent her some of his own poems and water-colour sketches and also had one of his books specially bound for her " so that it should be in some way worthy of passing through the most beautiful of all hands," and the Duke visited him in Weimar.[3] The Duke and Duchess also belonged to the principal Liedertafel of the city.[4]

The Duke and his wife travelled considerably about Germany and took the yearly cure at Ems, Wiesbaden and Carlsbad. The Duke made a long journey to Poland in 1819, where the charm and courtesy of Warsaw society and the splendour of the Polish cavalry delighted him,[5] to Vienna and Hungary in 1822 and to Paris twice,[6] besides annually attending the Prussian Army manœuvres. Only seldom did he visit Hanover, and then only for a few days at a time and often incognito as Count of Diepholz, for he did not wish to embarrass his brother in any way.

Back in England the scene was rapidly changing. In 1820 the Duke of Kent died and a short time afterwards the King. Years later, the Duke's son described to a friend how his parents had been invited to a ball at Princess Radziwill's and how the Duke had asked his wife to go alone as he did not feel well. When she returned she found him in tears. " The King is dead, my father is dead ! " he told her. She asked if a messenger had arrived. No, he said, he had had a presentiment. She tried to convince him that there was no cause for worry, but he insisted and put the household into mourning. A full week later the messenger arrived with the news that the King had died that very day and that he

[1] Afterwards Emperor William.
[2] H.A. Joint report of the Prince's birth. Hann. Des. 9 K.G. Dom. 217.
[3] See many references to the Cumberlands in the Briefwechsel zwischen Goethe und Zelter. Goethe's letter and sketches are in the M.A.
[4] A group which met for music and singing.
[5] For the Duke's visit to Poland see W.A. To Prince Regent, 6th November 1819 ; G.A. To Duchess, 11th–16th October 1819.
[6] In 1823 and 1825.

had noticed the Duke of Cumberland's absence at his bedside and asked to have him brought to him.[1] " Though to a certain degree I was prepared for this sad catastrophe," wrote the Duke, " yet when the certainty of the event arrived, it quite overcame me, for certainly there never existed a better father, Christian or man." All the more the Duke now thought of the unity of the remaining members of the family, and to demonstrate this he had intended to go to his father's funeral and to congratulate his brother upon his succession, but he forbore as he realised that enemies would attribute false motives to him.[2]

In March, however, the new King begged him and his wife to come to his coronation as he wished as many members of the family to be present as possible. Since the King very seldom wrote letters in his own hand, the Duke knew that he was in earnest and so he set about finding the means to meet his wishes, " thus proving to the world that there exists but one heart and one mind among the family, which God grant may ever be the case." Since his arrival in Berlin he had found that his income was insufficient for life in both England and Germany, but, after the deaths of the King and the Duke of Kent, he thought that some monies of the Civil List might have become available. At the beginning of June he received a letter from Lord Eldon, the Lord Chancellor, which dashed these hopes and ruled out the possibility of attending at his brother's crowning.[3]

George IV inaugurated his reign by a series of tours of those parts of his realms which had not seen their Sovereign for decades. Between visiting Ireland and Scotland, he went to Hanover in October 1821,[4] and there he was fêted and celebrated as he had never been in his life. The Duke and Duchess of Cumberland were also in the city and took the opportunity of presenting their little son to him, but the Duchess, with her melancholy nature, was not happy in the city of her birth. " I confess to you," she wrote to her brother,[5] " the thought of Hanover makes me quite sad. I cannot let the Duke notice this since he loves it so much, but I am certainly happy not to be in the place of the Duke of Cambridge because of just these memories, for it would be good for the Duke and his love of activity. It would be really strange if fate were to ordain

---

[1] Von Malortie : *'Twixt Old Times and New.*
[2] W.A.* To King, 7th February and 25th March 1820.
[3] S.A. Duchess to Grand Duke of Strelitz, 28th March 1820.
[4] The King had intended to go to Hanover in 1820 but the trouble with his wife had caused him to postpone his visit (H.A.).
[5] S.A. Duchess to Grand Duke, 26th September and 6th October 1827.

that I should belong there and die there. . . . Ach! the *sensation* of treading the house and *room* where we were all born and where our dear mother ended her beautiful life! No, I cannot describe it! Many old playmates, old places, yes, even the old Leine [1] moves me, as with its unhinderable unchanging flow onwards it reminds me of Time. . . ." Little Prince George, however, did not forget his visit and sat silently upon his mother's lap for the whole journey home, then suddenly exclaimed, " I love Uncle George ! " [2]

The Duke of Cumberland had never abandoned the hope that some day he might be able to return to his native country, and he regarded his *pied-à-terre* in St. James's Palace as an earnest of this. Persons who did not desire his return were aware of his feelings and a plan was now put forward (1823) by which his apartments would be utilised by the guard. The Duke was so troubled at this that he hurried to London to protest at such a deprivation. " The poor Duke of Cumberland came in to me, here, on Saturday afternoon," wrote the Lord Chancellor, Lord Eldon.[3] " He is hardly treated. In the improvements at St. James's Palace, they are about to take away his apartments, so that, as he says, if he can ever return to stay, he will not have anywhere to lay his head. He was greatly affected." The Duke visited the Prime Minister, who could only tell him that he had not been informed of the proposed arrangements as they did not fall under the Treasury. At length, however, the Lord Chamberlain's Department was instructed not to proceed with the changes.[4]

The Duke found London so changed during his absence that he frequently lost himself, and his life abroad had disaccustomed him to the rush and whirl of the metropolis. " To be here for a short time one needs threefold strength and as many hours of the day, as one cannot catch up with oneself at all," he wrote. Of the innovations, he found Regent Street the merriest thoroughfare in Europe. But, he went on, " uncomfortable as I am here separated from all that I have, it will be very pleasant for me to sail across the sea again," and when he learnt that his mission had succeeded, he lost no time in setting out for home again. " I flatter myself that through my conduct I have brought many people who were not formerly friendly to me, if not actually to turn into friends, at least to lay aside their enmity, which is a lot in these times." [5]

---

[1] The river upon which Hanover stands.
[2] S.A. Duchess to Grand Duke, 3rd December 1821.
[3] *Twiss*, II, p. 474.
[4] Liverpool Papers (Add. MSS 38295 ff. 34,189).
[5] S.A. Duke to Grand Duke, 7th July and 4th August 1823.

Perhaps the greatest happiness to the Duke was his little son. He could not sufficiently talk about him and praise him to the world. Now the little Prince was growing up and thoughts were directed towards his education. He was almost exactly the same age as his cousins, Princess Victoria and Prince George of Cambridge, and so their cases were now dealt with together and Parliament asked for the means of providing for their education. Once again the Duke had to allow himself to be put into the pillory for whatever might be thrown at him.

On the 26th March 1825 the Chancellor of the Exchequer [1] proposed in the House of Commons that a sum of six thousand pounds should be paid yearly to the Duchess of Kent and the Dukes of Cumberland and Cambridge for the education of their children. The House re-echoed with the old insults and attacks upon the Duke of Cumberland. Brougham told the Members that there was a rooted dislike to him in the country—" it was felt by every man, woman and child." He then attacked the Duke *because he chose to live abroad*! " He lived abroad," he said, " not because he held any office, as the Duke of Cambridge did, but he lived abroad to please himself. . . . Why did he not show himself among them ? What was to prevent his living here ? " Bennet, true to form, congratulated the House. " When he saw gentlemen of different political sentiments uniting on a question of this nature, it almost made him doubt the necessity of Parliamentary reform." Sir G. Rose, who had returned from the Embassy in Berlin and was now in the House, testified that when he first had social intercourse with the Duke there, " some of his friends had remonstrated with him on the danger which he might run from the bad repute in which His Royal Highness was held. . . . He had never known any man to behave on all occasions in a manner more becoming his station or with more kindness and consideration for all who were about him. The behaviour of His Royal Highness was not purchased on his [Rose's] part by any servile compliance. On the contrary, he had upon some occasions felt himself obliged to differ from His Royal Highness, and on those occasions the Duke had acted with the greatest fairness. During his residence at Berlin, he had constant opportunities of seeing the Duke in his family, and he must say that he had never seen a more affectionate parent. . . ."

The Whigs and Radicals were in a dilemma. The young Prince might some day succeed to the Throne, and, as Hume said, " If left in foreign countries, it was impossible that they [Princes] should

[1] Mr. Robinson, afterwards Lord Goderich and Ripon.

not imperceptibly get impressions not congenial with the free principles of the British constitution." It was therefore a matter of interest to the Opposition to take the young Prince from the hands of his reactionary father—these were the traditional Opposition tactics since the days of George I—and here a new possibility revealed itself, for it was known that the Duke himself could not afford to reside in this country. A proposal was therefore suggested and adopted that the grant should be made conditional upon Prince George's receiving his education in England. The Chancellor of the Exchequer protested in vain against this attitude. " Whatever the honourable gentlemen might think of the illustrious Duke against whom so much animosity seemed to be felt, he could not agree with them that it was quite a matter of course that a child should be separated from its parents. They seemed to think it perfectly a matter of course that the Duke of Cumberland should be expatriated and that his son should be sent to this country to be educated." Even this did not please Brougham, who said that it was taking advantage " of a temporary and accidental coldness on the part of the people respecting questions of economy." Of course, the Duke did not send his son to England.[1]

By the year 1826 the Duke was suffering from a great weakness of vision in his remaining eye, and his doctor, Graefe, told him that a cataract was forming. In March 1827 Graefe told him that the very hazardous but necessary operation might be risked ; if it were unsuccessful, his sight would be totally and irrevocably lost. The Duke did not hesitate in the decision to undergo the horror of *an operation on the eye itself* without anæsthetic. He ordered that it should take place on the morning of the 5th, but no one was told apart from the doctors and the valet, not even the Duchess. The Duke rose and dressed as usual, in military uniform, and all the instruments were placed ready on a table in the ante-room. Dr. Graefe and his two assistants then entered and performed the operation in five minutes. The patient's eyes were then bandaged and he went to bed. For days he lay with his eyes bound, not knowing whether the operation had succeeded or whether he was a blind man for life. They were days and nights of acute pain and discomfort and in England rumours spread that he was already dead.[2] Ten days later it became clear that the operation had been

---

[1] Upon the recommendation of the Bishop of London, the Duke appointed as tutor to his son Mr. Richard Jelf (1798–1871), Fellow of Oriel College, Oxford, who became one of his closest friends and advisers.

[2] *Greville*, I, p. 92.

a success. The Duke begged that the Guelphic Order might be awarded to his saviour, Dr. Graefe. The King agreed and the Duchess herself invested the surgeon with it.[1]

Immediately upon his recovery the Duke received official notification that he had been appointed to the colonelcy of the Royal Horse Guards.[2] He was happy and proud at the news, since this had been his father's favourite regiment, but he was naturally sad at severing his official connections with the 15th Hussars, with whom he had been associated ever since he had held a commission in the British Army. Of course, his enforced exile meant that he could not take up actively all the duties which went with this situation, including those of the Gold Stick,[3] and his heart always remained with his old regiment, as he told Colonel Thackwell and the officers in a farewell letter.[4]

Early in 1828 the Duke's attention was again directed towards England. Events had occurred which caused him great alarm. Old Lord Liverpool, whose Ministry had held the country in relative peace since Waterloo, had been smitten with apoplexy in 1827 and was succeeded by Canning. The world knew that the new Prime Minister was sympathetic towards concessions to the Roman Catholics and his anti-European and pro-revolutionary policy was certain to incur the Duke of Cumberland's disapproval. The Duke could now no longer remain in exile in the confidence that all went well in his native land. Canning died, however, and a new Government was formed by the Duke of Wellington. The Duke of Cumberland hoped " from the bottom of my soul that the Duke of Wellington may meet with *that* support that his noble character has a right to demand from every loyal Briton." [5] But even now he did not feel completely reassured, since the Cabinet included many of the so-called Canningites and was by no means united under its leader. The Duke of Cumberland considered that the time might well come when his personal support would be indispensable, but he could not vote in the Lords, not even by proxy,[6] as he had not yet taken the Oaths there to King George IV. He decided to do that without delay and his presence in England would also offer an opportunity to acquaint his son with the country

---

[1] The account of the operation is from *Von Malortie*, pp. 32–34, and von Reden's reports to the King, H.A. K.G. Hann. 9 Dom. 247.

[2] The appointment was dated the 22nd January 1827.

[3] Who had to accompany the Sovereign and command the troops about him.

[4] *Wylly*.

[5] W.A.* To King, 2nd February 1828.

[6] Votes could be cast in the Lords by proxy until 1868.

and present him to his uncle and the English people. When his brother-in-law remonstrated, he replied,[1] " I thought that you knew me well enough to know that in things of substance I do not make an X for a Y. No, by God, as I said, the object of my journey is first, to take my seat and give my *vote* in the Catholic question, especially as *unhappily*, none of my brothers will do it and it is highly necessary that the *nation*, which is not at all Catholic-inclined, should know that there is *one* of the family who is truly and honestly Protestant."

Early in April 1828 the Duke and his nine-year-old son, accompanied by Captain Poten, Jelf (the Prince's governor) and Mrs. Ford (his nurse), set out from Berlin, and they embarked at Calais at one in the morning on the 21st. The sea was very rough and all the sailors praised the young Prince, who slept well, even though his nurse was suffering most audibly in the room adjacent. After a three-hour crossing and then breakfast in the Ship Hotel at Dover, they drove to London. They arrived at five o'clock in the afternoon and the Duke took his little son to the King.[2]

The Duke's fears as to the capacity of the Government to resist making concessions at the expense of the supremacy of the Church proved to be well-founded. Lord John Russell proposed the repeal of the Test and Corporation Acts for Dissenters (now, of course, a formality as an Act of Indemnity was passed annually negativing their effects), and the Government, though it was at first inclined to resist, found it wiser to agree. Of course, the Duke of Cumberland was not the man to countenance such a capitulation. As he explained to the Lords when he had taken his seat, " it was with unfeigned reluctance that he found himself compelled to dissent from the Noble Duke in the view which he took of the measure before the House. He never felt more concerned at any circumstance than at that of being obliged to oppose a Bill which had the Noble Duke's support and approbation."

" You know that my fate has always had something peculiar about it," the Duke of Cumberland wrote to his brother-in-law afterwards,[3] " and so it has been with me this time. Who would have said or believed that I, the friend, the great worshipper of Wellington, should have found myself obliged to give my *vote* against him, I, who was come to give it for him ? But before I

---

[1] S.A.   Duke to Grand Duke, 25th March 1828.
[2] G.A.   Jelf to Duchess, 28th April 1828.
[3] S.A.   Duke to Grand Duke, 1st August 1828.

did that, I was with him and told him of my situation and I must do my friend the justice of saying that he said to me, ' I am sorry, but you have no alternative.' I do flatter myself that instead of injuring him, I have helped *him*, and he is honest enough to admit it and *we are the best and most upright friends.*"

The second event which shook the Ministry was the election of the Irish Catholic leader, O'Connell, for Clare. This convinced them that Catholic Emancipation was no longer to be avoided and they resolved to bring such a measure before Parliament in the coming year. But according to the Duke of Cumberland's testimony, on the 9th August (five days before his departure from the country), he had a three-hour discussion with Wellington, when the latter spoke of Canning's plans to carry through concessions, stigmatised this as his " duplicity " and described his intention to negotiate with the Pope as a course forbidden by English law. The Duke of Cumberland then gave voice to his fears that the Government might compromise upon Emancipation as it had done upon the Test Acts. " You may depend upon it," replied Wellington, " as to Catholic Emancipation, I for one would never consent to it, for I know of no securities which I can admit as such." [1] But on the 3rd August, Lord Bathurst had written to Wellington to inform him that his wife had just received a letter from the Duke of Cumberland announcing his determination to leave his proxy in support of the Government and his intention to return himself should the issue of Catholic Emancipation be raised. " Has he any suspicions ? " he concluded.[2]

The Duke and his suite embarked at Deptford at dawn on the 14th August, but such a storm rose that the ship had to anchor for some time off Ramsgate before she could sail on to Calais.

The Duke of Cumberland devoted the remainder of the year to military activities. He attended the grand manœuvres in Silesia and then those in Hanover, where he took farewell of his old instructor, Count von Linsingen.[3] He had intended to visit his sister, the Queen of Württemberg, on his return from England, to show that he and his wife had forgiven her for the injury which she had done them.[4] The imminence of the manœuvres prevented

---

[1] G.A. Duke's *Memoir*.

[2] Wellington's *Despatches*, IV, p. 574.

[3] Von Linsingen, who had been raised to the rank of Count and lived at Herrenhausen, was not expected to survive the winter. He died on the 5th September 1830. He had joined the army in 1759 at the age of fourteen and thus completed seventy years' service !

[4] S.A. Duchess to Grand Duke, 27th October 1828.

this and while in Hanover he received the news of her death.[1]
" As I have never seen her since 3rd June 1797,[2] upwards of thirty-
one years ago, I have hardly a recollection of her," he wrote.
" However, one cannot help feeling deeply when one branch of
the old tree drops off." [3]

[1] For some details of this, see S.A., Duchess to Grand Duke, 14th October 1828.
[2] After her wedding.
[3] W.A.* To King, 13th December 1828.

CHAPTER XIV

CATHOLIC EMANCIPATION [1]

THE question of Catholic Emancipation, or the admission of Roman Catholics to sit in Parliament, was one upon which the Duke of Cumberland had held strong views ever since his political début. It presented problems of great complexity—so much so that it is impossible to enter into all its intricacies here—but for him and his colleagues, the so-called Ultras, the issue at stake was very simple.

As Lord Eldon pointed out, " The Whigs of former days, of whom some of the Whigs of the present day were the offspring, had constantly been the advocates of a Protestant King, a Protestant Government and a Protestant Parliament. The present race of Whigs through the issue of their loins had totally lost sight of their original distinctive characteristic." Now that Cardinal York and with him the threat of a Stewart Restoration were dead, Exclusion had served its purpose and the Whigs shifted the odium of responsibility for it throughout the last two hundred years upon the Tories. While Catholics were dangerous, they and the Dissenters had seen in their Church the great menace, but now that it represented no appreciable threat to them and, if free, would form just another religious group in the country, those elements were able to devote themselves entirely to weakening the paramount and privileged position of the Established Church, one of the pillars of the social structure of which they disapproved. They were eventually to gain far more from their strategy through the division which they caused in the ranks of the Tories than they had ever dreamed.

The Duke of Wellington had always been on principle opposed to Emancipation and even considered that in the last instance the Sovereign should withhold his consent from such a measure,[2] but now he thought that it could no longer be resisted and decided to introduce just such a Bill into Parliament himself. He thus separated himself from the Duke of Cumberland. That Duke would

---

[1] Where not otherwise noticed, this chapter is from the Duke of Cumberland's own memoir (G.A.).

[2] Wellington's *Despatches* (to Duke of Cumberland, 23rd June 1827).

not, as he expressed it, sacrifice principle for expediency, whatever the odds, and his courage and determination in the coming struggle were worthy of a better cause than that—Catholic exclusion from Parliament—which he was defending.

The return of the Duke of Cumberland to offer assistance to the King and (as he believed) the Duke of Wellington in their struggle against the measure threatened to frustrate all the Government's plans. The Duke of Wellington therefore wrote to him personally and prevailed upon the King to send Sir William Knighton to Berlin to dissuade him. With that, he was quite confident, as he told Princess Lieven, that " the only man that I fear " would remain in Germany.[1]

For the Duke of Cumberland the year 1829 opened in the normal way. On the 2nd January he went with his brother Adolphus to Magdeburg for a week, and he also paid a visit to Brunswick nearby. On the 2nd February he found on his return from a shoot that the English mails, which had been delayed by frost and contrary winds, had arrived. Among the letters was one from Lord Eldon, answering his question as to whether he would be needed in the coming session or not. Eldon did not doubt that Emancipation would be brought up and would let him know when, but, he said, it might come too quickly to allow for this. Lord Farnham also wrote to him that the question would arise " and I have every reason to believe that every engine is set on foot to gain the Consent, in a certain quarter, which Your Royal Highness alone can perhaps prevent."

The Duke's mind was made up—he was being called to his post. The undisturbed peace and happiness of the domestic life which he had been leading for the past ten years was over. That night was the first of the Carnival and Prince and Princess William dined with the Cumberlands early so that they could go to the opera. The Duke returned to dress and found then a fresh arrival of mail with a letter from Wellington, apparently explaining his reasons for recalling the Marquess of Anglesey, the Lord-Lieutenant of Ireland.[2] He was in full accord with his friend, the Prime Minister, who, he gathered the impression, was as staunch against Emancipation as ever. On the way to the opera, the Duke told his wife that he had received letters which made his immediate departure for England necessary.

[1] G.A. To Duchess, 21st February 1829.
[2] Lord Anglesey had been very indiscreet in displaying his conviction of the necessity of Catholic Emancipation.

On the 5th February the Duke took leave of his wife and son, to set out through the bitter winter to where duty called him. It was no light sacrifice to leave loving arms for the country where he suffered only misery, persecution and humiliation. " You can easily imagine," he wrote to his wife that night of his journey through the snows to Halle, " that my heart is very heavy and that my thoughts are unceasingly with you, my dearest angel. I have diverted myself every hour in thinking of what you would be doing at that time, so that I pictured you to myself, at half-past one, as you went to Charlottenburg." [1] It was bitterly cold and the journey continued to Frankfurt through deep snow ; there the Duke spent the afternoon with his sister Elizabeth and then drove on to Mainz, where he crossed the frozen Rhine on a sledge. After travelling down the river through Coblenz, Bonn and Aix-la-Chapelle, he arrived in Brussels on the evening of the 12th, in time to dine with the English Ambassador, Sir Charles Bagot.[2]

Eagerly, the Duke asked for the latest news from England. What was in the King's Speech at the opening of Parliament on the 5th ? he inquired. Catholic Emancipation was to be granted, the ambassador replied with some satisfaction (for he was a Canningite), and he gave to his guest a copy of the speech. For the first time the Duke learned of his colleague's sudden desertion of the Protestant cause. " No words can express my astonishment, my sorrow and my internal rage," he wrote. " Still, however, I forbore expressing any sentiments, being so astonished that I really could hardly believe what I had read."

The prospect of the Duke of Cumberland's arrival filled the Government with alarm. " Cumberland is coming over. The Duke had written to stop him. It is feared the letter may miss him on the road. The King is afraid of him, and God knows what mischief he may do," wrote Lord Ellenborough.[3] Knighton, who had been sent to head him off, had taken a different route. The Duke of Cumberland, seething with rage, lost no time and drove on the next day through deep snows to Lille and Calais. There he saw Captain Lyon of the packet-boat, who told him that the tide would be favourable at five the next morning. The weather was warm, and after a three-hour crossing the ship arrived off

---

[1] G.A. To Duchess, 5th February 1829.

[2] Belgium was at this time united to the Netherlands and the Court resided alternately in the two capitals.

[3] *Diary*, 13th February 1829. Ellenborough was Privy Seal.

Dover between eight and nine o'clock on the morning of the 14th February.[1]

News had been spread of the Duke's approach and the quay was lined by crowds of Protestants waiting to greet the arrival of their champion. As he landed, they gave three cheers and accompanied him to Wright's Hotel; there the Collector of Customs, an old acquaintance, told him of the state of Protestant feeling. Along the whole road to London, and wherever he changed horses, he was greeted with enthusiastic demonstrations, and at Canterbury Protestant crowds threw newspapers which supported their cause into his carriage. He arrived in London between nine and ten o'clock that night and wrote a brief note to Eldon announcing his arrival—"I am *aghast* and surprised, as you may conceive," he said. Then he enjoyed the first real sleep which he had had for a long time. The struggle was to begin on the morrow.

The Duke drove to Windsor early. He was immediately admitted to his brother, the King, who showed great astonishment. "Good God, what, you here?" he exclaimed. "Have you not received a letter from me?" The Duke answered that he had not and asked what it contained. His brother explained that the Duke of Wellington had prevailed upon him against his own conviction, "not exactly to desire you not to come, but to express to you the difficulties you might be placed in, and thereby place me in." The Duke then said that though he might have excused himself by saying that he had not received it, he was bound in honour to declare that had he done so, he would have set off "the moment I had known the contents of the *Speech*."

The King was taken aback at this. "There is nothing in the speech to alarm you?" he asked. "Not to alarm me!" exclaimed the Duke. "Why, it is holding out Emancipation!" "Who has put that idea into your head?" "Nobody, but by reading the speech itself, and that is the general feeling throughout the whole country, and everywhere else, you may depend upon it."

"The King seemed perfectly astonished at my declaration," the Duke wrote, describing the scene, "and positively told me: that the Duke of Wellington had told him, that all that he wanted was, an inquiry into the state of Ireland, and that he could assure him, that nothing should be done without his complete assent and acquiescence and that he was bound to do nothing, and that in the case of difficulties, the King might rest assured, that *he*, the

---

[1] The account of the journey is from the Duke's letters to his wife, G.A., 5th–14th February 1829.

Duke of Wellington, would stand in the breach, and that hereby, the King pledged himself to nothing. . . . The King positively declared to me, that he *never* would give his consent to such a measure. . . ." and added that Lord Lyndhurst, the Lord Chancellor, whom he looked upon as a pillar of Protestantism, had promised the King that he might rely upon him to stand by *him* should there occur any unpleasantness with the Duke of Wellington.

The conversation had begun at nine, and at one Lord Lyndhurst was announced. The King asked him to wait and continued talking with his brother, whom he desired to see Wellington. The Duke of Cumberland agreed to do so, though he could see no purpose in such an interview. He had deliberately seen no one before coming, so that it might not be said that he had been influenced. At three o'clock he reminded his brother that Lyndhurst was still waiting. They took farewell of each other and the King made him promise to come down again on Tuesday (the 17th), asking him to exchange a few civil words with the Chancellor on his way out.

Lord Lyndhurst seemed surprised to see the Duke. He hoped that he had come to give his support, he said. If he meant to Catholic Emancipation, replied the Duke, that he never could do, and he could not believe that Lord Lyndhurst could either, after his speeches in 1827 and 1828, " to which I blush to say," wrote the Duke, he replied, " A political man must learn to forget to-day what he had said yesterday." " Your Lordship's opinion upon the character of a politician," retorted the Duke coldly, " differs so widely from mine that I must suppose that we shall now differ *entirely*." He then asked if Wellington would be at home, to which the embarrassed Lord Chancellor replied in the affirmative.

The Duke drove straight to Downing Street. The Duke of Wellington was still at a Cabinet meeting, so the Duke of Cumberland waited until he arrived at eight. Wellington was very cordial, but he expressed his surprise at the Duke's presence. This the latter considered affected, for he must have known by every stage-coach from Dover since early that morning that he had arrived. Wellington asked him if he had received his letter, which he had sent through Knighton, advising him not to come, to which the Duke replied that he had not, but that had he done so it would have made no difference. He could not go into details now as he had hardly been in bed for ten nights and was dog-tired, so he suggested a meeting in the morning. Wellington agreed, but pressed him to stay to dinner. The Duke of Cumberland pondered a moment. "Duke," he said, "I do not much like to dine with you, not thinking it right to dine with a man whose measures I shall probably feel it my duty to oppose most strenuously in a very few days." "That's nothing," replied Wellington, "we shall understand one another perfectly well and settle everything." "Be not too sure," said the other as he accepted the invitation.

The dinner lasted until eleven and domestic politics were not discussed. Afterwards, Sir Henry Cooke, one of the guests, accompanied the Duke home in his carriage. Wellington, he said, had convinced all the great Tory interests of the necessity of his measure. The Duke was puzzled and asked him if *he*, who had always been a staunch Protestant, was going to give him his vote. "It's all nonsense, opposing," Sir Henry replied evasively, "for the Duke has them all in his pocket." The Duke of Cumberland was taken aback, but he could not doubt it, for he had seen all the Protestant interests represented by the guests at the dinner with his own eyes. "I certainly therefore returned home under considerable dismay," he wrote later, "and astonished when I recollected my brother's having told me, but a few hours before, that there was not the least idea of Catholic Emancipation, rather intimating that it was a *phantom* that I had conjured up in my own head."

He realised now that it was to be a lone fight of himself and his friends for the cause which they conceived to be sacred, since they faced both the Government and the Opposition. "No one has ever been placed in such a terrible position as I am," he wrote to his wife. "But God will help me and I will do my duty as a man of honour. I have only one line to follow and that is the straight line. If I had been so weak as to have been kept back,[1] I would have dishonoured myself and never have been able to show myself to the world again, and you would have had to despise your Ernest, for he would have despised himself."[2] To follow this straight line, he resolved to read no newspapers so that he might not be drawn by flattery or intimidated by the most horrible libels and slanders which were being spread against him.[3]

At nine o'clock the next morning (16th February) the two Dukes met again with very cordial greetings. Wellington began by expressing his conviction that if the Duke of Cumberland listened without prejudice, he would be bound to come to the same conclusion as he himself had done, and he explained his

[1] By the efforts of the Government to dissuade him.
[2] G.A. To Duchess, 18th February 1829.   [3] See appendices.

grounds in detail. The Duke of Cumberland, however, could see in them not one reason for not having granted Emancipation twenty years ago, and yet he had always assured him, as late as last year, that he would resist it. Every detail, every small point was thrashed out, but, at the conclusion of the discussion the Duke announced that he was gratified for the conversation but his views were unaltered and he would oppose the measure to the end.

The Duke of Cumberland then visited Lord Eldon, who was astonished by his account of his audience with the King and the latter's disavowal of his consent to the measure. From there he went to see Princess Lieven [1]; he had declined her invitation to dinner last night as he felt that all eyes would be upon him and everybody on the *qui vive* for what he might say. She told him he had been right, for every time the door had opened, all eyes were turned upon it expecting to see him come in, and rumours were rife since his going to Windsor and his dining with Wellington that if he did not support the measure, he would at least return to Berlin and merely leave his proxy-vote. After this, the Duke went for a short time to the House of Lords. He was greeted enthusiastically by the Ultra-Protestants, who were glad to have their champion in their midst again.

As he had promised, the Duke returned to Windsor on the morning of the 17th and related to his brother all that had taken place. "When I told him that the Duke of Wellington had made no secret of his intention of granting the Catholic Emancipation, he flew out in the greatest *rage* and said that he *never* would consent to it; that if the Duke pretended to say that such was the meaning of the speech he had *deceived* him most grossly." He remained in the Castle that day and the next, and had a very interesting discussion with Lady Conyngham. She told him of her conviction that the King had so enervated himself through his habit of taking laudanum that he knew nothing of the contents of the speech read at the Council. Afterwards, he had called her assertion that Emancipation was to be granted " nonsense " and said that he had only consented to the appointment of a commission to inquire into the means of tranquillising Ireland.

On the 19th the Duke returned to town, stopping on the way at Kensington to visit his sister Sophia. There he met the Duke of Dorset and they walked together through the Gardens to the Park. The other Duke, a staunch Protestant, commented upon

---

[1] Wife of the Russian Ambassador. She held a very important position in London society and also in politics.

the strange times in which they were living and asked if there were any truth in the report that the Duke of Cumberland had joined the Government side. When he arrived at Lord Eldon's he was told of the same report, and two or three Protestants whom he met on the way home repeated the question. Finally, he found Sir William Best [1] waiting for him, very agitated, with the same news. He resolved, therefore, to declare his sentiments in the Lords at the first opportunity.

It was then five o'clock when the Duke went to the House of Lords and took his usual seat next to the Archbishop of Canterbury. He was immediately assailed by the Bench, and the Bishop of Bath and Wells expressed the hope that they would hear a declaration from his own lips that he was determined to uphold the Protestant Church. The Duke assured him that they would, but as to-day's business was the presentation of petitions and he had none to present, he could not make it then. There were many ladies in the House and the Duke joined Georgina Bathurst, Lord Bathurst's daughter ; she conveyed to him an invitation to dinner from her mother, but expressed her regret that the Duke had come and her hope that he would not speak. " What, you, Georgy ? " exclaimed the Duke in astonishment. " The staunch Protestant ? "

At that moment he heard his brother, the Duke of Sussex, who took the side of the Whigs, rise to oppose a petition presented by the Bishop of Bristol. In his peroration he said that Catholic Emancipation would immortalise the Duke of Wellington more than all his victories in Spain or at Waterloo. " This was more than human flesh and blood could bear," the Duke of Cumberland tells us, and he immediately rose to reply. But seeing that the Bishop of Bristol also did so, he sat down again, whereupon the House cried out, " Duke of Cumberland ! Duke of Cumberland ! " In this way he was moved to make his declaration quite unprepared and unrehearsed.

He never rose to address Their Lordships with more painful feelings than he did at that moment. Indeed, he begged to assure Their Lordships that nothing but the duty which he owed to that House, to the country and to himself would have induced him then to trespass upon their indulgence. But, feeling as strongly as he did the importance of the subject, he thought it his duty to let the country know, not whether he said this or whether he said that, but what he was. It was a source of painful regret to him to differ on any measure from the Noble Duke at the head of the Government, with whom he had long been on habits

---

[1] Afterwards Lord Wynford.

of intimacy and for whom he entertained the highest respect. He would put it to Their Lordships, whether they were prepared to say—for that in fact, was the question—whether this country was to be a Protestant country with a Protestant Government or a Roman Catholic country with a Roman Catholic Government. This was the question, and none other. The moment that there were Roman Catholics admitted into that or the other House of Parliament, their House and the House of Commons must cease to be a Protestant House of Peers and a Protestant House of Commons. Although as much a friend as any Noble Lord within the reach of his voice to toleration, he was not prepared to admit the Catholics to seats in that House, to become members of the Cabinet, to be eligible to the high and confidential situation of Lord Chancellor, nor to that of Lord-Lieutenant of Ireland. He was unwilling to say more at present, though he would confess that he believed there were many Roman Catholics who were just and worthy men. He felt sorry that he had been called, as it were, somewhat out of place, to interrupt the regular proceedings by this avowal of his sentiments on this most important subject. It had cost him some effort, but he felt, considering the turn which the debate had taken, that this explanation upon his part could not be avoided.

In no time the news of the Duke of Cumberland's speech was spread about London, and as he installed himself in his carriage a crowd of four thousand was assembled which cheered him as far as Westminster Bridge. On the 21st February he went to Windsor and the King expressed his full approval of his declaration, saying that he had not spoken one word too much or too little.

The Duke returned to town the next evening, and as he had a letter to deliver into the hands of the Duchess of Clarence, he went to see her the following morning. The Clarences' apartments were being renovated and Princess Augusta had lent them her own. The Duke of Cumberland found his brother there alone and they sat together for nearly half an hour—" Nothing could be more friendly or more amicable than he had been towards me, we talked of indifferent things, but not one word of politics." The Duke of Clarence told him that he would find his wife at their sister Mary's so he proceeded there forthwith. As he walked down Piccadilly, he was approached by the Marquess of Thomond, who told him that, according to rumour in the Lords, the Duke of Clarence was to come down to the House and make declaration.

The Duke of Cumberland gave the letter to the Duchess of Clarence and then visited his sister, Princess Mary. " Have you seen William ? " she asked. " Yes," he replied. " How did you find him ? " " Why, looking much better than I had any reason to expect." " No, no, I do not mean that, but how did you find

him in his manner ? " " Perfectly friendly and amiable." " Well,"
she replied, " you do surprise me, for he has been sitting here for
an hour and he has frightened me to death ; he swears that *your*
having made this declaration in favour of the Church and the
Protestant cause, he must go down and avow his opinion to be
completely *for* the measure. I asked him if he had the King's
consent so to do. He replied, ' Certainly *not*,' and he needed
nobody's consent. I begged and beseeched him to consider well
over what he was going to do, and advised him strongly before he
took such a step to let the King know it, to know what he thought
about it ; that certainly there could not be any necessity for his
being in such a hurry, and I begged and prayed him to listen to
my entreaties." The Duke said that his brother had not hinted a
word about it but he had just heard of such a rumour in the Lords.
The sensational scene which followed can best be described by the
Duke of Cumberland himself.

I went as usual to the House of Lords where I found the Duke of
Clarence already arrived, and all his daughters drawn up in array under
the Throne. I went up and shook hands with him. Approaching the
Woolsack, the Lord Chancellor addressed himself to me, and said : " So I
understand, His Royal Highness the Duke of Clarence means to make a
Declaration this evening." " In what manner ? " I inquired. The Chancellor answered " I know nothing but it is so rumoured in the House,
and I received a note from His Royal Highness requesting me to give
an order of admission to his daughters." The House began to fill, and
on the Duke of Wellington's coming in, William went and sat next to
him, and shook hands with him (this was the first time I had seen them
meet, since their quarrel about the Admiralty).[1] Shortly afterwards,
the Duke of Sussex and Lord Holland, whom I had seen talking together
in the Robing Room as I passed, entered the House and took their
usual seats, and the Duke of Clarence instantly left the place he was
sitting on, and went over to the Duke of Sussex, with whom he spoke
a few minutes. He then got up and placed himself on the Woolsack
next to the Lord Chancellor. I must here make a remark : that during
all this period of time, one could easily perceive, by his whole manner,
that he was excessively agitated and nervous as he kept constantly upon
the move. The Duke of Clarence got up from the left side of the
Woolsack and with the Woolsack behind him, and in the most unusual
manner spoke from *that place*.

The business of the day began, when the Duke of Clarence made
his Declaration and made use of such *strong* and *violent* language against

---

[1] The previous summer the Duke of Clarence, as Lord High Admiral, had issued
sailing orders to the Fleet without reference to the Admiralty and his resignation had
become necessary. The Duke of Cumberland sincerely regretted this.—*Wellington's
Despatches*, Duke of Cumberland to Duke of Wellington, 7th October, 1828.

all those who had declared themselves *adverse* to the measure and resolved to oppose it, terming such conduct as *infamous* and *factious*, that the very moment he sat down, I felt myself called upon, however painful and disagreeable it was to my feelings to get up, *repelled* such an accusation, expressing my sorrow that such an attack should have come from so near a relative. I naturally guarded myself from saying anything to irritate him more, though I decidedly declared : that I neither could, nor would, permit any man, either in that House or out of that House, to cast *such* an imputation, either upon myself or upon any of those with whom I acted, feeling that it was unjustified. Upon this, the Duke of Sussex arose, and (*whether* intentionally or unintentionally I do not pretend to say) but made the thing *worse*.[1] However, having, as I thought, *completely repelled this unjustifiable attack*, I determined to take no further notice.

As soon as the House had broken up I got home. I instantly wrote to the King, to give him a detail of this most unpleasant scene, for certainly nothing could be more so than *three brothers* of the highest rank in the country, thus disputing publicly in the eyes of the whole country. However, as I felt, that I had not given rise to this, but had been, for my own character's sake, and that of those with whom I was acting, forced unwillingly to act as I had done, I could make myself no reproaches.

In the evening I went to Princess Lieven's, who had heard all that had passed, and she told me that having seen a great number of Members the general opinion was : that I could not have acted otherwise than I had done and that the manner in which I had spoken had shown a firmness and at the same time a moderation and a dignity, which had been highly approved of and universally acknowledged by those who are adverse to me in their views of the subject.

Mylord Eldon perfectly approved of all I had replied, and said, that it came much better from me, than if any other Peer had taken it up, but that if I had not done it, he *certainly* should have felt himself called upon to have *rebutted such* a charge ; the more *necessary* coming from so high a quarter. We both lamented, as I believe the majority of the country did, not only the *scene* that had taken place, but the *unfortunate Declaration* of the Duke of Clarence, he being the Heir Presumptive to the Crown. The Duke declared, in the course of this speech, that he meant to attend regularly the progress of these measures, which, however, he never did. He likewise threatened us with many more speeches and especially

---

[1] The Duke of Cumberland had denied that he and his colleagues-in-opposition were acting " basely," " infamously " or in a manner to justify any other of the epithets which his brother had applied to them in supporting the Government " when he saw them so unjustly if not infamously attacked." The Duke of Sussex then said that he was not taking his brother's words as they were meant, but " if his illustrious relative chose to take the expression to himself, it was an affair of taste with him to do so." The Duke of Clarence then rose and denied that he applied those words to his brother, and " could not help suspecting that his illustrious relative had been so long abroad that he had almost forgotten what was due to the freedom of debate in this country." Certainly, most persons would interpret such words as referring to the Opposition, and it is difficult to see how, in rebutting them, the Duke was in any way forgetting what was due to freedom of debate.

attacked violently the Bench Bishops. To the best of my recollection, he only appeared once more in the House and that was the first night of the 3rd reading of the Emancipation Bill, but he stayed merely a couple of hours and never returned. The fact was, that he felt that he had committed a gross folly, and I happened to know from a person intimately connected with him, that he had been urged to this step partly by the Duke of Sussex and partly by Lord Holland, through the medium of the former and his own daughter, married to a natural son of Mylord Holland's. I also know that he felt this so deeply that it brought on a very severe fit of sickness, from which he did not recover till late in the summer.

The next day, after routine business in the Lords, the Duke went to Princess Lieven's again " and there heard that everyone, even those most anxious for the success of the measure, deplored the scene that had taken place the night before, and that it was called ' the Night of the Three Princes.' " The following day (the 25th), the Duke received an invitation from the Duchess of Clarence to lunch with her at their sister Mary's. " I immediately comprehended her object, and not wishing to prolong any further my variance with my brother, I immediately went over. Nothing could be more kind and amicable than she was ; I observed at the same time, by the trembling of her hand, how nervous she was. We naturally neither of us talked of what had occurred. In a little time my brother came in and asked me : how I did. We talked of indifferent matters, when my sister Mary came in. After the luncheon was over, he proposed to me to fix a day and dine with him at Bushy, which I considered as a desire on his part to forget all that had passed, and I accordingly fixed the Sunday se'nnight."

The next day, the 26th, the Duke of Cumberland went to Windsor as the King had requested him to do when he was there last. The previous day there had been a meeting with all the Ministers and it had not been at all agreeable. The King had stood firm and Wellington had again assured him that it was not Catholic Emancipation which was intended. He had also expressed the desire to have another talk with the Duke of Cumberland and the Duke agreed to this, though he could see no useful purpose which could be served by one ; he would not be convinced by Wellington, nor did he think that he would alter Wellington's views. The following morning, the 27th, the Duke of Wellington arrived precisely at a quarter to twelve. The Duke of Cumberland was still with his brother but he immediately went to the Library, where the discussion took place.

Since the Duke of Cumberland's arrival, the Duke of Wellington began, there had been a complete change in the opinions of the King. He had written with the King's permission to point out to him (the Duke of Cumberland) the difficulties in which he would place the King if he came to England ; the King's health was precarious and he, his brother, might soon be called upon to be Regent in the case of a minority.[1]

For the Duke of Cumberland, however, it was principle and duty which were important and, he replied, " Even if such a calamity were to occur, as you have referred to, I look upon it that by no act of my life could I prove myself so worthy to the country or place myself in a higher and more dignified situation, than by following the line of conduct I am now pursuing, which is, standing up for those principles to defend which and to uphold which our family was called to the Throne." The Duke of Wellington was staggered. He paused for a moment and then asked whether, now that he had made his declaration and the country knew his sentiments, he could not leave his proxy-vote in the hands of Lord Eldon and retire abroad. Again, the Duke retorted characteristically, " I certainly could do that, but I should think it unmanly and unworthy of my own character, especially being perfectly well aware that there may be very serious and, I am sorry to add, very disagreeable, nay dangerous scenes occur, not, I mean, so much in Parliament as in the country at large, and what would Your Grace say, supposing prior to the Battle of Waterloo, any General Officer had come to Your Grace and said : he had business which required him to go to his family ? (the only excuse which I could offer for my leaving the country at this moment). Your Grace would naturally look upon such a General Officer, and with reason, as a rank coward. Now I do not know why you should or wish to classify me as such."

If there were any wish which the Duke desired might be gratified, Wellington said, he would do all in his power to be of assistance, but he felt it his duty to warn him that if he acted contrary to the law, the Government could not shelter him. This the Duke of Cumberland took as a bribe and a threat. " I would rather lay my head on the scaffold, feeling that I died in a good cause, than lead a life with shame and disgrace at the end of it," he said angrily,

---

[1] That is, in the case of the death of the King and then the Duke of Clarence, neither of whom was expected to live long, when the Crown would come to the young daughter of the late Duke of Kent, unless the Duke of Clarence had an heir born to him in the meantime.

" and I must desire that you go no further in this strain for I shall look upon it as a personal insult to myself, which I shall reveal."

The Duke of Cumberland then countered the charge that he had altered his brother's opinions. The King had never given his assent to Emancipation, but had been deceived, he said. Wellington grew very irritable, and looking at the clock which now stood at two, he said, " Sir, you must not go from here now ; the question must be immediately decided ; I must be at five o'clock at the House of Lords, for the reading the third time the Bill to put down the Catholic Association, and His Majesty must therefore instantly decide whether he chooses to keep his present servants or order Your Royal Highness to form a new administration."

" I smiled, half with rage and indignation, and half at his folly and absurdity," wrote the Duke later. " Really, My Lord Duke," he replied, " I do not know what reason you have to take me for a fool. How is it possible the clock being now past two, Your Grace being obliged to be at five in the Lords, and all this mighty business is to be decided : first, Your Grace must see His Majesty. You must come to an explanation with him ; supposing His Majesty dismisses you, then comes the question : whom His Majesty may think proper, the entrusting the formation of a new Government."

" Why, to be sure," said Wellington, in rather an impertinent way. " You are the only man he can look to." The Duke looked at him seriously. " My Lord Duke," he replied, " there are two persons whose consent must be had for that ; the first is His Majesty—whether he will make me that proposal—and secondly myself—whether I would accept such a task, and now My Lord Duke, it is high time for you and I to part and put an end to a conversation which can lead to no advantage," and so saying, he rang the bell and left the room. He immediately told his brother everything which had been said and promised him, at his earnest behest, to remain in the Castle in case needed. The Duke of Wellington then went in to the King and remained with him from three o'clock until about half-past seven, during which time the Duke of Cumberland walked up and down the Gallery in close conversation with Lord Farnborough. When the audience was over, the King sent for him and told him that he was nearly exhausted, but *had not given up one point*, though Wellington at one time took his hair in his hands and exclaimed, " Would to God the Earth opened itself and would swallow me up ! " Sir William Knighton then came in with a message from Wellington, who was taking refreshment below before leaving, desiring a further conversation with the Duke of Cumberland. The Duke was surprised and sent back word that he would call at Downing Street at twelve o'clock on his return to town the next morning.

As the Duke of Cumberland drove from Windsor, he reflected upon the disagreeable conversation which he had had and realised that the same scene might now be repeated. On his arrival, he therefore wrote a very civil note to Wellington, pointing out that his visit could not go unobserved and therefore he must consider himself at liberty to inform his friends of what passed at it. Wellington had intended to make another attempt to persuade him to return abroad [1] again and this he did not wish to be made known, so the Duke's note disturbed him. Late in the afternoon his answer reached St. James's. " The Duke's answer was couched in the most extraordinary language that was ever penned," the Duke of Cumberland recorded, " and certainly not in that style of civility and good breeding in which I trusted mine to him was. It was evident that my letter had put him into difficulty and consequently out of humour." He wrote, " I have just had the honour of receiving Your Royal Highness's letter of 1 p.m. I assure Your Royal Highness that I have nothing to talk to Your Royal Highness upon respecting which I care not whether it is stated to the whole world. I have no business to transact excepting His Majesty's, and I do not care who knows what I say or do in the transaction of that business." [2] The Duke of Cumberland's first reaction was, of course, that he would not go, but then it occurred to him that if Wellington *did* have a proposal to make after all, he would injure his cause if he, Wellington, could say that he had not wished to come.

I therefore swallowed the affront and proceeded, through the Park and the Horse-guards, on horse-back to his front-door in Downing Street, fully determined that the whole world should know that I had been there openly and not clandestinely and I particularly ordered my groom to parade with my horses before his door. I was instantly introduced into his library where I found Lord Aberdeen sitting with him, but who immediately retired. The Duke began talking of the wind and the weather, and after my waiting a full quarter of an hour, finding he had nothing to say to me, and, God knows, I had nothing to say to him, I took my leave and rode back the same way I had come, feeling myself not a bit wiser for our meeting. Thus ended all further communication between His Grace the Duke of Wellington and myself. . . .

[1] *Wellington's Despatches,* Duke of Wellington to King, 18th February 1829.
[2] *Ibid.,* V, p. 513.

The Duke of Wellington rightly saw that he could not persuade his opponent to leave the country. The Duke of Cumberland was not here for pleasure ; it was one of the greatest sacrifices of his life to give up the happiness which he had so long enjoyed with his family and friends for the tumult and persecution which were his lot in England. His wife was ill. She pleaded with him to return. " Ach, God, how I wish I could," he wrote to her, " but when I tell you that *my presence is of vital consequence here now*, you would be the first to say *stay*. Do not think, dear angel, that when *I* say I am of *vital consequence* I am vain enough to believe that my talents can save the country, but *placed* as I am, alas the *only* one of the Royal Family except the King who is *Protestant*, faithful to this holy cause, if I quit, *all is finished*. Would I so be able to answer to my duty, to my country, if I let my personal feelings lead me to neglect the public duties to my country which call me ! ! ! Adored angel of my heart, you know your Ernest, you know that he adores you, that he adores his child as no father could, and when I tell you all that passes in my soul, in my heart, you could only believe that only one object could have induced me to undertake this journey, the feeling of *Duty*." [1] To render his anguish complete, he learned that his son had been taken ill—so seriously that his life was despaired of—and this was at the height of the political struggle and personal persecution. He passed days in fear and torment and beseeched the Almighty to have mercy on him. One morning, as he was praying for his child, there was a knock on the door. He waited until he had finished the prayer, and then was given a letter in his wife's handwriting. He opened it with trembling hands and read, " God be blessed thousand and thousand times, I can give you the very best news of our little angel." [1]

The evening after seeing the Duke of Wellington, the Duke of Cumberland went to Lady Bathurst's party at her house in Great Cumberland Street in accordance with her invitation. The Cabinet was having a long meeting, so Lord Bathurst and its members did not arrive until later. When the Duke of Wellington entered he " wanted to be very familiar and very friendly, but as I was determined, after all that had occurred of late between him and myself, that everyone should understand the real footing upon which we were, I was excessively grand and formal, but civil. He wanted to shake hands, which I declined. Lord Aberdeen followed him, and to make a difference, having no personal quarrel with him, and

[1] G.A. To Duchess, 25th February 1829.

wishing to show at the same time that political difference had nothing to do with private friendship, I shook hands cordially with him." The company, of course, noticed the strained relations ; everyone was tense and on the look-out for any expression which might fall from the Duke of Cumberland's lips. For this reason he spoke to his neighbour at dinner, Princess Lieven, in German most of the time. The dinner was so hurried " that what is very unusual in *that* house, the gentlemen did not remain ten minutes before they proceeded to the Drawing Room."

The Duke found his hostess and Lady Lyndhurst, the Lord Chancellor's very attractive wife, seated upon a couch opposite the door, and as there was a vacant place, he took it and began conversing with Lady Lyndhurst. " So, sir, you are come to turn us out ? " she asked. The Duke replied that he had no such intention. " Oh, I know you are a very wicked man, and as mischievous as the Devil ! " she responded. " At least," rejoined the Duke, " give me the credit of being a *bon* Diable." " Very agreeable, I acknowledge," she said. " But pray have pity on my *poor* husband ! Do not turn *him* out, I beg and beseech you ! if not for his sake, at least for mine." " Do you take me then to be so hard-hearted ? " asked the Duke. " No," she replied, " especially when a *handsome* woman asks it upon her knees, which I would do, if you would call upon me." She then reproached him for not having visited her at all. " Don't say so, Lady Lyndhurst," the Duke answered, " for I not only recollect a most elegant dinner at your house, but assisted at a squeeze or rout, where Your Ladyship was devilishly out of humour and if anybody ought to feel hurt, it is myself, as you did not think proper to invite me to your haymaking parties at Wimbledon, when I understand it went off magnificently." He could not call now, however, he told her. " What ! " she exclaimed. " Not call upon me ! Oh fie ! Not when a handsome woman asks you ? " " I do not deny that the temptation is very great, but circumstanced as I am, it would be highly improper for me to enter the enemy's camp."

" I merely mention this conversation," wrote the Duke later, " as this conversation led me to expect, from the extraordinary style of it, that an anecdote I had heard a few days before from a particular friend, was true : namely, that the Duke of Wellington had said : in case he could not succeed in persuading me to leave England, that they must try to throw some handsome woman in my way, to engage my attention, and thus divert it from politics."

The next day the Duke again met Lady Lyndhurst,[1] who complained that she was late and that her dinner had been delayed. " I suppose you have been at some of your mischief again," she said, " for my husband, coming up to town at five o'clock, found an order from His Majesty to proceed directly to Windsor." This news puzzled the Duke and his mystification was increased the next morning when George Bankes called on him to say that he had seen the Lord Chancellor arriving home at eight o'clock in the morning in a hackney-chaise. " Your Lordship has taken an early drive to-day ! " commented the Duke when he met him in the Lords, and he pointed out that when a Lord Chancellor went to Windsor, he could not do so incognito. The astonished Chancellor was taken off his guard. " That is really most extraordinary," he exclaimed, " for in order that nobody should know it, I sent for a common hack-chaise and got into it at a corner of Regent Street." Several days later the Duke saw his brother at Windsor and learned what had been afoot.

The Duke of Wellington had written to the King a very strong letter urging the absolute necessity of his insisting upon his brother's leaving England, since his presence was causing such embarrassments to the Government. The King therefore sent for the Lord Chancellor, who did not arrive until dinner, which the King allowed him to join, although he was still in his travelling clothes and boots. Afterwards, he told him of the Duke of Wellington's message, and the Chancellor expressed his full agreement with it. " Well, then, My Lord," he said. " *You* are the proper person to go to my brother and state this to him, as coming from me."

Lord Lyndhurst remained with Knighton until late, and when the King had retired to his bedroom Knighton came to him and said that as the matter was so serious, the Lord Chancellor felt scruples in taking such a step without first consulting the Prime Minister and would therefore call in at Strathfield Saye [2] on the way back to town. But the night was dark, the roads were bad and he did not arrive until three o'clock in the morning. The whole house-party was asleep and he had difficulty in obtaining admittance. The Duke of Wellington, awakened and disgruntled, violently upbraided him for his folly in taking anything written, as that would put fresh ammunition into the Duke of Cumberland's hands. He had wished the message to seem to come from the King alone and upon his own initiative ; he remembered the Duke

[1] At Lady Salisbury's.
[2] Strathfield Saye is the Hampshire seat of the Dukes of Wellington.

of Cumberland's warning of the day before that everything would
be communicated to his friends. The Government did not wish
to appear responsible for the suggestion, but the King had most
artfully caused it to recoil upon them, and in an audience the next
day he positively refused to take any other course than that which
he had suggested to the Chancellor.[1]

Hitherto, the Duke of Cumberland had regarded his old friend,
the Duke of Wellington, as " infatuated and, as it were, acting
under a spell," but when the whole measure of Catholic Emancipation was laid before the House on the 6th March, and he saw that
there were no securities whatever for the Protestant ascendancy,
which Wellington had promised, his wrath knew no bounds. Now
Wellington was to him an opportunist seeking only his own power,
and the Duke of Cumberland determined to oppose not only the
measure but the Government with all means at his disposal.

But here a false impression, hitherto prevalent, must be corrected—that the Duke of Cumberland succeeded in bringing about
the resignation of the Ministry, but that as he was powerless to
form a new one, he had to admit defeat. His own memoirs prove
the falsity of this idea.

I never have been able to get to the bottom of the history respecting
what I have already alluded to, to the meeting which took place on the
Wednesday between His Majesty, the Duke of Wellington, the Lord
Chancellor and Mr. Peel, except partly from expressions which fell
from time to time in various conversations that I have had with my
brother, as well as from what, I know, has come from the Ministers
themselves and their adherents. For example : I know that Lady
Bathurst told the next day a friend of hers, most confidentially, that they
were *all out*. The first time after this scene that I saw my brother, *he*
mentioned to me, in general terms, that he had had a very unpleasant
scene with these gentlemen. . . .

It appears, however, perfectly certain that in fact the Ministers were
all out that evening, and I have every reason to believe that during
48 hours there was no Ministry at all, but that during this period,
Lady Conyngham on her side, the known and avowed advocate and
supporter of Catholic Emancipation, did all in her power to persuade
His Majesty to come to some compromise with the Duke of Wellington,
but to obtain this, it was necessary for her to have an assistant, and she
could not fix upon a more eligible person than Knighton, who, being
the rankest political coward existing, feared on one hand that if a change
took place, his situation might be more difficult and being fully aware
that if it came to a crash there must be a number of curious scenes, and
many things known, which perhaps he thought might as well be kept

---

[1] Greville's description of what was observed this evening tallies exactly, I, p. 185.

secret, and that in fact a great deal of his own power, whether real or imaginary, would probably be put an end to, he thought proper, however much he hated and abused Lady Conyngham, as I have heard him often and often do, to buckle to her and join in her views in trying to bring about a reconciliation between His Majesty and the Duke of Wellington,

and Knighton went to the Lord Chancellor and persuaded him to resign with the Ministry, in defiance of his promise to the King always to remain by him personally.

The Duke of Wellington now announced to the House (10th March) that he had the full support of the King for his measure. As he did so, he turned pointedly to the Duke of Cumberland, at which his colleagues cheered him vociferously. This the Duke of Cumberland considered the height of indecency, for he knew very well from repeated private conversations where the sympathies of his brother lay, but the Prime Minister knew that he could not divulge these in the House, and " I took this opportunity of publicly showing how deeply I felt the insult so unworthily offered me by His Majesty's Ministers, by taking my seat upon the Cross-Bench, which was immediately understood, not only by the House, but by the country at large, and thus now openly showed myself as one of the leaders of the Opposition. I was told afterwards that this nettled the Duke of Wellington *much*."

The Duke of Cumberland presented two hundred petitions to the King in person and over one hundred and fifty to the House against the measure. On one occasion he dealt summarily with the Lord Chancellor who falsely called him to order. " I must beg to state to that Learned Lord on the Woolsack," he said, " that having now had the honour to sit precisely thirty years in that House, I never have yet been called to order and I believe no Peer is less willing to act out of order than myself, but I can assure that Noble and Learned Lord, that I never have seen *less* order come up in this House than since *His* Lordship sat on the Wool-sack, and I recommend him to learn what are the orders of the House before *he* presumes to *call* to order, and had the Noble Lord taken the trouble to have inquired *before* he called me to order whether I was *out* of order, *he* would not be *out* of order as *I* mention he is now." Afterwards the Chancellor complained that Lord Grey and Lord Holland had incited him and the Duke replied that they had made a fool of him.

The most important of the Duke's petitions was that of the Protestants of Dublin, which three men had to carry and the parchment for which cost over five hundred pounds. Such a petition

The King visiting the lead-factory at Osterode, in the Harz Mountains, 1839

(*By Riepe*)

The King arriving at his Palais in Berlin, 1843

He rented the house for a few months in 1819, during which time
Prince George was born there, and purchased it in 1839

(*By Brücke*)

he considered worthy of a speech; he asked Wellington what he had meant by assuring the House recently that there would be " securities " for the Protestant Church, and he assured him, looking him steadfastly in the face, that though he would always obey his commands in the field, in this House he would oppose both the measures which now lay before it.[1]

So the Bill for Catholic Emancipation was in its last stages and there was little hope of preventing its passage. The Duke of Cumberland had intended to recount to the House all the " tricks and falsity " of Wellington, but decided not to do so, and determined to say no more upon the subject, but merely to give his " decided vote against it." But towards the close of the last evening of its passage, countless Peers came to him and said that it was absolutely necessary that he should say something

. . . and I can say that I never in my life did get up to speak with greater difficulty than I did then, feeling not only that the eyes of the whole House, but I may say, of the whole country were at this time turned upon me, therefore I felt that every word that fell from my lips was of the greatest consequence, and having been seated from one o'clock till eleven at night without ever leaving my seat, was little prepared for such an undertaking. The goodness of the cause and the zeal that I had for it are the only reasons that I can give for having succeeded as well as I did upon that trying occasion.

The Duke assured the House that he had listened to everything which had been said most carefully, but had heard nothing to cause him to change his original opinion. " In the opposition which I have given to it, I have not been actuated by any feelings of opposition against Roman Catholics, but I am unwilling to sanction a measure which I consider to be a breach of the constitution . . ." and he announced his determination to continue his opposition to the last.

Thus the Bill had passed both Houses of Parliament, and it remained only for the sanction of the Sovereign to pass it into law. Determined, however, to make one trial more, I wrote a long letter to my brother in which I stated to him all that had passed, calling to his recollection the many and various confidential conversations that had taken place between us during the progress of the measure. I beseeched him to weigh well in his mind what he meant to do ; saying, that if he still felt as he had done and was determined to refuse his Consent, I was willing to take upon my shoulders the responsibility of having given him that advice, which as a Privy Counsellor I had a right to do.

---

[1] See the usual Parliamentary reports.

E.A.—7

I understood from a person who had been by chance in the room when he received my letter that he read it several times over with the greatest attention, and that it had the effect of making him shed tears, but alas ! he had not the resolution to do that which would have immortalised him, have secured him the affection of his subjects and have taught the Duke of Wellington that he would not submit to his overbearing and dictatorial manner.

This picture of the two Dukes waging war upon each other in this way is hardly an edifying one, and for the country it was a tragedy. Here were two great men whose courage, determination and tenacity might have saved everything a few years later, dissipating their energies in a stupid feud over an issue which was to them politically irrelevant. The Duke of Cumberland's adherence to principle and obligation, as laid down for his House in the Act of Settlement, certainly approached the quixotic, and the fact that in the campaign against " popery " he had the mob on his side, that he enjoyed popularity during those weeks and was in the same camp as the Radicals and revolutionaries, should have opened his eyes. On the other hand, the Duke of Wellington was as foolish in blindly persisting in splitting his party on this issue in an endeavour to steal the thunder of the Whigs when he might as well have remained neutral. He gained no credit thereby ; he sacrificed his convictions, the interests of his party and, worse, of his country to no purpose, as he himself recognised within a couple of years.

So when the real crisis came and the two Dukes saw dangers threatening which dwarfed that upon which they had wasted all their energy, they found themselves impotent spectators. In this way the opportunist Whigs had used the Catholic problem first to extinguish the power of the Stewarts and then that of their successors.

CHAPTER XV

1829–32

THE Duke of Cumberland's mission had been unsuccessful and he wished only to return to his family and friends and the peace and quiet of his life in Berlin. " I must thank God," he said, " for having saved me from an illness from all the biliousness from which I have suffered these two months, for, by God, I was not in the country *twenty-four* hours but the scene commenced—all the most infamous and diabolical calumnies." [1] At last he was able to fix a day for his departure.

On the 28th June 1829 he held a conference with Eldon, Falmouth and Mansfield to decide upon the line which they would take should Wellington seek to rejoin their party. They must, he said, oppose all further concessions to Catholics and, above all, parliamentary reform.[2] On the 3rd July the Duke went to take leave of the King, who desired to contact Lord Lansdowne's party with a view to opposing further concessions. The Duke said that he would endeavour to arrange this as quickly as possible, so that he could leave and rejoin his family. This shook his brother. " I hate, I cannot bear the idea of your leaving ! " he cried. The Duke then went on to Lord Eldon, who told him, " If you go, *all* will be lost. You must stay ; your presence is absolutely neces-sary." [3] The Duke was upset by this. He could hardly leave his friends and colleagues in this predicament. It cost him a great struggle with himself, but finally he decided to renounce the prospect which he had been enjoying of returning to the peace of his home abroad. He was his brother's only support and the mainstay of the non-Wellington Tories. He would therefore remain and establish his wife and son at Kew.

No sooner had the news of the Duke's determination leaked out than a great slander story about him burst upon the headlines of the scurrilous Radical papers, one of just such a nature as to give a man cause for wishing his wife well away.[4] Indeed, the

[1] G.A. To Duchess of Cumberland, 16th April 1829.
[2] *Ibid.* To Duchess, 28th June 1829.
[3] *Ibid.* To Duchess, 5th July 1829.   [4] See appendix.

precise timing of these slander-campaigns gives the lie to their origin and purpose. But the Duke did not flinch, though his feelings were those of any other human creature. " I have been occupied with one of the most serious, delicate and difficult affairs that I have had to deal with in my life," he told his wife, " and that often makes me wish in the agony of my soul, ach! if only I were again in Berlin, ach! how joyfully I would breathe without worry, without trouble, with all that is dear to me in this life ! " [1]

Far away in Schloss Schönhausen the Duchess was expecting a letter announcing the date of her husband's coming. Instead, she learned that she and her son were to leave for England eight days later. After years of happiness here, at the very moment when she was looking forward to her husband's return, she was suddenly to leave for that land which for her had meant nothing but three years of deepest degradation and humiliation. For the first day, she could only sob, then, as she told herself that it was her duty and her husband's honour was at stake, she regained her composure, but she left her home, friends, relatives and children " with a thousand tears." [2]

For the Duke, however, the thought of her coming conquered all his misery at having to remain. " Ah ! How my heart burns when I think that in three weeks I will be able to press my dearest, my finest Ike to my heart ! " he wrote. [3] He went to Kew to see how the furniture and carpets were being arranged and the trees in front of the house thinned to give more light. The King was also looking forward to his sister-in-law's coming. " When you see the Duchess of Cumberland come into a room," he told the company at dinner, " then you will see what are manners. I have never seen anything like her yet, and if you were to meet her on the high-road all covered in rags, she would so strike you that you would stop to look at her." [4]

The Duke himself went to welcome his wife and son and their escort, Colonel Poten. The meeting took place at Lille, for the Duchess had spent a day with her niece and nephew [5] in Brussels, dining at Laeken and going to the opera to Auber's *Muette* [6] in

[1] G.A. To Duchess, 6th July 1829.
[2] S.A. Duchess to Grand Duke of Mecklenburg-Strelitz (her brother), 7th August 1829.
[3] G.A. To Duchess, 10th July 1829.   [4] *Ibid*. To Duchess, 24th July 1829.
[5] King William I of the Netherlands was married to her sister-in-law, Princess Wilhelmina of Prussia, his son Frederick to her niece, Princess Louise, and his daughter to her nephew, Prince Albert, both children of King Frederick William III.
[6] It was the performance of this opera a year later that gave occasion to the Belgian revolution.

the evening.   On the 6th August the Duke and Duchess arrived at Calais, supped and boarded the steamer *Lightning* (so called because of her speed).   She weighed anchor and was in Deptford in exactly twelve hours, at three o'clock on the afternoon of the 7th.   The King had sent horses and coaches to meet them and an hour later they were in London.   A reception of the customary sort had been prepared—" I see *The Times* is already beginning its attack on her," wrote Princess Lieven on the 5th.   " This is really too bad." [1]

As soon as they had settled down, the Duke lost no time in taking his wife to Windsor to present her to his brother and the Court.   On the 12th they arrived at Cumberland Lodge and stayed there for three days.   On the 14th, after fourteen years of marriage, the Duchess was at last received into the family.[2]   The King took her by the hand and introduced his sisters Augusta and Mary and the Duchess of Clarence.   They all shook hands and embraced.   The King then presented all the ladies and gentlemen present, including the Duke of Wellington, Lord Lyndhurst, Lord Aberdeen, Prince Eszterházy and his wife, Theresie, the Duchess's niece,[3] who embraced her.   The King led his two sisters-in-law to the table and sat between them ; after dinner there were music and cards.   In the first week of September there was another party at Windsor, but this time the King was unwell ; he was almost blind, but his little nephew George lightened his mood.   Every evening there was harmonium music and Prince Lieven played the piano.   On the way back to London the Duchess visited her sister-in-law Mary, the Duchess of Gloucester, at Bagshot.[4]   The coming of the Duchess was a tonic for the Court, which had so long been starved of legitimate female influence, but it was a source of resentment to at least one member, Lady Conyngham, who conspired with the Ministers to secure the removal of her supplanter in the primacy.[5]

[1] To Lord Grey, I, 262.
[2] S.A.   Duchess to Grand Duke, 12th August 1829.   Princess Lieven told Lord Grey that the Princesses had determined to follow the late Queen's course of not receiving the Duchess, but that the King had commanded it and Sir Herbert Taylor had carried out negotiations with Princess Augusta, who, as senior, agreed to take the lead in doing so.   This can only be accepted with reserve, for the Duke's relations with his sisters during the meantime contradict it strongly.   On the other hand, Ellenborough also says (19th July) that the Duchess of Gloucester intended to refuse to receive her.   On this, see below, p. 201, note 2.
[3] Daughter of her sister, the Princess of Thurn and Taxis.
[4] S.A.   Duchess to Grand Duke, 9th September 1829.
[5] Princess Lieven's letters often tell us of this tug-of-war between the two ladies about the King.

The unambiguous manifestation of the Duke of Cumberland's determination to remain at the head of the Opposition in England had, of course, put renewed fear into the hearts of the Ministry and set them about thinking how they might yet secure his departure. This was not so easy, especially as one solution— that of giving him his brother's post in Hanover—they found to be impracticable.[1] They should try, Wellington told Peel, to induce the King to forbid him his presence. " The difficulty will be to prove a case of which we can take notice, and upon which we can proceed to extremities. . . . For this we must have a clear case against the Duke. . . . All that we can say at present is that the Duke of Cumberland is a great inconvenience, as he has always been . . . and we cannot attempt to remove him from the King's presence until we have a complete case, without exposing ourselves to the blame of all good men in the country." [2]

The Ministers did not have to wait long for their opportunity. The Powers had just decided to recognise Greek independence and discussions were in progress as to who should be called to occupy the Throne. The English Ministers had suggested Prince Leopold of Coburg (who had been living in retirement at Clare- mont since the death of his wife, Princess Charlotte), but they did not inform the King of their act as they were aware of his dislike for their candidate. The King of Prussia, however, wished to nominate his son-in-law, the Duke's brother-in-law and cousin, Prince Charles of Mecklenburg-Strelitz, and this desire he conveyed to King George IV through a letter to the Duke of Cumberland at the beginning of December 1829. The Duke immediately spoke to the King upon the matter, and the King called Aberdeen, his Foreign Minister, on the 7th. Lord Aberdeen told him nothing of his promise to support Prince Leopold and received his master's instructions to further the cause of Prince Charles, as if he were in full agreement. The Duke of Cumberland then wrote to his relations saying that all was settled as they desired.

In Ministerial circles this was far from the case. In the first place, the King was more or less a prisoner. It was, said Wellington, unheard of " for the King of England to receive letters from other Sovereigns, letters which do not pass through the hands of his Ministers," and it was " ungentlemanlike " for anyone to deliver such a letter except a Minister ! Of course, when the King showed any sign of independence or stood up for his rights, it was easy to

[1] Duke of Wellington to Sir William Knighton, 26th June 1829 (*Despatches*).
[2] Duke of Wellington to Peel, 24th July 1829 (Parker's *Peel*).

guess the source of his resolution. They could not doubt who was behind it all, wrote Wellington. " The point is, can the Ministers allow of this transaction passing unnoticed ? Rely upon it that the only safe course for us to take is to strike at once at what is a grave constitutional irregularity. . . ." So the disobedient King was to be called to account lest he take it into his head to become insubordinate upon any other occasion. Peel agreed enthusiastic-ally. Now, he said, had come the time when they could destroy the Duke of Cumberland's influence by discrediting him in the eyes of the King and the public.

But they would also take the opportunity of ridding the Govern-ment of another thorn in its side, the Russian Ambassador, Prince Lieven, who was not in favour with it for reasons of Oriental policy. Lieven had learnt of Prince Charles's candidature only through the Duke of Cumberland, and though he had often seen Lord Aberdeen, the latter had never spoken a word upon the subject. A week later, he learned that Aberdeen had been to the King and complained of the obstinate resistance of the Russian Ambassador. Though he, Aberdeen, had named Prince Charles at the King's express wish, Lieven insisted upon supporting Prince Philip of Homburg ! The King was, of course, angry, and Aberdeen then remarked that the conduct and interference of Prince Lieven in general were such as to render his recall desirable. This inter-view was reported word-for-word by the King to his brother, who told the Ambassador.

Now, said Aberdeen to Wellington, the handwriting of the letter in question was not that of the King of Prussia and the signature was that of some German name with which he was not acquainted ; it was, the King had told him, that of someone only employed in matters of the strictest confidence. The thought occurred to him that the whole proposition was an intrigue of the Duke of Cumberland, who was using the King of Prussia's name fraudulently to give it greater weight. He at once despatched an order to the British Ambassador in Berlin to give the *Government* of Prussia an *official* answer of the English Government declining the entirely personal and confidential suggestion of the King of Prussia. But he found out from the Prussian Ambassador that he had shown the British Government to be unworthy of trust and con-fidence to no object. " We shall evidently have a storm at home," he wrote. " Bülow was with me to-day and it really appears that the King of Prussia has interested himself very much about Prince Charles of Mecklenburg." He proceeded to lie to von Bülow, saying that he knew nothing of the King's sentiments as conveyed by the Duke of Cumberland, though he had expressed his full agreement to the King personally and had officially informed the King of Prussia through the Minister in Berlin of his master's opinion ! Not until January 1830 was the King informed of the choice of Prince Leopold,[1] and " that the whole public knew a fact of which the King alone was ignorant." It was represented to him, as had been intended, as a *fait accompli* of the Great Powers. The King expressed his regret, but he did not doubt of the Ministers' story.[2] The Ministers dined with him on the 28th. " It looks as though he were trying to atone for his sin in having shown a momentary spark of courage," Princess Lieven wrote. " I think Cumberland will die of rage ! " [3]

But the Duke was already ill again. On the 22nd, Princess Lieven had had to cancel a dinner that she was to have given in his honour as he was " back in bed once more ; he returned from Windsor yesterday as sick as a dog." [3] By inducing the King to show that " momentary spark of courage," he had been asking for another dastardly plot to be perpetrated to secure his removal, especially as Parliament was shortly to meet. This time it was one which was to cost a man's life. As the Duke and his wife both lay ill at Kew and the snows covered the Green outside, a new slander campaign began upon the lines expounded by Don Basilio.[4] " It is disgusting," wrote the Duke in his wrath, " to live in a country where every man's character is at the mercy of hirelings who, to carry out any purpose or gratify any party motive, can insinuate the greatest lies against anyone." [5] But it was very opportune to the Ministry, as we know from Lord Ellenborough's diary, in which he wrote that the affair " will drive the Duke of Cumberland from the field." With an ordinary man it might have succeeded in doing so. Even those who knew the Duke did not believe that he could survive this campaign in England.[6] But the Duke himself

---

[1] Eventually, Prince Otho of Bavaria became King of Greece, and Prince Leopold became King of Belgium the following year.

[2] This account of the negotiations for the Greek candidature is from the correspondence between Wellington, Aberdeen and Peel in the former's *Despatches*, from Princess Lieven's account, from S.A., Duke to Grand Duke, 18th December 1829 and Duchess to Grand Duke, 19th June 1830, and from G.A., several rough notes and diaries of the Duchess.

[3] To Lady Cowper, 29th January 1830.

[4] See appendices.   [5] Eldon Archives, to Lord Eldon, 14th February 1830.

[6] See, for example, the Duke of Rutland to Lady Shelley, 24th February 1830 : " I understand the Duke of Cumberland will leave this country as soon as he can do so without *appearing* to have been driven out of it by implication in the late melancholy catastrophe."

was writing to Lord Eldon, " they may as well move St. Paul's to this place as get me to *flinch* ! " [1]

Now was the opportunity to destroy the Duke of Cumberland's influence once and for all. If the King saw him, it would imply that he did not believe the slander; if, however, he declined to receive him, the Duke would be branded to the world as guilty in the eyes of the King and the highest quarters of the State. For this reason, one of the most unscrupulous arch-intriguers about the King, Knighton, hurried to Windsor to recommend his not seeing his brother. Whether or not he were innocent, he said, the public was in no state to believe it and the King would only injure himself and do no good to his brother by seeing him.[2] However, on the 1st March, the Duke, though not yet convalescent, went to Windsor. The King received him most cordially and did not touch upon the unpleasant topic; he commented upon his brother's thinness and changed appearance and he assured him that he had done all in his power with regard to Greece, but his Ministers had ill-used him. " My having been full *two* hours with him will put an end to *all the lies* on *that score*," [3] he wrote.

While this campaign against him was at its height, the Duke was conducting negotiations for a Royal donation towards the enlargement of the village church, immediately opposite his windows, and he announced his brother's generosity at a public Vestry meeting.[4] He was still unwell when the Duchess's birthday came round on the 2nd March 1830. As the date was given incorrectly in the Court Calendar, they were not troubled by official visitors, but gave a tea-party for the Eszterházys, Lievens, Münster, the Bülows and the Duchess of Clarence. Suddenly, loud reports boomed from the Green outside and the Duchess was terrified at the shock; then they learned what had happened.

[1] To Lord Eldon, 14th February 1830.

[2] W.A.* Sir William Knighton's *Diary*, 9th February 1830: " I went down to Windsor for the express purpose of recommending the King, if possible, to avoid seeing the Duke of Cumberland. Whatever might be his innocence as to intrigue with Lady Graves, the public were in a state of mind not to believe it. The King, by seeing much of him, would involve himself without doing any real benefit to the character of his brother. I succeeded in convincing the King that I was right, but only through the agency of the Duchess of Gloucester." It is quite impossible to find one's way through these intrigues against the Duke of Cumberland. Certainly, his sister Mary, the contrary to Augusta, had never shown great affection for him during the years up to 1818, but her letters to him during the intervening years of exile (G.A.), her conduct during the Emancipation crisis and her apparent Conservative sympathies would have led one to discredit such a report.

[3] To Lord Eldon, 2nd March 1830.

[4] To Sir William Knighton, 2nd March 1830.

The villagers had just discovered that it was her birthday and had hurriedly borrowed the Lord Mayor's cannon and fired a salute as they hoisted the flag on the church in her honour.[1]

All the trials of the last few months had, of course, increased the Duke's hostility to the Government. His policy was, as he termed it, one of "red-hot opposition."[2] After Wellington's somersault with regard to Emancipation, he expected a similar antic when the question of parliamentary reform became acute, as, it was quite clear, it eventually would—"he merely wants to see *what* is the predominant feeling, the moment he can ascertain that, directly he adopts it, be it in direct contradiction to everything that he has said or done before."[3]

"Unless something is *done* and that too *very shortly*, I am perfectly convinced that we shall have some violent commotion in the State,"[4] he wrote. Patriotic men of all parties could see this, he considered, and he urged them all to unite to rid the country of the Ministry which was leading it to Jacobinism and ruin. They should, he suggested, bring forward only such general measures as could gain the support of men of all parties and lay aside points that divided them; they could not go on as hitherto, "like a pack of hounds without huntsmen or whippers-in."[5] Alas, he still thought of politics as they had been in his youth, when parties were largely family affairs and differed little in principles, but he was more far-sighted than his aristocratic opponents and believed that they would unite in the face of common danger. He did not know what the real objects of his fellow-opponents to Wellington were; he took them for patriotic men also seeking to save the country from Jacobinism. "A sort of understanding ought to exist between *us* and the *moderates* of the other party," he wrote. "With respect to Whigs and Tories *now* it appears to me that that idea should be laid completely aside now and the main and great consideration for us to take in view is this—whether the country is or is not in the most imminent danger: distress and rebellion the natural consequence *staring us* in the face, and from my conscience, I believe the *epoch* not *far distant*."[6] The Duke of Cumberland's mistaken views of the Whigs' desire to ward off rebellion was to be of fateful consequence for the country.

[1] S.A. Duchess to Grand Duke, 20th March 1830.
[2] Encombe Archives. To Lord Eldon, 24th January 1830.
[3] *Ibid.* To Lord Eldon, 14th February 1830.
[4] *Ibid.* To Lord Eldon, 10th March 1830.
[5] *Ibid.* To Lord Eldon, 14th February 1830.
[6] *Ibid.* To Lord Eldon, 21st and 23rd February 1830.

Periodically throughout March 1830 the Duke went to his brother at Windsor. He hoped to warn him of the danger of the present Ministry, but intended that the King should introduce the topic himself. He thought that the King was becoming more communicative when, on the 26th, he found him so unwell and wretched in appearance that he remained only a quarter of an hour with him.[1] The King's condition soon became grave and it was clear that his end was near. From his sisters the Duke heard a description " that went to my very soul, loving him as faithfully as ever one brother did another; for this I can say, I loved him for himself, and never have I had any sordid or interested view in my affection for him, but that of purest love and attachment. . . . God preserve him for us all! " [2] On the 8th May the Duke, the Duchess and Prince George were with him. Early on the morning of the 26th June he died.

The position of the Duke of Cumberland underwent a drastic change overnight. No longer was he the chief support and confidant of the King, no longer was he a figure at the Court. The new King William IV was well-meaning but naïve. He desired the affection of his subjects and thought that he could gain this by displaying exaggerated liberal and nationalist sympathies. It needed only a few months for him to see his own folly and that his reign was, as it were, the liquidation or winding-up of all that had meant England. One of his first acts was the dismissal of the late King's German musicians and French cooks. He now intended to show to the world that the Duke of Cumberland no longer had any influence and the occasion for this was even before the late King was in his grave.

In the normal way the Household Cavalry present at the funeral would have been under the command of Gold Stick, who was directly responsible to the King. But the King announced that upon this and all future occasions Gold Stick was to be subordinate to and take his orders from the Commander-in-Chief like any other officer. The post ceased thereupon to be of military significance and became merely that of that officer detailed to command the troops at Court functions. The Duke informed the King through Sir Herbert Taylor that he would in that case resign the position. He was, he pointed out, the Senior Field-Marshal of the British Army after Wellington and so he could not take orders from an inferior general. The King announced to Wellington

---

[1] Encombe Archives. To Lord Eldon, 27th March 1830.
[2] To Knighton, 1st May 1830.

that he intended to accept his brother's resignation if proffered. Wellington himself, now more inclined towards the Duke, had great misgivings as to the loss of power and dignity to the Crown through the intended change and attempted to pour oil on the troubled waters by suggesting alternative mutually acceptable measures.   But the King was adamant in his determination to humiliate his brother, even if he suffered himself loss thereby. After the funeral the Duke wrote a long and passionate letter to him explaining the wishes of their late brother, his own attempts to fulfil his duties conscientiously and his regret that he was not to do the same about the present King's person, that the King had the right to order as he pleased, he said, but that in this case it would not be compatible with the honour of a Prince of the Blood and a Field-Marshal to remain in a position so altered.   To this the King replied curtly that he had received his letter and regretted that he considered it necessary to resign his office in consequence of the new arrangement.   So, after thirty-one years and a fortnight of service, the Duke of Cumberland left the active list of the British Army.[1]   The King was to learn by bitter experience who was right.   Certainly, he was an ungrateful man, for his brother had loyally supported him in a similar dispute when he had not had right on his side.

Amidst all these rebuffs, however, the King did grant one boon to his brother, that of a suitable residence.   The Duke's present house at Kew was only suitable for a bachelor.   Kew had ceased to be important as a Royal residence with the death of Queen Charlotte—besides the Duke of Cumberland, only the absent Duke of Cambridge had a house there now—and its gardens were now already cultivated primarily for botanical purposes.   The Duke had thus become more or less the squire of the village, who interested himself in all its affairs and activities, and so it was a happy idea to give him (for life and as a jointure for his wife) the large empty house owned by the Crown on the north side of the Green beside the entrance to the Gardens.   So great was the joy of the pair that, according to John Smith (a curator of the Gardens), who witnessed the scene, the Duchess fell upon her knees and thanked the King.   Their new residence was a fine red-brick Georgian house with extensive grounds containing many fine old elms and cedars.   They extended to the bank of the Thames and included the long thin island in its middle, while on one side

---

[1] See the correspondence in Wellington's *Despatches* and Sir George Arthur's *Household Cavalry*.

they bordered on the Royal Gardens, to which access could be had through a small gate. The old house by the church was the Duke's own property and he now intended to use it for the accommodation of guests. The Duke and Duchess interested themselves in the work being undertaken on their new house, and on the 16th July 1831 they were able to open it with a fête in honour of the King. Three hundred persons were invited, but as the dining-room held only twenty-six, only the Royal table was indoors and a large red-and-white striped marquee was erected in the garden. There the party ate, danced and listened to two orchestras, but unfortunately it rained and, though everyone was happy and contented, for the Duchess the whole afternoon was spoilt.[1]

In politics the King gave his full support to Wellington and it might have seemed as if the Prime Minister's position had been strengthened. But it was now that the division between Wellington and the Duke of Cumberland became of such moment to the country. Riot and disorder had been a settled feature of the English scene since the beginning of the Industrial Revolution and there was nothing in the country which portended great developments. When Parliament met in October 1830 there were no Reform and Anti-Reform parties, not even Whigs and Tories, for both parties were broken into splinters. Wellington had estranged first the Canning or, as would be said to-day, left-wing, and then the Cumberland, or right-wing, of his party, and the Whigs were similarly divided between aristocratic Grey and plebian Brougham. But that month these Whig fragments reunited on the common ground of their hatred of Wellington, and thenceforth the disunity of the Tory groups meant suicide. Of course, the Tories new nothing of this; as has been seen, the Ultras regarded Grey as in a similar position to themselves and so believed a non-party alliance feasible. But now there was this secret Whig conspiracy, for that is what it was.

Under the guise of their moderation they would gain sufficient support to defeat the Government, then they would work up support outside—in effect, by riots and burnings—to frighten the moderates. That this is no exaggerated view, I quote deliberately from the most biassed and question-begging book which could be found in favour of the Whigs,[2] " It was determined to combine

---

[1] S.A. Duchess to her brother, Grand Duke of Mecklenburg-Strelitz, 19th July 1830.
[2] Trevelyan's *Lord Grey of the Reform Bill*.

and throw the Government out; if nothing else turned up first, then let it be on Brougham's motion for Reform, which had been drawn up on ' moderate ' lines, to attract as many votes as possible in the House. It was therefore less thorough than the Government Reform Bill of the following year, which was drawn up on the opposite principle of winning such support in the country as to overawe ' moderate ' opinion in the House." On the day before Brougham's motion was to have been put, the Whigs voted against the Government upon a detail of the Civil List, while most of the Ultras, unaware of what was to be the result of this apparently routine debate, abstained. There was a majority against the Government and Wellington resigned.

Thus the Duke of Cumberland's ambition had been realised. Now he set about approaching Grey with a view to forming an all-party Government against the dangers of Reform and Jacobinism. Wellington, he said, deliberately let himself be beaten as he knew that he was bound to fall shortly. " Although I am certainly not a Whig," he wrote, " there is no doubt, I must admit, that Grey is a man of character, and that he has changed since he defended those old theories and doctrines and is an honest man who loves his country." [1] Wellington also had confidence in moderate, aristocratic Lord Grey and recommended the King to send for him as his successor. There is something pathetic in the picture of these two hostile leaders, united only in respecting and trusting their common deceiver. The Duke of Cumberland tried, then, to contact Grey, and he hoped that Princess Lieven, the latter's great friend, might arrange a meeting at her house. [2]

All this confusion was created deliberately by the Whigs. Not to appear in their true colours and thus reveal the dangers and unite the Tories, they began a campaign of severe suppression of riots and disorders. Noted Radical spokesmen were prosecuted, men transported and some executed. For a few months, while consolidating their power, they could afford to be unpopular as reactionary. The most important thing was to keep their enemies divided and complacent while they marshalled their ranks. Another move of the same game, with the same object of drawing wool across the eyes of their enemies who still believed Grey to be almost a Tory—as he wished them to believe—was the formation of an almost entirely aristocratic Cabinet. Again, historians—and Whig historians—unblushingly admit this. Says Trevelyan, " In

[1] S.A. Duke to Grand Duke, 16th July (?) 1830.
[2] On these attempts, see Princess Lieven's *Letters*.

that age, with that King, with those nobles, a less imposing and aristocratic personality than Grey with his ' patrician thoroughbred look ' that Byron ' doted on,' would have failed to create and hold together a Government capable, under the existing Constitution, of peacefully handing over the power of the aristocracy to the middle class. People complained then and complain still that Grey's Government was very aristocratic in its personnel. It certainly was, but it passed the Reform Bill ; and the question is whether it would have been permitted to do so if it had not been so largely made up of aristocrats ; for the measure was, in effect, one by which the aristocracy, under the combined influence of persuasion, cajolery and intimidation, laid down its monopoly of political power. It is almost impossible for people now living to realise the difficulties of the task Grey accomplished in 1830-32, the immensity of the chasm which he bridged, or his need of stressing the conservative elements of his Government in order to persuade the King and the aristocracy to surrender to the people." [1] However much one may admire the cunning and astuteness of these men, the perfidious deception and dishonesty of their methods should rouse feelings of the deepest disgust. Their opponents were of a different stamp.

Brougham, the Duke of Cumberland's great antagonist, wrote of him, " I respected the courage with which he faced the odious charges made upon his reputation, the effect of which courage had been clear to him ; I also held him to be a fair open enemy, and not one who pretended to more liberality than he possessed, but was content to appear what he really was—a rank, violent, ultra Tory of the strongest Orange breed, and whose principles and propensities were purely arbitrary." [2] If the Whigs had been as honest, they would never have been able to pass their cherished Bill.

Unfortunately, the Duke of Cumberland was now also cut off from the King, who, simple and trusting as he was, was left to deal with Grey alone. As Trevelyan delicately puts it for his republican readers, " it was then the custom of the Constitution " that the King had to agree to the measures which were to be introduced in his name. The Prime Minister deceived him, though Trevelyan makes the unconvincing excuse that " the King was deceived by his own simplicity." " Grey persuaded the King that the Bill was an ' aristocratical ' measure, designed to save the Constitution from more revolutionary changes. And so it was in

---

[1] *Trevelyan*, op. cit.   [2] His *Life and Times*.

Grey's mind. Its ' democratical ' implications only began to be
apparent to William after it had become public, when the joy of
the Radicals of whom he lived in terror, and the rage of the Tories
with whom he lived in intimacy, gradually made him realise what
he had done." But amidst all this deception, Trevelyan ends by
deceiving himself, for he gives a list of Tory prophecies of 1830
which did not come about—not, that is, in 1920. But most of
them were realised a few decades later.[1]

The King, the Nobility, the Tories, the Dukes of Cumberland
and Wellington, even many of the Whigs, all successfully misled,
there remained only one danger—that the truth might leak out
prematurely. To guard against this, the Whigs had recourse to an
unprecedented expedient. As Trevelyan explains, " To prevent a
premature outburst of Tory rage from frightening the King and
the moderates in the Cabinet before they were irretrievably committed, was one of the many grave reasons for secrecy during this
critical period, and it is to the credit of all concerned how well the
secret was kept to the very last day. Several of the ' Grey Ladies '
were made partners in the secret as amanuenses, to prevent the
employment of clerks. Durham's wife and eldest daughter had
helped to make copies of the report of the Committee of Four."[1]
The phrase " to the credit of all concerned " can only be intended
ironically.

So, of course, the Duke of Cumberland had no idea of what
was going on behind the scenes, though the atmosphere was
growing tenser and, he wrote from Brighton (where the Court
spent the end of 1830 and the commencement of 1831), " The fires
are frightful and continue. There was a terrible one near Worthing
last night. The threatening letters have been very odious, but we
are determined not to worry ourselves with unnecessary fears.
The stories afloat are very alarming, but Augusta and I keep up
the courage of our neighbours. . . . We must hope that strong
measures may be adopted to stop the mischief, for it is not
pleasant . . ."[2]—and, of course, he had full confidence that the
Government would adopt those measures.

The Duke of Buckingham now tried to negotiate a reunion of
the Tory party under the Dukes of Cumberland and Wellington.
The former would not hear of such an idea. He had determined,
he said, never to act with Wellington in politics again after his
apostasy, as he could not be trusted. He much preferred Grey's

---

[1] Trevelyan's *British History in the Nineteenth Century*, p. 237.
[2] To Lady Shelley, 22nd November 1830.

Government. "I myself," he said, "will never make a factious
opposition to the present Government, though not being able to
support them in all their measures, at the same time without pledg-
ing myself, but being always on the watch, and if I observe that
they contravene or bring forward measures to overthrow the
Constitution, I shall oppose them. As far as I can as yet judge,
they are doing *all* in their power to save us from that abyss in
which we were placed by the Duke of Wellington." This was
written on the 9th February 1831.[1]

On the 1st March Lord John Russell announced to the House
of Commons his Government's proposals. No one will deny that
they involved the destruction of all that had meant England,
though of course its consummation would never be seen by these
men ; but without going into such fundamental issues, it must be
emphasised that the battle of the Reform Bill was not one of classes.
It was the final act of the conquest of industrialism and the industrial
society, with all the changes in philosophy which that implies.
Hitherto, power had resided on the land, in the villages, the market
towns and ancient cathedral cities. Now it was to be transferred
to the teeming industrial centres with their shafts and smokestacks. Trevelyan agrees that this was no question of oppressors
against oppressed ; indeed, the most extreme Reformers were the
bullies of the children in the factories. It was a clash of ways of
life and philosophies. "The one feeling," he says,[2] "that the
starving operatives shared with their employers, whom they regarded
as their tyrants, was a passion for the Bill to destroy the aristocratic
rule which they both detested." And when the House realised
what the measure meant, no one took it seriously—Members sat
and shook their sides with laughter. But they had reckoned without the "support from outside," which was soon to manifest
itself. The war-cry spread like wildfire to the mobs all ready to
be mobilised and go into action at a signal.

The two Dukes, Cumberland and Wellington, saw that for the
last years they had been living in fantasy throughout the last few
years. There was now no further cause for their estrangement—
it was clear that Wellington was no Jacobin and also that his rival
had been right as to the pacifying effects of his policy. What was
more, their reconciliation was vital for the country and all that was
dear to them. This conclusion they both reached independently.
"Nothing can be more gratifying to me," wrote the Duke of
Wellington, "than to find myself acting with those from whom I

---

[1] G.A. To Duchess of Cumberland.   [2] *Lord Grey of the Reform Bill.*

have never ceased to regret the separation." He also wrote to the Duke of Buckingham on the 5th April of his desire for a reconciliation, and this note the latter showed to the Duke of Cumberland.[1]

After clearing up a few matters of difference, the Duke replied to him,[2] "However, now I am sure I am, under present circumstances, the last person to touch upon these past events. . . . It appears to me that, in times such as these, it is necessary for every well-wisher to his country, who is attached to the Monarchy and the Court, to meet and resist the Revolutionary Bill now pending in Parliament; which, if carried out, must, according to my humble opinion, annihilate all our institutions both in Church and State. . . ." So, at last, the old friendsip between the two illustrious Dukes was restored, and continued until the end of their days. Wellington became the Duke of Cumberland's hero, as he himself called him. Ernest Augustus's loyalty to his friends was second only to his loyalty to principle. For this, he would divide from his most intimate associates, but once he saw that he had been mistaken he was the first to renew all his old affections.

The reconciliation took place none too soon, for the revolution was gathering pace. The Duke of Cumberland's suggestion that the Government's boast of a large majority were a "*ruse de guerre*" brought forth Grey's anger and alarm, for the Bill was to be passed by sheer terror and any suggestion of bluff or compromise would have endangered everything. The reconciliation between the two Tory groups had caused him enough anxiety. "There is no species of misrepresentation to which they are ashamed to resort," he wrote. "Their last attempt to propagate a belief that we were willing to compromise the efficiency of the measure has been, I trust, completely defeated. . . . The Duke of Cumberland's conduct in circulating the scandalous libel is of a piece with all the rest." [3] This indignation ill became one who, with his colleagues, had for three months deliberately deceived everyone and everything.

On all occasions mobs were posted to frighten the conservatives and "overawe" the moderates. Going to the theatre the King's carriage was attacked and little Prince George received a stone in his lap. Of course a mob was always detailed to threaten

---

[1] Wellington to Lord Falmouth, 3rd April 1831 and to Duke of Buckingham, 5th April 1831.—*Despatches*.

[2] To Duke of Buckingham, 8th April 1831.

[3] To Lord Wellesley, 15th April 1831.—*Wellesley Papers*.

and insult the Duke of Cumberland, but its members might better have employed themselves against others for all the impression which they could make on him. At the Coronation, which took place only at the Duke of Cumberland's representations,[1] mobs cheered Grey and Brougham, then changed to insults and jeers as the Duke of Cumberland's carriage passed. This, of course, he expected, but he did not hide himself or hesitate to show himself in public on foot or on horseback. This personal blackmail and threat of violence plays a large but conveniently-forgotten part in the story of Democracy.

To these threats and Grey's cajolery, the poor King fell victim and humiliated himself publicly at his Minister's behest. " Grey knew exactly how to treat William IV," Trevelyan tells us,[2] " and took infinite pains about it. It was fortunate that it fell to him, out of all the Cabinet, to conduct the correspondence and interviews with their Royal Master."

After elections carried out under every form of duress, Parliament came together again and the Lords threw out the Bill on the 8th October. By law and constitution, the Whigs and Radicals had failed. Now force and bloodshed—revolution—were invoked. The Duke of Cumberland, after the rejection of his grant in 1815 and 1818, and the Tories after 1832, remained law-abiding citizens. Not so the Whigs and Democrats when *their* measures failed to become law by lawful means. On the 13th the two Dukes were hanged in effigy by a mob at the Tyburn. In Newcastle a colossal image of Death holding a tricoloured spear in one hand and the bleeding heads of the two Dukes and Lord Eldon in the other and trampling upon a coronet and a mitre, was paraded by riotous mobs. Everywhere gentry were attacked and their houses in town and country sacked. The Duke of Newcastle's castle at Nottingham was burnt by the mob. Everywhere was terror and anarchy reminiscent of the Jacquerie. In Bristol, as the Assizes were opened, battle was joined, the city was sacked and looted and a great part of it, including all the more important buildings, burnt down. Afterwards, the bodies were collected in heaps in the squares and the stench was unbearable. Nowhere in any of Europe's revolutions was there such widespread violence and destruction.

---

[1] Taylor to Grey, 2nd July 1831. The King had wished to dispense with a Coronation, but his brother pointed out its constitutional necessity.—*Correspondence of William IV and Grey.*

[2] Op. cit.

All this is conveniently forgotten to-day, when English historians and politicians tell continental peoples that English history
is one of peace, law and orderly development. The truth, which
should be widely known, is that spread over this decade there was
more violence in England than in any of the European capitals in
1848, and that the Reform Bill was passed by blackmail and bloodshed without any pretence of legality or morality. This was how
the Duke of Wellington saw it when he wrote, " But, it is said,
if this course be not adopted, we shall have insurrection and civil
war. What have we had throughout the year 1831 ? Is it tran-
quillity ? Is it the British Constitution ? Is it security to anyone
for his property, his rights, or even his life ? " [1]

The King prayed his brother not to come to London for the
session, but, of course, nothing held him back. Great mobs were
in the streets and surged round the Duke's horse, but he rode on
without taking any notice. One day the police begged him to dis-
mount and be escorted to St. James's. One person who tried to
pass through the mob as the Duke made his way on foot heard
one of its members say, " We must be ashamed of what we are
doing " and many remarks of admiration at the Duke's courage.
Poor Lord Londonderry was struck unconscious by a stone thrown
at him upon the same occasion.[2]   Another time a mob surrounded
the Duke as he left the House, shouting " Kill him ! " The Duke
turned and looked them steadily in the face " to let them see that
I treat them with contempt and am not *afraid*." At this, many
applauded him.[3]   Towards the end of November the Duke went
to stay for a few days with Lord Eldon at his seat at Encombe, in
Dorset. They were lucky, indeed, that a house was there, for
shortly before, a mob in the nearby town of Poole had planned to
burn it down. A farmer had learnt of the project and removed all
the boats along the bank of the intervening river, thereby checking
the rabble on its mission of destruction.[4]   Such were the conditions
of danger in which these dauntless men lived out their everyday
lives, with nowhere safe for them.   " It cannot be denied that
Lord Grey and his colleagues are real *traitors* ! " The Duke wrote
from the house which had so narrowly escaped destruction.[5]

Against all this, however, the Tories remained only an inco-
hesive group suddenly awakened from their internal feuds. The

[1] To Lord Strangford, 13th January 1832.—*De Fonblanque.*
[2] S.A. Duchess to Grand Duke, 20th October 1831.
[3] G.A. To Duchess, dateless.   [4] *Twiss*, II, p. 159.
[5] G.A. To Duchess, 25th November 1831.

Duke of Cumberland saw the need to form them into a strong
party with leadership to fight the battle with as much organisation
and cunning as their opponents. It was necessary, he told Wellington, that for the next session they should come to an understanding
with one another as to what line they were to adopt. A large
meeting would only lead to much speech-making and discussion
but no decisions or action. He therefore suggested the formation
of a committee of seven to nine of the most capable and trusted
Peers, including Wellington, to guide their course, and all would
bind themselves to follow its decisions—he would be the first to
do so.[1] Throughout the first months of 1832, he was always at
his post, despite mobs, despite recurring illness—once he had to be
carried from the Lords in a delirious fever.[2] He was frequently in
the House all night and only Wednesdays and Saturdays did he
have any relaxation, air and movement in the country at Kew.

In May the whole battle reached its climax. Men were arming
and drilling, gun- and swordsmiths were doing a roaring trade and
the so-called Political Unions, the chief of which was that of
Birmingham, were preparing to seize power if it were not made
over to them. No longer was the violence merely sporadic, or
simply the spontaneous expressions of rage ; it was organised and
controlled and this gave to the country an ominous appearance of
calm after the last year. The rot was now too far gone. The Tories
and Peers could only hope to save the constitutional principle by
enacting a measure of Reform themselves, rather than that the
precedent be set that a decision of Parliament could be flouted by
force. No doubt this was mere hair-splitting. As Dr. Trevelyan
puts it,[3] " 'The ' Days of May ' were brought about by an attempt,
not indeed to destroy the Bill or even pass seriously to cut down
its provisions, but to reassert the power and prestige of the House
of Lords by taking the conduct of the Bill out of the hands of the
Ministers and handing it over to the leaders of the Opposition."
But now, things had travelled so far that not merely the Bill was
wanted, not merely Parliamentary Reform, but the affirmation of
the principle employed in carrying it. Freedom and Democracy
without force, but by the operation of the law and Constitution,
would have drained the cup of its flavour ; Dr. Trevelyan and his
Liberals wanted their liberties to be consecrated in this way. " The
people did not become sovereign in Germany," he writes proudly,[3]

[1] To Wellington, 26th April 1832.—*Despatches.*
[2] S.A. Duchess to Grand Duke, 23rd February 1832.
[3] Op. cit.

" when Bismarck granted limited popular rights, because those rights had not been won by the action of the nation itself, as the First Reform Bill had been won."

Grey resigned and Wellington was asked by the King to form a Government.

The revolutionaries now had to seize power. English historians have a remarkable insularity and lack of logic in never applying the yardstick by which they measure others to themselves. The organising cells of this revolution, which corresponded to the Jacobin Clubs of the 1790's or the " Workers' Soviets " of 1918, became something quite different in their eyes, the " outlet of the English genius for local self-government, voluntary combination and self-help . . . improvised by the British people, they constituted the strongest proof of its fitness to work self-governing institutions of a more official character." [1] First, they would create a run on the banks—one cannot refrain from asking what would be the cry had the Tories sought to create a financial crash to bring down a Government—and if, in spite of the country's financial ruin, Wellington still became Prime Minister, then the barricades were to be manned, banks closed, mobs of idlers turned on to the streets through the cessation of business and the unemployment which was to be brought about—it is all described in Trevelyan's book.[2] When the news came that the Duke was already Prime Minister, there followed " a general suspension of work and business in the big towns. . . . Pikes were hammered in Sheffield without concealment. Employers and workmen prepared to act together even in Manchester. . . ." And yet, after writing this, the author adds after an interval of three pages, " The change was so profound that in most countries it would only have been effected by civil war. Therein lies the measure of Lord Grey's achievement." That is because in most other countries, burning, killing and arming and threatening against the law and constitution would be called civil war, but in the terminology of English Liberal historians it is not, so long as it takes place on this side of the Channel.

The King was frightened. At last he decided to accede to Grey's demands and make a mass creation of Peers for him. So all was over. The Tory Peers decided to attend no more debates. Wellington called a meeting of them, to which he specially invited the Duke of Cumberland, and explained that he had given up his commission.

[1] Trevelyan's *British History in the Nineteenth Century*, p. 238.
[2] *Lord Grey of the Reform Bill*.

In this sad struggle the Duke of Cumberland had been able to do little for his cause, quarantined as he was from the King [1] and without any organised party or platform. It was tragic that he and Wellington had wasted all their energy and talents upon the irrelevant issue of Catholic Emancipation, but, at least, the Duke of Cumberland was a man who did not make the same mistake twice. All his efforts from now on were directed towards establishing a determined, united and organised Conservative party to stop the destruction which was threatening all. His future status was merely that of one of the leading Peers ; all influence with the King and Court, which themselves no longer had anything to say in the affairs of State, was useless. This was proved by the Duke's remonstrance with his brother as to the danger that the so-called Political Unions might usurp the government of the country. The King fully agreed with him and demanded that Grey should take action, but if the King thought that his representations would have any effect upon his Minister, he was mistaken. Grey, respectful and civil as ever, was influenced not in the slightest and refused to do anything about the matter. The King protested, but could do no more.[2] Now he must have looked upon his brother in a new light and regretted those deliberate little provocations which he had offered to him in the not-so-far-off days of inexperience, when his brother was so unpopular and he felt secure in the devotion of his Ministers and the love of his people.

.   .   .   .

But if all was lost in England, at least the Duke of Cumberland now had the prospect of putting his principles into practice elsewhere, for now he was recognised as the Heir to the Kingdom of Hanover.[3] In a few years, at the most, he would be called to the Throne. But that was all the more reason that the Radicals in Hanover should seek to deprive the Crown of its powers before then, while the weak and timid Duke of Cambridge still ruled there and his similarly inoffensive brother in England.

So, as the Duke of Cumberland was so desperately striving to hold the forces of destruction in England, the storm had broken

[1] Grey had forbidden the King to correspond with his brother.—Arbuthnot to Peel, 9th March 1831 (Parker's *Peel*).
[2] See *Correspondence of William IV and Grey*, 1830-32.
[3] This had become virtually certain after the beginning of 1832. Queen Adelaide was then in the hopes of providing an heir, but had no better fortune than on similar occasions previously. See, in particular, S.A., Duchess to Grand Duke, 12th February 1832.

out in Hanover, which he had regarded as the true, loyal, peaceful and secure homeland of his House. Under the weak government which it was experiencing, everything was going to ruin. All over the country the class of pettifogging lawyers was seeking to stir up trouble and win thereby power for itself, for the profession of law had quite a different prestige and standing there and elsewhere on the Continent from in England, and its members were recruited from a different class of person. Everyone held them in contempt; the examination required to enter their ranks was of such a low standard that no one had been known to fail it, and those rejected as candidates for official positions, or who had failed the necessary examination, all became advocates and sought to revenge themselves upon society by sowing seeds of dissatisfaction and discontent. They were not content with using merely the pen, but openly led disorders.

It so happened that a man in Göttingen had dared to write a book defending Legitimacy, and such was the tyranny of these gallant fighters for Democracy, as we are usually accustomed to hear them described, that a mob under the leadership of two of these lawyers forthwith attacked his house, then, enjoying the experience of disorder and plunder, seized the Town Hall, armed itself and soon had the city completely in its hands. Now it was time for the Government to intervene and General von dem Bussche was ready with troops to restore order.

But the Duke of Cambridge was so weak of resolution that he hesitated to take any step, though urged to do so by Freiherr von Schele, one of the most accomplished men of affairs in the Kingdom. To his entreaties were added those of General von Alten, the veteran of Waterloo, and eventually the Duke gave the order, the troops marched in and, of course, there was no resistance. Everyone in the city breathed a sigh of relief at the restoration of order.

But the Duke of Cambridge was badly shaken.[1] As Governor-General, he had very little to say in the government of Hanover; the Ministers and Münster had a free hand and he occupied himself with the social life of the city and the pleasures of the table. Through his affability and good humour he became beloved by the citizens, and he was always to be found in their houses. With politics he had little concern.

[1] G.A. Duchess of Gloucester to Duke of Cumberland, with reference to his suggestion that the Duke of Cambridge should be appointed Commander-in-Chief in 1828 : "When it comes to *act* and take *upon himself*, I feel sure he has no nerve for it." See also the Duke of Cumberland's own comments. W.A.* To Sir William Knighton, 10th November 1828.

Now, he made a visit to the scene of the late disorders, then a further tour to the Harz. The stage was carefully set for him. Everywhere, frightful tales were told to him, petitions and disguised threats presented, all couched in terms of utmost loyalty and devotion which moved the guileless Duke ; all the blame for the troubles of the country was put on to the shoulders of Count Münster. The alarmed Duke, believing the Kingdom lost if he did not yield, decided to report to the King stressing the urgency of giving way to the agitators, of dismissing Münster and throwing himself to the mercy of the Chambers. He therefore sent recommendations to the King through Colonel Prott and two others, which resulted in Münster's immediate dismissal and his own installation as Viceroy with full powers. His pliancy which had rendered him so acceptable to Count Münster made him as convenient to the latter's opponents who were now on the road to power.

On the 10th February 1831 Colonel Prott came to the Duke of Cumberland with a letter from his younger brother in which he asked him to consider thoroughly the proposals for a change in the Constitution which the King would communicate to him. However, the Duke heard no more and Prott returned to Hanover without seeing him again, but he already knew what was afoot. The Duchess dreamed that night of a plan to usurp his Throne and wrote of her forebodings in her diary, " The real plan goes much deeper, and is, to make the Duke of Cambridge so popular and to cultivate such revolutionary feelings in the land that, when the King dies, the people will *proclaim the Duke of Cambridge King*, to exclude the Duke of Cumberland and his son Prince George." [1]

Of course the person most intimately concerned with the future of the Hanoverian Crown, the Duke of Cumberland, was not consulted, for these were measures designed expressly for his benefit. The principal of them was the transfer of the Crown Domains and their revenues to the control of the Chambers. We know from English history, as the Duke of Cumberland also knew from his own personal experience, the significance of such a step. Hitherto the Crown had been independent, enjoying its own revenues ; now it was to be dependent upon a civil list, though, to save the King's feelings, it was not so called and somewhat disguised. The Chambers would have the upper hand in the country and the King, in time, become a mere figurehead. There was the moral aspect—a King can no more be dispossessed of his

[1] G.A. Memorandum of Duchess upon the subject.

private property than any other citizen. One further flaw, how-ever, rendered the whole legally invalid. The King personally was not absolute, but suffered a check. He could dispose of or alienate family property or rights only with the consent of every Agnate, or male member of the family, since he was also dealing with his family's and his successors' interests.[1]

It has not been sufficiently observed that, like all " Constitu-tions," this had only been brought about by force or the threat of force, and it is a universal juristic principle that contracts made under duress have no moral or legal validity whatever. No court of law would for one moment accept such promises as those extorted by murderers made in revolutions as legally binding.

On the 16th August discussions began upon the new Con-stitution between the Duke of Cambridge, the Ministers and Dahlmann.[2] On the 5th October, Falcke [3] left for London and laid it before the King, who, his morale already broken by events at home, was in no state to resist and reluctantly gave his consent. He then ordered the proposals to be shown to his brother, the Duke of Cumberland, though he did not ask any opinion from him. In October 1831 Falcke and the Hanoverian Minister in London, von Ompteda, came to him in the midst of all the work and worry with which he was beset during the political crisis in England. London was being endangered by the mobs, Bristol actually burning, and the affairs of Hanover must have seemed very small then. Von Ompteda quickly read through the pro-posals " at full gallop " and in the elaborate German legal phrase-ology in which the Duke was not yet practised ; then, having discharged their duty, the two visitors withdrew. Even so, the

---

[1] The Kingdom of Hanover had come about through the devolution of all the possessions of the House of Brunswick-Lüneburg upon the one line. This was regu-lated by family treaties of 1636, 1646 and 1640, and the will of the Elector Ernest Augustus, upon whom all the lands and rights devolved, of the 23rd October 1688. The latter laid down that they were to be inherited as belonging for perpetuity to the whole House and expressly forbade any alienation by any individual member of that House, with or without the consent of any Estates or Chambers. Such would be " void, invalid and without power, would have no legal effect and not bind the successor either in the direct or collateral line in the slightest." The Duke had special researches into this testament made in the Royal Archives at Hanover and this convinced him of the invalidity of the present proposals.—H.A. Hann. 9. Dom. 288a. It is on a similar principle that in England the surrender of the Crown Lands by one Sovereign does not bind his successor and the legislation embodying it is re-enacted at the commencement of each reign.

[2] 1785–1860. Professor at Kiel University 1818–29, then at Göttingen, drafted the proposed new constitution as head of the doctrinaire liberals.

[3] 1783–1850. Privy Cabinet Counsellor, ennobled by William IV. He pointed out to the Government the necessity of the Duke of Cumberland's signature, but was ignored.

Duke, with his parliamentary experience, had immediately detected some flaws which he mentioned to the King in his letter of thanks for having had the proposals read to him. For example, he said, the payment of Members for the time that they were sitting would lead to their dragging out debates for more money, and publicity would mean that they spoke not to the Chamber but to the public. The King thanked the Duke of Cumberland for his observations, saying that he had no doubt that these points would be amicably settled. Copies of the correspondence were sent by Sir H. Taylor to the Duke of Cambridge and there the matter rested, and the Duke of Cumberland turned himself to the urgencies of the situation in England.[1]

[1] H.A. Hann. Des. 92 I, iv. nr. 36 : Duke of Cumberland to Duke of Cambridge, 30th October 1831 ; Sir Herbert Taylor to same, 7th November 1831 ; Duke of Cumberland to King, 31st October 1831 ; King to Duke of Cumberland, 3rd November 1831. Hann. 9 Secreta Domus IV, 48 : Duke of Cumberland to von Falcke, 18th December 1835.

CHAPTER XVI

1832–34

THE Duke of Cumberland had not recovered from the effects of the political disasters of the last few years when the greatest personal tragedy of his life came upon him. His great pride was his son. Everyone who came into contact with the young Prince had only praise for him. Handsome, healthy and talented, he seemed assured of a fine future. Though he had been brought up in Berlin, his education, conducted by Mr. Jelf, had been English, and when he came to join his father in England in 1829, and was thus eligible for a parliamentary grant towards it, his father had carefully selected a school for him where he could be assured that he would receive a fitting training. His choice fell, naturally enough, upon the Eldon School at Vauxhall,[1] and there the young Prince soon distinguished himself. The possibility that he might succeed to the Throne of Great Britain was always before the eyes of his parents, for only the young Princess Victoria stood between, and the Duchess also treasured the hope that the two cousins might fall in love and marry, thus preserving the union of the Crowns. Prince George had, therefore, to be foreign neither in England nor Germany, and it was intended that he should, when old enough, be sent to study at Göttingen as his father had been.[2]

But, as the Duchess wrote, " Since *something* always disturbs human perfection, so it is here too," by which she meant the loss of Prince George's right eye as the result of an inflammation during his illness several years before.[3] The doctors were always afraid that this would eventually affect the other, and because of this weakness he was always warned to be especially careful of it. His youthful buoyancy could no longer be allowed full freedom.

---

[1] Founded by Mr. Charles Francis "to perpetuate the memory of John, Earl of Eldon, Lord High Chancellor of Great Britain, and to commemorate his able, zealous and constant defence of the Protestant Reformed Religion against every innovation." It provided education for a hundred and fifty boys who were examined annually on Lord Eldon's birthday, when there were many distinguished visitors and a banquet.

[2] S.A. Duchess to Grand Duke of Mecklenburg-Strelitz, 11th September 1830.

[3] *Ibid.* Duchess to Grand Duke, 12th November 1831.

On the 11th September 1832 the thirteen-year-old Prince was playing in the garden at Kew when he saw some poor people on the Green outside. He hurried out with his purse and gave them some money, then he ran back, feeling very happy at having helped the needy, and in his high spirits he swung the purse merrily in a circle about him. But in so doing he struck his left eye with the full force of one of the ivory acorns and the silver ornaments to it. Holding his eye, he ran in to Mrs. Ford, his nurse, and she washed it with lavender-water. At that moment his mother and Sir Charles Wetherell came back from a walk and he told her what had happened. Now, he said, his eye was much better and he would go riding. Though she did not consider the hurt grave, the Duchess thought that ill-advised and suggested that he should drive with her and Wetherell to meet his father, who was returning from the Garrison Dinner held at Windsor the previous day. He sat still in the carriage and did not seem to see properly. It became clear to his mother that he was *quite blind*.[1]

For two days the Prince saw nothing and his parents were in despair. The first specialist summoned, Mr. Alexander, doubted that he would ever regain his sight. But for a time his condition began to improve, then relapses followed, alternating with encouraging symptoms, so that Waller believed in the possibility of his recovery if for two years he lived only for his health and gave up riding, dancing and anything which might bring blood to the eye. He should go to live quietly by the sea, he recommended, and Hastings was chosen as it was a quiet and lonely fishing-town, warm and sheltered from the north and east winds.[2]

In the midst of all this distress the Duke's character was assailed by the last of the great slander campaigns of his life.[3] He had, indeed, had enough, and now he considered prosecuting the culprits, the scurrilous *Times*. Only when the campaign had died down could he leave the town with honour. He himself was fond of company and society so he did not relish of the idea of leaving Kew and London for deliberate seclusion. To his wife, on the other hand, the removal was welcome, for she had no very favourable impression of England. " The district and the countryside will please you," she wrote to a friend who had expressed a hope of visiting her,[4] " but not the people. I admit, I know as good as nothing of the country, as the Duke is not to be moved and only

---

[1] M.A. Duchess's diary ; S.A. Duchess to Grand Duke, 19th September 1832.
[2] S.A. Duchess to Grand Duke, 21st October 1832.   [3] See appendix.
[4] S.A. Duchess to Countess von Voss (née von Berg), 28th November 1832.

believes that he lives when he drives or rides from London to Kew and then back again to London. The people, however, I know all the better, and alas! not their most advantageous side, with few exceptions. The *party-spirit* so demoralises them that it tears the most sacred bonds. I know of brothers and sisters who did not speak together during the time of the Reform Bill and let sad events in the families of brothers or sisters pass by without any feeling or sympathy simply because the one was *for* and the other *against* the Bill. When *such things* can take place inside *families*, you can imagine the *spirit of persecution* towards other persons, of which so much is directed against the Duke. I assure you that many people have turned their backs upon *me* merely because I am his wife." So appeared Liberal England to one from abroad in the nineteenth century, a very sobering account.

Hastings consisted of two parallel streets of fishermen's houses and a recently-built Marine Parade extending westwards under the shelter of the cliffs. At the extremity of the Parade was an elegant terrace, and that was the only foothold of fashion in the town. To avoid all excitement for his son, the Duke declined an official reception by the Mayor, but as they arrived people cheered them. The coming of a Prince of the Blood to live in this remote little town was a cause of great excitement, and when he rode along the coast to Winchelsea one day he was recognised and enthusiastically received.[1] He had the satisfaction of seeing his son's health improve daily and wrote of it very confidently to Wellington.[2]

Wellington had invited him to stay at Strathfield Saye, his seat in Hampshire, before Christmas and he accepted eagerly. The two Dukes had worries enough. It was now proposed to dissolve Parliament and elect a new one, and it was clear that if elections took place with the present Ministers in power, they would be so influenced that a change of Government could follow only with a further dissolution.[3] The country was still largely in the hands of the so-called Political Unions, and the Duke of Cumberland, knowing that the King was as much averse to them as he was himself, did not cease to urge him to insist upon some action against them in accordance with existing statutes.[4] At the same time he had not the same access to the Court as during the late reign; he could only see his brother if he demanded an audience

[1] S.A. Duchess to Countess von Voss, 28th November 1832.
[2] Duke to Duke of Wellington, 21st November 1832.—*Despatches.*
[3] Encombe Archives. Duke to Lord Eldon, 12th September 1832.
[4] *Correspondence of William IV and Lord Grey*, I, p. 262.

and what he wanted was an informal personal discussion. He
therefore charged Taylor to report to him verbatim his and Lord
Eldon's views upon a dissolution.[1] But, of course, the King was
no longer master of the situation and the dissolution followed.

Its effects were felt in the quiet coastal town where the Duke
was living. A large Radical meeting was held, and suspended
across the street between two houses was a red flag with *Elphinstone
the Friend of the People* inscribed in large black letters. " But," the
Duchess wrote after passing under it,[2] " as a proof of how interested
these sorts of people are, the butcher, the baker and several other
of our tradesmen have declared that to honour the Duke they will
vote for the Tory candidate, although hitherto the Whig candidate
has always received their votes."

The result of the elections was, as the Duke of Cumberland
had foreseen, disastrous.[3] Even the Government was frightened
by the forces which it had conjured up. " To describe to you *all*
I feel," wrote the Duke to Lord Eldon,[4] " *all* I think after the
result of last week's elections is hardly possible ; to conceive such
men as Wetherell, Sugden, Follett, Croker, all able men and excellent
debaters, out of Parliament speaks more for the downfall and ruin
of this once blessed country than all the letters and folios that
could be written on the subject. . . . I am dreadfully in the
dismals." The growth in the strength of the Radicals was " *such*
as must make every thinking mind shudder from the contemplation
of the dangers that await us when St. Stephen's is opened." [5] As
Princess Lieven wrote, Grey " would long for his enemies when
he found himself face to face with his new friends." Lord Grey
himself had, indeed, already become an anachronism.[6]

The Duke of Cumberland lost no time in reacting to the blow.
On the 30th December he wrote to Wellington a long and detailed
letter pointing out what in his opinion were the blunders made by
them in the last session and urging upon him the necessity for a
meeting of the leaders of the party to work out a plan of campaign
for the future to prevent a repetition of the same mistakes.[7]

On the 3rd January 1833 the Duke had to leave his wife and son
and return to London as he could no longer endure the toothache

[1] Eldon Archives, 12th September 1832.
[2] S.A. Duchess to Countess von Voss, 28th November 1832.
[3] Parliament was dissolved on the 3rd December 1832 and assembled again on the
29th January 1833.
[4] Encombe Archives. To Lord Eldon, 16th December 1832.
[5] Encombe Archives. To Lord Eldon, 19th December 1832.
[6] *Trevelyan.*
[7] Encombe Archives. To Lord Eldon, 1st January 1833.

from which he had for some time been suffering. He visited the dentist to undergo " a cruel operation " and passed several days of unrelieved physical torment. But he did not slacken in his work and he took the opportunity of his presence in town to see his friends and discuss politics. Lord Sidmouth he found angry at their leader's apparent apathy and he himself was most unpleasantly surprised by the answer which he received from Wellington to his letter. " As to smaller meetings," he wrote, " I know not of what use they are, for they lead to no decisive measures." [1]

" In a word," wrote the Duke of Cumberland,[2] " I see that he is *beaten*, and that his great soul has lost for the moment its energy and resource." The Duke of Cumberland realised that it now depended upon himself. " Now, though God knows," he wrote,[3] " no one sees things more thoroughly than I do in the way they ought to be looked at and as they deserve, and that I am as fully convinced as anyone can be that the revolution has not *only begun*, but even made *greater progress than* I had *expected or suspected*, still, I say, instead of being cowed or appearing to give up everything as lost and irreparable, we ought to be the firmer united and stand boldly and appear undaunted, do the best we can, not to sit with our hands crossed before us. . . . Measures for proceeding ought without loss of time to be *adopted*, and this can only be done with any use and for any good that possibly can result from it, by our now meeting without loss of time, I mean, the leaders and great guns, to talk over matters and come to a closer union which can only be effected by the most perfect *harmony* and *cordial co-operation* forming but *one Conservative Party*. Let me tell you, our numbers though actually lessened still are respectable and may act, if harmony, unanimity and good fellowship are the rules we go by. In this sense I address myself to all those I am connected with. . . ."

There was no cohesive Conservative Party with a common plan and leadership. Events of the past had left their mark in personal hostilities born of recrimination, and everyone was particularly angry with Peel for his equivocal conduct during the last session, when he had not supported Wellington in his Ministerial attempts. His cold nature had always repelled his colleagues. Since the break-up of their Ministry he had been on hostile terms with Wellington, and before the Whigs published their Reform Bill he had not been far from separating himself from the party.

[1] G.A. Duke to Duchess, 3rd, 4th, 6th and 7th January 1833.
[2] *Ibid*. To Duchess, 6th January 1833.
[3] Encombe Archives. To Lord Eldon, 1st January 1833.

The Duke of Cumberland saw now that this loose group of individuals would never achieve unity of itself. Its former leaders were paralysed, the Duke of Wellington was discouraged and it was he himself who would have to forge it into a party. First, he said, they had to ask themselves, " Who are we ? How many are we ? " ; they had to forget all past differences, unite and remain united.[1] These were the lessons which he had been learning since the tragedies of 1828 and 1829.

The Duke of Wellington's house-party had been postponed owing to the elections, and now he sent invitations for the middle of January 1833. This fitted into the Duke of Cumberland's plans admirably. There was a large gathering, the Duke had many discussions with his host and they played whist until after midnight. He was delighted to find, after all, that he was interested and determined and he desired only to induce him to come to London before the opening of Parliament on the 5th February so that together they could concert their party beforehand. As a device to this end, he invited him to come shooting at Kew on the last day before the close season, 1st February, and the invitation was readily accepted. He considered that he had gained an important point, for Wellington had not intended to come to town until the day before the session opened. After lunch on the 25th, the Duke returned to London, stopping at Kew on the way to see that the house and the horses were in order for the party. He learned that Wellington had now communicated with many Peers asking them to come up for the session and was giving a dinner at Apsley House on the 2nd, so he felt that his representations to him had been of avail.[2]

The Duke of Cumberland now decided to carry his plans a step further by bringing in the leader of the third faction of the Tories, Peel, between whom and Wellington there were such cold relations. He therefore invited him to come to his shooting-party at Kew, too, besides Wetherell, Rosslyn, Salisbury, Chandos, Burghersh and Holmes (the party's whip). Peel was flattered by the invitation and accepted.

At one o'clock on the 1st February the Duke of Wellington and his sons, the Marquess of Douro and Lord Charles Wellesley, arrived, and after them Chandos, Holmes and Peel. The party then went out with their guns. Wellington was given the best places ; Peel and Chandos showed themselves to be poor shots. Wellington was in high spirits and his host was pleased to see that

[1] G.A. To Duchess, 6th January 1833.
[2] Ibid. To Duchess, 19th, 22nd, 24th and 31st January 1833.

E.A.—8

he and Peel spoke much together. Afterwards Wellington told him that he was well satisfied after having a long conversation with Peel. Dinner was at seven. Rosslyn and Wetherell arrived beforehand and the Duke had also invited the officers of the guard. All ate and drank well and went up to the drawing-room for tea and coffee at ten o'clock in high spirits. There the conversation continued. They agreed to remain firm to their principles and cede nothing. The Duke told them that he was giving a dinner at the Carlton Club. " Then I will make a point of dining there," said Wellington. " Thus," the Duke of Cumberland wrote to his wife at Hastings, " you see that my plan has succeeded perfectly." At eleven, the party broke up and the company went to bed, except the Duke and Wellington and his sons, who played billiards until midnight.[1]

So the next day saw a gathering of the leaders at the Carlton— Wellington, Peel, Chandos, Aberdeen, Rosslyn, Strangford, Lynd- hurst and all the others who were recently drifting and divided.[2] The Duke of Cumberland had cause to be satisfied with himself. " The question is neither more nor less than this," he told Lord Eldon that day,[3] " we must either act as one body, or we fall to the ground and everything is lost, and become the laughing-stock and disgust of the country. If we are prudent and act as I have now explained to you, believe me, the time will come, and that perhaps sooner than any of us are aware, of throwing them all out. . . ." He had some minor points of disagreement with the Duke of Wellington, " but these I will willingly give up, being fully convinced in my mind that the unanimity and the direct com- munications between his partisans, the Peelites and mine are neces- sary to save us, and on this I am decided." The Duke of Bucking- ham had meanwhile suggested that as Wellington had " given up the game," the Duke of Cumberland should put himself at the head of the Ultra-Tories. " To this I reply, the *Duke of Wellington and I* are *one* and the same, and I never will nor can countenance any schism among us. You and I have so far succeeded to have got not only the Duke of Wellington to come up to town and put himself directly in communication with all the Tory Peers, but I have been the humble instrument of bringing Peel to meet him at my house and they have communicated, nay, moreover, I have got the Duke of Wellington to come and meet a large party of Conservatives at dinner yesterday at our Club, and I feel convinced

---

[1] G.A. To Duchess, 1st February 1833.
[2] *Ibid.* To Duchess, 2nd February 1833.
[3] *Ibid.* To Duchess, 3rd February 1833.

that if such a dinner were regularly fixed for *one* day in the week for the Members of the two Houses, it would do invaluable good." [1]

So, when the session of Parliament opened, there was a regular forum and meeting-place for the leaders of the party, at which the Duke of Cumberland presided. At first, the dinners were held in the library of the Club, which would only allow twenty-four covers to be laid, so the Duke proposed to the committee that the so-called coffee-room, which could seat fifty, should be set aside for this purpose one day in the week. At Peel's suggestion, suppers were also inaugurated so that Members could come after the sittings in the House. "I am sure that nothing will serve to consolidate the party more than these very dinners," the Duke wrote, "and we are determined to break through the crust of little *underlings* who are trying to tyrannise over the Club, but which must give way the moment they see that the leaders of the party are determined to have matters carried in *their way*." [2]

But when Parliament opened, with a Whig majority faced by the three groups of Tories, Radicals and Irish Members, the Tories themselves were still not sure of what course to adopt and Peel was still suspect. The old school, to whom he had never been congenial, did not trust him, and it was the Duke of Cumberland who, as its leader, kept its members firm in his support. He did not consult them and the Duke frequently had to soothe their ruffled tempers. One day he heard that there was uproar at the Club and he hurried there to find that accusations were being made that Peel wished to break up the party. "No," said the Duke, "I cannot for the life of me see this. We all know *he* is a *shy man* and *this* must explain to us how difficult it is for others of that nervous disposition to come forward and hold *meetings* of this sort. As to myself, you might think me *impudent*, not pretending to have Peel's talents, but I should never hesitate if I thought it right to call a meeting and state boldly and manfully my views and opinions, naturally not pretending to be infallible, and, therefore, if anyone differed from me and could convince me by argument that I was in error, I should acknowledge myself to be in error, but if I did not think myself wrong I should equally fairly and honourably maintain my opinion. If the *party thinks*, which *I* for one do not, nor *ever could conceive* for one moment, that *Peel* would act unfairly, they ought to call upon him and explain themselves to *him*." [3]

[1] G.A. To Duchess, 3rd February 1833.
[2] *Ibid.* To Duchess, 11th and 25th February 1833.
[3] *Ibid.* To Duchess, 2nd May 1833.

There were two courses open to the Tories. They could support the Government against the Radicals or they could remain neutral. Peel counselled the former. He would lend his support whenever possible, he said, though he realised the paradox of his actions, in writing, " What are we doing ? We are making the Reform Bill work. We are falsifying our own predictions . . . we are protecting the authors of the evil from the work of their own hands." The Duke of Cumberland, on the other hand, was firmly opposed to such a course. Grey, he said, was playing the Conservatives and the Radicals off against each other and enlisting the support of the one against the other as the nature of his legislation required. The Conservatives should not fall into this trap. They should oppose all Radical measures, but when Grey brought forward such Bills as to incur the displeasure of the Radicals, they should let them fight them out among themselves.[1] He had learnt from his own bitter experience what dissension in a party meant. " The more I reflect upon the conduct that we Conservatives should follow," he wrote,[1] " the more I am convinced that we can only act as a corps of observation." He warned against all precipitate action, and when, in March, the Duke of Buckingham expressed his anxiety to turn out the Government, he pointed out, " No one can be more anxious than myself to get rid of these vagabonds, but are we ripe enough to do that ? Can we form an administration to *act* and do the business of the country ? "[2] He was highly satisfied to learn from Princess Lieven that Grey had told her, " There are some of the moderate Tories who I believe would be inclined *not* to trouble and harrass us as some did last year, but then there are *such* violent wrong-headed ones among them that prevent the others from taking this line." [3]

The Duke thus realised that his presence was necessary to prevent a split between Peel and the old Tories. But nothing was more painful to him than to have to remain while the Duchess was going through torments of anxiety at Hastings. The young Prince had repeated relapses and underwent excruciating physical pain, but he had now resigned himself and asked to begin lessons again. It was clear to the Duke from the letters, in which the Duchess reproved him for staying in London, that she was nearing a nervous breakdown. He went to Hastings as often as he could. " God knows I have had worry and vexation enough this last stay here,"

    G.A.   To Duchess, 3rd February 1833.
   [2] *Ibid.*   To Duchess, 11th March 1833.
   [3] *Ibid.*   To Duchess, 6th January 1833.

he wrote from London at the beginnning of April,[1] " for at one
moment I really thought *all* was going to break up, but now I hope
I have got everything in its proper train again." At last the time
came when his wife and son were able to join him again, and on
the 11th May he rode out to meet them late in the afternoon on the
road between Camberwell and Bromley. He was able to occupy
himself with the political struggle with an easier mind now.

It was again the question of Ireland, which baffled so many
Governments and has left a chapter of unjustifiable conduct in the
biographies of so many great men. To conciliate their recent
allies and to render more palatable the strong measures necessitated
by the lawlessness and anarchy prevailing there, the Government
had decided to introduce measures affecting the Established Church
in Ireland. This institution was a part of the Anglican Church in
a country where ninety per cent of the population were Catholic.
It is not to be wondered that this was a grievance, and the Government now proposed, among other things, to reduce the number
of Bishops (there were twenty-two) by ten and apply the revenue
thus made available to education. Even some of its own members
were shocked at this, so it can be imagined how the High Churchmen and the Duke of Cumberland felt about it. To him, it was a
direct attack upon religion and property—*spoliation* he called it.
It would be a precedent for similar agitation in England and would
lead to the destruction of the Church of Ireland and the Union.
The logic of his argument was clear enough, but he does not seem
to have realised that he might be defending an institution which
was intrinsically unjust. Indeed, this was one of the few cases
where he did not apply his maxim of study at first hand before
forming judgment.[2] He treated of the Church of Ireland's status

[1] G.A. To Duchess, 30th March 1833.
[2] There is no record of the Duke's having visited Ireland and he had little concern
with the non-religious affairs of Trinity College, Dublin. One case where he did was
when he told the Bishop of Armagh that the introduction of wives and families inside
the college walls might lead to mischief. " Why, My Lord," he said, " suppose the
wife of one of these Fellows is a handsome sprightly dashing Irish woman or has
daughters, handsome and flashy, are you not aware that the young men may be led to
intrigue with them ? . . . Do you mean to tell me that when a boy at Eton, for Your
Grace is of the same standing as to years as myself, do you not remember a Mrs.
Langford, the wife of the Second Master there, well known for her gallantry ? "
" I must own she was a handsome woman, and there were others," agreed the Bishop.
" Well, then, if this took place with the older boys, is it not likely that the young men
at Trinity and *all* Irish men are more inflammable, may make it a comical scene ? "
" But," objected the Bishop, " now the *Provost* may marry." " Yes, and so also the
Heads of Houses, but then they are generally old men and their wives are sober, but
this proposal is for the Junior Fellows, all young men from twenty-four to thirty-six
years old, who are not likely to take themselves ugly and old wives, but handsome ones."

as if it were comparable to that of the Anglican Church in England.[1] Perhaps this was because it was for him a religious question and a matter of conscience. The duty of preserving the Established Church was imposed upon him and his family by their dynastic obligations. It was 1801 and 1829 over again.

The proposed measures, he said,[2] were " in open *defiance* of the King's *oath* taken at the Coronation to maintain the rights and revenues of the Protestant Church, and as by the Act of Union the Irish Protestant Church is declared to be *one and the same with that of Great Britain he* is *equally bound* to one as to the other. 2nd, it is thus equally in open *defiance* of the *Act* of *Union*, and therefore if *this Act* is done, a part of the Union becomes *virtually repealed* and then how can they cry out against those who are so loudly calling out *for* the *Repeal* ? " With his conception of the sacredness of oaths, that was the crux of the question. " He could not for the life of him see how that [the Coronation] oath was to be got over in the present instance," and he read to the House of Lords that passage of the Coronation Service in which the oath was administered. He urged the Bishop of Armagh to encourage the whole Episcopacy in its resistance to the measure, asking him, " Is this country to be still blessed with a National Church ? " [3]

This was the Duke of Cumberland's principal interest in the session of 1833 and he was disappointed that some of his colleagues were half-hearted in it. He had doubts about Peel when he heard from the gallery the speech (" the most shuffling I ever heard in my life ") in which he said that he would accept certain aspects of the Bill and he reproached him with desiring the King to break his Coronation Oath.[4] When he learned that the Duke of Wellington had decided not to contest the second reading, his anger knew no bounds. " *Tout est perdu !* " he cried and asserted that Peel was at the bottom of it.[5] But he had learnt his lesson and was not going to split the party, however angry he might be with his colleagues in it.

He did not consider that his efforts during the session had been in vain, " as," he told Lord Eldon,[6] " they have been in keeping people together and preventing a schism in the Conservative Party, which, though I say it, is, as you know, perfectly *true*, that

[1] For example, " Surely, if this position is admitted as a ground for extinguishing the Irish Church rate, it equally applies to the English ones."—To the Bishop of Armagh, *van Thal*, Appendix.
[2] G.A. To Duchess, 26th February 1833.
[3] See the Duke's letters to the Bishop of Armagh in *van Thal*, Appendix.
[4] G.A. To Duchess, 7th May 1833.
[5] *Ibid*. To Duchess, 23rd July 1833.
[6] Encombe Archives. To Lord Eldon, 19th September 1833.

I alone have succeeded in preventing this session." The Government was steadily losing popularity and there was no doubt that a reaction towards Conservatism was taking place. This bore out the soundness of the Duke's advice at the beginning of the session that they should have patience and remain united.

There was also a gleam of hope for the Duke in another direction. Waller believed that an operation by Dr. Graefe, who had saved the Duke's sight, might also save that of his son.[1] The Duke immediately decided to follow his advice and place his son under Graefe's care. But the doctor could not leave his practice in Berlin, so he resolved to go there. The session was over and, after spending a few days with Lord Salisbury at Hatfield at the beginning of September, he left Kew with his wife and son on the 1st October 1833 and drove to Walmer Castle, the Duke of Wellington's residence as Warden of the Cinque Ports. They spent the night there and embarked the next day upon the steamer at Dover. Wellington's son, Lord Charles Wellesley, accompanied the Duke as A.D.C.

The journey did not go well with the Duchess and when they arrived at Homburg, the home of the Duke's sister Elizabeth, she had to take to bed for several days with headache. The Princess was shaken by the arrival of her nephew. " Never did I exert more not to show what I felt at our first meeting, for to see that lovely creature led about is not to be told. His good humour, his sweet way of expressing himself, his gratitude for every kindness is not to be expressed." [2] On the 13th they were in Weissenfels, the next day in Wittenberg and then, at last, in their home in the Prussian capital. Life resumed its old ways, but for the melancholy background of the cause of their return. It was clear that the course of treatment for Prince George would be a long one. The Duke, meanwhile, revisited all his old haunts, took up old friendships and acquaintances and lived again among the relatives who meant so much more to him than any left in England.

But no sooner was the Duke of Cumberland back in Germany than he was again involved in the developments in the land of which he might any day be King. The negotiations over the new Constitution had been continuing and they were accompanied by many unprecedented proceedings. The Estates were dissolved and elected by the new law, as promulgated by the Government in the interval, though legality required that Estates elected under the old electoral law should first have approved the new and *then*

[1] M.A. Duchess's diary.   [2] Her *Letters*.

an election held according to its provisions. Debates followed and the original proposals of Dahlmann, which had received the King's consent, were so altered in every way that they were no longer recognisable. One great disappointment to the Liberals was the figures of the Domain finances, now to be taken over by the state. There was no golden mountain, as they had been promised for years. On the contrary, the Treasury might find itself with a liability. But that did not matter—the important thing was that the independence of the Crown was at an end and this assembly of, for the greater part, disreputable small lawyers would have the country in its hands. On the 13th March 1833 the Chambers approved the new Constitution and it was sent to the King. His horror and indignation at what was now laid before him for his consent knew no bounds and he could not see in it that which he reluctantly approved the previous year. But the Ministers pressed him to sign the law, and the old King, weary of reigning both in England and Hanover and told by his easily-alarmed brother of the necessity of yielding if he were to retain the sceptre in the latter country, at length consented, though to save his face the Ministers suggested that he should make a few minor alterations, fourteen in all, which in no way affected the substance of the law. The Constitution was promulgated on the 26th September 1833 as the Staatsgrundgeſetz or Fundamental Law of State.

It could not fail to strike anyone that nowhere in all these wrangling proceedings was the Duke of Cumberland mentioned, although he was far more affected by their outcome than the present King. The latter, living in England, could be indifferent to his affairs and finances in Hanover, but his successor, whoever he might be, would be King of Hanover alone and dependent entirely upon his Hanoverian revenues. Again, the childless King had little interest in such questions as appanages. There had been, in all, so much deceit and so many stratagems and ruses that the propriety of the whole proceeding would have to be questioned. But above all, it lacked the consent of the Agnates of the House and particularly of the Heir. This was especially vital in view of the alienation of the properties and revenues of the *entire House*, for they did not belong to the *Crown as such*.

The Duke had, of course, followed all this keenly and he now understood the full import of what was intended. Far more perspicacious and strong-willed than his brother, he, like him (though to a far greater extent) had experienced what the financial

dependence of the Crown on an assembly meant. What had originally been a contract, the surrender of the Crown Estates in return
for a Civil List, had been forgotten and the latter was regarded as
a favour bestowed or withheld by Parliament at its own sweet will
and after its own taste in persons every time that it came up for
discussion. The origin of the Civil List was forgotten; people
spoke of the Royal Family as a burden on the nation and asked
why they should have to pay taxes to support it—as if this were
not just the solution desired by all the agitators of this time in
every land and opposed by the sovereigns themselves.

The Ministry knew very well what the sentiments of the Duke
of Cumberland would be, for he was the one man of whose principles and beliefs no one could have been in any doubt since the
turn of the century. They dared not approach him, therefore, for
his consent, but they trusted that they might gain their end by
presenting him with a *fait accompli* and could excuse their silence
hitherto on the ground that they had believed since 1831 that he
was in agreement with the law, with three reservations. They
conveniently forgot that what had been read to him when he made
those objections was the original proposal, which had been completely destroyed during the discussions which followed and to
which, in any case, he had not given his consent. In accordance
with this plan, they did not now formally ask him for his consent
but treated this as already given, and respectfully reminded him,
in a letter of the 16th October 1833, delivered through von Müch-
hausen (the Hanoverian Ambassador in Berlin) that he might now
take his seat in the Upper Chamber.[1] The Duke, as they might
have expected, indignantly rejected this suggestion and its circuitous
way of trapping him into recognising the new Constitution. He
put on record the manner in which he had been ignored throughout the negotiations. In a declaration of the 29th October 1833
he thanked the Ministers for their communication but stated that,
as he had been informed of nothing since 1819, he could not consider himself bound by any law enacted since then which required
his consent.[2]

The Hanoverian Ministers should have known their man
better. They had placed themselves in a situation of great
embarrassment, and von Stralenheim had to instruct von Ompteda
to acquaint the King with what had happened.[3] He endeavoure¹

---

[1] As they had done the Duke of Sussex through von Ompteda.
[2] H.A. Hann. Des. 92 I iv Nr. 36.
[3] *Ibid.* Hann. Des. 92 I iv Nr. 36. 14th November 1833.

E.A.—8*

to prove by juristic casuistry that agnatic consent was not necessary and attempted to explain away the awkward development. They saw no alternative but to continue their feigned ignorance of the Duke of Cumberland's dissent and sent corresponding instructions to the Chancery in London.[1] Of the Duke's protest, they said, they could not, after careful examination of its form and contents, consider it an actual protest against the law, but merely an answer to the letter, explaining why the Duke was not acting upon their suggestion by securing his seat in the Upper House, and they had to avoid giving greater importance to the document than the Duke had intended ! So his outright protests and warnings were deliberately ignored.

With the New Year the Duke's thoughts were once again directed to England, where the parliamentary session would soon be resumed. Remembering his part last year, he realised that he could not live peacefully in Berlin confident that all would be well in his homeland as he had done in the 1820's. He would have to return for the session, though his wife and son had to remain. As the day of departure approached, their life became more and more subdued and the Duchess could not hide her emotions. The Duke said nothing of his impending departure to his suffering son and took farewell of him as he was dressing on the 11th January ; he left hurriedly so that the boy should not be affected by the emotions which he found it difficult to conceal.

So the Duke set out on the long winter journey across bad and frozen roads. " Each moment that I go farther from you, darling, the sadder and more miserable becomes my heart," he wrote to his wife, " and when I think of all that I will have to endure in these times and all the difficulties which I will have to overcome, I am taken with fear. . . ." At Calais, storms prevented the steamer's crossing the bar, so he had to be rowed out to her. He passed a horrible night aboard, he said, though the accommodation was luxurious. He was not actually sick, but giddy, and when the captain had given him some cognac and ship's biscuit, he threw himself on to the sofa and endeavoured to sleep. Off the coast at Ramsgate, they ran into a " really frightful tempest " and anchored for twelve hours. The ship manœuvred for some time to enter the Thames for Woolwich but she was frustrated by the winds, and the Duke decided after dinner to land there by boat, at Northfleet, " a little village near Rochester, where we lunched, if you remember, on the way to Walmer." Thankful to be on

---

[1] H.A. Hann. Des. 92 I iv Nr. 36. 13th December 1833.

firm ground again, the Duke and Charles Wellesley took a hack-
chaise and drove to London, where they arrived late in the evening
on the 22nd January 1834. They were not expected at St. James's
as the wind was so violent, but there was soon a fire blazing in
the Duke's room, and after writing a few lines to his brother (who
was leaving for Brighton the following day), he threw himself
into bed to sleep off his headache.[1]

He merely announced his arrival to the King and left it to him
to invite him or not, as he did not wish it to be said that he had
forced himself upon him. Two days later, he received a message
from the Queen asking him to come to Brighton, and he arrived
before dinner on the 25th. He found the King harassed and
unable to understand properly what was going on. Though
unwell himself, he hurried back to town to start laying plans for
the coming session. First of all, of course, he discussed everything with Lord Eldon, then he visited the omniscient Princess
Lieven and the Carlton Club to find out the latest events.[2]

The Duke was soon back at work encouraging flagging spirits.
He was alarmed by the ignorant apathy of many who did not seem
to realise what was at stake. He found Lord Sidmouth depressed
and disgusted and determined not to set foot in Parliament again,
but succeeded in inducing him to promise to come whenever
summoned. " My dear Lord," he exclaimed, " you that had the
courage of a lion, I do not understand or comprehend you. . . .
Then I suppose you mean to sit quiet with your hands in your
pockets and allow the Church to be separated from the State and
the Monarchy to be turned into a republic ? " Describing the
episode to his wife,[3] the Duke added, " It is just this *insouciance*,
this apathy, that, according to my beliefs, has been and will be the
misfortune of the country, that these gentlemen do not wish to
sacrifice their comforts, their pleasures, and so go to the devil."
On another occasion, at a time when he frequently had to go
without food or rest for long hours, he wrote that " thoroughbred
like a horse, I go on till I fall from fatigue. And work at present
is the more terrible as those who should contribute to it absent
themselves and do nothing from frivolity, indifference and sulkiness." He then instanced Mr. Smith, M.P., who, when supposed
to be present for a division, replied, " That he would see the House
d——d before he would come up and give up a day's hunting,"

[1] The account of the journey is from G.A., To Duchess, 11th–23rd January 1834.
[2] G.A. To Duchess, 24th January 1834.
[3] *Ibid*. To Duchess, 28th January 1834.

and commented, " So Old England is and will be totally sacrificed by the folly and wickedness of those who might at least stem the torrent raging against us." [1]

The Duke was alarmed when he compared this easy-going attitude of many of his fellows with what he considered the desperate unscrupulousness of his opponents. " The Tories were *honest men*," he said.[2] " They told you what they would do and stood by what they said, but these Whigs were rascals, they pledged themselves to measures, said they would stand or fall by them and then quietly turned upon them and to keep *place* did the precise contrary." But he could still only counsel patience. The Ministry, he knew, was torn by internal dissension and personal jealousies. " We must keep *quiet* and aloof," he said,[3] " and not take any step, so that if they fall, it will be their own act and deed, and not appear to be effected by any intrigue of ours. . . . When rogues begin to quarrel among themselves, honest men may live."

The Duke's activities commenced, as last year, with a three-day shooting-party at Kew at the beginning of February immediately before the reassembly of Parliament, and he developed his theme to his guests.[4] " I said that according to my belief, the chief point seemed to me to be the *Church*, and that it was on that that our *principal stand* ought to be made." To objectors, he pointed out that it " was a question which touched more or less everyone here." To explain his views as to the paramountcy of religion in all matters, he asserted upon another occasion that " without it, what would become of the world ? It is only religion and the respect for it which can hold us together and prevent our cutting one another's throats." [5]

The measures proposed for this session which the Duke of Cumberland considered dangerous to the Church were a commission to inquire into the exact revenues, properties and numbers of the respective churches in Ireland, which seemed to him the first step towards appropriating any supposed superfluous properties, one for commuting tithes in Ireland and another for doing

---

[1] G.A. To Duchess, 8th March 1834.
[2] *Ibid.* To Duchess, 9th February 1834.
[3] *Ibid.* To Duchess, 29th May 1834. Yet we read in E. L. Woodward's *The Age of Reform*, p. 96, " The King's brother, the Duke of Cumberland, a stupid and savage Tory, was wild enough to consider the possibility of a military *coup d'état.*" How a historian who wishes to be taken seriously can make such a wild assertion as a statement of fact without giving any sources to support it is incomprehensible. In any case, at the time in question (the crisis at the end of the year), the Duke was not even in the country.
[4] *Ibid.* To Duchess, 2nd February 1834.   [5] *Ibid.* To Duchess, 29th March 1834.

away with certain abuses in the Church, among which was listed the plurality of livings. In the background was the agitation for the admission of Dissenters as teachers at the universities and the legalisation of Dissenters' marriage ceremonies. All of these the Duke was determined to resist.

He delivered a petition of the Lord Mayor, Sheriffs and Commonalty of Dublin against the first measure and asked if the proposed census of Catholics and Protestants in every village of Ireland was "the way to pacify Ireland or satisfy the loyal Protestants of that country? Was it not, on the contrary, throwing a firebrand into that country? Was it not calculated to set one sect more violently against another than was the case at any former time?" He complained that the income of the poor clergy had been cut by two-thirds through the Government's legislation of last year, and he himself subscribed to a fund to alleviate distress among them.

As to the correction of abuses, he wished as much as anyone, he said, to see genuine evils in the Church reformed, but he considered pluralities essential to the character of the Church in cases where livings were too small to support a clergyman in any gentlemanly way of life. He compared the clergy of England to their counterparts in states of Germany and other Protestant countries whose social status and prestige were so much lower, and pointed out that there certainly no Nobleman would ever take Orders. He believed that there should be a church in every parish, but considered it matter of little importance whether the duties were discharged by a rector or curate.

The Duke was particularly alarmed at the lack of spirit shown by the Bench. On one occasion when the Bishop of London was dining with him, he was shocked by his levity in discussing the proposals for Dissenters' marriages. "He did not care twopence about it," he said, as it did not concern the clergy, but would lead to confusion among the Dissenters and that was their business. "My Lord," replied the Duke, "what, then, if *this* is so, *what* security can there be for any marriage? Why, if that is now allowed, every marriage performed by a blacksmith or shoemaker will be valid, and is not that the next thing to overthrowing everything that is sacred and divine? and every man will become a Dissenter to avoid paying the fees." [1]

The Duke of Cumberland's pertinacity in ecclesiastical affairs may seem somewhat misplaced to-day, when the Irish Church has

[1] G.A. To Duchess, 2nd February 1834.

ceased to exist, and few would excite themselves over pluralities, for this was the time when some of the forces which were to alter the course of history and unleash misery, bullying and robbery as the normal apparatus of governing and living in communities were already taking shape. But the Duke of Cumberland had observed these too and that was more than many of his fellows. " In the north, the strikings are now general," he wrote,[1] " and despite all, one cannot but smile at what the miserable Duke of Cleveland, the great *orator*, said for Parliamentary Reform, and now *troops* are being sent to him as he has fears for his aunt and daughter."

He learned that the Chartists and trade unions planned a grand procession in April, and though troops were under arms, he could not understand why it was not forbidden by an Order in Council. A deputation of local shopkeepers waited upon him and expressed to him their fears. " Gentlemen," he told them, " everyone has a right to defend his house and property, but, mind, this must be done quietly and not in a manner contrary to the laws, for the Ministers, if they knew their duty or had the courage to act, could have issued a proclamation forbidding all large assemblies of people at this moment, and called in their loyal and faithful subjects to be ready to come forward and form themselves into bodies to assist the authorities in putting down all riots and tumult." The Duke, in accordance with his principle of observing everything with his own eyes, went to see the procession from Green's, the silversmiths on Cockspur Street, as it passed down Regent Street. The masses were, he said, quiet and orderly and there was no cheering. In fact, their behaviour was unexceptionable. But it gave him occasion for some of his frequent grim and prophetic meditations. " In reflecting upon all this," he wrote, " two thoughts have come to my mind. Firstly, that the greater part of these poor devils were only instruments or puppets in the hands of certain masters, and that is at least comforting, for I have never seen a more *good-natured* or more inoffensive mob, and that is the good side of the thing. But, in the second place, I think that that *such* a *mass* can *exist, so organised*, strong and well-managed, can meet and assemble, the disorder that the mass could cause is frightening." It was only harmless, he said, because no one had the courage to lead it. " There is no doubt that no time should be lost in meeting the danger and putting down these unions, as it is too much to be every instant at the mercy of a mob like that." [2]

[1] G.A. To Duchess, 12th April 1834.
[2] G.A. To Duchess, 12th–21st April 1834.

From such sights and sounds it was only natural that the Duke should have endeavoured whenever possible to escape to the quiet of Kew, where, as a village squire, he participated in the life of the old England which, up in Westminster, he was fighting to preserve. There he was known to everybody, interested himself in all parochial affairs, attended whenever possible the vestry meetings and donated regular sums to the local charities. He spent every week-end there and frequently invited groups of his friends. We read, for example, of a dinner with Lord Lyndhurst and the Speaker. "We dined with the windows and the door into the garden open, so that we could enjoy the divine fragrance of the flowers." [1]

The Duke of Cumberland was now the recognised champion of the Church and it was not surprising that he should receive an invitation to visit one of its strongholds, the University of Oxford. He valued this so highly that he disengaged himself for the only week in the year which he spent away from London and his Parliamentary routine.

On the 9th June he arrived in the city and was welcomed by Jelf, who was a Fellow of Oriel, and placed his rooms at his disposal. The Duke of Wellington (the Chancellor), the Vice-Chancellor and Wetherell called on him, and he went with the latter to see Magdalen College with its " unequalled chapel." The city was full, there were Peers and distinguished men everywhere and he was meeting acquaintances the whole length of the High Street. "Here I am in the most learned city, I believe, as to literary connoisseurs, that there is in Europe," he wrote. "But although too convinced of my ignorance to pretend to be worthy of comparing myself to these learned men, nevertheless, I see that as to knowledge of *men* and living objects, I believe that I am perhaps more learned than many of these *very learned personages*."

The next day the Duke appeared at the first function of his visit. "There are neither words nor expressions strong enough to describe to you the manner in which I have been received in the theatre," [2] he wrote. He entered before the procession and instantly the whole hall broke into cheering. Afterwards, there was dinner for one hundred and twenty persons in University College. The following morning the Duke went for a walk in the city for some fresh air and exercise, and as he was going up a narrow street to Exeter College, and passing Lancaster College, an undergraduate stopped him. "Sir," he said, "there is in this

[1] G.A. To Duchess, 9th June 1834.   [2] The Sheldonian Theatre.

small college a chapel well worth your notice on account of its beautiful windows and carvings." The Duke went in and found that what the young man had said was true. His guide then said that he would inform the Warden and in a few minutes five or six Fellows who had been at table were showing the college to the illustrious guest who had been unexpectedly gained for them by the undergraduate's enterprise. Several members requested him to protect their rights and privileges, and he assured them that they could put their trust in him. After giving him three cheers, they accompanied him through the street back to Jelf's. The Duke expressed similar sentiments when he dined at St. John's the next day, that he " could never act against the principles and the *solemn* compact on which the family was called to the Throne of this country, and it was to this I had acted up to and pledged myself ever to act up to."

On the last day of his visit, the 14th June, the Duke saw the Cathedral, Chapter House, Worcester College and the Clarendon Press, where he spent two hours with Jelf and the Dean. He found it very interesting, but the new building did not please him, " as it seems to me that in a city like Oxford, where the greater part of the buildings are Gothic, it should have been built in that style." The staff of one hundred and fifty was also new after the recent political disturbances. The next day the Duke returned to London and wrote of his stay in Oxford that his only regret was that his wife was not with him—" Everything together has made upon me an impression that nothing could ever make me forget." [1]

The Duke had hoped that Parliament would adjourn in June ; he could then join his wife and son who were going to take the waters at Pyrmont. But discussions upon the Irish Church revenues continued and disagreements among the Whigs led to the retirement of Grey and his replacement by a reluctant Melbourne. The Duke of Cumberland had always predicted such a split and he was now confirmed in his belief that it would only be a matter of time before the Conservatives were called to office again. But politics were at last over, or seemed to be, for the year and he made to leave for Berlin. Before his departure he spoke to the Duke of Wellington and he related to his wife [2] with some pride that Wellington told him that the party owed everything to him and only he in his situation could have held it together. " Sir," he

[1] The account of the visit to Oxford is from G.A. To Duchess, 9th–14th June 1834.

[2] G.A. To Duchess, 15th August 1834.

said, " be not angry when I say I regret that you are under the
necessity of leaving the country at this important juncture, for you
are our *mainstay* and prop, we all look to you ; your decision,
coolness and moderation have done all and I implore you for the
salvation of all that must be dear to us not to abandon us, but to
be back whenever Parliament meets again."

The Duke of Cumberland visited Windsor from Kew for the
King's birthday and to take leave of him, and soon after seven
o'clock in the morning on the 24th August 1834 he left for Deptford and embarked an hour later in the *Lightning*. This time he
sailed direct to Hamburg. It was a two-day crossing and there
was a violent stormy night as they entered the Elbe Estuary. The
pilot lost his head when he saw a brig bearing down upon them
and heard the captain cry, " Steer to the right ! " [1] In a panic he
let go of the wheel, but fortunately a sailor sprang to it just in
time, so that the two ships passed each other slowly. Nevertheless,
there was a terrible shudder as they came together. The Duke was
resting on the sofa and just falling asleep when he heard and felt
the crash, followed by movement and shouting. He ran on to the
deck and saw the other vessel drawing away. They had all had a
narrow escape. Shortly afterwards the waves calmed, and as they
would have to wait for the tide, the captain suggested that the
Duke should land there by boat. He and his party followed the
advice and landed at six o'clock in the morning at a village some
miles from Hamburg—the Duke, Jelf, Captain Slade (his A.D.C.)
and Holmes, who was also going to the Continent.[2]

Once again, the Duke passed several months uneventfully with
his family, his relatives and friends.

[1] As the Duke reported. Presumably the captain would have used the nautical
term. Such an incident is not surprising, for the pilotage from which the Heligolanders
had earlier made their living had, from a variety of changes in the life of the island,
deteriorated in quality.

[2] G.A. To Duchess, 26th August 1834.

CHAPTER XVII

THE DUKE OF CUMBERLAND AND PEEL (1835-37)

WHEN the Duke of Cumberland was away from the English
political scene the crisis within the Cabinet suddenly reached
its climax. Lord Althorp had been called to the Lords after the
death of his father and in the consequent reshuffling in the Cabinet
the King, who was weary of the Whig régime, thought that the time
had come to change it. The country was steadily moving towards
the Conservatives and, as the Duke of Cumberland had always
said, only patience was required on their part. But the King was
not possessed of this and by his precipitate action he prolonged
the life of the Whig Ministry by several years. He " dismissed "
Melbourne early in December and sent for Peel to form a Ministry,
though he knew that it would have to face a Whig majority in the
Commons. Peel was in Italy but he started for home on receiving
the summons and Wellington took over in the meantime.[1]

The Duke of Cumberland had just celebrated Christmas in
Berlin when news of this development reached him. He had no
doubt as to where his duty lay and he took the painful decision to
leave at once. " I am in the act of starting this very evening for
England," he wrote to his brother on Boxing Day, 1834,[2] " having
received again *this day* most pressing letters for my attendance
there from so many of my political friends that I feel in honour
bound to go there." He drove through Cologne and Brussels to
Calais without incident and there took the Dover steam packet,
which, as she had no mail to take to England that day, was returning
empty and could go to Woolwich. Anchor was weighed at three
o'clock and for once the winter crossing was " superb." At four
o'clock in the morning she arrived inconspicuously at Woolwich
and the Duke and Jelf went on foot to find a hack-chaise. They

---

[1] Of his decision, the Duke told Wellington later, " that of all his heroic actions,
of all the victories he had gained and the signal service he had rendered his country,
this appeared to me to have been the *greatest*, for to fight and fall in action was one thing,
but here boldly to step forward and take upon his own shoulders the sole and total
responsibility was an act of courage, self-sacrifice that *none* but himself would *at once*
have undertaken, and that must immortalise him."—G.A. To Duchess, 11th January
1835.

[2] Linsingen Archives. To Duke of Cambridge.

were going into a public-house when they saw that it was full of
Radicals. The Duke said that he would not patronise such a
place ; they would walk on and he would order a cab to catch up
with them. So they began walking, expecting a cab to overtake
them every minute, but had gone some six miles on foot to the
Elephant and Castle and none had arrived. There they hired one
and arrived unexpectedly at St. James's at six o'clock on the
morning of the 4th January 1835, when it was still dark.[1] At
seven the Duke went to breakfast at the Carlton and there he met
his nephew, Lord Adolphus Fitzclarence.[2] Lord Adolphus wrote
of his uncle's arrival to his sister, Sophia,[3] who was with the King
at Brighton, and when she mentioned it to her father he requested
her to ask the Duke to come to see him, though there was no room
in the Pavilion. The Duke was still anxious not to appear to be
pressing himself upon the King.

Accordingly, the Duke of Cumberland went the following
afternoon to Brighton and spent over three hours with the King
at the Pavilion. The King, in the crisis which he had precipitated,
wept and begged him to stay for several days, and the Duke
promised that he would do so the next week ; at the moment he
had to be at his post in London. The King had now long seen
the folly of his past conduct and the wisdom of his brother's advice
which he had ignored. Now, it would seem, he begged his brother
to use his influence on his friends to support Peel's Ministry, for
they knew that many were loath to do this. On the 12th January
the Duke returned to Brighton, where he took rooms at the York
Hotel. He was anxious about his brother, as he seemed to breathe
with difficulty. He spoke of the elections with him and discussed
politics with the Queen, who considered that the fire which had
burnt down the Houses of Parliament was a divine retribution for
all the wickedness that had taken place in them so recently.[4] She
suggested a promenade the next day and they walked the whole
length of the West Cliff, above and below, for some two miles.
Afterwards, they went in their coaches to Kemp Town for lunch
and then the Duke again accompanied his sister-in-law to see the
Chain Pier. He left Brighton after lunch on the 16th and on his
arrival in London in the evening went straight to the Carlton Club
for the latest election results.

[1] The account of the journey is from G.A. To Duchess, 27th December 1834–
4th January 1835.
[2] Son of William IV by Mrs. Jordan.
[3] Daughter of William IV by Mrs. Jordan.
[4] G.A. Queen to Duke.

Peel had, of course, dissolved Parliament and gone to the country with the principles of his " New Conservatism." The first impression which the Duke received upon his arrival in the country was that the election was being bungled. " Naturally," he wrote,[1] " in public I am *confident* and speak courage, for I believe that at this moment all depends upon putting on a good face and not appearing to be afraid. But it seems to me inconceivable that in such a crisis and at such a critical moment as that of a general election, there is no one here to arrange the whole and, I beg you, it is only since *Holmes's* return that they have seen their folly and confusion." The Conservatives, though they doubled their representation, did not have a majority over the Whigs and Irish Members together, and it was obvious that the experiment of Peel's Government would be short-lived. However, this election is always considered a milestone in the history of the party, for it was in his constituency upon that occasion that Peel issued his celebrated " Tamworth Manifesto " setting out the principles by which it would be guided in the future. Peel, according to a generally-held view, was trying to formulate a positive and reasoned policy, but was hampered by the old aristocrats and diehard Ultras with their negative attitude and their jealousy of this Radical plebian. If this is so, it is interesting to see the Duke of Cumberland's attitude.

His was no blind and selfish spirit of opposition, and where he could make concessions without sacrificing principles, he was quite prepared to do so. He therefore gave the Tamworth policy his full approval, though he did not agree with courting popularity by such means.[2] He would, he said, consent to the legalisation of Dissenters' marriage services, if there were safeguards against their being carried out clandestinely, and to the abolition in general of pluralities, with specific exceptions ; as to Municipal Reform, we will see his views upon that. He had thus made substantial concessions and gone as far as his principles would allow him.[3]

But he was thereby placed in a very difficult position, for Peel had made no corresponding sacrifice to his group, the so-called Ultras. He was himself disgusted with the appointments which he had made, where all of the group were simply passed over, in many cases for men of doubtful loyalties. He regarded it as scandalous that Wetherell received no attention and he heard similar stories from all his most personal and intimate friends ; the most

[1] G.A. To Duchess, 6th January 1835.
[2] G.A. To Duchess, 20th July 1835.
[3] G.A. To Duchess, 28th January 1835.

critical case was that of the Duke of Buckingham. The Duke of Cumberland shared all his friends' resentment, but he did not allow himself to show it.[1] " I perfectly agree with you and hear many things that displease me mightily," he told Eldon,[2] " but then we must make the best of it and consider the salvation of the whole." He had to persuade his colleagues, the Ultras, to support the Prime Minister, who had so grossly snubbed them, and his influence was thus a very important factor in the life of the Ministry, however short; a split between Peel and the Ultras would have brought it down at once, as such a split had Wellington's in 1830. As one of the Duke of Cumberland's greatest triumphs, the disgusted and offended Buckingham wrote to him,[3] " Though I feel I am put on the shelf, I shall always feel happy to *obey* your summons and will come to town for the meeting of Parliament."

The Duke mentioned this to the King later, when he was returning to the Continent. " Now," he said,[4] " I hope you will agree that my coming as I did, upon the call of the party over here last January, was not so idle or out of the way, for had I not those six weeks before me to soothe and soften down the feelings of our party to Peel's Government and thus amalgamated them, never could I at this very important crisis have gained that ascendency and influence over them. Did I not get completely hold of Buckingham, Newcastle, Falmouth, Winchelsea, Chandos and many others ? *This* was not the work of a day or an hour, but *days* and hours, both by day and night, and I am happy to say that you now see there has not been a split and even Wellington has thanked me and said he owed all to my conduct. What does Lyndhurst say ? Rosslyn and all of them ? "

But Peel was a difficult man to help, " not a communicative man and always what I call *cold* and *repulsive* in his manner, which in the present circumstances does not make for friendship and *bonhomie*, which does all and is of the first importance." [5] He did not consider the delicate position of the Duke, who was making such sacrifices to support him. In speaking in Parliament of the Church, for example, he made use of the word *abuses*, knowing that the Duke had so often denied that there were any—they were only, perhaps, what he would term *irregularities*.[6] The old antipathy

---

[1] G.A.   To Duchess, 6th January 1835.
[2] *Ibid.*   To Duchess, 10th January 1835.
[3] *Ibid.*   To Duchess, 6th January 1835.
[4] *Ibid.*   To Duchess, 26th August 1835.
[5] *Ibid.*   To Duchess, 12th January 1835.
[6] *Ibid.*   To Duchess, 19th January 1835.

between Peel and Wellington also began to make itself perceptible again, though the Duke of Cumberland had always suspected that the latter had not been pleased at the Government appointments.[1] " To steer a middle course is very difficult," wrote the Duke,[2] " but all that I desire, all that I implore is that the most perfect harmony may exist between the two great movers and supporters, Wellington and Peel, that no jealousy or misunderstanding may break out there. . . . This repelling manner of Peel, which no one can suffer, is not intentional, but is, unhappily, his nature. But in persons who are great, either by birth or through their position in the world, all depends upon *manners*." He considered it only fair to state in advance that his support for the Ministry would not extend to sacrificing his basic principles. " No one could be more ready to support the present Ministry than myself," he wrote,[3] " but at the same time, if I see any signs of its wishing to sacrifice the privileges of the Church, and thus for what I termed expediency give up the rights and privileges of the Church, to that I could not and would not be a party ! "

So the Duke had to defend Peel among his friends and make excuses for him which certainly did not convince himself. He even had on one occasion to subdue Wellington, whom he found very violent and abusive of him. " The difficulty which I have had to keep all the Ultra *party* in order demands such a wisdom and prudence," he wrote to his wife of his thankless task,[4] " that I swear to you, I reflected well last night as to whether I should not withdraw my pin from the game and betake myself in peace and quiet to the bosom of my family and all that is dear to me. . . . *Holmes*, to whom I spoke this evening after dining alone with him, said to me, ' Sir, I can perfectly enter into your feelings, and am not surprised at your wish, but allow me to say without flattery, you are the only man who can keep them together. Who could have tamed the Duke of Buckingham last year ? Who managed that difficult family but you ? Peel said so last night and Rosslyn said in my hearing this day at the Club to at least twenty members that you *alone* had and have a patriotism, a knowledge of mankind and a prudence that the party could not nor ought to forget.' All this is very flattering to me, but it does not take all the weight off me and all the responsibility of a *leader*, which is the most ungrateful

[1] G.A.   To Duchess, 12th January 1835.
[2] *Ibid.*   To Duchess, 20th January 1835.
[3] *Ibid.*   To Duchess, 28th January 1835.
[4] *Ibid.*   To Duchess, 19th April 1835.

and the most difficult *métier* in the world.   In a word, to be *master*
it is necessary to be *slave*.   This sounds nonsense, but it is true in
the meaning of the word, for to be master or leader it is necessary
to sacrifice all one's comforts and so it truly is slavery."

The Duke described how his time was spent to his old equerry
Poten.[1]   "You know that I have hardly time to deal with all the
business in the twenty-four hours that the day is long and the
times at present are such that I have hardly the *time* either to lunch
or to sleep, for already at nine in the morning I have people of all
sorts coming on business, Members of Parliament, lawyers, agents,
Peers, etc., so that I can only with difficulty take a sandwich and a
glass of wine in between. . . . Would to God it were all over,
for it is too fatiguing and I sense that my powers are feeling it.
During the last fourteen days before the recess, I never came home
before one or two in the morning, and was up again at eight.   One
cannot keep this up."

His relaxation was still the week-ends which he spent at Kew
among the villagers and his closer circle of friends.   He went out
to watch the hay-making in his fields, attended the services in the
church and went riding.   "You have no idea how *beautiful* and
delightful Kew is this evening," he concluded one of his letters to
his wife.[2]   "Wetherell and I went for a walk from seven till eight
in the arboretum and round our dear garden.   The hortensia are
more beautiful this year than I have ever seen them and the verdure
magnificent.   There, my adored angel, is my story of to-day.
Alas, I must go to bed . . . for it is so tranquil and peaceful here,
but the village clock has just struck I'm ashamed to say two o'clock
and I must put myself to bed."   From Kew he visited all the
social events of the neighbourhood, Epsom, Ascot, the Duke of
Northumberland's grand garden party on the other bank of the
Thames at Syon [3] and the Montem at Eton.[4]   On another occasion
he attended a dinner in Woolwich and to reach it he had to pass
through narrow streets where they could only go at a walking-
pace.   Everyone was respectful, some shouted "No Popery ! "—
"and when I think of the difference between now and how the
times were *three* years ago, it is too remarkable." [5]

[1] 14th May 1835, Vaterländisches Museum, Celle.   Peel's Government had at last
resigned on the 8th April after repeated defeats brought about by a combination of
the Whigs with the Irish members.
[2] G.A.   To Duchess, 6th June 1835.
[3] On the 19th June 1835.
[4] 9th June 1835.   See the description of this visit by Princess Victoria in *The Girlhood
of Queen Victoria.*
[5] G.A.   To Duchess, 24th July 1835.

But the Duke's most important invitation of the year was to Cambridge—no doubt anxious not to be out-done by its sister-university—which he received in the middle of June and, of course, accepted.   On the afternoon of the 6th July he arrived at Trinity College and was received at the gate by the Chancellor of the University, Lord Camden, the Master and Fellows.[1]   He then had *déjeuner* with the Master and Fellows of Sidney Sussex College even before he had had time to retire.   In the evening he attended a dinner given in his honour at Jesus College by the Master, Dr. French, who was also Vice-Chancellor of the University, " a very distinguished man, a perfect gentleman, the best chairman that I have ever seen, violently conservative " ; it was to have been held in the court, but threatening weather caused a change of plan and it was held in the Hall.

The next day the Duke rose and went down to breakfast in the Master's Lodge.[2]   After introductions, the Master was about to say prayers when the Duke noticed that three or four women, one of them exceedingly corpulent, had just entered and were standing some way from the table.   Believing them to be the wives of his hosts, he courteously said to them, " Mesdames, won't you please take your places at the table ? "   To his astonishment Lord Harding said to him, " Not yet, first we have the prayers."   The Master took out a book and said prayers, then the women departed and the Duke realised that they were the cook and housemaids.   He was so overcome with his own stupidity that he could have " collapsed with laughter at the thought of it." At eleven he went to the Senate House, where doctorates were to be conferred, and as he entered he was received with enthusiastic cheering and applause.   In the evening there was a grand dinner. The Master, in introducing the Duke, coupled his name with that of Dublin and expressed his confidence that they could safely entrust the defence of their rights to him.   The Duke was loudly applauded when he replied that they most certainly could do so. Later he went for a walk with Lyndhurst round several colleges and halls, comparing them with those of Oxford.   " Those of Oxford," he said, " are the more beautiful, but King's College is superb and above all the old part and the church of such beauty." He also viewed the pictures presented by Lord Fitzwilliam.   He

---

[1] Apart from this description of his arrival, the Duke does not name the College where he stayed, but from all the details which he mentions in connection with it, it seems certain that he resided at Trinity.

[2] See Note 1.

had been told, he said, that the townspeople were all Radicals, but everywhere he found them polite and they raised their hats to him.

On the 8th the Duke continued seeing the sights in the morning, lunched at Downing, dined at St. John's and went to the Town Hall for the ball in aid of Addenbrooke's Hospital in the evening. The following day he attended service in King's College Chapel—it was very beautiful, he said, the organ and choir were magnificent, but the solo-singing " nothing special." In the afternoon there was a fête in the grounds of Trinity College. Tables had been arranged for two thousand in the cloisters of the court, which were decorated with an abundance of flowers and there were pretty alleys under the great trees. At five o'clock they went in procession to King's College for dinner and returned again on foot when it was dark. The court was illuminated, the tables removed and two floors put down for the dancing, with the orchestra in the middle. At a certain time they went into the garden again for fireworks and there were illuminated boats on the water. On the morrow the Duke continued his tours with Wetherell. They went to Corpus Christi, not on account of its " Radical Master," Dr. Lamb, but to see its chapel and the beautiful missals and letters of Henry VIII, Ann Boleyn and Queen Elizabeth in its library. Then they visited the head of Peterhouse, Dr. Barnes, who, although a nonagenarian, was as lively as a man of fifty and related to the Duke his memories of the '45. After strolling along the beautiful promenades in the environs of the city, the Duke left at five o'clock and passed the evening at Wimpole, Lord Hardwick's house some thirteen miles away. He left at midnight and arrived in London at six o'clock the next morning.

" And now I am going to give you my opinions as to the differences between the Universities of Oxford and Cambridge," he wrote to his wife. " The first I find preferable as it is a single *body* and has no other object than the *good* of *all*. Cambridge, on the other hand, is very diverse, the colleges are jealous of one another, and in consequence there is little harmony among them. Cambridge is more sceptical and so I myself give my preference to Oxford. But when I say this, I do not wish to deny the great merits of Cambridge. The buildings of Oxford are more beautiful, except King's College, which is truly *unique* in its kind and should strike *everyone* ; the Chapel is superb." [1]

[1] The account of the visit to Cambridge is from G.A. To Duchess, 7th-12th July 1835, and the *Cambridge Independent Press*.

The last important controversial measure of the year was the Municipal Corporations Reform Bill, which aimed at giving a uniform constitution to the boroughs of the country now governed so diversely. Here again the Duke of Cumberland's readiness to reform where there seemed to be need for it was evident. Peel had supported the principles of the Bill against, we read, his bitter and jealous Ultra colleagues, who cut it up in the Lords and all but led to a clash between the two Houses. Again, the Duke of Cumberland's part is interesting and proves him to have acted quite differently from what would generally be supposed. Before the second reading, he presided over a meeting of some eighty leading personalities and Peers of the party. The Duke of Wellington opened it with a description of the situation ; then the Duke of Cumberland called upon Lyndhurst, as the only Law Lord present, to give his views. Lyndhurst said that the Bill was bad, but there were many acknowledged abuses and it would make propaganda for the Radicals if the Lords rejected it offhand. The Duke himself then said that " I had given myself every possible pain to hear from those among us the general feeling and opinion and that as far as I could perceive there seemed to be a doubt as to the question of *principle*, which, though I certainly felt disinclined as much as anyone to sacrifice, I think after the explanation of the learned Lord I may to a certain degree admit is not given up, as there is a general acknowledgement, it strikes me, on all sides, that there are corporations fatally fallen into confusion and where original objects have been so vitiated that they absolutely demand correction. Therefore . . . *I will accede to the second reading*," if they were not pledged beyond that and could still hear evidence at the Bar.[1]

When the committee stage was reached the Duke of Newcastle and Lord Falmouth moved an amendment condemning the Bill and the attempt of the Commons to bully them. The Duke of Cumberland therefore rose and explained that, although he was equally opposed to the " encroachment on the rights and privileges of the people and on chartered rights, for which he for one would constantly stand up," he could not vote for their amendment and " it only remained for him to say that he should give the measure his most serious attention, and he hoped and trusted that when the Bill was read a third time he should be in a situation to give it his hearty support." Brougham was taken aback at this line of

[1] G.A. To Duchess, 24th July 1835. Various municipalities claimed a right to be heard, saying that the commission collecting evidence for the Bill had proceeded unfairly.

the Duke, than whom, he said, " I must say I never knew, generally speaking, a more fair, open, above-board antagonist, and
knowing therefore his strong opinions on this and all similar questions, I certainly expected to have found him supporting the proposition of the Noble Duke—' But no,' he says . . ." and the
speaker lapsed into sarcasm which had its object in sowing dissension between the Duke and his followers. However, Newcastle
did not press his amendment and there can be no doubt that in this
he was influenced by the advice of his leader.

Upon another issue which became acute during the session,
however, the Duke of Cumberland announced his opposition in
no uncertain terms. That was the railways which were now being
built or applying for Parliamentary sanction. In them, he saw the
latest threat to the English countryside and its way of life. During
the Royal visit to Eton, as the party was passing the large grass
court, a letter and bundle of papers from the Provost and Fellows
had been pressed into his hands, and when he opened them back at
Kew he found that they contained a protest against the proposed
railway line passing close to the College.[1] A few days later he
rode from Kew across Brentford and Ealing to Pinner to see the
proposed route of the railway there. One of the farmers accompanied him and showed him the beautiful houses, farms and farm-
land—" jewels," the Duke called them—which would be affected
by it.[2] On another occasion he made a detour when riding into
town to see the work in progress on the Southampton Railway at
Wandsworth. Fifty to sixty navvies were at work in an excavation
forty feet under the road and he spoke to the engineer in charge.[3]
He made up his mind to oppose these developments with all his
might, as if he saw before him the hideous monster which London
with its suburbs was to become.

There is no doubt that the Duke had the majority of the country
behind him on this issue. But he did not wish to be unjust, for,
as he told the House, " if he thought that he could gain popularity
by going to that window, when he believed that such a step would
be attended by injustice, he would not stir an inch for that purpose." So he attended every committee on the Great Western
Railway and heard all the evidence. The only sittings which he
missed were those which were held during his visit to Cambridge
and the evidence which had been given then he read with great
care. He was present when the committee examined the under-

[1] G.A. To Duchess, 9th June 1835.   [2] *Ibid.* To Duchess, 27th June 1835.
[3] *Ibid.* To Duchess, 22nd February 1836.

master of Eton, who stated that the railway would jeopardise the character of the school. " The thought that the speculations of merchants and people of that class should outweigh the institution which gives us statesmen, politicians, Ministers, Archbishops, Bishops, lawyers, etc., is too melancholy and how little it is *desired* to maintain that which is good and fine and *everything is to give way to the recklessness of change, eternal change* ! ! ! " [1]

This moved him to declare, when the Great Western Railway Bill was being debated in the House, that although no one could desire the welfare of Bristol and Ireland more than he, the evidence before the committee had destroyed the grounds upon which the Bill rested, for if a shorter unobjectionable route to Bristol could be taken, why was it not ? " One of the chief objections, however, which he felt to the line of the Western Railway was its proximity to Eton. The consequence of its adoption, as he understood from some of the masters, was that the whole system of discipline would necessarily be changed, and a much more contracted system adopted." An equally good line to the west could be obtained by the Southampton Railway, he said.[2]

With that, the session was over and the Duke could return home, highly satisfied with the success of his efforts. " In short," he wrote of his acknowledged position as leader of the Ultras,[3] " I may with pride and satisfaction to myself say, ' I have saved the whole ' and this the enemy knows and never will nor can forgive." After going to Frogmore to visit the King (who spoke of the possible necessity for a regency in the future), the Duke embarked at Woolwich on the 4th September 1835 on the *Firebrand*.

The following evening she reached Heligoland and, on the evening of the 6th, delayed, Hamburg. A few days after the Duke's arrival in Berlin he left again, this time for the Russian army manœuvres at Kalisch, in Poland, just across the Silesian frontier, then he went to Prague. Two Emperors and hosts of Princes were staying there, and the Duke was particularly impressed by the happiness of the inhabitants and their enthusiasm for their Emperor.[4]

The Duke's next call came from Hanover again, the country where his succession was now a matter of certainty, possibly of

---

[1] G.A. To Duchess, 11th August 1835.

[2] It will thus be seen that the question was, which of the two proposed routes should be adopted, and it cannot be said that the Duke opposed a railway to the West Country on the grounds that it would disturb the boys of Eton, as it has been written.

[3] G.A. To Duchess, 11th August 1835.

[4] See the account of the visit to Prague in G.A. To Duchess, 3rd–7th October 1835.

imminence. The new Constitution had been in operation for two years, despite the fact he had never ceased to protest against it and to point out its illegality. By the end of 1835 the increasing urgency of the matter led the Hanoverian Ministers to realise that they could no longer brush aside the objections of the Heir as of no consequence. The morrow he might be King, and what then? As he was again in Germany they decided to take the opportunity of pressing him to go there, confident that they would persuade him by their arguments to recognise the new Constitution. Again there was a trap into which one not so astute as he might have fallen. In 1831 a House Law for the House of Brunswick had been adopted by its two branches to settle problems caused by the dissolution of the Empire and its ordinances, mainly with regard to marriages. The Duke of Cumberland, of course, did not dissent, but in 1833 there had been some alterations.[1] The Duke, who was then about to travel to Berlin, had had no time to examine them, but he told von Ompteda after a glance at it that he could never agree to some points.[2] However, the overriding ground for his refusing his consent was that the intended House Law made several references to, and thus seemed to derive its authority from, the new Constitution, and that by consenting to the former, the recognition of the latter would be automatically implied.[3] The Duke of Cumberland was, of course, the only member of the House to whom this whole transaction was of any consequence. Now the Ministers had such confidence in their powers of persuasion and the pliability of the Duke that they were certain of being able to convince him of their case if only they could have a personal discussion. They asked him to come to Hanover and in December he acceded to their request.

The Duke's visit opened with a house-party at Derneburg, Count Münster's seat.[4] There he met many of his old friends and

[1] To regulate the succession in view of the possibility that the Duke of Brunswick might die childless and that the Crowns of Hanover and Great Britain might shortly separate as William IV had no sons. A woman could not succeed in Hanover as long as Agnates or male members of the family survived. It is incorrect to represent the Salic Law, under which no woman might succeed, as prevailing there.

[2] Such as that only children of the King and the Crown Prince should enjoy the predicate "Royal Highness," which, the Duke said, would put the other Princes on the footings of those of Grand Ducal Houses.

[3] The House Law was actually drafted by someone who was quite unassociated with the House, Dahlmann, a prime mover of the 1833 Constitution.

[4] The former monastery which had been presented to Count von Münster by the King. There, after his dismissal, he lived quietly, occupying himself with art, study, entertaining and the education of his children, visiting Hanover rarely and only when absolutely necessary. He had nothing more to do with politics or his successors.

they told him of the chaos and discontent brought about by the new state of affairs. Even those writers most enthusiastic for the new Constitution [1] do not claim that the masses had any great esteem or affection for it. In Hanover the Duke saw Rossini's *Tancred* at the Opera, and as he entered his box, enthusiastic clapping and cries of " Vivat ! " came from the audience.[2] Von der Decken introduced to him the most brilliant of the Conservatives, Edward von Schele,[3] a man who, like himself, did not take refuge in subtleties. The Duke was delighted at his frankness, his honesty and his evident ability, but, he wrote to his wife, he would reflect well and hear quietly *all* explanations, though they were unlikely to alter his opinions. The Ministers he believed to be " honest men, but of such a feebleness and pusillanimity that in the first moment of difficulty they are ready to surrender everything. . . . They have been so much fêted and spoilt that they believe themselves to be above their masters." Von Schele told him that " the good Duke [4] means everything for the best, but he has no *nerve* and lets himself be led about by anyone who approaches him."

As a man of honour, the Duke of Cumberland told the Ministers, he could not be ambiguous, and they could not deny that if he were to sign the Family Law in its present state he would recognise the recent changes. Rose, the Under-Secretary, tried to bluff him by the assurance that there had been no change in the real state of affairs, but, wrote the Duke, " he saw that I would not let myself be led astray by his subtleties and official phraseology." " Every Sovereign," the Duke told him, " should have the good of his people at heart, and that is the principle which has always distinguished the Sovereigns of this country. . . ." He could not sign the new Constitution since " *I* am one of those who keep their promises." The Minister had not expected these remarks and could not offer a word in reply.

Falcke also tried to convince the Duke of the validity and desirability of the new Constitution. The Duke listened quite quietly and did not show the slightest trace of excitement, Falcke reported ; at the end, he told him to put his points in writing and said that he would communicate his decision.[5] So the Minister saw that they had miscalculated. " I have a suspicion," the Duke

---

[1] For example, von Treitschke and Oppermann.
[2] The Court Opera was then immediately adjacent to the Palace.
[3] Freiherr von Schele had filled many situations in the administration and been dismissed from office during the French occupation.
[4] Of Cambridge.
[5] H.A. K.G. Hann. 9 Sec. Dom. IV 48.

told his wife after the interview, " that many of these gentlemen have such an easy conscience that they now try their best to persuade me to put my name to it, saying that I can always change, but I am neither such a fool nor such a vagabond ; when I put my name to a document, I regard that as *sacred*. I said, ' Gentlemen, I reject nothing, but I must first become conversant with everything ; I cannot accept everything merely as it is read to me ! " Ah, he sighed, he had to work here harder than in London, for he had to watch for himself and his son and could not go to a Wetherell or an Eldon for advice.

Soon afterwards Falcke submitted his paper which, he claimed, " would not compromise him." The Duke saw its subtleties at once. It was a trap, he told the Duchess, but " I pretend not to have noticed it and to be such an *idiot* as not to see it, but I wrote him a very polite reply, sufficiently detailed that I do not think he can see that I am not so stupid and absurd, but I do not deny to you that *this* proves to me what a task my poor brother has, for I have astonished them by the patience that I have shown towards their verbiage "—as Falcke's report confirms—" and that I did not allow myself to say a single word that would bind me, but only that I would reflect well and not decide myself in a hurry. I have perplexed them much and they see that they cannot make ducks and drakes of me and that I have nerves and am not the person to be intimidated. They thought and I have found out the object of my being *so much pressed* to come *here* that they would persuade me to sign these papers, but no earthly power will make me."

To Falcke, he wrote a long letter explaining his grounds for refusing to sign the Family Law.

I am too honest a man ever to put my name to any paper or document unless in so doing I meant honestly and truly to act up to it. . . . I must now be the more cautious as you showed me the copy of a letter which I am stated to have written to the King in the year 1832, in which having objected to only one or two articles and having said I was satisfied with the whole, it is understood that I made no further opposition to the Staatsgrundgesetz. Permit me therefore to make this remark, that when you and Baron Ompteda read the Staatsgrundgesetz to me, my first object was to thank His Majesty for the communication that he had made to me . . . At the same time, there were still some few points which struck me at the time that I animadverted upon them. . . . You must remember that the whole you read to me on that occasion took up about from three to four hours. Now, it is hardly possible to be supposed that any man, however accustomed he may be to public affairs, could possibly understand a matter of this importance when read to him, as I may say, in full gallop as it was and in a foreign language—even now, that I have been for the last week taken up with discussing and demanding explanations from various members of the Government, I feel the greater difficulty in comprehending the whole, for I plainly see that *one* change has led to *another* and that even up to this hour, no man can exactly tell me where it is to end. Besides, I really cannot see the necessity of hurrying this " family law," as in fact it can only have reference to myself and my son, there being one clause which positively states that no member of the family shall be admitted as an appanagé unless he becomes resident in the country. Now, I should hardly believe that whenever that unfortunate event shall arrive for such a decision, that any member of the family will settle at *Hanover* and quit *England*, and therefore it can only concern myself and my son.

But, he said, his principal objection to signing it was that, " talk of it as you may choose," it always referred to the great change that he had ever deprecated, particularly the surrender of the Domains, however advantageous that might be pecuniarily.[1]   Then, to put an end to all doubt and discussion upon his attitude to this question, he issued a formal declaration in English and German that

> I can only resolve to express my assent to the Royal Family Statute under the reservation that *from this assent* a recognition of the contents of the Fundamental Law of the State above alluded to, whether in general or as far as they are quoted in the Family Statute, shall neither be deduced nor implied.[2]

From now on everyone knew what to expect from him.

Yet the Ministers still would not face the consequences of their actions ; they lived from one day to the other exactly as the Duke had written. On the 28th December, von Stralenheim reported these events to von Ompteda in London for the King. . . .[3] " It is already known in the whole country that His Royal Highness will not recognise the Staatsgrundgeſeħ," he said. " We must indeed despair that the Duke, even if the reluctant conviction of the necessity of upholding the present Constitution should force itself upon him, would permit himself to express it. Under the circumstances, it has not seemed to us advisable to drive the affair to the most extreme point at the present moment without the probability of a favourable result, especially as the experience of history shows that the political views of heirs to Thrones often undergo considerable modifications of their own accord when

---

[1] H.A.   K.G. Hann. 9 Sec. Dom. IV 48, 18th December 1835.
[2] *Ibid.*   K.G. Hann. 9 Sec. Dom. IV 48.
[3] *Ibid.*   K.G. Hann. 9 Sec. Dom. IV 48, 28th December 1835.

A characteristic command

On the margin of an official document: "For the future I must forbid the sending of paper to me which stinks so disgracefully of tobacco.—E. A."

The Duke's House at Kew

finally it comes to practising them." So they buried their heads in the sand and dismissed the principles of this now elderly man of the world as if they were the product of youthful exuberance and inexperience. With this ended their attempts to gain his acquiescence in the new order in Hanover. " The more I investigate the true state of affairs," the Duke told von Stralenheim, " the more I see the gallop continuing, and, forgive me, you must not always play into their hands,[1] for it is to me as clear as the sun that the whole thing spells *ruin*." [2]

The Duke arrived in Berlin on the afternoon of Christmas Eve and in the evening he and the Duchess went to the Prince of Prussia's Palace where the Christmas presents were being distributed.[3] Poor Prince George had to stay at home, but his turn for enjoyment came on Boxing Day with a visit to the Opera. On the 27th the Duke was seized with shivering and had to go to bed with a fever.[4] But a week later, on the 3rd January 1836, we find him writing,[5] " Alas, alas ! To my despair I must alas go to *London*. I am inconsolable. I had flattered myself that I could postpone my departure until March, so that I could still be here for Ike's birthday, but unhappily yesterday I received such pressing letters from London. . . ." His followers were in trouble again.

So the Duke set out upon another of his long wintry journeys.[6] " What a horrible day ! " he wrote. " I did my best to control myself, seeing you so sad and discomposed, but when I had passed out of the court of our house I could no longer restrain my tears, and I prayed fervently to dear God to have mercy and that I might be able to rejoin you soon, for it is too cruel to be thus separated from wife and child. At least, you can be sure that my heart belongs to you *alone* and that you are always present before my eyes and in my heart."

The journey was terrible. Past Cassel they ran into a snow blizzard. Three times they had to be dug out and in places the drifts were six feet deep. Travelling by way of Cologne, Coblenz and Brussels, they eventually arrived in Calais and there the S.S. *Ferret* was waiting. The tide was for a long time unfavourable, but the next day the captain suddenly appeared during dinner to

---

[1] The Liberals, Radicals and Revolutionaries.
[2] The account of the visit to Hanover, where not otherwise noticed, is from G.A. To Duchess, 28th November–20th December 1835.
[3] In Germany this takes place on Christmas Eve.
[4] S.A. Duchess to Grand Duke of Meckleburg-Strelitz, 29th November 1835.
[5] *Ibid*. Duke to Grand Duke.
[6] The account of the journey is from G.A. To Duchess, 17th–26th January 1836.

say that the wind was changing and they must be aboard at eleven. It was not until four, however, that they passed over the bar. It was an excellent crossing as far as the Nore, but there, at eleven, they ran into fog so thick that they had to drop anchor until seven o'clock in the evening. " I have seen many frightful things," the Duke wrote afterwards,[1] " but must own a fog at sea is the worst, for when once in it one runs the risk either of being run down oneself or running others down." They dined aboard, then the captain announced that the fog was clearing, and as soon as the moon rose they proceeded. At ten o'clock that night they landed at Gravesend. The Duke and Jelf took a hack-chaise and arrived home at one in the morning (of the 26th January 1836) " after a most tiresome, painful and tolerably dangerous journey, having risked being lost both by land and sea." [1]

The political situation which the Duke found on his arrival was far from satisfactory. When he went to visit his friends and acquaintances the next day, they told him of the way in which Peel was departing from the principles which they had always understood to be those of the party. The Duke was very grieved at this, for it meant that Peel had been misusing him last year. He was determined that that should not happen again, and when Lyndhurst told him that his arrival was " hailed by all " and that " now they talked of Peelites and *Cumberlandites*, and that he had no hesitation in saying that in the Lords, if noses were told, the *latter* had the majority," he replied that " This was highly flattering, but that I wanted but one united party and that this was my primary object, but that I never would nor could allow myself to be led as I was last year, or allow any man to tell the Lords that we were to follow blindly as slaves the orders of a man who chose to allow his temper and his vanity to get the better of his reason, and that I must demand a full explanation as to what line of conduct was to be pursued and not allow us to be told the moment one thing and then again because Sir Robert Peel changed his views, we were instantly to change our line." [2]

The Duke's policy was quite different from that of former years. Then he had counselled patience until the time came when the party would be called to power again through the course of events. The King's ill-judged actions at the end of 1834 had altered that. Now, the Duke was convinced that they had to make a continuous attack upon the Government, for " every hour

[1] M.A. To Duke of Brunswick.
[2] G.A. To Duchess, 26th January 1836.

the present people remain in office, every hour affairs will worsen." [1]
Others felt this, but Peel, despite promises that he would go on
to the offensive at the first moment, was not taking such an energetic
line. He was again on bad terms with Wellington, who also advo-
cated a more active policy.[2] The situation in the party was thus
thoroughly unsatisfactory.

All the Peers, however, were anxious to know the line which
they were to follow, and Wynford and Kenyon suggested to the
Duke that if no one else would do so, he should himself call a
meeting to settle one. The Duke felt that he could not do this
without first waiting to hear Wellington's plans, otherwise it
would seem as if there were a schism, " which it is our duty and
my most ardent desire to prevent." [3] But Wellington, he heard,
was so angry with Peel that he had left town saying that he would
not set foot in the Club or the House until June.[3] Shortly afterwards he learned that a reconciliation had taken place,[4] but the
two men no longer communicated to him what went on and he
could only know from hearsay. He certainly did not know of the
terms in which they were writing to each other about him.[5] After

[1] G.A. To Duchess, 30th January 1836.
[2] Londonderry told the Duke that Wellington had said, " All I can say is that if
Sir Robert wants to speak to me he knows were he can find me and *all* I have to say
to him can be said in one half hour."—G.A. To Duchess, 30th January 1836.
[3] G.A. To Duchess, 11th February 1836.
[4] At Lord Chesterfield's. Londonderry reported this to the Duke.—G.A. To
Duchess, 12th February 1836.
[5] Wellington wrote to Peel on the 11th February 1836 :—

There is no person who feels more than I do the inconvenience of the Duke of
Cumberland. I feel it every day. I feel it every day, and all day. Others feel it
only occasionally. But I can't see a remedy. His whole business is to pass the
time. His amusement is mischief, preparing for it, hearing about each other, and
talking of it afterwards. But I never could discover that he felt any real interest
in any question, or entertained any serious opinion. As long as we are engaged
in measures which have for their object only to prevent the Government from doing
mischief, I don't see what harm the Duke of Cumberland and those whom he affects
to lead can do, excepting annoy me and the few persons who must keep him in
order. If a Government, or any other combination, were to be formed to direct
a course of proceeding in which the Duke of Cumberland should think proper to
interfere, it might be necessary to cease all communication with him. But till
this time comes, I am convinced that, however inconvenient to me personally, it
is best to bear him, and to have his support."—Parker's *Peel*.
This letter is very difficult to explain. In July Strangford told the Duke of Cumberland
that Wellington had said to him, " Well, by God, my only hope [on a particular occasion]
was the Duke of Cumberland. He knows better than me to manage men, and no one
but him could have effected this. . . . How the devil he manages I cannot explain
to myself, but where there is difficulty, and God knows we have had several very ticklish
points, when before meetings I have despaired, he always somehow or other hits the
nail upon the head and manages to say more in a few words, and those so concise and
clear that they bring all right."—G.A. To Duchess, 10th July 1836. This is, it is true,
a second-hand account, but the Duke's descriptions of conversations, where they can

all the Duke of Cumberland's efforts and sacrifices of last year, on the very day that, out of consideration for Wellington, he had declined to preside over a meeting of the discontented Peers, Wellington was writing to Peel the most violent invective against him. It is certainly very difficult to find one's way about the kaleidoscopic personal intrigues of politics and refreshing to find in the Duke of Cumberland at least one man of whose sentiments one can never be in doubt. Peel and Wellington must have been finding him a thorn in their side with his insistence upon combat and action. He would willingly leave the direction of the main attack in Peel's hands, he said, but that did not mean that they should be idle ; they should have daily attacks and always have a full attendance.[1]

At a dinner at the Carlton on the 24th February Peel told the gathering, " He rejoiced to see the harmony which existed in the party, that he felt certain that the line he was adopting was the wisest, not to try to turn them out, but merely to watch and stop any of their mischievous plans." Then suspicions began to creep into the Duke's mind. " It is sad that a leader has such an idea, but unpardonable and impolitic to say it," he wrote,[2] " and I swear to you that I do not know when I have passed an unhappier and uneasier day, as I begin to fear that there is some truth in it that *Peel* will ally himself with a part of the present Cabinet, by which he will ruin himself and lose his character. . . . God grant that I am mistaken, but I swear that I was so overwhelmed by this that I do not know what I should believe."

The Duke was in despair, " for with the suspicions which I have of a sort of tacit understanding [3] between Peel and members of the present Government, we are betrayed and sold." When one thought over Peel's course of action since leaving office, he said, there was cause for suspicion as to the fidelity of the leader. It was not a case of a mediocre man bungling ; all the troops were there with powder and fuse waiting for orders to march, when he had thrown cold water over everything, as the Duke put it.

---

be checked with others of the same, are astonishingly accurate and in some cases almost literal. He was a great admirer of Wellington and could have had no idea that he was writing such a letter to Peel. On the other hand, he often complained of his sulkiness and moods. " Wellington is so stubborn that when he has once taken something into his head, he will never retract nor let himself admit that he is wrong. This is like a *spoilt child*."—G.A. To Duchess, 5th June 1836. It would seem that Wellington wrote the above letters in such a mood.

[1] G.A. To Duchess, 11th February 1836.
[2] *Ibid.* To Duchess, 25th February 1836.   [3] *Sous-entendue.*

Wetherell agreed that " to tell us *sixty* Members of the two Houses of Parliament, all staunch and determined men, that we are to do nothing, that we are to expect nothing, not to turn out these rascals who are daily pulling down the Monarchy by every overt and clandestine act—why, sir, it is a perfect farce to tell me that Sir Robert is an honest man. I deny it. Depend upon it, he is, if not directly, at least, trying to get into a parley with them, to enter into negotiations of some sort." A proof of Peel's guilty conscience, said the Duke, was that in the month that he had been in town, Peel had not honoured him by leaving his card, though all the other Members of both Houses had done so—" And to whom is he more indebted than to *me*, who worked so hard for him and his Government ? " [1]

Wellington's silence and lack of communication was also incomprehensible to the Duke. " No one feels more deeply or more thoroughly the mischief, the difficulties that this throws on us," he told Lyndhurst,[2] " and *I* must feel this doubly, as you know that I am connected with men of strong feelings and passions, and they are driving me to call a meeting at my house to deliberate upon what is best to be done on the present occasion. Flatly to refuse would be to lose my hold over them. I temporise and say that the Duke will of himself see the absolute necessity of coming up and at least showing himself."

But the bitterest experience for the Duke was a sudden attack which was made upon his personal character to discredit him and raise suspicions of personal ambition and high treason against him. Russell and other Whigs had for some time been contemplating a move against him on account of his leadership of the Orange lodges, but they could never surmount the difficulty caused by the fact that so far as the Duke had anything to do with them, they were scrupulously law-abiding.[3] As he told them himself,[4] " I must beg to call the serious attention of all my brother Orangemen to the necessity of avoiding all transgression of the law, for to do otherwise would be to put arms into our enemies' hands. Remember, we are to support and maintain the laws of the country and not to infringe them." It remained for the Radical, Joseph Hume, to " unearth " an Orange plot to pass over the Princess Victoria and put their Grand Master on the Throne upon the

---

[1] G.A. To Duchess, 24th February 1836.
[2] *Ibid.* To Duchess, 4th March 1836.
[3] See the correspondence between Russell and Melbourne upon this.
[4] *The Answer of H.R.H. the Duke of Cumberland to the Address of the Grand Orange Lodge of Longford,* from Berlin, 12th August 1835.

death of the present Sovereign.¹ To facilitate this *coup d'état*, he said, they had formed lodges in the army and navy, a proceeding expressly forbidden by the Commander-in-Chief. He drew the attention of Parliament to the existence of the lodges on the 8th February 1836, and again on the 23rd. As recently as the previous Thursday, he said, the Duke of Cumberland had presided at a lodge in Portman Square and he also cited his reply to the Longford men of last year. He was still a Field-Marshal, he said, and regarded by the Orangemen as successor to the Throne—" The Duke of Cumberland, he thought, was a dangerous man, whose connection with such a society required to be carefully and closely watched." The House of Commons passed a resolution condemning Orange lodges and it was made known that the King would consent to their suppression.

The feelings of the Duke of Cumberland can well be imagined. That *he*, the champion of Legitimism, should be accused of conspiring against the Throne was one of the bitterest blows which he had ever felt. He rose to defend himself in the Lords on 7th March. " It is idle for me to tell you," he said, " that I have been, for the last six months, abused, accused and treated in the most cruel manner that ever a human being was treated—nay, if what has been said of me were true, instead of standing here in my place as I now am, a member of Your Lordships' House, I ought to be at that bar for the crime of high treason." He would be mad if the charges were true. " . . . My Lords, ever since I have had the honour of a seat in this House, I have been the firmest, strongest and most determined supporter of all Legitimate Government." He would shed his last drop of blood for his niece should she succeed, he said; these slanderers were not champions but plotters against the Monarchy.² The King had consented to his becoming Grand Master in 1827,³ and if now he disapproved he would give up the situation. He himself had expressly forbidden the formation of lodges in the army.

¹ Hume had produced a letter purporting to be from a Colonel Fairman to the Duke, which seemed to lend colour to his charges. " This famous letter that Hume pretends to have found, *mark* well, it is without *name or address*. How, then, can he state that it was *intended* for me ? I never had any connection with that man, never received him at my house, never was in company with him in the whole course of my life, except when he brought me as secretary warrants to sign, or at the great meetings."—G.A. To Duchess, 6th March 1836.
² It was not so much from the Catholic as from the Radical side that this attack was coming, which had little connection with either the religious or the Irish questions.
³ Upon the death of the Duke of York.

Upon Lord John Russell's sending to him notification of the resolution condemning the Orange lodges (on the 26th February),[1] he replied, " Before I had received Your Lordship's communication, I had already taken steps, in conjunction with several official and distinguished members of the Loyal Orange Lodge in Ireland, to recommend its immediate dissolution in conformity with the loyal principles of that institution. I have only to add, I shall take immediate steps to dissolve the loyal Orange institution in Great Britain." [2] He wrote to the Irish lodges that they should not appear to give conditional loyalty ; loyalty to the King was their first principle.[3]

To his wife he poured out his true feelings. " I cannot describe to you," he wrote,[4] " how my heart boils with rage at all these attacks of Hume and company which I have to suffer, but that Peel and company who personally owe *so much* to me could have permitted people to talk like that, to publish these falsehoods, these atrocities against me and so many respectable men without saying a single word in our defence, I swear to you that I am so indignant and outraged that I am not certain that after my explanation to-morrow, I will not go and place myself on the cross-benches and declare myself aloof from them."

The possibility of either his or Peel's leaving the party now crossed his mind. " I am so disgusted with all that is taking place," he told his wife,[5] " that I would give anything to be able to quit the field of battle, for the moment that honour and principle are sacrificed for expediency, there is nothing more sacred in the world." He said openly, " I am no party man ; it is not men I oppose, but measures,[6] and if those with whom I am acting fly

---

[1] The Duke of Cumberland had called a meeting of the Imperial Grand Lodge at Lord Kenyon's house on the 1st September 1835, which resolved to condemn Lodges in the army and grant no warrants for them, and the minutes of this meeting were published. On another occasion, the Duke rebutted a charge in Parliament that he had established a Lodge in Trinity College, Dublin. That bearing the name, he said, had no association with the College, but had only taken it from its geographical locality.

[2] G.A.

[3] *Ibid.* To Duchess, 25th February 1836.

[4] *Ibid.* To Duchess, 6th March 1836. That Peel and Wellington did not eye these attacks on the Duke entirely with disapproval is shown by the above-mentioned letter of the latter, when he continues, " I am inclined to think that the Radicals in the House of Commons will make a serious attack upon him and his foolish Orangeism, which is probably, however, though inconvenient to others, the best thing that could happen to him."

[5] *Ibid.* To Duchess, 1st April 1836.

[6] *Ibid.* To Duchess, 11th March 1836. Peel, on the other hand, once wrote, " No one can feel more strongly than I do the absurdity of the doctrine that because a certain course was taken one session, it must necessarily be taken the next, with reference to the same measure."—Parker's *Peel*, II, p. 199.

from those sacred principles I maintain, I will be the first to leave them."

"My meaning is plain and distinct," he told Lyndhurst,[1] "that I cannot and will not go on thus temporising, giving up one point after another, sacrificing principles to your new-fashioned ideas and favourite expression of expediency." Lyndhurst agreed, but protested that he had talked of voting against them. "Yes," the Duke replied, "if you go on following the Radical line Peel is taking, I look upon it as not only ruining the country . . . we are endangering our honour and character and you cannot expect me to be a party or lend my hand to that." "Why, if you do that, the party is split!" exclaimed Lyndhurst. "I cannot help that, but if we are to amalgamate ourselves with Melbourne and company we dishonour ourselves and I will out and fly and return as soon as I can to my wife and family. I have sacrificed enough and I cannot in my conscience nor can it be expected that I should dishonour myself." Lyndhurst expressed his horror at such a prospect, which would mean the retirement of the Lords. "Well, then, My Lord," the Duke told him, "if this is correct what you say, follow my principles and we may still save something; be firm on the Municipal Bill."[2] The Duke agreed to attend further meetings, "but mind, I shall certainly make a bargain that we are to be staunch to our colours and not allow ourselves to have all our efforts foiled and overturned by waverers."

On the 15th March the Opposition moved for papers on the Government's education policy in Ireland, which, the Duke claimed, was riddled with deceit and duplicity to the detriment of the Protestants. Melbourne refused, and when he gave the House assurances upon this, "the waverer Harrowby" said that he would trust to the Government's honour and not press the matter to a division. Never was the chance of giving a "complete thrashing" so thrown away, said the Duke; the numbers were there, the cause brilliant. "Disgusted with all this, I rose and left the Chamber, my heart full of bile and rage," and he played four rubbers of whist with Arthur Stanhope in an effort to distract himself.[3]

"I swear to you, it is pitiable," wrote the Duke to his wife. "One great struggle would give us the day, but by this shuffling game we are lost." Peel, as usual, communicated with no one

[1] G.A. To Duchess, 12th March 1836.
[2] The Irish Municipal Reform Bill. Though carrying out the principles of its English precedent, its implications were different, for it would have resulted in a shift of the power from the Protestants to the Catholics in most of the municipalities.
[3] G.A. To Duchess, 15th March 1836.

and there was such an outcry against him in the Carlton that the Duke no longer went there.[1] " To me, the thing is clear," he said.[1] " *He* temporises and wishes to try to form a new party of *Tories* who approach more the moderate Whigs, and who are not the supporters of the Church, what we call the High Churchmen, who are inconvenient to him, that is to say, the Rutlands, Beauforts, Newcastles, Lonsdales, Winchelsea, Hertford, the old staunch Tories, who wish to do all to maintain the Church and the ancient laws of the country." If that succeeded, the Duke intended to lose no time in returning to Berlin, for, he said, he could not compromise his honour.[2]

As the session proceeded, the Duke's suspicions of Peel lost some of their violence—he even complimented him upon one or two of his speeches [3]—but his enthusiasm for the struggle was gone. He thought now that Peel was possibly more incapable than treacherous. " It is very sad," he said,[4] " but the truth is that Peel, by his indecision, his lack of communication with the different Members, has so disgusted them that they are no longer to be held in order. Holmes has worked for four days like a coalheaver to do what he can. I do not know what to think of it, for the proud follies which we have committed and all the wet blankets thrown upon our endeavours make my blood rise, and for me it is most essential to gulp all that, to keep the rest steady and right. . . . A little energy now followed by an attack could decide the thing, but God knows what Peel will do. I will try to search his brains, but he is the closest and most inaccessible person whom I have ever met in the whole course of my life. My angel, how I languish for your letters. I am in such a painful state, with an uneasiness and an anxiety to get away that I cannot possibly describe. A ship, a ship, my Kingdom for a ship ! " And, at last, this bitter and humiliating session drew to its close. The Duke could not wait to leave and Holmes went to Mr. Burrows, at the Admiralty, to inquire when a ship would be available. Through him he learned that the *Firebrand* would be able to take him direct to Hamburg.

The Duke took farewell of the King at Windsor on the 7th August and " opened his eyes to the position." The King was very grateful for all that he told him and as he was about to leave he pressed him to accompany himself and the Queen to Virginia

---

[1] G.A. To Duchess, 29th March 1836.

[2] *Ibid.* To Duchess, 28th March 1836.

[3] For example, on the 21st April (in rebutting attacks upon foreign Sovereigns) and the 4th June 1836.

[4] G.A. To Duchess, 1st and 4th July 1836.

E.A.—9*

Water. They went on the water in boats. The weather was beautiful, the King was in his best mood and " it was delightful." The Duke stayed until half-past eleven and arrived back at Kew at between one and two in the morning.[1]

On the 8th August he boarded H.M.S. *Firebrand* before midnight and slept soundly until she sailed at seven the next morning, after a delay caused by fog. Though the wind was unfavourable, the crossing was not difficult and at five o'clock on the morning of the 10th the ship, sailing north of the Frisian coast some four miles out to sea, lay opposite the island of Norderney. This was the resort for sea-bathing which had been recommended to Prince George, and as he was now there, the Duke decided to pay him a surprise visit. He was rowed to the beach and spent the afternoon there. He then continued his journey to Berlin,[2] where he resumed his old way of life and attended the usual parades and manœuvres. Towards the end of this year he paid another visit to Hanover. He arrived in the afternoon of the 27th December. A guard of Grenadiers was mounted at the Fürstenhof, and crowds in front of the railings cried " Long live the Duke ! " The Duke visited his brother and afterwards went with his sister-in-law to see the last act of the *Marriage of Figaro*. He found his nephew and niece, George and Augusta, very much grown, and the little Mary [3] asked who were the strangers. The atmosphere was different now. By some intuition, everyone had the feeling that this was probably the Duke of Cumberland's last visit to Hanover as such. Von Stralenheim frankly confided to him his condemnation of what the Government had been doing, but the Duke replied that what he wanted was deeds, not words. The Minister then invited him to dinner—" *C'est entre nous une vraie sacrifice que je fais, car c'est diablement mauvaise que sa cuisine,*" the Duke observed to his wife. There was a grand ball at Court, where the Duke led the polonaise with his sister-in-law. He noticed the difference in the manner in which he was treated and reported it to his wife. " Everyone is attentive. I do not know their motives [*leur* Daher] but I see that even the Ministers feel quite differently towards *me* and they think to themselves, ' He may be our King one day.' I do not know if they like me, but at least they respect me or know that I have sufficient spirit that they cannot make me swallow all that they have proposed *yesterday*."

---

[1] G.A. To Duchess, 7th August 1836.
[2] The account of the journey is from G.A. To Duchess, 9th and 11th August 1836.
[3] The mother of Her late Majesty Queen Mary.

New Year's Eve, or St. Sylvester's Night as it is called in Germany, arrived and there was a grand ball at the Duke of Cambridge's. As the clock struck midnight, the company congratulated one another, but the Duke prayed " God send sight to our son in the year 1837 ! " After more balls and dinners and a hunt at Ahlden, he left on the 6th for Derneburg, where he visited Münster. He chose that day for his departure, it is said, as the Chambers of the illegal constitution assembled then and he lost no opportunity of demonstrating his disapproval.[1]

Politics did not call the Duke of Cumberland so early in 1837 as they had done the previous year. His great rôle in the party had ceased and he was disillusioned. The ever-increasing universal awareness of the imminence of a change limited his freedom of action and he was concerning himself more and more with Hanoverian affairs. But he still had his duty to do ; he was still a Peer and a Conservative. On the 11th March 1837 he set out on " the most horrible journey " which he had undertaken. The roads were piled high with snow and in one place the four horses became firmly locked in it through the stupidity of one of the postillions. The Duke visited his brother in Hanover and the Dutch Royal Family in The Hague. At Rotterdam he boarded the packet-boat *Batavia*. It was bitterly cold and there was a thick fog from five in the morning until two in the afternoon, but the ship was luxurious, and dinner, which the Duke took not with the passengers but with the officers, was superb. The vessel was so delayed that instead of arriving at the Tower at noon, it was ten o'clock at night before he disembarked there.[2]

But the Duke was no sooner in England discussing politics with his old friends and embroiled in the continuing struggle against the Irish Tithes Bill, than the German affairs of his House suddenly thrust themselves upon him again in an unexpected way. It has been seen how the Duke of Cumberland had condemned what he and most others rightly or wrongly considered the mad acts of his cousin of the reigning line of his family, the Duke Charles of Brunswick, which had culminated in his sending a challenge to the King (George IV) through a horse-dealer. The Duke of Cumberland had exerted himself to obtain a recognition from the Sovereigns of his cousin's incapacity to rule, with the result that he was succeeded by his brother, the Duke William.

---

[1] The account of the Duke's visit to Hanover is from G.A. to Duchess, 27th December 1836–5th January 1837.
[2] The account of the journey is from G.A. To Duchess, 12th–19th April 1837.

It seemed then that a very delicate and combustible affair had been settled and all was peace again.

On the 5th May 1837 the King's Hanoverian Minister in London, von Ompteda, came to the Duke of Cumberland. He talked for three hours and " you know how prolix he is, and how difficult it is to understand him. However, I listened to him with Job's patience " and found that it was proposed that should the two Brunswick brothers marry, the children of the younger, the Reigning Duke, should have the right of right of succession. As an Agnate, if the Duke of Cumberland withheld his consent, the alteration could not be put into effect, for this was a matter of persons and the position now was so different from that of a couple of years before that he could not be ignored. He refused categorically to associate himself in any way with the proposed arrangement. He had the greatest respect for his cousin William, he said, and the greatest detestation for Charles. " Still, as an *honest man*, I never can allow myself to concur in what I consider would be an act of gross injustice and violation of those principles for which I have ever stood out and for which my character is universally known." It would, he said, be punishing an innocent child for the sins of its father. But, countered von Ompteda, William being the Reigning Duke, his elder brother was considered dead politically and constitutionally. This, of course, the Duke dismissed as absurd. Duke William was reigning only on account of the incapacity of his brother, and if von Ompteda's contention were correct, why was any new provision necessary ? " I reject with *horror* and can never soil my name or character in consenting to it." [1]

When he had returned to Kew, on the 7th May, the Duke drew up a letter to the Minister, dictating it to Jelf in the presence of Wetherell, who assured him that the words in it could not be construed as offensive to the King.[2] After declaring his positive refusal to the proposed arrangement, he wrote :

I am convinced day by day of the necessity of carefully and scrupulously upholding all questions of Legitimate Succession, and I must recall to your mind a circumstance, of an expression which fell from you to me last year, which has made a deep impression on my mind, and in doing this, do not think, I beg you, that I mean anything in the slightest degree offensive to yourself, though I do not deny to you that at the time my feelings were deeply wounded. I mean, when you

[1] G.A.   To Duchess, 5th, and to Duke of Cambridge, 21st May 1837.
[2] *Ibid.*   To Duchess, 19th May 1837.

stated to me that on account of the unfortunate situation in which my son is placed at this moment (from loss of sight), but which under the blessing of God we may soon have the happiness of seeing him relieved from, that objections might possibly be made to his succeeding to the Crown of Hanover. What was my reply to you then? That I had not the slightest anxiety on that point, for that I felt certain, that the first person who would stand up and fight for his right would be the Duke of Cambridge himself. With this staring me in the face, or even the bare possibility of the thing, should I not myself be authorising a doubt upon that point if I could sanction the proposal made with reference to the children of Duke William?

Again, I must be particularly cautious in all my proceedings, as you will remember that (however incredible it may appear), I was accused last year most calumniously of having got myself placed at the head of the Orangemen of Great Britain and Ireland for the purpose of altering the Dynasty of England, and in the event of my brother's demise, seizing the Throne of Great Britain. What was my public reply in the House of Lords to this insane and wicked insinuation? That I had been and should ever be the strongest and firmest upholder of the Legitimate Succession, and that so far from allowing a single hair of Princess Victoria's head to be touched, I would sacrifice the last drop of my blood in her defence and the maintenance of her unquestionable rights.[1]

The King, the Duke heard, was very grieved and angry at his action when von Ompteda read out his letter to him; he particularly resented his use of the word "unjust." The Duke said that he would then delete it, but he would not alter the spirit or meaning of his refusal. No doubt the King was annoyed when he realised what he had done. "What gives me even more *pain*," wrote the Duke,[2] "is that in this whole transaction the poor King has been led by the nose by the Ministers." He was convinced that had he studied the case himself and not merely heard from von Ompteda, he would have felt differently about it. "I can only look at it as a question of conscience and am deeply sorry to have to say that it seems to me that Ompteda looks at it as nothing but a political question, in a word, as a matter of expediency. . . . The King, according to what Ompteda says, is very *indignant* that I have refused to sign, but believe me, *this* is not *his* doing, for he is too just to wish to do what is unjust, but I cannot say as much of Ompteda and I fear that certainly *he* seeing that I am too astute and too clear-sighted not to discover the *rottenness* of his plan, which is in fact an act of expediency and that my *refusal* stops the whole business into which they have inveigled the King, Ompteda sees he has gone *too far* and my heady adherence to principle checkmates

[1] G.A.   [2] *Ibid.* To Duchess, 19th May 1837.

them. Between us, it is a base intrigue." [1] He was waiting for the Minister to send him more documents on the case, when a letter arrived at breakfast on the 22nd May from his sister Mary who was at Windsor, with the news that the King was unwell, having recently suffered from oppression of the chest during the night. He decided to go straight to Windsor, but his brother seemed to have recovered, though at his age there was always cause for anxiety, so he returned. [2]

For the Duke life went on quietly. He was at Kew, where he walked round the garden after breakfast through the lilacs, which, he said, were as thick as a forest and filled the whole garden with their scent. One day he mounted his horse and rode over to visit the local Poorhouse, which he had not seen since the new Poor Law Act had been passed in 1834. He did not announce himself in advance and so he saw everything in its true state. There were 198 inmates, men, women and children, and the Duke considered that the governors and master were to be complimented on the excellent management of the establishment. He was detained some time since they wished to show him every corner ; he sampled their food, which he found excellent—he could have taken a whole dish of the soup, he said—and he asked all of them if they were happy, which they said they were. [3]

Two days later, on the 7th June, the Duke met Melbourne riding in the Park and asked him what news he had. " *Very bad*," he replied ; " the King has had a bad night and Hudson has come up express to fetch Halford and Chambers directly." [4] The next day Wellington approached him in the House of Lords.

" I want to speak to you," he said. " Have you made your arrangements to be off, for your situation will be greatly changed and I should think that your presence will be highly necessary in Hanover in a very short time." The great change which would certainly shortly take place in his circumstances was brought home to the Duke, and he said that he would like to discuss everything that evening after a meeting of Peers at Apsley House. He had decided that " the moment that I have taken my oath of obedience to the new Queen, *which* is most *advisable* and *wise* on my part, and taken my oaths in the House of Lords as *Peer* of Great Britain, I shall start instantly for *Hanover*. This is my present *plan, for* I must

[1] G.A. To Duchess, 16th and 20th May 1837.
[2] *Ibid.* To Duchess, 23rd May 1837.
[3] *Ibid.* To Duchess, 5th June 1837.
[4] *Ibid.* To Duchess 7th June 1837.

secure my rights here and take *all* the necessary formalities here, and then proceed to Hanover to my fate and from there try to get *four* weeks at Carlsbad,[1] *if it is in my power*, but all this has fallen upon me like a bomb on my head. I must be prepared for anything."

That evening the Duke of Wellington told him, " You are in a very delicate position, first, if His Majesty dies, you are instantly King of Hanover. But you have also a great stake here for yourself and your son and this is what I must call your attention to." The Duke said that he would take the oaths " to prove that I was a British subject and thus take my lawful rights and not allow them to be questioned or a false interpretation put upon my absence." Eldon agreed that he must do this and gave precedents. The Duke said that he would do it, " for I have to prove in the clearest and most distinct manner *my* determination of upholding and acknowledging the Queen's lawful and undeniable right to the Throne." If he were in the country and did not take the oaths, it would look as if he had abandoned his position there, and in this Wellington agreed.[2] The King's condition was becoming more serious, and on the 12th June, Melbourne told Greville (the Clerk to the Privy Council) to begin making arrangements for the Accession Council. There were two points to be decided : whether the Duchess of Kent should accompany her daughter and whether the Duke of Cumberland could attend, since he would then be King of Hanover.[3] Of course, there was no question as to the latter's right, but this showed how necessary was the Duke's care and caution.

The next day the Duke was dining with Eldon and Wetherell at the former's when he learned that the Queen wished to see him at Windsor. He arrived at ten and was met by Lord Howe.[4] When the Queen entered the room she told him that the King had said to her, " Tell him if he can wait I will see him by and by but I am *still* too weak." After a while, the Duke was called. He was shocked as he beheld his brother, gasping for breath and hardly able to speak, so that he had to put his ear close to him to understand him. On the 17th the Duke again hurried to Windsor. He was greeted by George Fitzclarence with the news that his father was not expected to live long. In the passage the Duke encountered Howe, then the Queen came out of her husband's room and said that he had no strength and Davis had little hope

---

[1] For the Duchess's annual cure. They had planned this before his departure for England.   [2] All these discussions are from G.A. To Duchess, 7th June 1837.
[3] *Greville*, III, pp. 409–410.   [4] The Queen's Chamberlain.

for him.   She brought him a last request that a cousin, Prince Gustav of Hohenlohe-Langenburg, should be awarded the Guelphic Order.   The Duke then returned to Kew and arranged to meet Halford on Kew Bridge for tidings as he returned the next day.[1]

Early the following morning (the 18th) the Duke received a message from Wellington, " Tell the Duke that my advice to him as one of his truest friends is, as soon as the fatal event comes to take the oaths and then instantly be off to Hanover ; tell him *I* will take the greatest possible care of his *interests* and *his honour* and that I will lay down my life sooner than *any one of his rights* or those of his son should be in any way impaired." [2]   He filled in the time pacing in his garden and in the alley beside his house until Halford arrived.   The conversation which he had with him was not heartening and when letters followed from Windsor with still more discouraging news he decided to proceed there at once.   He took a coach and arrived there at about noon, on the 19th.   Everyone was in despair.   " He knows you are here," the Queen told him of her husband, " and says he will see you presently, but *now* he cannot " ;   he wished to be left in peace, but he would speak to his brother in the morning if he survived the night.   The Duke therefore slept in the Castle.[2]   At five o'clock in the morning, on the 20th June, he was awakened by Lord Howe with a note from the Queen informing him that the King had breathed his last.[3] The Duke of Cumberland had become King of Hanover.

His first reactions, however, were grief at the loss of his brother and anxiety to fulfil his duties as an Englishman and demonstrate his loyalty to the Queen, his niece.   Early in the morning he drove alone to St. James's and after a discussion with Lord Lyndhurst, who called upon him immediately, he went to Kensington Palace for the Accession Council.   Nearly ninety Councillors were seated round a long table in the Red Salon, and the Lord President, Lord Lansdowne, informed them of the King's death and the Queen's accession.   The Archbishop of Canterbury, the two Royal Dukes (of Cumberland and Sussex), Lord Melbourne and the Lord Chancellor then went into the adjacent room, where their young Sovereign received them.   They returned, the folding-doors were thrown open and the two Dukes advanced to conduct the Queen to her place.   When she had read her speech and signed the oath for the security of the Church of Scotland, the Privy

---

[1] G.A.   To Duchess, 17th June 1837.
[2] *Ibid.*   To Duchess, 18th June 1837.
[3] *Ibid.*   To Duchess, 20th June 1837.

Councillors were sworn in, commencing with the two Royal Dukes. " As these two old men, her uncles, knelt before her, swearing allegiance and kissing her hand," wrote Greville, who recorded the oaths, " I saw her blush up to the eyes, as if she felt the contrast between their civil and their natural relations, and this was the only sign of emotion which she evinced." [1]   On his way back through Green Park and outside his apartments at St. James's, hostile groups had assembled to hoot and hiss the new King of Hanover, but, of course, that no more worried him as King than as Duke.   In the evening he went to Gloucester House to dine with his sister and the next day he drove to Windsor to take leave of the calm but weeping Queen Adelaide and the remains of his brother, since he would not be present at the funeral.   His indignation was roused, however, when he found that the coffin had already been sealed down.[2]

On his return from Windsor he found Londonderry in his library with an article from the *Morning Chronicle* upon the subject of his Peerage, and he also received a message from Buckingham, " for God's sake not to *lose* a moment's time in taking my seat." The King had returned late in the afternoon and, when he went with Londonderry to the House, it was already up and so they had to wait until the morrow.   In the meantime they discussed the matter with Eldon, Lyndhurst, Wynford, Wetherell and Buckingham.   Lyndhurst told him that the Lord Chancellor [3] had announced that if the King of Hanover presented himself to take the oaths, he would refuse to accept them, but all the legal experts agreed that there was no doubt that the King's rights as Duke of Cumberland were quite unaffected by his succession and the records were searched for a precedent.

At two o'clock the King went to take his seat.   When he heard that the Whigs intended to contest his right, " this made me *determine* to do it, fully resolved to fight it *out* myself in that case in the House, which I should have done and, to tell you the truth, I should have liked, for it would have afforded me an opportunity of *speaking*, and we should have had a warm and probably— [illegible] debate, and I had *all* the best authorities and speakers to fight with me, and, as they said, for their *Leader*.   But when I came down accompanied by Londonderry and Lyndhurst, and when I went to the *Table* and demanded to be *sworn*, Mr. Birch,

---

[1] The account of the Council is from *Greville*, III, pp. 415, 416, and the Queen's own description in *The Girlhood of Queen Victoria.*
[2] G.A.   To Duchess, 21st June 1837.   [3] Lord Cottenham.

the Chief Clerk, gave me the Bible and the formula of the Oath and I believe I never took it or spoke it more *clearly* and more *distinctly*, and then signed it, so that now it *stands* recorded in the *Rolls* of Parliament and at my death George has no further difficulties in proving *his right* to demand his writ. There were many of the *public* in the gallery, which was very good. Then I went to Kensington to take leave of the little Queen, who was very friendly, and I embraced her tenderly and said, ' My dear, you may depend upon me on *all* occasions in support of your rights and I will stand by you in all danger.' " [1]   After calling upon the Duchess of Kent, the Duchess of Gloucester, Princess Augusta and Lord Eldon, the King left to enjoy Kew for the last time. He rose at six the next morning to see the hay-cutting which had been in progress two days and at midday he received an address from the villagers expressing their regret at his having to leave them. [2]

He then went into town and received many visitors, including von Ompteda, now as *his* Minister; all the intrigues which were such lively and important affairs a month before had now faded away. The next day, Saturday, the 24th June 1837, at four o'clock in the afternoon, he left in his private carriage for Woolwich, where, without any ceremony, he embarked in H.M. Steamship *Comet* and set sail for his Kingdom.

" My angel," he wrote to his wife, [3] " I cannot say or express to you all that passes within me, for to think that in effect I *bid adieu* to my native country is a hard and cruel feeling, the more so *at my age* ; all the weight and responsibility which now lie on my shoulders give me much to think and reflect upon, and I pray to the Almighty every day to guide me, to lead me, in my new career, so that I can be of some service—*all* this disheartens me, *mais que faire* ! ! "

---

[1] The account of the events of this day is from G.A. To Duchess, 23rd June 1837.
[2] See *The Times*.   [3] G.A. To Duchess, 23rd June 1837.

CHAPTER XVIII

ACCESSION

"I AM commencing a new epoch of my life, one of the most difficult moments of my life, and I pray to the Almighty every morning that He may have the grace to guide me with His Holy Spirit, that I may be able to conduct myself in such a way as to gain the hearts and serve the good of my subjects—and that is, God knows, my most ardent wish." [1] These were the thoughts of the King of Hanover as the steamer ploughed through rough and stormy seas and he made his way to the land over which he was to reign.

He might well have felt some trepidation. He had been accustomed all his life to opposing or urging other men to action, and now for the first time power and responsibility were his own. He had the opportunity of putting those ideals into practice for which he had been mocked as an old-fashioned diehard or denounced as a blackguard, and most Englishmen confidently expected to see him back again within a few months, dethroned and exiled. This supreme test was being imposed upon him at an age when most men thought only of quiet and a peaceful evening to their lives, and added to all these discouragements were the hazards of uncertainty. Since his youth Ernest Augustus had been deliberately kept at arm's length from his future realm and its affairs. " I know neither the things nor even the men here," he wrote.[2] " I am as if I had fallen from Nowhere, and as I had not my own means here for learning of what went on, I am arriving here as an *ignoramus*." He resolved therefore, before embarking upon any definite course of action in politics, to give himself time in which to study all the circumstances of his new Kingdom.

It is a remarkable fact that though Hanover was so closely bound to Great Britain for one and a quarter centuries, very little has been made known about it, and this may be a suitable point at which to describe its state upon Ernest Augustus's accession.

[1] G.A. To Queen, 29th June 1837.
[2] S.A. To Grand Duke of Mecklenburg-Strelitz, 7th July 1837.

Hanover was one of the constituent states of the German Confederation which had been established at the Congress of Vienna as a successor to the Holy Roman Empire dissolved in 1806. Austria, Prussia, the other Kingdoms and Principalities and the Free Cities were members and all of them sent delegates to the Diet at Frankfurt. In effect, the principal concerns of the Confederation were the defence of its territories against attack from outside, for which each member-state furnished a specified contingent, the settlement of relations between member-states and the maintenance of peace within the federal frontiers. It was not otherwise empowered to interfere in the internal affairs of member-states. In case of disobedience to an act of the Diet, a member-state was liable to suffer a federal execution, that is, the forcible putting into effect of its decisions.

The Kingdom of Hanover [1] had grown out of the ancient Guelphic Duchies of Lüneburg, Calenberg and Grubenhagen, which together formed a long north-to-south oblong from the Elbe to the frontiers of Hesse. Lüneburg, the most northerly, was a vast sparsely-populated heath, and its bleakness was accentuated by the scattered juniper bushes and the stone blocks and slabs which marked the graves and places of worship of its early inhabitants. The city of Hanover lay in the centre of the very fertile and intensely cultivated plain of Calenberg, enclosed on the west by a range of low wooded hills, the Deister, and a large lake, the Steinhuder Meer. In the extreme south and west rose the rolling pine-covered Harz Mountains, the home of ancient Nordic legend, where the witches gathered on Walpurgis Night. Now silver and almost every other mineral were mined and smelted in the mountain villages.

To these ancient lands George I had acquired in addition the Duchy of Bremen [2] from the Swedes in 1719, and East Frisia, Osnabrück and Hildesheim had been added as a result of the Napoleonic wars. East Frisia—flat, treeless, desolate and boggy, and secured from the sea by dykes—was geographically an extension of Holland eastwards. This newly-acquired coastline with the port of Emden in addition to the old Electoral port of Stade, gave Hanover alone in Germany an extensive maritime interest and this was furthered by her connection with England. Osnabrück and Hildesheim were ancient ecclesiastical territories secularised in

[1] The Electorate of Hanover had been raised to the rank of Kingdom in 1814, after the powers had decided not to restore the Holy Roman Empire.
[2] The Duchy of Bremen is not to be confused with the independent city of Bremen.

the Napoleonic era.   The former had, in fact, long formed part
of the Guelphic dominions, for a Prince of the House had held
the See as titular Bishop alternately with a Catholic Prelate.[1]

The Kingdom was one of the most prosperous states in Germany. Its people had more than their wants and even imported
large quantities of colonial wares and luxuries.   The Industrial
Revolution had passed it by and distress and discontent were
unknown.   Only in the last decade had a party of innovation
sprung up in the Kingdom, and then not on a popular basis but
originating in the circles of lawyers and professors. This minority
is always honoured with the appellation " public opinion," but in
this case it was evident that the people as a whole had no interest
in its innovations, for the publication of the journals of the proceedings of the constituted Chambers had had to cease simply
because no one had bought them.[2]

King Ernest Augustus was determined to win back all that had
been lost through violence and illegality under his predecessor.
Right and justice were to be re-established as the foundation of
power in the realm in the place of party intrigue and blackmail,
and nothing was more abhorrent to him than the abstract but
omnipotent modern " State " where no one could be held to
account for its actions.   According to his theory, people should
not face an impersonal machine but a monarch of flesh and blood,
who felt the same emotions as they did.   From this conception of
kingship, Ernest Augustus developed his ideal of becoming
Landesvater, or Father of his People, secure in their trust and
affection.   We will see how he set about the task of realising it.

His sentiments had long been known to the Hanoverians and
they were eager for the end of the corrupt and inefficient régime
or Schlendrianocratie [3] under which they had been suffering
during the last decade. After 123 years Hanover would once again
become a Royal residence, society would come to life and everyone
would derive employment and prosperity from the glittering Court
which it was certain the new King would establish.   All along the
route from the frontier to the capital, preparations were being
made to celebrate his progress in a manner expressive of the
universal joy.

At noon on the 26th June 1837 the King landed in Rotterdam,
giddy after a very disagreeable nocturnal crossing, and, after a

---

[1] The last Bishop of Osnabrück, when the Bishopric was secularised in 1803, was
the King's elder brother, the Duke of York.

[2] *Rosendahl*, p.774.   [3] Bungling bureaucracy.

conversation with the King of Holland in a hotel there, he set out in his coach for Hanover.[1] The next day he crossed its borders at Nordhorn,[2] near Bentheim. Before a triumphal arch the Mayor, the clergy and the whole population of some 1400 souls were gathered to welcome him as he set foot upon the soil of his Kingdom. He did not tarry, but drove on to Lingen, where he arrived at eight o'clock in the evening. At the canal bridge on the city boundary, the Municipal Corporation welcomed him and in the city itself a battalion was drawn up for his inspection. He only stayed an hour, however—so that he could take light refresh-ment and a short walk—then, to the cheers of the citizens, he resumed his journey. Throughout the night he drove eastwards and arrived at six o'clock in the morning at Osnabrück. Again he only stopped to acknowledge the official welcome and drink some coffee, then he left on the final stage of his journey to Hanover. Count von Kielmannsegg, the Master of the Horse, joined him in his coach, and so they entered Hanover together as in 1813.

The triumphal progress continued throughout the day. In every wayside village the whole population was assembled in the street and every cottage festively decorated. All along the route triumphal arches had been erected and the procession had to stop repeatedly to receive loyal addresses, poems and garlands. In the capital, tension had risen to a climax—there had been a false alarm the day before—the streets were full, all windows along the route to be taken by the King were occupied and the most prominent citizens in their most splendid clothes and mounting their finest saddlery were riding out to greet him. To reach the city before nightfall, the King took a short cut across his neighbours, Schaum-burg-Lippe and Westphalia, and re-entered his Kingdom at Wennigsen, where the provincial officials were gathered to receive him, then the procession made its way along the road, now thickly-lined without interruption by peasants and inhabitants from all the neighbouring villages. The escort of Garde du Corps was left behind and the King proceeded accompanied only by the citizens who had ridden out from Hanover. Through semaphore signals his approach was announced to the city, and, late in the afternoon of the 28th June, the officers posted on the top of the Waterloo Column could see the procession approaching past the Benther

---

[1] G.A. To Queen, 26th June 1837 ; F.O. 35/205, Sir Edward Disbrowe's report.
[2] The account of the King's journey to Hanover is from G.A. To Queen, 29th June 1837, the Hannoverſche Zeitung and *Von Malortie*, pp. 40-41.

Hill through their telescopes and gave the signal to the troops assembled on the Square below.[1]

From the high bastion planted with chestnut trees the batteries boomed out in salute and the crowds burst into frantic cheering as the King's carriage with its escort of mounted citizens drew up at the entrance to the Calenbergstrasse. There a great arch had been erected and Stadtdireftor [2] Rumann, at the head of the City Council, presented to him the keys of the City on a silk cushion. So accustomed to persecution by mobs, the King was overwhelmed by his reception and thanked his subjects. " You know my love for this land and this city, where I spent my youth," he said simply. " It has pleased Providence to call me to the Throne of my fathers. I will be for the Hanoverians a just and gracious King." These few spontaneous words, in the King's own style of German, had a magical effect and the crowds broke into deafening applause. As the procession passed down the Calenbergstrasse the tall over-hanging houses were full of cheering spectators and dense crowds were held back by the troops lining the narrow thoroughfare.

The King alighted at the Fürstenhof where, as Duke of Cumberland, he had always resided on his visits to the city. The Duke of Cambridge and his son were waiting to receive him and, in full view of the crowd behind the railings, the two brothers fell into each other's arms.[3] Together they went up to the King's rooms and both showed the greatest tact, for if this was a joyous day for the King, his brother could not but be sad at taking farewell of the life which he had led for so many years. The King therefore ordered that he should continue in the enjoyment of all former privileges and facilities until his departure. The Ministers and officers of the Household were assembled in the salon and " I said something amiable to each of them," the King reported.[4] As he appeared at the window, the crowds filling the narrow street below and the square at the side of the house greeted him with wild cheering, and it was more than an hour before the streets in the neighbourhood were passable again. The Cambridges returned to their palace, Montbrillant, and the King followed them to dinner, remaining much longer than he had intended as the little Princess Mary begged him to stay. He returned home through the streets of the city, which were illuminated

---

[1] The account of the King's entry into Hanover is from *Von Malortie*, pp. 41-42 ; *Von Hassell*, and *Hartmann*, p. 77.

[2] The Stadtdireftor was not merely an honorary official but one with the executive functions of an English town clerk.

[3] *Von Malortie*, p. 41.   [4] G.A. To Queen, 29th June 1837.

everywhere in his honour [1] and $\mathfrak{Freiherr}$ von Schele [2] was waiting for him. The ceremonies were over and the great task of his life had begun.

No time was to be lost. At the beginning of the year von Schele had posed the question as to whether the King held himself to be bound by the illegal Constitution or not and, he had said, it was one which had to be decided then. The King had never wavered in his determination and so it was now a question not of the end but of the means.

The principal difficulty, von Schele pointed out, was an external one. The Act of Confederation in 1815 had declared that all constitutions " in recognised effectiveness " were under the protection of the Confederation and could only be altered or modified by constitutional means. He therefore urged the King not to base his objections upon moral grounds but upon juristic argument. It was important to uphold the federal power, he said, for any weakening would allow France to indulge in her old pastime of fishing in troubled German waters, but there was a great danger that the protagonists of the 1833 Constitution might endeavour to intimidate the King into its recognition through the other states in which they had the whip-hand. They would have no case if the Constitution could be proved to be illegal in the terms of the 1815 Act, and this was simple enough, for the Constitution in " recognised effectiveness " in 1833 had not been altered by the means required by that Act—the mutual agreement of the King and the Chambers then existing. Instead of this, a new assembly had been called, differing from the old in many points, some of them suggested from the side of the King, others from the side of the Chambers, and this assembly had passed the new law. " This new assembly," said von Schele, " had no authority for its existence than precisely this new law upon which it rested. It was not competent either to accept it or to reject it. . . . The requisite agreement between the ruler and the Chambers could obviously only take place with the Estates in recognised effectiveness, that is to say, those elected under the Constitution of 1819. These should therefore have been summoned once more and the new law laid before them for their acceptance." The logic of this was so simple that no doubts could be entertained of the illegality of the 1833

---

[1] It is thus not true that the King did not trouble to see the illuminations, as Frensdorff writes.

[2] Von Schele's arguments are from his memorandum to the Duke of Cumberland, 8th January 1836, printed in *Von Hassell.*

Constitution according to the terms of the Act of Confederation. Once decided, von Schele concluded, the King must act with decision and frankness so that no seeds of suspicion of his good faith could be sown among his subjects.

The King was in full agreement with these views and so he wrote to his wife, in Berlin, the next day, " I have had a long conversation with Schele until *one* o'clock in the morning and, as a result, I have given the order to M. de Schulte to adjourn the Estates to-day. This is to prevent all caballing and to give me time in which to reflect well and think well about what it is advisable to do, and to make myself conversant *with everything*. You can be assured that I will not act in haste and will conduct myself with great caution in all that I do. At ten o'clock I will sign the paper." These were the King's favourite maxims—decision, but detailed study and mature reflection. Already their practice was imposing a great strain upon him, and when von Schulte, the Minister whom he had summoned, came to ask for his instructions, the King had been doing so much work that, he said, " I know not if I stand on my head or my feet." He handed him his signed commission and with that the die was cast.[1]

The Chambers were serenely unaware of what was before them. Everyone knew, of course, that the King, as Duke of Cumberland, had lost no opportunity of protesting against the illegal Constitution and had reserved to himself the right to act as he might deem necessary should he ever succeed to the Throne. But it did not occur to anyone that he would actually *dare* to take such a bold step at a time when other monarchs were on the defensive and the examples of the Duke of Brunswick and the Elector of Hesse-Cassel were still fresh in men's minds. So, as the Chambers were finishing debating some outstanding business on the criminal law, von Schulte arrived and handed to the President of the Upper House the King's message adjourning them indefinitely. It was read out and, with a " God Save the King ! " the members left ; then it passed to the Second Chamber, where Rumann, the Stadt= direftor, was President. He, in turn, read it out and asked for observations. Only one member, Stüve, made any comment. He did not believe that the King had begun to reign yet, he said, as he had not yet taken the oath to the Constitution—which was, of course, begging the question of the latter's validity. The Chamber then dissolved. The quickness and resolution of the old King had taken it completely by surprise. Now the resistance to him would

[1] G.A. To Queen, 29th June 1837.

have no rallying-point or platform and, above all, he had time for thought.

The same day the King summoned each of the Cabinet Ministers —von Stralenheim, Count von Alten (for War), von Schulte and von der Wisch—for a separate audience. He explained that what he needed was time to make himself conversant with conditions in the Kingdom and a man of sound and tested principles who could advise him and in whom he could have confidence; he would therefore appoint von Schele to the leadership of the Government as Minister of State. Following this, he called von Schele to his room and swore him in. The King's first day in his capital had certainly been an eventful one. [1]

The next day the army swore allegiance to its new Sovereign. The King received the officers of the garrison in the Palace and throughout the following weeks he was receiving deputations from all over the Kingdom, one after the other. Despite his weariness there was neither rest nor exercise. He was, he told the Queen, as tired as a child. In London at least he knew " the way of things from top to bottom and the people with whom I had to deal, and as the language was more familiar, I did not have to be on my guard with every word that I uttered." [2] Every day he dined with the Cambridges. His brother was quite lost in wonderment at his strength and resolution which contrasted so much with his own display. It was a fine beginning, he said, to have prorogued the Estates without consulting the Ministers and that would show them that he had a will of his own.[2] One evening the whole family drove out to the rococo Palace and Gardens of Herrenhausen. The King was awed as he stood upon the ground trodden by his ancestors. " It is *noble*," he wrote afterwards,[2] " and one realises the antiquity of our House. I could see Madame, the Electress Sophie, in those beautiful garments walking there with her Ladies-in-Waiting and Chamberlains in perruques, and to see the sentry of to-day—you know what passes within me at such moments."

After church on the morning of the 3rd July he drafted the text of his accession proclamation with von Schele and on the 5th it was completed. " To-day," he wrote,[3] " I will sign my public declaration and I hope that everyone will be satisfied with it. *Cela* naturellement est a very ticklish thing et qui m'a donné beaucoup à faire." As he wished, it was firm and unambiguous. In it he

---

[1] G.A. To Queen, 3 p.m., 29th July 1837.
[2] G.A. To Queen, 1st July 1837.   [3] G.A. To Queen, 5th July 1837.

announced his determination to act only for the good of his subjects, but he found no guarantee for this in the 1833 Constitution ;
he was bound by it neither morally nor legally, but it was far from
his intention to decide without due examination and reflection.
He would therefore, he said, consider whether it was desirable to
modify the present Constitution or to return to that previously
in force. To his wife, the King described the proclamation
as " right mild and cautious—it promises nothing and refuses
nothing. What is good I will retain ; what is shameful I will
reject." [1]

Von Schele read the contents of the proclamation to the other
Ministers, who were ordered to listen with great attention. When
he discussed it with them the next day (the 6th) he found them
somewhat nervous at taking such a bold step. Could not the
King merely make alterations and modifications ? they asked.
But von Schele had already seen the danger of doing anything
which might imply recognition of the Constitution at the outset
and the King would not hear of it. " I do not find it in accordance with my dignity to let my true opinions be a matter of doubt,"
he declared,[2] " and so the completed patent stays." As all the
Ministers were more or less compromised, von Schele counter-
signed it.[3] The King had, of course, foreseen the timidity of the
Ministers—which was one of the reasons for von Schele's appointment.[4] He knew that they desired nothing so much as the abolition
of the Constitution, which they agreed they had found an impossible
one, but " they did not see how they could *rid themselves* of it and
go back from that which they had the stupidity to propose." [5]
The King, therefore, had to inspire courage without undermining
their self-confidence, a task which called for much tact and delicacy.
He was not angry with them for carrying out the wishes of their
late master, he said ; that was their duty, but now *he* was their
Sovereign and they must act in *his* sense ; they were his Ministers
and not those of the Chambers.[5] At the same time he assured
them, " I will not be precipitate in anything. All that I demand
is to see all and hear all and only then, when I have considered
everything most thoroughly, will I be able to come to a decision." [4]
The King knew men—" What a good fortune it is," he wrote
after haranguing his Ministers, " to have had such rough company

---

[1] G.A.   To Queen, 7th July 1837.
[2] *Von Hassell*, quoting *Von Treitschke*, IV, p. 752.
[3] G.A.   To Queen, 5th July 1837.   [4] *Ibid.*   To Queen, 30th June 1837.
[5] *Ibid.*   To Queen, 3rd July 1837.

in Parliament. That has given me an acquaintance into things of this sort and an insight into the character of men." [1] But, he also wrote,[2] " I regard myself by no means as infallible. On the contrary, very much so (*bien bien de cela*), and that is why I like to hear opinions given frankly from every quarter, then I reflect well on all that has been said to me, and it is not until after very seriously considering all the *pros* and *cons* that I *decide* and take sides, but then my decision remains firm." His success in winning the confidence of the Ministers was shown when von Alten came to him to say that he had intended to resign upon his accession but had now resolved to remain.[3]

The King's proclamation was well received and the people were impressed by his frankness and sincerity. As to the astonished politicians, they could say or do nothing in their stupefaction ; it would require a little time for them to recover their spirits and open a campaign of opposition. This is a point of some significance, for the people generally manifested no great excitement at the King's adjournment of the Chambers and his declaration. On the contrary, they displayed a marked indifference towards politics and " their " new democracy. It was no storm of rage and indignation that arose as soon as the King's intentions were published. Only after a time did the burrowing and scheming of certain persons and cliques begin to make themselves felt.[4]

Far more interesting was the change which was coming over the city now that it was once again a Royal residence. After the late King's funeral on the 7th July, Court functions began, and on the 14th the Queen and the Crown Prince arrived from Berlin, where the Duke of Cumberland's establishment, much to the regret of the tradespeople of the city,[5] was now dissolved. The King had ridden out to the frontier at Schladen early in the morning to meet them. An arch had been erected and crowds were gathered where the Queen set foot on Hanoverian soil, and she was moved to tears by the speech of welcome of the local notary, who recalled that her sister, Queen Louise, had passed by this same spot in 1806. The King and Queen spent the night as guests of Count

---

[1] G.A. To Queen, 3rd July 1837.
[2] S.A. To Grand Duke, 19th April 1838.
[3] G.A. To Queen, 2nd July 1837.
[4] See *Rosendahl*, p. 785, where he demonstrates the fallacy and self-contradiction of von Treitschke upon this subject.
[5] Enemies of the King spread the story that he had left large debts in Berlin. As von Malortie, who had charge of the movement of the Court, testifies, not a penny was owing. It is regrettable that Pollard perpetuates this legend in the *Cambridge Modern History*, X, p. 379.

Münster at Derneburg and then drove to Hanover, fêted in all the wayside villages and towns. As they approached the capital, the King left the carriage and rode on horseback before it. Early in the afternoon the brilliant procession, with its escort of Garde du Corps, entered the city to the thunder of cannon, the pealing of bells and the cheers of the crowds, and proceeded up the long avenue of limes leading to the Palace at Herrenhausen. The King dismounted under the balcony of the portico and escorted his wife up the stairs to the hall above where the Ministers, the Diplomatic Corps, the Household and the Corps of Officers were assembled. In the evening the whole city was illuminated.[1] A few days later the Queen made her first public appearance when her husband persuaded her to accompany him to the Schützenfest, the great annual fair centring round the marksmanship competitions of the Schützen.[2] The crowds—ten thousand persons—had not known that they were to honour it with their presence and as soon as they learnt that their King and Queen were among them they lost no time in demonstrating their loyalty.

But beneath the jubilating populace there was a stratum of jealous and embittered malcontents. By varied means that group, dominated by ambitious lawyers, had succeeded in taking the government of the country into its hands and tasting for four years the pleasures of power and the flattering sensation of importance. Now those days were over and back in the towns and villages the prospect opened before them of a return to pettifogging and the old unrewarding way of life. " The feeling of offended vanity that they—the great heroes of Liberty—had been so unceremoni- ously sent home now mounted to an immeasurable bitterness." [3] At their desks they brooded upon means of revenge and thought out how they might humiliate this defiant old man. As they arrived from Hanover they began spreading sedition and sowing fear and distrust of what he might do next. Soon they were travelling throughout the states of Germany relating the fearful misdeeds of their new Sovereign. Articles were written in foreign newspapers and sympathisers in other national assemblies demanded that their governments should intervene to restore them to power.

---

[1] The account of the Queen's journey is principally from the Hannoverſche Zeitung.

[2] In the Middle Ages the citizens of each street in a German city were allotted a section of the wall to defend in case of emergency. These thus formed Marksman Companies, or Schützengeſellſchaften, and have survived to the present day as clubs with many and various traditions. Once a year they hold competitions between each other and these are the occasion for a vast fair and carnival.

[3] *Von Hassell*, p. 372.

The King was aware of the dangers inherent in this situation and fully weighed the consequences of each step which he took. To gain expert advice on the legal aspects he appointed a commission of five recognised jurists from various parts of the Kingdom. Like the Ministers, they hesitated to follow von Schele's bold plans and recommended to the King that he should modify the existing Constitution. It was not a question of law and justice, they felt, but one of practicability. That the old King, supported only by von Schele, could leave the struggle upon which he proposed to embark victorious seemed to them out of the question.[1] It now remained for the King to hear the opinions of the rest of Germany, which, in effect, meant Austria and Prussia. His success depended upon their support and so his journey to Carlsbad was particularly opportune.

The minerals of this cosmopolitan Bohemian spa had been highly recommended to the Queen by her doctors, and the King had planned to take her there in July before he left for England. When the Crown Prince had gone to Norderney for his regular course of sea-bathing, the King set out with his wife for Carlsbad. That it was not merely a cure or holiday that he had in mind was shown by the fact that von Schele's second son accompanied them. Immediately after his arrival the King received Metternich and the Prussian Ambassador in Vienna, von Maltzan, in audience. Both of them were astonished at his sobriety and moderation. " He does not even go as far as he could," the Imperial Chancellor told the Ambassador. The King explained to them that although he did not regard the new Constitution of Hanover as in any way binding upon him, he would proceed very cautiously and base his objections upon purely juristic grounds. Metternich urged him to do nothing that might oblige the Diet to take notice of Hanoverian affairs and hoped that in this way his endeavours might be rewarded with success. A conference was then held under the Chancellor's presidency at his neighbouring castle of Königswarth between the Austrian President of the Diet, Count von Münch-Bellinghausen, von Maltzan, the young von Schele and the Hanoverian Ambassador to Vienna, von Bodenhausen, and it was agreed that Austria and Prussia would support the King of Hanover as far as the laws of the Confederation would permit, while he, in his turn, assured them of his intention to do nothing in conflict with those laws. The front was sealed and Ernest Augustus, now that he felt sure of his ground,

[1] *Von Hassell*, pp. 371–72.

did not hesitate in his resolution to carry out von Schele's recommendations in their entirety.[1]

The King had no time for any political steps immediately upon his return to Hanover as the University of Göttingen was celebrating its centenary and he particularly wished to be present at the ceremonies. In all the towns on the way from the capital to the city, he was received with the usual triumphal arches, bells, artillery-salutes and speeches, and on the 17th September he made his ceremonial entry through the Weender Gate in the walls. With the usual ceremonies, the keys of the city were presented to him, and as he returned them he thought of the other jubilee which he had celebrated there fifty years before. " I passed three years of my early youth in this city," he said, addressing the crowds, " and I could never forget all the proofs of attachment shown to me at that time. I trust in this same loyalty now. My sole object is to do my utmost to make all my subjects happy and contented, but I cannot cause miracles. I am mortal as everyone else, and all that I can promise is that I will do everything to prove to you that my intentions really are what I am saying to you now."

After a service in St. John's Church he watched the unveiling of the monument to his brother and predecessor, William IV, from a window of the university building; then he dined in the Aula and visited the only survivor of his own instructors, Blumenbach, now a very aged man. After a few days in his nearby hunting-lodge of Rotenkirchen and some days hunting with his neighbour and kinsman, the Duke of Brunswick, he returned to Hanover on the 19th September.[2]

The King's visit to Göttingen has given rise to a number of legends. Von Hassell asserts that he was in a conciliatory mood towards the Estates after his return from Carlsbad, but that the provocations which he suffered during this visit decided him not to compromise. There had been much ostentatious praise of William IV for his supposedly liberal views; a doctorate had been conferred upon one of the leaders of the Opposition, Stüve, and petitions had been presented on behalf of revolutionaries in confinement for offences in 1831. Von Treitschke writes that as the veil fell from the statue of William IV the King turned his back.

---

[1] This account is from *Von Hassell*, pp. 375–80. The Queen wrote to her brother S.A. 12th August 1837) that Metternich agreed, " not only with *what*, but with how." The King and Queen left Hanover on the 2nd and arrived in Carlsbad on the 5th August; they arrived in Hanover again on the 8th September 1837.

[2] Hannoverſche Zeitung; *Von Malortie*, pp. 44; *Von Hassell*, I, p. 381; G.A. To Queen, 18th September 1837.

That these were intended provocations there can be no doubt, but the King, perhaps through the novelty of the circumstances, does not seem to have appreciated them. None of his feelings are ever concealed in his letters to his wife and in his accounts of this visit there is no trace of offence. He described how he went to the Aula " and I saw the statue of William IV unveiled to the public. It is very well executed. After that . . ." [1] It would seem, then, that von Hassell's deduction is incorrect and von Treitschke misinformed, if nothing more sinister.

On his return to Hanover the King lost no time in giving effect to his decisions. On the 11th November the patent appeared enumerating the legal failings of the 1833 Constitution and declaring it null and void. Estates would be summoned under the provisions of the 1819 Constitution and proposals would be laid before them for " completely and precisely defining it." Through the grace of the Sovereign, laws enacted since 1833 would remain in force until repealed, and in the coming year there would be a reduction in taxation of 100,000 Thaler.[3] The significance of this reduction did not pass unnoticed, for during the life of the 1833 Constitution, the burdens upon the people had been continuously increasing. Finally, the King announced the principles which were to guide him throughout his reign. " Our loyal subjects can be assured that Our feelings for them are those of a father for his children," he concluded. " We have taken the irrevocable decision to amend the national Constitution so that that ancient trust between the ruler and his people, which evil-minded persons have sought to destroy during the last few years, may be maintained and strengthened."

[1] G.A. To Queen, 18th September 1837.

CHAPTER XIX

1837–38

KING ERNEST AUGUSTUS had always been convinced that the 1833 Constitution did not enjoy real popular support and he had felt no anxiety on that score when he repealed it. But he was very keen to see how his action had been received among the people and he did not entirely trust official reports or newspaper accounts to give him a true picture of the state of public feeling. He decided therefore to form his own impressions by going out into the country and mixing freely with the population wherever he went. Ostensibly he was travelling to a hunting-party in the forest of Göhrde on the Elbe when he left Hanover in mid-November 1837 with his stepson, the Prince of Solms.

His first halt was in Celle, the legal capital of the Kingdom.[1] All Hanoverian towns had preserved their mediæval character and many—Hildesheim, Goslar, Hamelin (the city of the Pied Piper) and the capital itself—were the prototypes of a city as it is depicted in pantomime and fairy-tale. Celle was one of the finest examples, with its small, overhanging, half-timbered houses and their sharply-pointed gables. An arch had been erected before the castle—the castle in which the King's aunt, the unhappy Queen Caroline of Denmark,[2] had died an exile while he was still a child—and the City Councillors and the Guilds were assembled by it. The King spoke some time with these citizens, then he and his party drove on to Medingen, a village to the north. The inhabitants were all gathered to greet him and he did not make a formal or platitudinous speech in reply. " At one time," he said, " the relations between the Prince and his people were those of a father towards his children and of children towards their father. What on this earth could be more beautiful and more bountiful than such a relationship ? " He would do all that he could for his subjects, he explained, but he

---

[1] The Supreme Court had been established in Celle in 1711 as a compensation for the loss of the city's status after the death of the last Duke.

[2] Queen Caroline, the sister of George III, had been exiled from Denmark on a charge of adultery with Count Struensee, who was beheaded. She lived in Celle and died there in May 1775. On account of mourning, Prince Ernest Augustus's birthday on 5th June was not celebrated that year.

was only a mortal of limited capabilities.[1] Similar scenes took place in Uelzen, in the middle of the vast heathland, and when the Royal party arrived at Hitzacker, in the Göhrde.

The first snow of the year had fallen, it was foggy and later rained, so that the hunt could not have afforded the King much pleasure. But that was of secondary importance to him. After-wards he went to the chief forester's house in a mule-carriage and the day ended with a torchlight procession and serenade by hornists.[1] The King was so impressed with the neighbourhood that he selected a site for a hunting-box and ordered construction to begin at once, for, he learnt to his anger, the castle of the Elector Ernest Augustus had been demolished by the Government in 1826.[2] He left on the 19th November and arrived in Lüneburg, the ancient home of his ancestors, late in the afternoon. A great reception had been prepared by the townspeople and he invited the most important to dinner in the castle, where he took up residence. " It was very merry ! " he told the Queen.[3] In the middle of the proceedings a torchlight procession passed before the castle. The King opened the window to watch it and, in the glare of the flames, the crowd could see that he was moved by their demonstration of loyalty. He ordered his carriage and drove through the narrow streets of the city with his stepson. All the people were wearing yellow and white flowers (the Hanoverian colours) in their hats and the houses were similarly decorated. The following evening five hundred burgesses were invited to a ball in his honour in the City Hall and the King opened it himself by dancing the polonaise with one of the local ladies. The next day he returned to Hanover.[1]

King Ernest Augustus was highly satisfied with his journey. The manifest loyalty of his people had exceeded his most sanguine expectations and now he had no doubt that they were firmly behind him. " I am fully convinced," he told the Queen, " that my tour is *worth millions* and I am certain that my declaration has worked wonders." [4] To his brother-in-law he wrote, " I am extremely, yes, I can say with truth, delighted with my tour, for everywhere that I have been, I have witnessed the greatest proofs of love, respect and loyalty. Peasants, you know, are not courtiers, or make pretences [*sic*], so that if they come eight to twelve miles [5]

[1] Hannoverſche Zeitung.
[2] Hannoverſche Zeitung and Von Hassell's account of the visit to the ruin.
[3] G.A. King to Queen, 20th November 1837.
[4] G.A. To Queen, 20th November 1837.
[5] Presumably English miles. A German mile is approximately four and one-half English miles.

on foot in rows, yearning only to see their King and master and
to give a cheer for him, then it is their genuine taste that moves
them. Naturally, *Messieurs les avocats, les canailleurs et les libéraux*
do not approve, but thank God my country is *free* of these abominable principles. I flatter myself that on this journey I have gained
the good opinion and the confidence of those whose confidence I
desire." [1]

When the King returned fortified from his tour the most
momentous act of his reign had already taken place—momentous,
at least, in the sense that, whatever its importance at the time,
subsequent historians have never ceased to dwell upon it. On the
14th November the Cabinet, as a routine matter and in accordance
with universal precedent and practice, had ordered all the King's
servants to renew the oaths of allegiance which they had made to
the late Sovereign. The form of the declaration was, word for
word, that used upon the accessions of George IV and William IV,
except that the oath to the latter included in addition a solemn
undertaking to subscribe to the same oath to his lawful successor.
The contents of these declarations were those usual for oaths of
allegiance everywhere and there was no mention of any controversial political or constitutional issue in them. For some reason
their exact text has never been published in subsequent histories
and so all the ensuing events have been misunderstood. Von
Hassell, for example, a historian certainly not hostile to the King,
writes, " The Royal servants had to decide whether they would
declare that the oath which they had sworn to the Constitution
some years before was invalid, or whether they should provide
their subordinates with an example of disobedience to the King."
But they had to decide nothing of the sort. By the required oath
they swore that they recognised King Ernest Augustus, in accordance with the law of primogeniture, as their sole and rightful
Sovereign and would faithfully serve him. *These obligations obtained
under the Constitution of* 1833. But, in any case, the King did not
desire insincere or unwilling servants. " I will compel no one to
serve me against his will or conscience," he wrote.[2] " I will therefore release those who find it impossible to serve me on my principles. I only wish to be served by those who act according to
my principles."

Among the civil servants from whom the oath of allegiance
was required were the professors of Göttingen, the university

[1] S.A. 24th November 1837.
[2] G.A. To King of Prussia, 10th January 1837.

founded personally by George II, of which the Sovereign was Rector.[1] But just some of these men were the figureheads of the group which had come to power in 1833. They were, in any case, so accustomed to exercising tyranny in their respective spheres that it seemed incumbent upon them now to demonstrate their power. It did not occur to them that the old King might dare to take action against them ; others trembled indeed at a stern look. And one of them was *Dahlmann*, the author of the 1833 Constitution, who could hardly have viewed the sudden depreciation of his own importance with equanimity. Obviously, he was an interested party, and now, at a stroke, he resolved to avenge himself and make the King cry *peccavi*.

He summoned six of his colleagues together and told them of his plan. Under the guise of explaining their grounds for refusing to take the oath of allegiance to the King, they would issue a public declaration. They would suggest to their fellows all over the Kingdom to do likewise and, in particular, to sabotage all acts of the Government by obstructing or boycotting any elections which it might order. Of course, had they genuinely felt that they could not conscientiously do what the King required of them, they had simply to resign, as the King had recommended, and there was an end to it. To declare publicly to their employer—were he King or commoner—that they did not recognise his authority, to accuse him of crimes and to promise that they would seek to frustrate his will and induce others to do the same, and yet to expect to remain in his pay and service was a sufficient measure of their audacity and arrogance.

It is not clear why all of these seven men considered themselves qualified to adjudicate upon this question—George Gervinus, author of the *History of German Literature* ; the brothers William and Jacob Grimm, the philologists who developed the law of the sound-shift and wrote the children's fairy-tales ; William Weber, who studied the dynamo and helped to invent the telegraph ; and Heinrich Ewald, author of the *History of the Israelite Peoples* and a Hebrew grammar. Only Dahlmann and William Albrecht, as lawyers, were in any way concerned, but, worse still, only one of the seven, Ewald, was a Hanoverian, and he eventually became a champion of the Royal House, for which he suffered imprisonment under the Prussians. (Perhaps that is why von Treitschke gratuitously excepts him from the praise which he bestows upon

---

[1] The Sovereign was always Rector of the University and the head of the academic staff was the Prorector.

the others and attributes his actions now merely to " professorial arrogance.")

The insubordination of seven men would not be an episode deserving special treatment were it not that it is their profession which has principally written history since then and so amplified their importance, while through their colleagues and connections in other parts of Germany they were in a position to cause a storm of slander and abuse which has scarcely settled.

On the 18th November the seven men sent in their solemn declaration to the Curator [1] of the University, who earnestly begged them to withdraw it. Besides losing their situations, he said, they would bring the University into politics and endanger its repute. Haughtily, Dahlmann replied that they could not display such servility. In their protest, they declared that the King's grounds for annulling the 1833 Constitution were not legally valid ; they must therefore regard themselves as still bound by it and were thus unable to take the oath to him or to participate in any elections for the revived 1819 Chambers ; it was their duty as teachers of the young to set an example in the observance of oaths. This text they handed to their students, who made copies all night and sent them all over the country and to the other states of Germany.[2]

The step which the professors had taken was indefensible on innumerable grounds, both moral and legal. In the first place, it was not genuine. If their motives had been as they pretended, they would have sent their declaration to the Government privately and then resigned ; they would not have distributed it all over the country before the Government even knew of its existence. In the second place, their conduct would be inconsistent and illogical. Did they expect the King to continue employing and paying them after this public denunciation and announcement of intended disobedience ? Their objections to taking the oath were obviously unsound. Only the King had required them to swear observance of the 1833 Constitution. He could require this no longer, for it is quite clear that whoever binds a person to an oath or promise can release that person from it. Furthermore, if the 1833 Constitution were illegal, as it had been proved to be, the oaths taken to it were also illegal and conflicting with those already binding.

---

[1] The Curator of the University was the official appointed by the Crown for the administration and non-academic management of the University.

[2] See *Oppermann* and other opposition books which abound in accounts of the procedure adopted in formulating and distributing the manifesto.

But, of course, this whole affair of the " Göttingen Seven " was humbug. The oath which ostensibly gave occasion to it required no pronouncement whatever upon the validity of any of the disputed constitutions, nothing more than a recognition of the King's right to the Throne. Not even the professors questioned that right. It was embodied in the 1833 Constitution and by reaffirming it now they would be acting *in accordance* with that Constitution. As it was, they were *committing a breach* of it. Furthermore, they were *breaking their oaths*, for in that to William IV they had undertaken not only loyalty to him, but also that they would swear the same to his lawful successor. Under the guise of upholding the sanctity of oaths, they were breaking them, and under the guise of defending the 1833 Constitution, they were defying it.

In any case, historians have always lost sight of the moral origin of the question. There had been actual and threatened bloodshed. To this the King had yielded and his agreement in 1833 therefore bore the imprint of *duress*. That blackmailers— political or otherwise—should be able to extort a valid oath to render permanent the result of their pressure is legally and morally absurd. To-day we see all this in better perspective, for it is held that one of the cardinal principles of constitutional government is that civil servants carry out the orders of the Government without question—that Conservatives, for example, carry out measures of Socialism—and as to all this mention of oaths, it is a compliment to the times that they were taken so seriously. If they were regarded so carefully in the twentieth century, no republic could have come into existence.

The action of the seven professors thus stands condemned by both contemporary and modern standards and the consequences were only to be expected. By declaring their refusal or inability to serve the King any longer, they had, by all ordinary interpretations, vacated their positions of their own accord and not as a punishment inflicted by the King.

On the 24th November 1837 the King repaired to Roten- kirchen,[1] where his brother had built a house for hunting-parties round the tower and remains of the fortress of their thirteenth- century ancestor, the Duke of Grubenhagen. On the 28th, he was awakened as usual by the reveille sounded by the keepers on their horns, and after breakfast he was just considering whether to hunt or not when he received an urgent message from von Schele recommending the immediate institution of disciplinary proceed-

[1] Rotenkirchen lay on the road to Einbeck not far from Göttingen.

ings against the seven mutinous professors. Their object, he said, was to spread sedition and persuade others to follow their example, especially in obstructing elections ; they had compromised themselves irrevocably, for their manifesto was already as far abroad as France. " The affair seems to me to be *serious* in its object," the King wrote to his wife,[1] " but thank God of less consequence through the folly and stupidity of the provocateurs, for they have betrayed themselves in that they have compromised themselves [*sic*]. What they say of duty and *conscientious scruples* cannot be accepted ; that is what they hope to insinuate into the minds of others and even publish in every way. To me, that shows the malice of their conduct. But with reason and wisdom we can turn the affair rather to our advantage, for they can do less damage through their present behaviour than had they confined themselves to secret intrigue." To his nephew [2] he wrote, " If each of these seven gentlemen had addressed a letter to me expressing his opinion, I would have had no cause to take exception to their conduct. But to call a meeting and publish their opinions even before the Government had received their protest—that is what they have done and that I cannot allow. . . . No one respects Göttingen more than I do, having been brought up there, but I have my duty, which is, to maintain order, good spirit and sound principles in my realm." The King was in no fear of these men. He gave von Schele his instructions and did not alter his programme lest he appeared uneasy.

On the 14th December Leist drew up a rescript announcing the dismissal of the seven professors from their posts. Three of them, Dahlmann, Jacob Grimm and Gervinus, all of them non-Hanoverians who had helped to distribute the manifesto, were ordered to leave the country within three days or stand trial and face the normal legal consequences of their actions.[3] Such were the extremes of " tyranny " in those days.

The professors had been confident that they could attack their King and master with impunity. Now they were stunned by the blow and the sympathy of their fellow-agitators was a poor comfort. In all countries, institutions and journals, Liberals denounced this " atrocity." Von Treitschke tells us of a poem entitled *Anno*

---

[1] G.A.   To Queen, 28th November 1837.
[2] G.A.   To King of Prussia, 10th January 1838.
[3] The King examined each case on its own merits. " I have acted with moderation," he wrote to his nephew, " for I have made a difference between the three who have published their opinions and the four who have not, in ordering the three former to leave Göttingen and the country within three days and permitting the four latter to remain, providing that they keep the peace."—G.A.   To King of Prussia, 10th January 1838.

1937, in which an old woman relates to her little grandson the deeds of the evil King and how he dismissed seven professors and ordered three out of the country. In wide-eyed incredulity exclaims the little boy, " Such things could not possibly take place in Germany ! " No one will deny the innocence of von Treitschke and his fellow-Liberals.

The men of 1833 at last began to feel that their sun was setting. The King was clearly not going to be cowed or blackmailed. All the more the foreign press raged against him and renewed pressure was brought to bear upon the other states of Germany to intervene. The forces opposed to revolution and destruction took heart and the King's less intrepid fellow-monarchs were full of admiration for the man who had dared to do what they had never had the confidence to attempt. They did not re-engage the three ejected professors at their own institutions, nor would an employer in any walk of life select candidates with such a record. But in those days, individuals—even the opponents of governments—still had means and independence. An association was formed at Leipzig to provide an income for the three men and off this they could live the whole time. They should, indeed, have been grateful to their times that the protest of seven men, whether profesors or not, should have become a matter of such importance.

Contemporary opinion was by no means in favour of the seven professors. It was a self-assumed rôle on their part to speak in the name of learning, or even of the University of Göttingen, but historians have given no prominence to the disavowal by others just as worthy of consideration—the mathematician Gauss, for example, or Otfried Müller, the classical philologist. There was widespread indignation that at the moment when the country was beginning to feel the new vitality and prosperity brought to it by the presence of the Court and the enthusiasm of the King, these men had sought to hurl a brand into it. The Curator's fears for the University were realised. It had become notorious now as a centre of political agitation and its name appeared in every revolutionary pamphlet and placard. Its prestige diminished accordingly, and from almost a thousand students in 1837 its numbers fell to 664 by Michaelmas 1838.[1]

When the three expelled professors left for Cassel their friends and students demonstrated in sympathy, but the citizens of the town remained aloof. Throughout the last twenty years they had been terrorised by the members of the University. Any trifling

---

[1] *Von Hassell*, I, p. 494.

offence against a hooligan who belonged to it had always been followed by the breaking of windows or even the demolition of houses.[1] Now the townspeople had cause to be grateful to a King who was enforcing the law. The King was still at nearby Roten-kirchen, and on the 29th November between six and seven thousand peasants of Grubenhagen (the county round Göttingen) formed a torchlight procession to his house. He invited their leaders indoors and spoke to them personally. " I observed how delighted they were to be with their King," he wrote to the Queen,[2] " and, I am told, they say, ' Now at last we have our King.' That is good. It must be confessed, everything seems to show that the spirit of the people is *good* and that the city of Göttingen feels acutely the *folly* and infamy of these seven professors and I believe they wish to send a deputation to me from the city."

On the 30th, after dressing upon his return from the chase, the King found the Prorector and the four Deans of the Faculties of the University waiting to see him. They told him that they were charged by the University to declare its horror ($\mathfrak{Abscheu}$) of all that the seven professors had done. The King expressed himself " *très clairement et distinctement avec sagesse, prudence mais vigueur.*" The citizens of Göttingen also sent a delegation to describe the terrorism which they had suffered through the machinations of the professors in 1830 and expressed their hope that the King would not attribute to them any part in such actions and sentiments ; on the contrary, they were delighted to see an end put to that Constitution and that Chamber ; it had been a weight round their necks. Afterwards, the King received the Town Council of Einbeck and everyone sat down to dinner—" *Ainsi j'ai rendu tout le monde content.*" [3]

[1] In one case a student sheltered from the rain among the stalls of the meat market and roughly pushed aside a boy whom he fancied deliberately stood in his way. One of the stallholders indignantly asked him if he did not know that there was no right-of-way through the market. After altercations, the student had his ears boxed and was ejected. Humiliated, he ran to the students' union and the dreaded summons, " Out, boys ! " was shouted round the streets. Students swarmed to the offender's house and broke the windows in the traditional style, then entered and proceeded to ransack the house, destroy the furniture and demolish the structure before the eyes of the owner, his wife and his daughter. The work of destruction only ceased when its executors discovered that they had come to the wrong house. The mob then went to the magistrate's house and smashed the windows, for his not having punished the offender. Eventually, a squadron of Hussars had to be summoned to restore order.—*Von Hassell*.

[2] G.A. To Queen, 27th November 1837.

[3] When the official account of the University deputation's address was published, the Opposition attempted to deny that this had been said, but that it had only assured the King of its loyalty and not mentioned the professors who had been dismissed. Nothing further was known of the contents of the speech until the above, written by the King to his wife, from whom he never concealed anything, especially his feelings when he was vexed, as these excerpts will have shown.—G.A. 30th November 1837

E.A.—10*

The King emerged from the trial of strength with the Hanoverian Liberals with renewed confidence. Metternich was already becoming impatient for the next step. " But why are there still no Estates ? " he asked the Hanoverian Ambassador, von Bodenhausen. " Why such a long delay with what is so urgent ? " It was vital that there should be Estates in " recognised effectiveness " before the meeting of the Diet on the 20th January 1838.[1]

On the 11th January, therefore, the King signed a proclamation ordering elections to be held, according to the now valid Constitution of 1819. This was a necessary risk. The legal and electoral machinery of the country was still in the hands of the lawyers who were the Government's principal opponents and now they had had time in which to organise themselves. Above all, they controlled most of the electoral colleges.[2] These local bodies were not supposed to have a will of their own ; their duty was to organise the expression of opinion of the electors upon such subjects, not to express it themselves. However, many of those bodies now refused to participate in the election, or did so only with the reservation that they did not thereby disavow the Constitution of 1833. To understand what this might have meant, it must be imagined that to-day electors could not send a member because the Returning Officer belonged to the opposition and was, as would be said to-day, on strike. In any case, the suffrage (under all these constitutions equally) was restricted to a small minority, and it was these jealous little oligarchies entrenched in the seats of power which formed the principal opposition to the King ; when they spoke in the name of democracy, it was only to preserve their own power and privileges. For both these reasons, it is quite misleading when it is written in the histories that Osnabrück, Emden, Hadeln, Buxtehude and other towns refused to send delegates, and Hanover, Lüneburg, Hildesheim and others only with the reservation that they still upheld the 1833 Constitution. In this way a comparative handful of men was seeking to prevent the Electorate expressing itself and to render the elections null and ineffective. Their accomplices in the other states would then bring the matter before the Diet of the Confederation. They failed, however, and on the day fixed for the opening a quorum of forty-seven members was present.

The King appeared in person and made a short speech from the Throne. He denounced the insinuations of the Opposition.

---

[1] H.A. Hann. Des. 91 v. Schele Nr. 6. Report of von Bodenhausen, Ambassador in Vienna, 3rd January 1838.
[2] The so-called Waȟlmänner, through whom the electors chose their member.

" I have always detested arbitrary rule," he declared. " I wish only to govern my beloved people according to laws and rights." This would be proved, he said, by the proposals for a new Constitution which would be laid before them. A grand banquet for all members followed and the session had begun.

The Opposition members at once occupied the Chambers with debates as to whether they were competent to legislate or not. Some asserted that if they themselves accepted their salaries they would thereby recognise the 1819 Constitution. Eventually, a compromise was reached by which it was agreed that the case would not be prejudiced, and then the King announced that he would pay them himself as their salaries were such a burden on the people. Irritated by their manœuvres, he refused to adjourn them at Easter and granted them no more than a week's holiday. The leaders of the Opposition, Stüve, the Mayor of Osnabrück, Rumann, the Stadtdirektor of Hanover, and several advocates made use of the time for a meeting in Bremen, an enclave in Hanoverian territory, where they discussed future plans. Those to date had certainly failed miserably. Their next inspiration was to render the Chambers ineffective by absenting themselves from the debates and preventing the attendance of a quorum. If this scheme were to fail, the electoral colleges under their control—and here we see the absurd nature of the whole proceeding—would hold all unheld elections. Of course, these bodies had no right to elect or not elect as and when they chose, but by this means, the leaders of the Opposition hoped to obtain a majority which would declare its incompetence to legislate and thus oblige the Confederation to intervene. They had given up all hope of defeating the King by their own resources.[1]

For a time they did prevent the attendance of a quorum, but on the 3rd May the session was resumed. The alternative plan had therefore to be adopted. New members arrived, declared their recognition of the 1833 Constitution and left ; others embroiled the Chambers in wrangling over the question of competence. Debates became more and more heated, members quarrelled among themselves and the whole speedily degenerated into a bear-garden that proved, if other evidence were lacking, the complete absurdity of rule through such bodies and the necessity for such reforms as the King was set upon introducing. Weary of all this, he now turned once again to his people.

[1] See *Oppermann* and others for accounts of the activities of the leaders of the Opposition.

CHAPTER XX

THE KING AMONG HIS PEOPLE

IN the "constitutional" monarchies which were evolving during the nineteenth century the ruler was becoming increasingly isolated in his capital and known to the great mass of his subjects only through his cypher on the public buildings. When he appeared among them he was surrounded by a screen of rigid formality, and when he spoke it was only to utter platitudes. This was not Ernest Augustus's ideal of monarchy. His principles were patriarchal and he wished to be known personally to his whole people, to be accessible to anyone who wished to see him. He had set himself no easy task, for in these days before the era of centralisation, only a fraction of the total population ever came to the capital. He decided, therefore, to undertake a series of tours and on them he would see if the machinations of the Liberals and revolutionaries had met with any success in estranging the affections of his subjects.

The scenes of uproar in the Chambers were still at their height when the King left Hanover on the 18th June 1838. His first halt was in Celle. It was a warm day and he inspected the garrison in the courtyard of the castle. All the local personalities were invited to dinner and the day closed with a military torchlight parade. When the King continued his journey the next day the inhabitants of all the wayside villages turned out on foot " *et les paysans dans le meilleur esprit du monde,*" he wrote. He took some relaxation in the woods of the Göhrde before making his ceremonial entry into Lüneburg in the evening. This vast heathland was the stronghold of royalism and all the way to the illuminated city the route was lined by cheering crowds. The next day was a very strenuous one for the King. It began with a cavalry review and then there was a series of visits—to the Academy of the Nobility, the Grammar School, the new prison being built, the convent of Lüne and the plantation of the local agricultural superintendent. Finally, there was a reception for the civic authorities. The Mayor expressed his disgust for the agitators and told the King that the citizens had disavowed their deputy to the Chambers since he had joined the

Opposition. " I have *full confidence* in the people of Lüneburg and of the country generally," replied the King, " but unfortunately the Town Council is in the hands of the advocates and the whole world knows that they have nothing to lose and everything to hope for from trouble and eruption. But despite this, they cannot achieve much."

The King spoke as forcefully when, as he continued his journey on the morrow to Stade, he stopped to see the damage done at Winsen by a burst dyke the previous March. It had destroyed a bridge which was indispensable for the livelihood of the inhabitants and the King had personally provided the funds necessary for its replacement. The countrymen were very grateful and when they had shown him how the disaster had happened, he spoke to them in his usual style. " I do not care for words, but deeds," he said. " I wish to prove to each of you that I really mean what I say and that I have only your welfare and happiness at heart. I demonstrated this when I came to your aid in your time of need. I lay great value upon seeing things for myself and would have helped you immediately after the accident, but I was ill in bed at the time. Do not, then, believe all this nonsense (Dummes Zeug) from newspapers and evil-minded people. These people do not desire your happiness. Their only wish is to cause unrest and dissatisfaction among you. Just trust your King, who is really sincere with you, and you will be happy." The tour resembled a triumphal progress as it continued towards Harburg. " I can only pride myself on the reception which I have met everywhere," the King wrote to his wife, " friendly faces and hearty greetings which one could see came from the heart, all villages decorated with flowers and garlands, the streets packed, the windows full, and the women waving their kerchiefs."

At Harburg, the Hanoverian port on the Elbe opposite Hamburg, an envoy from the Hansa City waited upon the King to present the compliments of the Senate. The King invited him to dinner and told him of his irritation at the libels which were written about him in the Hamburg journals. He had been advised, he said, to prohibit their introduction into the Kingdom, but he had declined to do so as he did not believe that the loyalty of his subjects could be affected by such propaganda.[1] After dinner, undeterred by a thunderstorm and violent rain, the King went along the shore to see the devastation caused by the recent eruption of the North Sea. Seaweed was lodged high up in the trees and in one place there

[1] Hamburg City Archives. Cl. 1 Lit. 5 d. Nr. 5, v. 2. Report of Syndicus Sieveking.

was a precipice thirty to forty feet deep where gardens had been. "It is horrible to see where the water has been," he wrote. "The *gratitude* and feelings of the people defy description." At eight o'clock the thunder of cannon announced the King's arrival in the city of Stade, where he had first set foot in Hanover fifty-two years ago. He alighted at the residence of the Landdroſt [1] and then proceeded to the Town Hall for a civic ball. He opened the festivities by dancing the polonaise with the Mayor's wife and stayed until two in the morning. The next day (the 22nd) he made a tour of the town, visiting the barracks, the bastion and the house of the captain of one of the Elbe frigates; he also saw the Schwinge canal and went a little way into the Altes Land along the Elbe.

Everything interested him and he reported all the details of the life of his people to the Queen. "At this moment," he wrote, "I have just returned from my tour of the Altes Land, which is superb as to the richness of its fields, pastures and well-kept farms. There are about twenty thousand inhabitants in this country and the women still wear their very original ancient dress of large coiffes of stiff white linen like the bonnets of Dutch. Their dresses are of blue. The men, however, have abandoned theirs. Their houses are large. In the entrance is the stable, with the horses on one side and the cattle on the other, and the living-rooms are beyond—an excellent drawing-room with tiled chimneys in rococo."

The same day the King received a message from von Schele on the political situation in the capital. Von Hassell, in a misguided apology for King Ernest Augustus, asserts that his political "mistakes" were to be attributed to von Schele's influence, but from this episode it is clear that the King always followed his own judgment. His Minister's letter, he wrote in his entangled phraseology, "makes absolute nonsense to me. That is to say, he asks me for an order about which I had clearly explained myself in a conference lasting over two hours the day before my departure, where I put to him my reasons for determining not to dissolve the Chambers, but that if they persisted, that is to say, if the Second Chamber tried to start the discussion of the Constitution afresh, I would *never* permit it and I would prorogue them. He was of my opinion and so much so that he actually wrote the heads of the declaration which was to be published in the Act of Prorogation. Before deciding, it is necessary to reflect well and examine a question

---

[1] Hanover was divided into six Landdroſteien or provinces and the Landdroſte were the provincial governors.

from all standpoints, but once one has reflected well, one must remain firm. Now he says that it would be well to pretend to ignore what the Second Chamber does, as at least the First Chamber is not a party to it. That is no good, since, alas, the First has shown such a feebleness and fear of the Second that I cannot rely upon it. All this I told him before my departure and he was completely convinced that I was right, so I remain firm and will tell him so. The country will know of the infamy of the Second Chamber." [1]

Early the next morning the King took the road again. In each village the inhabitants were gathered before the church to greet him and every hut by the sandy wayside was decorated with festoons. At midday he arrived in the recently-founded port of Bremerhaven, where all the ships were flagged in his honour. He lunched with the local corporation in the harbour-master's house and then inspected the fortress. Afterwards he went on foot through the crowded streets as he was keen to see the architecture of the houses.

The King then left his realm to pass through the independent Hansa City of Bremen and up to a hundred of his own peasants escorted him on horseback. Though he had declined an official reception, the streets along the route were crowded with thousands of people on foot, horseback and carriage, and the whole garrison was drawn up at the entrance. When the King emerged from the gate at the other end of the city, he was " half-dead from the noise and the bustle." Back in his Kingdom the King proceeded up the Weser to Verden, where he sank exhausted into his bed at Count von der Decken's.[2] Despite the stifling heat the next day, he rode out to the military exercises, then he inspected the barracks and visited the cathedral. In the evening there was a ball. The following day was spent on the road and in the wayside villages. Just before midnight he arrived in Osnabrück.

Osnabrück was the stronghold of his political opponents and the King had therefore made a point of visiting it. On his arrival there was no sign of hostility. Before the illuminated gateway such a crowd was assembled that the King could not at first pass, and the civic authorities were waiting to present to him the keys of the city. It so happened that the Mayor was ill and the duty of officially welcoming him devolved upon his deputy. " I learned afterwards," wrote the King, " that this was the famous *Stüve*.

---

[1] G.A. To Queen, 23rd June 1838.

[2] Princess Louise of Hesse-Cassel (1794–1881), sister of the Duchess of Cambridge, had married Count von der Decken (1787–1859) in 1833 and they lived at Verden.

Nothing in the world could have been more loyal than his speech and he must have gone through suffocations of rage at having been obliged to speak in this way."

"I know that the citizens of Osnabrück are loyal and honest and cannot be deceived by phrases," the King replied. "You do not know me yet. You still have to become acquainted with me, then you will see that, by the Almighty, I speak the truth and mean everything that I say. I know well that the time will come when the Supreme Being will require from me an account of my actions. My only wish is to further the welfare of the citizens of Osnabrück and the whole country." Cheers greeted this short speech. The horses were taken from the King's carriage and it was drawn by the townspeople themselves through the densely-packed streets to the castle, where he was residing during his visit. On the morrow he set out as usual to tour the city—the cavalry barracks, some local monuments and Iburg, the castle of his ancestor and name-sake, the Bishop Ernest Augustus.[1] It was observed that he stood for some time in thought before his portrait.

That day an urgent despatch arrived from von Schele reporting that the disorder in the Chambers had reached a climax. Frightened and nervous, the President had left the chair and sat as an ordinary member, and the Vice-President, an extreme antagonist of the Government, had taken his place. The Opposition had then rejected the Government's proposals. The King was prepared for this and he immediately sent the courier back with the order to adjourn the Estates. "It's ridiculous to continue this farce," he wrote to the Queen. "As the Second Chamber became more and more insane, it was necessary to cut it short, to show them that I am serious."[2] A little while afterwards the King had occasion to see for himself the shallowness of the Opposition.

A request was brought to him to receive a deputation with a petition signed by 230 citizens for the restoration of the 1833 Constitution. "By all means," he replied, and asked the Landdroſt to be present as a witness. When the deputation entered and desired to read their petition, the King asked for the signatures, saying, "I do not doubt your statement, but, in all things, one must be correct, and as you are merchants, you know the necessity of never accepting letters of change without examining the signa-tures." "Of course," they replied, and hurried off to find the papers. "My friends," the King said to them on their return,

[1] Afterwards the Elector Ernest Augustus, father of George I.
[2] G.A. To Queen, 27th June 1838.

"I know the loyalty of the citizens of this town and you assure
me of it, but tell me, what is it in the law of 1833 that you believe
to be so necessary?" They all remained silent, so the King went
from one to the other for an answer to the question, but in vain.
"Can it be, then," he asked, "that you do not know the contents
of that Constitution?" Blushing at his folly, each member of the
deputation confessed that this was so. "Then why do you sign
something which you do not understand?" asked the King, not
angrily but more in the gentle way in which misguided children
are chided. "Do you not believe, then, that I have your good at
heart and only desire to see well-being, peace and contentment in
my land?" They were convinced of that, they replied. "Then
believe me," the King continued, "I have thoroughly thought
about the matter and see daily the necessity of doing away with
something which even the friends and authors of that Constitution
agree is incompatible with the existence of government." The
deputation agreed, and went away praising their King and his
wisdom.[1]

"I understand," reported Mr. Bligh, the British Ambassador,
"that his [the King's] reception everywhere has been very warm
and even enthusiastic."[2] But no attempt had been made to attract
the crowds and cheers. On the contrary, Bligh reported that at
Osnabrück the military and other authorities had wished to exclude
the civic bodies on account of their political behaviour and only
the temperate diplomacy of the Landdroſt had reconciled the
parties at the last moment.[2] "I went into the Den [of the Opposi-
tion]," the King wrote to an old friend in England, "and there all
was loyalty. It was easy to perceive that they had no concern
whatever with the magistrates[3] of the Corporation. They were,
if possible, more loud in their marks of loyalty than any other, and
gave most festive proofs from the expense they put themselves to,
uncalled for and even objected to by me."[4] Mr. Bligh, a typical
Englishman—always a Liberal where other countries are concerned—shook his head dubiously. "The reception which the
King will have met with during his progress through the country,"
he reported,[2] "will, it is to be feared, be construed into approbation
of his measures . . . and the disinclination of His Majesty to yield
any point will be confirmed . . . which will in all probability
sooner or later lead to some untoward results."

[1] G.A. To Queen, 27th June 1838.   [2] F.O. 34/27, 28th June 1838.
[3] Magiſtrat does not mean "magistracy" but the municipal corporation.
[4] To the Rev. D. C. Delafosse, 17th July 1838, van Thal, p. 294.

On the 28th the King left Osnabrück for Aurich. On the way he visited Lingen, exactly a year after his arrival there upon his accession. At all towns on the route he inquired of the population and its sources of food and posed all manner of other questions to which he demanded most detailed answers. Progress was slow, partly owing to the extreme sandiness of the roads and partly because the King had constantly to alter his itinerary to pass through villages where the inhabitants desired to receive him. In many cases they had erected triumphal arches and decorated all the houses in only three or four hours. At one village, he was almost suffocated by the crowds, and at another the thirteen-year-old schoolgirl who presented to him a bouquet asked if she and her playmates might accompany him as far as the next town. The King, who delighted in children, readily assented and spoke to them all the time.

Dog-tired after a day of the usual festivities in Aurich, the capital of East Frisia, the King arrived on the 30th in the North Sea port of Emden. This was the last visit of the tour, for the King returned thence direct to the capital, but it was marked by an event which no one in England in 1829 would have credited— his visit to the Catholic church there.

King Ernest Augustus had good reason to be satisfied. Despite the bitter stormings of the advocates, democrats and other revolutionaries against him, nowhere had he encountered a sign of hostility. He had never gone in a closed carriage in the middle of a great escort, but always among his subjects on foot in the streets and often so much pressed by the crowds that he was almost stifled. His speeches, too, had not been empty prepared formalities ; everywhere he had expressed himself most decidedly on the very lively political issues and everywhere he had succeeded in winning support, even from former opponents.[1]

The King's enemies became alarmed at the lack of sympathy which they found among the people and the almost feverish enthusiasm which was shown whenever he appeared. Their rôle had been that of leaders, champions and protectors of the people— now they saw that the people did not want them. Bitterly writes their historian, in all the rage of a frustrated democrat, " At the same time, one began to stir up the more insignificant and less-educated citizens in the towns against the councillors and mayors." [2]

[1] The account of the King's tour is from G.A. To Queen, 18th, 21st, 22nd, 23rd, 25th, 27th and 28th June 1838 ; the Hannoverſche Zeitung ; *Von Malortie,* pp. 61–66.
[2] *Oppermann,* I, p. 175.

Law-abiding citizens were, in fact, becoming indignant at the self-assumed rôles of the few men above who held important " strategic " positions and utilised them for personal politics. These men had spoken and written " in the name of " the cities in which they held office without reference to the citizens themselves. But now the citizens began to act for themselves. Those of Hildesheim, for example, signed a declaration—" We hereby solemnly declare that we have neither approved nor given our consent in any other manner to the petition for the maintenance of the Constitution of the year 1833 sent to the Illustrious Diet of the Confederation by a section of the Mayors, Councillors and Returning Officers,[1] and that this has taken place without our knowledge and against our will, and emanates from them alone." The citizens of Hanover followed this example and addressed a petition (18th January 1839) to the Councillors that they should express their loyalty to His Majesty and take steps to regain his goodwill. Münden, Osnabrück and other cities followed with similar declarations. The Opposition could not explain them away—Oppermann can only hint that he " knew how the signatures were obtained."

" His Majesty and those who are most in his confidence," reported the British Ambassador,[2] " argue from this [3] and similar incidents that the inhabitants of the towns are either indifferent or are favourable to his measures, and that they are made the tools of needy lawyers who gain by political agitation or of the corporations, in whom in fact is vested the election of the members of the States, and who fear that their local importance might be diminished by any change. On that account some would, I believe, go as far as to advise the King to enlarge the right of voting by giving it to all householders of a certain value which they think would ensure at the present moment an increase to the adherents of Government in the Chambers, while the measure would be popular as bearing the semblance of a liberal policy. But it is not likely that the King's repugnance to everything in the shape of Reform would be overcome so far as to induce him to try the experiment."

Mr. Bligh then described in detail the voting system in the towns. Thirty-two councillors formed the Electoral College or Corporation, and were elected, on the average, by only *eight hundred* citizens. There was, therefore, no question of the Second Chamber's being democratic or representing the people. It represented only a clique and nothing could be more misleading than to read, as one does, that one city boycotted an election, while the electors of

---

[1] Wahlmänner.   [2] F.O. 34/27, 12th July 1838.   [3] That in Osnabrück.

another sent in such-and-such a petition. " The partisans of Government confidently assert," Bligh continued, " that if the right of voting in the towns was open to the citizens in general, instead of being confined to the Corporations, the elections would not only take place, but would very likely be in their favour, in corroboration of which it is certain that in some places the citizens have endeavoured to persuade the Corporations to vote. It would be curious, though perhaps it may not be altogether out of the question, to see the Government of His Hanoverian Majesty extending the franchise and opening close corporations, as Parliamentary and Municipal Reformers." [1] But Ernest Augustus was no opportunist. He would use no measure to which he was on principle opposed, even if it would work to his advantage, so nothing came of these proposals.

Events in the Chambers made no sensation. The people were far more impressed by the glittering Court life which was now unfolding itself in the capital. Upon all ceremonial occasions the narrow street before the Palace was packed with spectators who had come to watch the arrival of the guests in their jewels and finery and see the liveried footmen on the steps of the grand portico, and if someone arrived in a style not befitting his rank or his known wealth great resentment was expressed among the waiting crowds. The King was also to be seen as he took his walks or rides or went visiting in the town. To go from the Palace either to Herrenhausen or, later, the station, he had to pass through winding streets between tall overhanging houses.[2] In this way everyone in the city came more or less into contact with him and, though it was an assassin's dream, he never experienced the slightest unpleasantness.

Wednesday was set aside as a day when anyone could request an audience and many amusing applications there were. Descriptions of two of these have come down to us. Frederick Schmidt was a toll-gate-keeper and spare-time tailor of Walsrode. He had applied to the officials for the medal and small pension which were due to him for his military service in the wars against the French, but, he complained, they sent him from one to the other and back again. At length he decided that his only hope lay in approaching the King himself and applied for an audience. But he had to dress suitably for such an occasion, he thought, and he made

---

[1] F.O. 34/28, 4th April 1839, and 19th March 1840.
[2] The Karmarschstrasse, breaking through the Old City, was not built until some forty years later.

himself from memory a Hussar's uniform of 1813. At the Palace he requested a room in which to change, and the footmen had to hide their smiles when they saw what came out of the bundle which he was carrying. The King saw the strange figure enter with a twinkle in his eye. "Yes," he said, looking more closely, "it's definitely a Hussar, an old Hussar!" and he asked where he had found the uniform. The man explained and related his war experiences. The delighted King listened intently and then asked him what he wanted. He should have the medal if he waited, he assured him when he was told, but the unhappy man pleaded that he dare not go back to his wife without it. This amused the old King. "Ah, hah!" he laughed. "A Hussar under the slipper! Well, you need not worry; you shall have it." The other case was that of old Sergeant Beyerstorff, the man who had saved the King's life by shielding him with his body in 1793. He had subsequently served in Spain with the King's German Legion, but as he received an English pension [1] he had been refused one by the Hanoverian authorities. He determined to tell the King about this. "I went into the Palace and said to the officer, he must tell the King that old Sergeant Beyerstorff was there. I had to go in at once and as I entered, the Prince asked, 'Well, Sergeant, how are things?' I said, 'Your Majesty, as usual, one gets old,' and he began immediately to talk of the battles which we had experienced together and we showed each other our wounds. I said, 'Your Majesty, my little George is waiting in the ante-room. Can he come in too?' He came in. Then the King asked, 'Sergeant, is there anything else that you want?' I said, 'They won't give me the Hanoverian pension. They say, I receive the English, but what business is the English pension of the Hanoverians?' Then the Prince said, 'You shall have it.' When I arrived home it was already there. If only he had become King earlier." [2]

Though the King and Queen spent their private lives in the modest Altes Palais, opposite the Residence Palace (where the functions of Court took place), and the summer in Montbrillant, another unpretentious palace on the way out to Herrenhausen, everything at Court was conducted with a splendour and orderliness which soon made it one of the most distinguished in Europe. It was especially noted for its hospitality; the whole year witnessed

[1] An English paymaster remained in Hanover throughout the King's reign for the payment of pensions to the veterans of the King's German Legion.

[2] These anecdotes are from the Deutsch-Hannoversches Taschenkalender für das Jahr, 1882; Von Malortie, p. 77.

an unending series of visits from crowned heads, especially those
of the neighbouring and related states, Prussia, Brunswick and
Mecklenburg-Strelitz.[1] The birthdays of the King and Queen
were also occasions for great celebration as well as New Year's
Day, for the King had a curious superstition that he would die in
the year when it was not so celebrated.[2] In all things at Court,
absolute correctness and rigorous etiquette were the rule. However accessible on the proper occasions, the King would tolerate
no deviation from this principle. Von Malortie, the Lord Chamberlain,[3] was also punctilious to the extreme, and such a prestige did
he win through his administration of the Court that his book
upon the subject became the standard work in all the Courts of
Europe.

Not least was the King stern with himself. " His Majesty
thinks it incumbent upon him to attend to the minutest details of
the administration of his country," wrote the British Ambassador.[4]
His work was long and tiring. Unremittingly he wrote and dictated ; he read or had read to him personally every request and
every complaint from any quarter. He studied all that went on in
his Kingdom and even had the ordinary police-reports sent to him
every morning—he once told a visitor that his home had been
burgled before the unfortunate victim knew it himself.[5]

The King's day was governed by a fixed routine. It began with
the toilette, and this lasted a very long time as he had a superstition that every place had to be washed with the sponge nine
times. While washing and dressing he received his physcian, the
chief groom and the Lord Chamberlain (with whom he discussed
the arrangements for dinner), and all announcements were conveyed to him by the valet. At about ten he stepped from the
dressing-room into his study, and when the connecting door was

---

[1] In July 1838 the Grand Duke (afterwards Emperor) Alexander of Russia arrived
in Hanover ill, and the Palace of Herrenhausen was placed at his disposal until he was
well enough to continue his journey.

[2] M.A. *Von Slicher* ; *Von Malortie*, p. 81.

[3] 1804–87, grandson of the Princes' governor at Göttingen. His father (1771–
1847) was Master of the Forests. He himself was a learned historian with much
research to his credit. In 1835 the Duke of Cumberland required a chamberlain and
von Malortie was recommended by the Duke of Cambridge. The Duke, however,
considered that only a military man could have the necessary qualities and replied,
according to von Malortie himself, " Keep away from me with a civilian," and so Major
von Spörcken was appointed. He was not happy in his position, however, and when
the Duke was in Hanover for the last time before his accession he consented to his
release and, upon the renewed recommendations of his brother, to the appointment
of von Malortie, who exceeded his expectations of a civilian.

[4] F.O. 34/27, 4th October 1838.

[5] M.A. *Von Slicher*.

opened by the valet, the A.D.C. on duty for the day took over. Until twelve, the King dealt with his very extensive private correspondence. He held it to be good form to answer every letter punctually and he was an extraordinary letter-writer. During his absence in England in the 1830's he had written letters to his wife every two or three days of up to *eighty* pages, reporting all that he did, heard and thought in the most thorough detail, though unfortunately all in his almost illegible script. Now he kept in touch with all his friends in England who still owned him, but only one of these correspondences, that to Lord Strangford, has, it seems, been preserved.[1]

At twelve o'clock the commandant arrived to report, then the King saw the Chief A.D.C. and others who had business to transact, concluding generally with the Cabinet Minister. The rest of the time before dinner was passed, when the weather permitted, riding. The King would keep up a brisk conversation with his equerry, beginning always with the question, " What news have you ? " or, " Whom have you seen lately ? " Perhaps through his leanness and lack of blood the King was quite insensitive to heat, and it always afforded him satisfaction after such a ride to ask his companion if he were warm. If the officer replied that he had perspired and was as if drawn out of water, he would comment, " Curious ! I am not at all warm." Correspondingly, however, he was very sensitive to cold.

Dinner and the conversation following it lasted from five until seven. The King ate very little during the day—a cup of tea and toast in bed in the morning ; one or (at the most) two mutton chops at one o'clock. For dinner he had something light, perhaps some oysters or some jelly with one or two glasses of champagne, then a cup of tea and a biscuit in the evening. He did not care for the cooking of the meat, and the courier who went to England during the first week of every month had to bring back with him a joint of beef roasted on the open fire.[2] " The Germans spoil their meat in their closed ovens," he said. " The sodden stuff is nothing like English roast beef."

After dinner, on non-theatre days, the King rode again. When the weather was bad he played billiards. From nine to eleven he played whist with three gentlemen specially invited ; then, after saying good-night to all, he joined the Queen.[3]

---

[1] Published in 1925 as the *Letters of the King of Hanover to Viscount Strangford, G.C.B.*
[2] *Wilkinson.*
[3] This account of the King's day is principally from M.A. *Von Slicher.*

In all things the King liked society and conversation. But in his old age his eccentricities became more and more overbearing and the persons about him often had a very difficult time. In particular, his sarcasm, which he had fought down and succeeded in keeping within bounds his whole life, now became uncontrollable. It was of a teasing rather than a malicious nature, but none the less unpleasant. After such a good " joke," he would say, " Oh, we've amused ourselves wonderfully ! " On one occasion his A.D.C. ventured to suggest that the guests were probably not amused, since they could not always distinguish between what was seriously intended and what was humorous. The King laughed. " Who can't take a joke is a silly fellow ! " he said.[1] He could not bear weak or easily-domineered persons ; they only invited more teasing. He demanded that others should be as forthright as he was, and it particularly pleased him when someone said boldly that he had " amused himself." His staff gradually learnt how to manage him.

Though he demanded strict obedience and punctuality, he could not suffer servility and affectation. Just as in his speeches to his subjects he never used meaningless phrases or made empty compliments, he could not tolerate it on their part, and when someone opened an audience in such a manner it brought forth his sarcasm. On more than one occasion someone who began with the form, " Allow me to throw myself at Your Majesty's feet ! " received the disconcerting retort, " Rubbish ! If you did, you would split your trousers ! " or, " That would be very unpleasant down there in the dirt ! " [2]

The King, so strictly religious, could not brook affectations or pietism there. " Isn't it so, Herr Superintendent," he once said to one of the high ecclesiastics, " the old faith of our fathers, of our youth, far from affected piety, tracts and meeting-house devotions [Winkelandacht], that was a much better faith ? " After dinner, he asked his newly-arrived English Chaplain if he had ever read Ogden's Sermons. As the answer was no, he replied, " Oh, I'll lend them to you. They were my father's favourite sermons— indeed, we all liked them very much. They are very short—none more than twenty minutes—but very pithy, without, I believe, a single unnecessary word. *Multum in parvo* we call them. No

---

[1] M.A. *Von Slicher.*

[2] *Ibid.* *Von Slicher.* Wilkinson also relates a story of the King's sarcasm at flattery. Perhaps the King did not quite understand that the expression quoted above is an idiom used in polite parlance in Germany.

doubt they were prepared with great care and, indeed, I have always been of the opinion that any clergyman who had made a sermon for forty-five minutes could always give us the real pith of it in twenty if he would only take the trouble." Turning to his secretary—" Desire the Librarian to send Mr. Wilkinson Ogden's Sermons," and the interview ended.[1]

But what brought down the full weight of the King's sarcasm was moral hypocrisy, especially when it was at the expense of another on the strength of rumour and scandal, He had suffered enough from this during his life to feel particularly bitter against its whisperers. In the most celebrated case, the victim of gossip was the young daughter of a deceased officer. The King had found a place for her in one of the Protestant foundations for ladies which in some respects resembled nunneries,[2] and whisperers now had it that she had spent a holiday with her mother in England to conceal the consequences of her misconduct. Without any investigation, the Abbess expelled her. Her mother, in distress, approached the King and he sent to England for an inquiry into the circumstances of her stay in a South-coast hotel. The result satisfied him that the story was utterly without foundation. Now the full blast of his wrath against rumour and scandal-mongers was let loose.

In the middle of the night an officer arrived at the establishment and demanded admittance with a message from the King which had to be read before all the ladies assembled. Hastily they dressed and gathered in the grand hall in great suspense, then the seals were broken and the letter, in the King's own hand, was read out to them. The King, after expressing his satisfaction with the evidence of the investigation which he had instituted, pointed out the dangers that could result from crediting unsubstantiated accusations. After all, he said, they could be brought against anyone. "What would you say, Frau Abbess," he concluded, " if it were said of you that in earlier years you had given birth to a pair of twins ? I would only believe the half of it." [3]

---

[1] *Wilkinson.*

[2] In the Guelphic dominions at the Reformation, the monasteries and convents were not secularised, but transformed into foundations for pious ladies, which they have remained to this day.

[3] One might not give credence to this story if Wilkinson alone had related it, knowing how far-fetched much of his book is, but von Malortie, pp. 49–50, also describes the incident, and neither of them would have known of the " only believing half," which is to be found in the parliamentary debate of 1815, from which the King no doubt drew his inspiration.

On another occasion an elderly lady arrived at a ball dressed as a young girl in virgin white decoltée, and this led the King to show his disapproval in no undecided manner. Coming down the line of guests, when he reached her, he turned his back and stood for a few moments there as if warming himself before what he took to be one of the decorative white porcelain stoves which heated the Palace. He was always very sensitive of dignity and correctness, as has been seen, and another time when he was going down the line to greet each guest with a few words at an Embassy ball and he came to a Nobleman untidily dressed, he said to him only, " What do you mean by coming in such a dress and in such a hat ? You look like an old cheese-monger ! " [1]

Travelling was still one of the King's great pleasures and he now began to pay regular visits to his neighbours. He frequently joined his cousin, the Duke of Brunswick, for hunts and house-parties, or his brother-in-law in Strelitz. He also attended the grand manœuvres at Magdeburg, across the Prussian frontier. On one occasion there was such a hectic programme that he stepped into the Prince of Prussia's coach as he was changing his grey field breeches for salon white, a contretemps which caused them much laughter.[2] In May and June 1838 the King and Queen visited Berlin and lived in their palace there in the old style. Upon their arrival all the servants in full livery and a guard of honour were drawn up at the door to receive them. The King also made less spectacular visits in his own country and concluded the year with one to the thousand-years-old walled city of Goslar on the edge of the Harz. He was received with all the usual ceremonies and festivities and two characteristics of the Harz—a musical procession by the miners and smelters with torches and mine-lamps and a whip-concert given in his honour by the mountain-waggoners of the Upper Harz. " Ma réception a été Rechtherzlich," the King wrote.[3] " It is not only touching, but really interesting to see all the good people."

---

[1] Wilkinson.
[2] G.A. To Queen, 13th September 1838. Prince William was afterwards the first German Emperor.
[3] Ibid. To Queen, 17th December 1838.

CHAPTER XXI

FEW persons abroad believed that the King of Hanover could emerge victorious from his struggle, and in England the Whigs relished the prospect of witnessing the humiliation of the man who had been such a dangerous opponent. His task was, indeed, much more difficult than it had been in the land of his birth, for there it had been primarily defensive. In Hanover, his enemies were already entrenched in power when he arrived and all the machinery of state was in their hands. Yet he had succeeded in reducing them to the point where they knew that their only hope lay in intervention from outside.

Stüve and his friends hoped to compel the Diet of the Confederation to declare the King of Hanover's actions illegal, and they sent petitions alleging this to Frankfurt. The Hanoverian Government pointed out in a memorandum that the Constitution of 1819 was in recognised effectiveness and that the King and the Estates were seeking to reconcile themselves.

The task of the Opposition, then, was to obstruct and prevent the functioning of the Estates, so that when the Diet met again the Hanoverian Government would not be able to point to Estates which were in " recognised effectiveness." When, therefore, the Chambers were opened again on the 15th February 1839, the leaders succeeded for several days in preventing the attendance of a quorum ; members arrived, were counted and then went home. Clearly this was a course which, if planned and followed in concert, would lead to the ineffectiveness of any Constitution, whether of the year 1819 or 1833, without regard to its legality. On the 23rd, von Schele issued an order explaining that when a candidate was elected, he accepted a mandate and a duty which he was bound to carry out conscientiously. If he ceased to do this, it was tantamount to a resignation. Those members, therefore, who had continuously absented themselves had, in fact, laid down their mandates of their own accord, and if they did not appear before the end of the month this fact would be officially recognised. Led by Christiani and Detmold—two lawyers, of course—twenty-three

Opposition members replied with a protest to the Confederation. They would only attend, they said, if the Diet or the Estates, with a quorum excluding themselves, declared that the Constitution of 1833 was invalid. The Government realised that it was useless to treat with them and adjourned the Chambers on the 2nd March. Elections were ordered to fill the places of those members who had declared their resignations by not attending at least fourteen days in the session.

" I have waited patiently," the King had written,[1] " but it will soon be necessary to take *more decided* measures to bring them to reason. It's an inexcusable stupidity, all this procedure." One of those who signed the members' protest told the King frankly that he was not convinced of its legitimacy, but had to do so to maintain his own influence.[2] The King wished that he could have adjourned the Chambers for longer than the by-elections, but the budget would soon be due. His own brother-in-law did not understand why he did not postpone summoning them. " You are right," he replied,[3] " and I would have done so had I not been in this position. Firstly, I wish to act strictly constitutionally and according to law. The budget has only been voted up to the 1st July, and I have observed all the manœuvres of the Radicals in the country to try to persuade the parishes and the villagers to refuse to pay taxes."

At the moment when matters were coming to a head in Frankfurt, the Opposition in Hanover suffered a severe setback. Beginning with that in Bremervörde, many of the electoral colleges which had hitherto refused to elect now expressed their readiness to do so, if the Government would make some statement about its conciliatory intentions. Of course, their members were denounced as traitors and mercenaries by the remaining Opposition, but the King was genuinely in a conciliatory mood and authorised such a declaration on the 3rd May, before the summoning of the Estates. " As I really wish to come to a union with them," he wrote to his brother-in-law,[4] " I will listen quietly and peacefully to all the propositions which they wish to make. If they are acceptable or worthy of consideration, I will not fail to act upon them." However, it was not conciliation which the Opposition desired. Its hopes were now centred upon an extraordinary and astonishing

---

[1] S.A.   To Grand Duke of Mecklenburg-Strelitz, 22nd February 1839.
[2] *Ibid.*   To Grand Duke, 4th March 1839.
[3] *Ibid.*   To Grand Duke, 13th March 1839.
[4] *Ibid.*   To Grand Duke, 27th or 29th May 1839.

assertion. If there were no quorum to approve the credentials of the newly-elected members, those members, it was claimed, could not take their seats. Since without them there could be no quorum, the Chambers would then simply cease to exist. No one, of course, considered seriously a theory which implied that any newly-elected member might at any time be prevented from taking his seat if a sufficient number of those already elected decided to absent themselves, and on the 7th June the Chambers met with a quorum. Another tedious session began, but on the 16th a rescript announced the immediate establishment of a commission for studying means of securing agreement between the Government and the Chambers, and at the same time expressed regret that slander was being spread against the King under the guise of defending the 1833 Constitution. The Chambers were adjourned on the 20th.

The probability that the Government would be able to announce to the Federal Diet a reconciliation with the Estates moved the frustrated opposition to measures of desperation. Something had to be done quickly, and on the 16th June its leaders on the City Council of the capital composed a note of protest to the Diet at the " illegality " of the present Chambers and the " tyrannical and despotic methods " used to bring them into being. The initiative came from the Stadtdirektor, Rumann. Even Liberals recognise that he was a social climber governed by ambition. At the King's succession he had, as President of the Second Chamber, made no protest at its dissolution and he had afterwards taken the King's part. He hoped to play a brilliant rôle in the regenerated social life of the Kingdom. He frequently dined with the King and in the New Year of 1838 he was created a Commander of the Guelphic Order. The King's prospects had dimmed, however, and he now thought it wise to re-align himself though the struggle had been in progress for months. " I regard him as the *only* really dangerous one," wrote the King,[1] " for he is a man of infinite resource, but a man without character and possessed with a bad heart."

The King could not afford to ignore this challenge in his capital and on the 13th July he summoned his Ministers for a conference at Montbrillant. They were unanimous in the opinion that the City Councillors had committed a criminal offence in libelling the King, the Ministers and the members of the Second Chamber. They also agreed that the case would have to be referred to the courts, but were of divergent views as to the disciplinary measures called for by those who held administrative offices. Some thought

[1] S.A. To Grand Duke, 26th July 1839.

that only Rumann should be suspended, but von Alten, the un-sophisticated War Minister, could not see that all were not equally involved. " It is high time," he said, " for a deterring example to be made, to curb the arrogance of many councillors in the towns." Von der Wisch and von Schele agreed and the King finally declared that this was also his opinion.[1] Landdroſt von Dachenhausen then pointed out that before all the posts could be filled, the administration would come to a standstill. It was decided, therefore, to suspend only Rumann and to replace him by the local Recorder, Heilige. As the latter was out of town at the moment, an official named Hagemann would temporarily exercise the func-tions. All of the signatories of the libel would be prosecuted. The following day the Landdroſt appeared at a session of the Council and demanded in the name of the King if those present had signed the criminal document. On the 16th, the proclamation announcing the measures decided upon was published.

" Every honest subject," it ran in characteristic tones, " can imagine the feelings which were aroused within Us when We saw Our most carefully-considered measures distorted and brought under suspicion in the most disgraceful and disrespectful manner by the representatives of a city which has always been favoured more than any other of Our Kingdom." [2] What was most irritating to the King and libellous against the Cabinet was the insinuation that it was acting without his authority. By this, the authors of the Opposition hoped to discredit the Government's measures in the eyes of the King's most loyal subjects, for they saw that a frontal attack on him was now purposeless. The King never sought to shelter behind others. The full responsibility was his, he declared, and his original patent had shown " that the *decision* of affairs deliberated by Our Cabinet lies with Us. We also hereby declare once more that We will never permit such a difference between Ourselves and Our Cabinet. We are not prepared to let this disgraceful offence pass with impunity." The King then announced the proceedings which he had instituted.

The Opposition was goaded to fury. The King replied to every step which was supposed to awe him by brushing aside the authors and declaring his intentions more unequivocally. On the 17th as the Landdroſt administered the oath to Hagemann in the City Hall, the Opposition, in an enraged mob, broke into the building

[1] See *Von Hassell*, I, p. 437.
[2] " It is certain that the angry King has hinted at the possibility of moving the seat of Government to Celle."—F.O. 34/28, 18th April 1838.

and unsuccessfully sought to defenestrate them. A deputation of the Councillors then led the mob out to Montbrillant and asked for an audience of the King. When he received them they pointed out to him that under paragraph five of the municipal constitution no civil servant could be a member of the Council. The King listened patiently, and replied that he would never wish to do anything unconstitutional; he was scrupulous in observing any law whose validity he did not challenge and so he decided to appoint instead Evers, a man who, though supporting the 1833 Constitution, guaranteed the peace of the city. Von Schele agreed with him that although they had the means to carry out their original intention if necessary, it was not worth while to make an issue of this incident. The King only yielded to legal arguments in this matter, and if the mob thought that it could force him to withdraw Rumann's suspension, it was mistaken, for he would not even discuss it. This was the only disturbance of the peace during the whole three years of the political struggle, which proves how little the popular passions were inflamed by the King's actions. As the King himself declared,[1] " The country is as happy as possible and it is only the *advocates* and the councillors in the towns who are causing all this bad blood." Those were indeed happy days when, we read, a tyrant was ruthlessly crushing all opposition, and not a life was taken, not a soul imprisoned and a sensation caused by the dismissal of seven professors and a Stadtdirektor!

The King's principal worries lay outside his own realm. The Liberals and revolutionaries, with a unity and consciousness of purpose which their opponents lacked, were applying pressure on the governments of the German Confederation to declare that he had contravened the Act of 1815 and to compel him by force to retract his measures. In the Chambers of the Middle and South German states they had the whip-hand, and their Sovereigns were not all of the mettle of King Ernest Augustus. The Kings of Bavaria and Württemberg, for example, expressed their admiration and sympathy for him and their hopes for the success of his efforts, but they regretted that they would have to instruct their envoys at the Diet to vote against him should his affairs be raised there.[2] Such weakness and lack of foresight appalled Ernest Augustus. He had already seen it when the Peers of England had chosen to go hunting while the Reform Bill was inaugurating the hundred

---

[1] S.A.   To Grand Duke, 19th April 1838.

[2] H.A.   Hann. Des. 91 von Schele, Nr. 6, von Stralenheim to von Schele, 8th January 1839.

years which were to extinguish them. "I give you my word of honour," he wrote,[1] "I would rather eat dry bread with honour than live in the greatest luxury, if my means were not my own, and I had always to beg from them [the Estates] the bread which I ate. The King of Bavaria's building and the King of Württemberg's travelling cost a lot of money.[2] That is the key to their conduct, for these monarchs are in their souls not just *monarchistic* but as great tyrants and despots as could exist."

But as long as Austria and Prussia remained united in their support there was still a prospect of success, though even Metternich was disturbed. "If you drive the matter to extremes," he told the Hanoverian Ambassador in Vienna, von Bodenhausen, with some asperity, "I cannot protect you from extremes."[3] On the 26th April 1839 the Bavarian and Badenese envoys at the Diet moved a resolution that it should inquire whether the Hanoverian Government had acted in accordance with the Federal Constitution in annulling the law of 1833. A minority—Saxony, the Saxon Duchies, Württemberg, Hesse-Darmstadt and the Hansa Cities— voted for it, but it was resolved that Hanover should furnish information within four weeks. Metternich was highly displeased to see such a grave matter going so far. The Hanoverian Government, he said, should not bother itself with rights and morals but should present an agreement with the Estates as a *fait accompli*. "Call the Estates together then all the trouble is at an end," he said.[4]

As has been seen, the Chambers had already been summoned and proposals for mutual conciliation announced. It could therefore be said that the Constitution of 1819 was in recognised effectiveness. But the Government had to be very careful in framing its explanatory declaration to the Diet; it must not compromise itself, "for," said the King,[5] "I maintain that I cannot pray the Diet to pronounce upon the validity of the 1819 Constitution as that is an internal affair and, I maintain, depends upon *me*."

Four months of diplomatic activity, highly interesting to the student of the internal politics of the Confederation, followed,[6] and finally a majority for Hanover was assured. On the 24th August

---

[1] S.A. To Grand Duke, 14th April and 19th August 1839.

[2] King Ludwig I had a passion for building and Munich owes it beauty to him. The peregrinations of the King of Württemberg have not left such an imprint in history.

[3] H.A. Von Bodenhausen to von Schele, 30th March 1839.

[4] H.A. Von Bodenhausen to von Schele, 4th May 1839.

[5] S.A. To Grand Duke, 2nd May 1839.

[6] Details had to be cut out owing to lack of space.

The King at manœuvres in the neighbourhood of the capital

(Artist unknown)

The Leinstrasse, Hanover

On the left is the portico of the Royal Palace. On the right, the Altes Palais,
where the King had his personal apartments on the ground floor facing on to
the street to the right of the far entrance; the Queen's were above them

(By Kretschmer)

the President of the Diet, the Austrian Count von Münch-Bellinghausen, brought matters to a close by proposing the resolution
that the Confederation found no cause to interfere in the affairs of
Hanover.   When it came to voting, Austria, Prussia, Hanover,
Hesse-Cassel, Luxemburg,[1] Holstein,[2] Mecklenburg and the 15th [3]
and 16th Curiae [4] approved, while Bavaria, Württemberg, Saxony,
Baden, the Saxon Duchies and the Hansa Cities dissented, though
the Duke of Saxe-Altenburg, who was outvoted in the preliminary
curatorial session, drew up a public protest at the decision of his
fellows.[5]   This, incidentally, helped to further the already friendly
relations between his family and Crown Prince George, whom they
met every year at the baths at Norderney.

The King received the news of the happy issue of the last of
his problems as he was leaving to visit Celle for the races (24th–
27th August) to present the Queen's Trophy.   He was delighted,
but he did not ascribe his success solely to his own courage and
abilities.   " Yes, dearest angel," he said to his wife,[6] " the Almighty
has supported me wonderfully and I can never be grateful enough
for His mercy and protection."

To his brother-in-law, the Grand Duke of Mecklenburg-
Strelitz, the King wrote at once from Montbrillant on the 24th,[7]
" I cannot go to bed without writing you a couple of words to let
you know that, thanks to God, I *have won my cause* at the Diet.   I
received this happy and blessed news by estafette this evening.
But at the same time, let me add that it is a battle that I have
won for *you all* to save the monarchical principle, and if it can be
added without appearing vain, I have stemmed the course of the
democrats."

Secure in his victory, King Ernest Augustus decided to undertake the second of his grand tours, this time to the south and east
of his Kingdom.   He had always been curious to visit the Harz
Mountains, a region quite unlike the rest of the country, and no
Sovereign had been there since George II's visit one hundred and
ten years before.

On the 15th September the King set out for a hunt at Rotenkirchen, to which he invited a number of guests, including Bligh,

---

[1] The Grand Duke of Luxemburg was the King of the Netherlands.
[2] The Duke of Holstein was the King of Denmark.
[3] Oldenburg, Anhalt and Schwarzburg.
[4] Hohenzollern, Liechtenstein, Reuss, Lippe-Detmold, Schaumburg-Lippe and
Waldeck.
[5] G.A.   Crown Prince to King, 3rd September 1839.
[6] *Ibid.*   To Queen, 24th August 1839.
[7] S.A.   To Grand Duke, 24th August 1839.

the British Ambassador. At the relay-stations on the way, crowds gathered and cheered their triumphant Sovereign. On the 18th the real tour began with his arrival at Osterode, on the edge of the Harz. There he visited the lead- and shot-factory, which was the most important in the country and employed some hundred hands. At the entrance a triumphal arch had been erected and all the workmen, dressed uniformly in blue with black leather bonnets, and women in blue with flowers were drawn up in line in the garden. The owner, very prosperous and very loyal, showed the King over the whole establishment, including all the amenities and facilities for the employees. After an hour's drive, along a way lined by cheering crowds from the villages, the King arrived at Clausthal early in the evening. It was very tiring, he told his wife, for on such a journey one had to remain alert to see all which came, while the scenery of the rolling pine-covered mountains held him under a spell. On the way he had to listen to some four or five speeches, and upon his arrival he was confronted with a magnificent spectacle. Eight hundred miners with their lamps and eight hundred smelters with torches had converged in processions with banners and music, and thousands had streamed from all the towns and villages of the mountains to greet him, and the civic authorities were assembled at the door of the house where he took up residence. After dinner and presentations, the day closed with a torchlight serenade of five thousand participants. In this little mountain town of wooden houses in the middle of the forests, it must have been a wonderful spectacle—" un coup d'œil superbe " the King called it—and Bligh marvelled at it.

After breakfast the next day the King made a tour of the twin towns of Clausthal and Zellerfeld. He saw the processing of silver in the Mint, and in the Mining Academy he was shown the plans of the various mines. He had lunch on the heights above Wilder Mann, or Wild Man, and then descended the extremely steep slope on foot to the town, where the Wilde Männer, masked inhabitants wearing moss and twigs of fir and pine, performed their dance from the far-distant past.

After this the King proceeded to inspect one of the Royal silver-mines of Andreasberg. The buildings were all decorated and at his request the shaft was lit. Saying that he wished to see all in detail for himself, he took a miner's hat from the Superintendent of the Mines, and went a little way along one of the galleries. The first thing which came to his mind was the safety and welfare of those working there and he demanded to see the procedure in

case of accident.   A man was lowered down the shaft in a form of
barrel to bring up a supposedly injured miner.   The King, who
hated all things concerned with industry, found it all detestable.
" It is very fine," he wrote to his wife, " but frightful."   He was
horrified to learn that for nine months of the year the silver-miners
saw little daylight, but when he expressed his views, those about
him assured him that they found pleasure in it, and that there were
too many aspirants for the career.   Unable to understand this, he
told his wife, " It is a horrible life, but they are as happy as could
be.   There is not a single mine that has no band and they dance
eternally."   They were " adorable, merry to excess, and when one
thinks of all the dangers to which these fine people are daily exposed,
one is astonished at their gaiety, but they believe in predestination
and, like the Turks, are prepared for anything.   Everywhere one
sees their gay nature ; they run like rabbits out of their burrows,
little ones roll down the mountains like monkeys, and it is for me
a real delight to see them."   All this was new to the King.

In England he had never visited the industrial areas, though,
of course, they bore no resemblance to these settlements up in the
forests and mountains.   Here the mines were Royal property
everything was strictly and systematically ordered and measures
for the welfare of those engaged in them—such as the prohibition
of juvenile labour—in force, while in liberal and democratic
England it was costing a handful of aristocrats a fierce struggle to
force such measures on to the statute book against the determined
opposition of the Whigs and progressives.

" You have no idea what a spectacle it was ! " wrote the King
to his wife, describing the progress ; the whole population, men,
women and children, followed him, climbing the mountains like
goats.   At six o'clock he held the ceremony of throwing silver
from the balcony of his room into the crowd on the square below.
Dinner followed with seventy guests and then the King made a
tour of the illuminated town.   All the miners had lit their lamps
and placed them before their houses, and the King, though now
dog-tired, was overcome by all the demonstrations of loyalty
which he received.   " This proves," he wrote, " a sincerity and
loyalty which goes right to the heart.   Never could I have imagined
to myself such cordiality and such a spirit of attachment as that of
these good mountaineers, who have not yet been gangrened or
indoctrinated by these new-fangled democrats.   Their *bonhomie*
and loyalty is not affected ; one sees that it comes straight from
the heart. . . . I believe in my conscience that here in the Harz the

people are *pure* and *loyal* and not of the modern idea. They have a spirit of adoration for their *Sovereign* which nothing could extinguish. One *sees* everywhere that this could not be affected or feigned."

After an excursion to Goslar the King left Clausthal and drove deeper into the mountains. The beauty of the scenery staggered him. " Really," he wrote to his wife, " if I had not seen it with my own eyes, I could not have imagined that there was anything so beautiful in this country. You must absolutely without fail make a tour here next year. . . ." The King inspected the forestry establishment at Bruchberg and then went on to Königshütte, where iron was smelted. As he approached, his monogram and " God Save the King ! " suddenly appeared from the dark hearth of the blast-furnaces in dazzling molten iron.

The King resumed his journey the following day to Herzberg, where he inspected the small-arms factory and went up to the old castle of his ancestors which dominated the town. That was the end of his mountain tour.[1] He returned through Osterode and Northeim to Rotenkirchen, where he arrived at three o'clock in the morning (on the 23rd). Before leaving for his capital he inspected the troops at Nörten and Einbeck. On the 20th the Göttingen garrison had marched out to the former place in preparation and it seemed to the citizens that the city was in disfavour. In alarm lest the professors might have caused the King to doubt their loyalty, the heads of the guilds and the leading shopkeepers assembled early the following morning, partly at the house of the town clerk, partly at the cobbler's guildhouse, and decided to send a deputation to the King at Rotenkirchen to assure him of the city's loyalty and to beg him to honour it with his presence.[2]

The King arrived in Hanover on the 24th September refreshed and with renewed confidence in the loyalty and affections of his people. " Amongst those who approached the King, and they appeared to be the entire population of the towns and country through which he passed," summarised the English Ambassador,[3] " there were no signs of their loyalty being in the least diminished by those feelings of dissatisfaction with the measures of the Government which exist among certain classes and in certain localities."

---

[1] This description of the King's tour in the Harz is from G.A. To the Queen, 15th, 18th, 20th, 21st, and 23rd September 1839 ; the Hannöversche Zeitung and *Von Malortie*, pp. 69-70.

[2] *Oppermann*, I, p. 210.   [3] F.O. 34/28, 26th September 1839.

During the remaining months of 1839 the King occupied himself with drafting the new Constitution which was to be laid before
the Estates to replace that of 1819, and he sat with the Council of
State every day. For relaxation he travelled into the country. He
was never so happy and convivial as at parties at his Jagdſchloß
deep in the forest, with only his most intimate friends. At table he
would become talkative and lead the conversation. His inclination
towards sarcastic jests disappeared. " Tell us a story, Linsingen ! "
he would say, combining familiarity with the regal dignity which
never left him.[1]

He also visited his cousin, the Duke of Brunswick,[2] at his
castle of Blankenburg in the Harz, and one such visit was notable
as being the first occasion upon which he travelled by rail. This
was on the line between Brunswick and Wolfenbüttel, where the
Duke had a hunting-villa.[3] The King complained of " All this
eternal bustle and noise that there is, for these trains go four times
a day the whole year and in the *belle saison* and public holidays as
many as eight times ; and the noise of such a cortège is enough to
chase away the Devil, with the smoke which it sends out. It was
the first time that I have ever ventured in such a machine. It is
comfortable, it is true, but if one looks at the objects as they pass
when it goes at full force, it is enough to turn the head and make
one giddy." [4]

The King had decided that the time had come for the country
to settle down. The Opposition was making its last stand on its
only remaining ground, those courts of law whose offices were
held by its members. It has already been noted that the lawyers
formed the great mass of the political opposition, and they did not
hesitate now to use their offices for political ends. The magistracies
of Hildesheim, Göttingen and Celle, for example, declared that
they would judge in accordance with the 1833 Constitution, and
this seemed to imply that they would uphold refusals to pay taxes.
It is, of course, a universal judicial principle that the courts are to
carry out laws and to play no part in the politics which lead to

[1] Communication of Baron von Linsingen-Gestorf. Ernst von Linsingen (1775–
1853), nephew of the King's old instructor, became Adjutant-General in 1838.

[2] The line reigning in Brunswick was the the elder of the House. Apart from this
relationship, the Duke, William, was the son of Duke Frederick William (brother-in-
law of George IV), who fell at Quatre Bras, and grandson of Duke Ferdinand, who died
of wounds received at Jena, and whose wife was the King of Hanover's aunt and sister
of George III.

[3] The railway from Brunswick to Wolfenbüttel was the second in Germany, the
first being that from Nürnberg to Fürth.

[4] G.A.   To Queen, 5th December 1839.

their making,[1] but that meant nothing to the men who used every weapon at their disposal to maintain themselves in power. On the 17th January 1840 the King issued a proclamation stating that it was outside the province of the law-courts to examine or question the laws which were promulgated. In so doing they were acting illegally and would draw upon themselves the logical consequences.

But the Opposition was already finished. The decision of the Diet had shattered its last hope. It was quite clear that the Government would always have a majority in the present Chambers and that the necessary reconciliation would take place. The last resistance, therefore, was directed at obtaining a dissolution, after which their members would endeavour to secure an assembly which would declare itself incompetent and so make the Diet intervene and start the whole story over again. Why they thought that the King should be so stupid as to grant a dissolution is not clear. At any rate, they begged for one in petitions and addresses couched in the most loyal language, promising that they would not abstain from electing—what an admission of the folly of their earlier proceedings ! It was a curious inconsistency first to boycott elections then to plead to be allowed to hold them.

In the country these politicians were now, of course, completely discredited. Their negative attitude of pure opposition might have been effective for a few months at the beginning, but it was an impossible one after three years during which, under the King's able and benevolent rule, the country was happier and more prosperous than it had ever been. Now the country saw them as selfish men intent only upon recovering their own power. In a typical democrat's fury, Oppermann betrayed how little the masses, for whom he and his fellows felt such contempt, had worried themselves or felt the effects of the 1833 Constitution in their lives. " One sought to stir up the lower classes, who had hardly an inkling of the meaning of the whole struggle, against the bourgeoisie from whom the resistance came."

The King, of course, paid no attention to the Radicals' call for a dissolution and summoned the Estates for the 19th March 1840, when proposals for the new Constitution were laid before them, and the King received their members in the presence of the Court

---

[1] The King would recall Liverpool's quotation of Lord Camden (1788) during the Regency debates, that " even if the Lord Chancellor should put the Great Seal by caprice to any commission, it could not be afterwards questioned, not even by the Judges themselves." If such an Act were " endorsed with the words *le Roi le veult*, it must be received as part of the Statute Law of the land, and could not be disputed."—*Yonge*, I, p. 351.

and Ministers. They brought him an address of thanks and he spoke in reply. "I can declare with truth," he said, "there is no chapter, no paragraph, no sentence in the whole Act which I have not thoroughly examined and tested. As you must know, I am not completely at home in the German language and so I must thoroughly examine and understand everything before I can sign my name beneath it. You know me; I am a man of my word. What I promise, I keep; I can assure you I have only one thought and I have never had another—the happiness and welfare of the country."

The new Constitution, of which the principal feature was the restoration of the integrity and independence of the Royal Domains, was then laid before the Estates for debate, and the whole three years' struggle ended in an anti-climax. Shortly afterwards, the whole capital celebrated the King's military jubilee; the garrison was reviewed; Herrenhausen Avenue and all the military establishments were floodlit.[1] By the end of July the discussions upon the new Constitution were completed and the Estates voted their approval. The conclusion of the struggle which had been so bitter passed almost unnoticed. An address was voted at midnight and on the morrow was presented to the King. "I understand," wrote the English Ambassador,[2] "His Majesty was quite overcome by his feelings whilst replying to it, which he did most graciously."

On the 1st August the Constitution was promulgated; the following day the King and both Chambers dined together in the Orangery at Herrenhausen, and on the 3rd the Estates, the last of the 1819 Constitution, were dissolved. Even von Treitschke, in his distorted account of the episode, cannot withhold a word of grudging admiration for the victorious King—" Thus the incredible had taken place. A Prince who at the beginning did not know what he wanted, supported by not a single man of importance, finally asserted his power against the law and public opinion."

The King himself wrote,[3] " I have all my *confidence* in the Divine Grace, which can all, will all and does all for the good, and it is to that alone that I attribute my success to this great affair with the Chambers." Everywhere the only man who had dared to punish the overbearing Radicals and revolutionaries was seen in a new light. Thenceforth Ernest Augustus was regarded as the

---

[1] For a description of these celebrations, see *Von Malortie*, Appendix III.
[2] F.O.   34/32, 3rd August 1840.
[3] G.A.   To Queen, 28th August 1840.

patriarch of the German Sovereigns and all came to him for advice upon their problems. " I was fully persuaded that I must succeed in the end," he said ; " doubtfulness or weakness shown on my side would have been destruction, and I boldly went on, but was ever prudent and cautious ; I thus always had my feet well secured ere I proceeded further. *Now* I am assailed with congratulations from every quarter, and they go so far as to tell me I have been the only King who could have stemmed the democratic spirit here on the Continent. My reply is very short—is this so ? Then aid me and stand by me." [1]

[1] To Sir Henry Halford, 22nd August 1840.—*Munk.*

CHAPTER XXII

1840–43

IN the years between 1840 and 1843, King Ernest Augustus was able to realise his ideal of becoming the " Father of his People." He was victorious in the struggle with his opponents and absolute power now lay in his hands, but he did not wish to flatter his vanity by dwelling upon that. On the contrary, it was a source of pain to him that such a struggle had been necessary and his first gestures were of peace and reconciliation.

Rumann, after his suspension from office in the capital, had been sentenced to eight weeks' imprisonment or a fine of eight hundred Thaler for his offences and the Councillors to corresponding fines.[1] " This verdict," reported Bligh, the English Ambassador,[2] " has not been productive of any popular demonstration whatever." All the sentences were now remitted and Rumann accepted the King's offer of a pension of three thousand Thaler from his own purse. The King also endeavoured to secure the return of those of the dismissed Göttingen professors who would make peace with him. In June 1845 he visited the University to express his joy that all misunderstandings had ceased and " how happy I am to declare that the past has been *forgiven* and forgotten."

In this way the Kingdom was soon at peace, and for the next few years politics virtually did not exist. Life and property were secure, personal freedom was jealously guarded, and the organs of state receded from the public consciousness.[3] The

---

[1] The prosecution had demanded a heavier sentence.

[2] F.O. 34/34, 26th August 1841.

[3] See Kobbe's Memoiren eines hannoverschen Landgendarmen for an account of the work of the policing of the Kingdom. Each gendarme had his own district, which he patrolled to his own time-table. Only once does Kobbe mention the State as such or anything bearing upon politics. The King interested himself personally in the judicial and police system of his realm, and it was his Constitution of 1840 and not that of the Liberals of 1833 which promulgated a new criminal code replacing that of the sixteenth century Carola Law. To him is thus due the credit for the abolition of torture to assist confessions, though, of course, the law providing for it was hardly more seriously interpreted than that ordaining drawing and quartering was in England in the 1870's, when it was last applied. It is on record, however, that a judge threatened its use in Meinersen in 1818. It was also under Ernest Augustus that, despite heavy opposition, the Jews received civic rights in Hanover.

true significance of these phrases is lost to the inhabitant of the twentieth century. The State is the determining factor in his life, and robbery and plunder—under other names—are taken for granted as its normal duties ; politics, more often merely the law of the mob, mould everyone's life in its most personal details and overrule all considerations of morality ; nobody knows how he stands from one five years to the next ; at any time he may be dispossessed or compelled to do something against which his mind rebels. Freedom from all this fear and misery was the boon of Ernest Augustus's system—a land without politics, in which all formed, as he had put it, one family, from peasant to King.

The land was wealthy and all classes prosperous and contented. Most of the people were peasants or craftsmen, with their own houses and fields or workshops ; unattached poor who wandered or filled workhouses did not exist in the Kingdom and anyone found on the streets without means of subsistence was apprehended. At the end of 1841 the British Government asked its ambassador for details of the conditions of the working-classes in Hanover. In the English sense, he replied, there were none ; there were no factories of any appreciable size and the only industry was that of the Royal mines in the Harz. He investigated in detail the working conditions and rates of pay in them and reported his findings to London. All apprentices had to be able to read and attend school besides work ; the employment of juveniles in the mines was forbidden. A welfare fund was provided, the greater proportion paid by the employer (the King), and sick pay was prescribed, as well as pensions for widows and their children under fourteen. There was also free medical treatment. When the price of corn rose, each employee or pensioner received cheap corn from the Royal Corn Magazine at Osterode, the amount varying according to the size of his or her family.[1] Yet this was the land and these were the servants of the most reactionary monarch in Europe, while in constitutional parliamentary England, blazing the path of Progress and Social Justice, it was to cost a group of aristocrats and humanitarians a bitter struggle a few years later to carry the most basic of measures for the protection of children in

[1] F.O. 34/37, 6th January 1842. For the Magazine at Osterode see Das Königliche Kornmagazin in Osterode, Heimatkalender, 1923. The system of so distributing corn dated from the scarcity after the Thirty Years' War and the Magazine was built in 1718–22. For some comments on the general absence of poverty in Germany see Greville, V, pp. 174, 175, 184.

industry, and their most resolute opponents were the Whigs and Liberals.[1]

The King devoted much attention to the problem of poverty. He was horrified to learn that paupers were often buried without the attendance of a clergyman and forthwith ordered that an end be put to this abuse and attendance strictly enforced. " I explained the horror of such an act," he told a friend.[2] When he learnt of the Irish famine of 1846, he immediately sent two thousand pounds towards its alleviation and advised the establishment of corn magazines as in his country. His munificence towards the poor was boundless and on all occasions and celebrations he distributed large sums of money amongst them. One of the charitable works which he furthered was an association of ladies for humanitarian work; he presented a home to them, which he named the " Frederica Foundation " in memory of the Queen, and to-day it is one of Hanover's principal hospitals. He received Elizabeth Fry during one of her visits and assured her of his support for her work.[3]

It was remarkable what was done in the Kingdom during those few years. After the chaos and misrule which immediately preceded the King's accession, everything was reorganised and rendered effective, discipline among officials was tightened and slackness and procrastination were no longer tolerated. One result of the improvement was misunderstood and unpopular. This was the changing of the scarlet of the Hanoverian Army, for which it had been famous in Germany, to blue. It has always been ascribed to the King's predilection for Prussian patterns, but in actual fact this unhappy decision had been made in George III's time and only financial difficulties had delayed its execution.[4]

---

[1] The King could not understand the struggles caused by the Factory Bill in his homeland, as he told Lord Strangford on the 19th May 1844. " I had hoped that yesterday's mail would have brought me a few lines, to explain to me how it is possible there should have been such a majority against Ashley's motion after all we have seen and heard. I am no advocate of tyranny or cruelty in any shape, still less where women and children are concerned," he continued, explaining that he had never had the time to visit the factories in England, but if such things went on, " surely there ought to be some legislative measure to stop such cruelties if existing. . . ." and " Equally do I agree with you, that it is a most lamentable thing for the country, the issue of the Factory Bill, for it certainly does not speak for the credit and honour of the House of Commons . . ." He also considered (29th May) that children " ought not to be confined so many hours in manufactories, where the air must be prejudicial to them, as they require both air and exercise to keep them healthy and make them grow."

[2] To Lord Strangford, 23rd January 1845.

[3] M.A. Privy Purse, VI 23. An appeal refers to " the well-known kindness shown by the King of Hanover to Mrs. Fry."

[4] Communication of Dr. Drögereit, of the State Archives, Hanover.

On the King's accession the capital was a city of mediæval houses densely packed within its bastions, far from the grand style of the usual German Refidenzſtadt. This state of affairs the King set about remedying as soon as he was free of the political preoccupations of the first years of his reign.

In 1838 he appointed as Court Architect George Laves (1789–1864), the man who had redesigned the Leine Palace and erected the Waterloo Column. Instead of razing the ancient city, as often happens in such cases, they decided to build a new district, the Ernſt Auguſt Stadt, or Ernest Augustus City, and this was to extend outwards from the avenues which, built upon the moat that had been filled in under George III, now bounded the city. Radial thoroughfares and avenues with long vistas were laid and the old ravelins became squares or gardens. Fine residences, Government buildings, the arsenal, the officers' school, pleasure gardens and, finally, the Court Opera House, formed the new city which surrounded the old mediæval cluster on three sides. The grandest of all was the Opera, built on the Georgestrasse, where formerly a windmill stood upon the ravelin. Before designing it, Laves was sent by the King to tour Italy and study all the chief theatres there. In fact, the Hanoverian Opera House became one of the finest in Germany, though King Ernest Augustus did not live to see its opening.[1]

No less was the King's building enthusiasm in the country. The restoration of his ancestors' palaces, including those of Celle, Lüneburg, Osnabrück and the Göhrde was a natural care for him, but he was keenly interested in other buildings of historical and artistic importance, and personally bought the fine old baroque house in the centre of Hanover in which Leibniz, the philosopher and adviser of the Electress Sophia, had lived and worked, when he heard of a proposal to break into its front and fit in modern shop-windows.

When the King had ceased to oppose railways—it will be seen how this came about—their construction was undertaken with great energy. The King insisted that they were to be Government enterprises, though this decision was not popular, as a burden upon the Exchequer was feared. The first was commenced in 1843 and opened the following year to Brunswick. In another few years the capital was connected with Hamburg, Bremen, Cassel, Minden (this extension completed the line from Berlin to the Rhine), Osnabrück and Emden. It had thus become a focal

[1] Begun 1845, completed January 1852.

point and all Royal travellers stayed a night or longer with the King. The Court was unrivalled for its brilliance and hospitality and the population of the capital lived largely from it. Everything prospered in what had been a few years before a dull and neglected provincial town and all this had been brought about by the accession of King Ernest Augustus. This alone would have gained him the respect and gratitude of his subjects, but not that personal love and affection which he had come to enjoy. It was his anxiety and paternal care for their welfare which forged that bond. Nothing pleased him more than to observe the happiness and prosperity of his people.

On one occasion there was great excitement among the peasants of Walsrode because the King was coming to hold a review during the manœuvres there. Some of them had decided to go to see it, but were concerned lest they should go in an unbefitting manner. They therefore hired a coach with the best black horses and engaged a postillion for the expedition. As they drove to the parade the spectators waiting along the road thought that the King was arriving and doffed their hats and cheered, so that the troops, hearing the cheering as the carriage approached, also took it for the King's. A general rode up to escort it to its destination. There, before all the troops drawn up, the door opened and the peasant occupants nervously alighted and bowed, begging the general not to be angry. In the middle of the universal laughter following the dénouement the King himself arrived and was told what had happened. " I am very pleased," he commented beaming, " that I have peasants in my Kingdom who can drive with a coach-and-four, and that they do it to see their King." [1]

On another occasion the King read in the newspaper that the postmaster at Celle, who often accompanied him when travelling in the district, had celebrated his fiftieth jubilee in service. He thereupon asked the Finance Minister why he had not been informed of this, and when he was told that such jubilees had not been considered important enough to justify a report, he replied that in future all such jubilees had to be announced to him. The next day he had dinner with the postmaster, for he held him to be an especially loyal servant. Another characteristic anecdote which shows the King's attention to the most trifling affairs of his people comes from Rabber, near Osnabrück. The church had just formed a brass band but the other parishioners complained that it disturbed them and addressed themselves to the King. The King

[1] Deutsch-Hannoversches Taschenkalender für das Jahr, 1882.

replied laconically, " The parishes have slept long enough ; it is time for them to be woken up." [1]

For the King himself, however, those years of success and fulfilment were the darkest of his life. No sooner were his political difficulties over than his wife died.

The Queen had been indisposed throughout the winter of 1840–41. On Easter Day she appeared at table for the last time. One day in May, however, the weather was so fine that she took a walk along her favourite route in the Calenbergerstrasse neighbourhood. Suddenly a violent thunderstorm broke out and she returned so shaken that an officer had to assist her to her room.[2] Though the doctors assured him that there was no danger, the King was apprehensive at the duration of her illness.[3]

On the 27th June the Queen's condition became so serious that she received the Sacrament from Mr. Hulme, the English Chaplain. During that day and the next the King remained with her the whole time and only went to bed himself at two in the morning, when she seemed to be comfortable. At seven he rose and, though hardly dressed, hurried up the little spiral staircase leading to her room above his, but she was sleeping so he withdrew again. At eight, the doctor summoned him and told him that a great change had taken place in her condition. The King went to her side, bowed down in his grief, and she put her left hand in his, saying, in English, " This is death "—the first time that she had mentioned the thought to him, though she had long been aware of the imminence of her dissolution. Her breathing grew fainter and fainter and, at twenty minutes past midnight, without any noticeable sign, she passed away, in the same room in which she had been born sixty-three and a quarter years before.[4]

" Alas, alas, all my happiness in this world is *finished*," wrote the King to her brother.[5] " At twenty minutes past midnight, our angelic and adored Ike *expired*. Oh, what a word ! Oh, dear friend, you know my adoration for that angel of a wife, for that is what she was. Certainly *I* have never known her like. She was the most faithful and tender wife, the best of wives, the most sincere, *amie*, noble, generous and charitable towards everyone, with no other thought or desire but to make those about her happy. . . . Oh, what an angel ; you know how much I loved

---

[1] Communication of Pastor Kasten, Rabber.   [2] M.A. Von Slicher's *Memoirs*.
[3] S.A. To Grand Duke, 8th June 1841.
[4] This account of the death of the Queen is from S.A. King to Grand Duke, 29th June 1841. See also that to Lord Strangford, 20th July 1841.
[5] S.A. To Grand Duke, 29th June 1841.

that adorable woman, for *me* she was everything in the world, for me, all is lost, for I can say that I lived only for her ; in her I found the tenderest wife, the most sincere *amie*, whom I consulted upon everything, and who always gave me the best advice, for it was always *disinterested*. Oh, my misery is great, the world holds nothing more for me." To a friend in England he wrote that what had supported him throughout all his struggles was " a happy home, domestic felicity—that is gone, and gone for ever, never to be recovered." [1]

On the 7th July the funeral took place. The King had himself discussed the arrangements for the melancholy ceremony with von Malortie, a most painful conference, for he burst into tears at intervals.[2] All eyes were upon him and hearts with him as he followed the coffin across the street to the Chapel, where it was laid in the crypt. " She is placed exactly opposite my window," he wrote.[3] " Only the wall of the Palace separates me from her, and I have had a key made so that I can go in and pray at her coffin. All will remain in her rooms as she had them ; nothing will be changed." Candles were lit and servants were in attendance every evening ; her books, even the bottle of Eau-de-Cologne, all were kept in their places, and the King used to go there for comfort before retiring every evening.[4] He resolved never to leave the Palais and thus gave up his and Laves's intention of demolishing it to allow a vista from the Marktkirche to the portico of the Palace opposite.[5] He decided to entrust to Laves the erection of a suitable resting-place for himself and his wife—" Laves is designing for me the plan of a Mausoleum, which I intend to have built in the flower-garden at Herrenhausen which she loved so much, and when he has drawn it I will send it to the King of Prussia, who has such good taste and knowledge, for his opinion." [6]

The King did not recover from his bereavement. " *Je ne veux rien plus pour ce monde,*" he said,[7] and to Lord Strangford he wrote,[8] " Her loss is to me irreparable and I can say life is now become to

---

[1] To Sir Henry Halford, 25th July 1841. At the same time Lady Cowper (Lady Palmerston) was writing to Princess Lieven, " They say that wicked husband of hers has already chosen a second wife."

[2] *Von Malortie*, pp. 111–115 and Appendix V.

[3] S.A. To Grand Duke, 8th July 1841.

[4] S.A. To Grand Duke, 23rd July 1841.

[5] A Royal suite was already being prepared in the Residence Palace which was to take the place of the Altes Palais.

[6] S.A. To Grand Duke, 8th July 1841.

[7] S.A. To Grand Duke, 15th September 1841.

[8] To Lord Strangford, 20th July 1841.

me a burden. . . . Nothing but a conscientious feeling that the preservation of my life is at this moment of use to my God and my country may make me wish still to lead on a life which, as I have said, can only be a burden."

After the funeral the King lived in retirement. His sole occupations were state affairs, his private correspondence and very long rides. The doctors were not happy and suggested that he should take a cure at Ems. Apathetically, he acquiesced, though he saw no purpose in what they recommended. After weeping and praying at the Queen's coffin, he left Hanover on the 1st August accompanied by his two stepchildren, Alexander and Augusta. "Throughout the journey," he wrote,[1] " I reflected upon all that had happened, the scenes of the last days, the words, the expressions, the feelings, in a word, all that had taken place, and unhappily, I have become so dim from my state of nerves that I have often not understood what has been said to me. Oh, what a sad and horrible position ! "

In Ems the King was at first very irritable. The waters, he complained, made him giddy and lose his appetite and his capacity for thought.[2] This was especially so after the morning cure and on the promenade. But there was society and gradually he began to take an interest in his surroundings again. The Queen of Greece [3] was able to reawaken his humorous moods, Sir Charles Wetherell was there, and Metternich, whose Rhine castle of Johannisburg was in the neighbourhood, often dined with him alone. They spoke of political affairs and one day the conversation turned upon the development of railways. The King had always been opposed to them, but Metternich now persuaded him that they were a " necessary evil " and that rulers would be wise to develop them as speedily as possible.[4] The words of the great statesman had weight with the King, and although he never overcame his personal dislike of them, thenceforth he furthered the construction of railways in Hanover with the energy with which he had formerly opposed them. The King arrived in Hanover on the 2nd September [5]—" The homecoming is terrible for me. Oh, I cannot describe to you what I felt in arriving back here, to enter

[1] S.A. To Grand Duke, 2nd August and 15th September 1841.
[2] S.A. To Grand Duke, 15th September 1841 ; M.A. *Von Slicher.*
[3] Queen Amelie, wife of the Wittelsbach King Otho of Greece, née Princess of Oldenburg.
[4] M.A. *Von Slicher.*
[5] The King travelled by steamer to Cologne, where he slept and saw the city. He also visited the small-arms factory at Solingen on the way.

alone into my rooms, for dear and adored Ike used to leave at the moment when I arrived, and came down to receive me with open arms. This time I went up to those dear chambers alone." [1] There he prayed every night before going to bed.

The remainder of the year passed quietly for the King, and the cessation of Court life through the mourning made the capital a very dull place. But the King was still superstitious about New Year celebrations and so ordered a hunting-party in the Göhrde and left Hanover on the last day of the year. On the way he was in a good mood and related experiences from his campaigns to his aide, but on their arrival at Uelzen, where he slept the night, the officer was astonished to observe what a change came over him. He wished to see no one and could only with difficulty be prevailed upon to receive the gentlemen waiting to greet him. Every word which fell from his lips was bitter, and it was not pleasant for the unfortunate officials at dinner in the evening. The King always sought to hide the softness of his feelings and so his moods seemed to be contrary to those which were to be expected. [2]

With the New Year and the cessation of official mourning— though the King himself never laid it off for the rest of his life— Court life gradually recommenced. In March the King paid a visit to Berlin to his old friends and acquaintances. [3] He frequently dined with the King of Prussia and it was on one of these occasions that he made the sarcastic remark which has since become notorious—" Professors have no homeland," he said jokingly. " One can have professors, comedians and loose girls for money anywhere." Von Humboldt, who was sitting at the table with them, was offended, but it was only one of the teasing remarks which his guests had often to tolerate, and those who knew him countered them in the same spirit. What the King could not suffer was anxiety or servility, and those who betrayed embarrassment were asking for more teasing. This was one of the curious and unpleasant eccentricities of the King's old age, but under the surface his feelings were of quite a different nature. " Ach, my friend," he wrote from Berlin, " each house, each stone here reminds me of my former happiness, and now I feel my very sad and lonely

---

[1] S.A. To Grand Duke, 15th September 1841.   [2] M.A. *Von Slicher.*

[3] After his accession the King had given up his Palace in Berlin, which he rented from the daughter of Frau von Berg, Countess von Voss. In 1839, however, he again desired a residence for his visits to Berlin and bought Count von Redern's house, the house in which Prince George had been born. The Hanoverian Ambassador was also to live there.

position a hundredfold." He also went on to Strelitz—" the dear village "—and there he revisited the scenes of his first acquaintance with his wife. " Many a tear have I shed on the quiet, but my heart is lighter and I find a sort of comfort in visiting the different places which I have seen with other feelings upon other occasions." [1]

At the end of August 1842 the King of Prussia invited him to the manœuvres on the Rhine, and there he was so ill that his life was despaired of by the doctors.[2] His eccentricities always appeared at their worst when he was unwell. He distrusted medicines and when they were prescribed for him he always told his valet to " put them in the cupboard." On one occasion when he recovered from an indisposition and the doctors were feeling satisfied with themselves, he opened the cupboard before them. " Yes, gentlemen," he said, " and do you think that I would have recovered if I had taken all that ? " [3]

The King regained his strength very slowly and was a source of anxiety throughout the remainder of the year (1842) ; when he went hunting in the Göhrde in December, great precautions were taken to prevent his catching cold, and huts with stoves were built at various points in the forest. But on the whole his health was improving and he was already attending evening parties again. Travelling became one of his chief joys and he was never in a better mood or more talkative than when on the road. There he could forget, or re-live, former days. Since Hanover now held sad memories for him, he was happiest when he visited his wife's daughter [4] at Dessau, or the scenes of his most treasured memories in Berlin, though now, as will be seen, political tensions had arisen which soured even this pleasure. On his return from a visit to Berlin in April 1843, he announced his intention of going to England as soon as he had despatched the work which had accumulated in his absence, but he would not bind himself to any date and there was always mystery and uncertainty about his movements.[5]

The King's bereavement, the burdensomeness of his life and his severe illness had led him to think more and more of his own death and of his son's future. He had carefully seen that his right of succession was upheld in the new Constitution—in that of 1833

---

[1] S.A. To Grand Duke, 8th March and 1st April 1844.
[2] For Dr. Baring's account of this illness, see *Von Malortie*, Appendix VI. So that the King could be examined by another doctor, something to which he would never have consented, a consultation was carried out in the dark, with Baring asking the questions.   [3] *Wilkinson.*
[4] Of her first husband. Frederica (1796–1850) married the Duke of Anhalt-Dessau in 1818.   [5] F.O. 34/39, 13th April 1843.

ambiguous phrasing, no doubt intentional, might have cast a doubt upon it—and he had initiated him into state affairs. During the discussions of the new Constitution in January of 1840 they together attended the Cabinet meetings almost daily, and the Crown Prince zealously approved of all which his father did. The King particularly ordered him to take the strictest care of his health, for he had not yet despaired of his regaining his sight. Successive painful operations yielded no result, but a more tolerable part of the treatment was sea-bathing on the North Sea island of Norderney, and his yearly visits established it as a fashionable resort. Members of other Royal Houses followed his example, and among them was the Duke of Saxe-Altenburg with his family.[1]

Every year the Crown Prince met his young cousin Mary and every year his affection for her grew stronger. Whenever possible he visited the little Thuringian Duchy of Altenburg, and in April 1842 he wrote home requesting his father's consent to their engagement.[2] The King was pleased at this, but counselled patience. They must look after their English as well as their Hanoverian interests, he said, and unless they were to lose their rights in England, the Queen had to give her consent as well in accordance with the Royal Marriages Act of George III's reign. The marriage of a Prince and Princess and their freedom in their own affairs could not be quite like those of a tinker, he pointed out.[3] The Duke of Wellington undertook to discharge all formalities in England. Queen Victoria gave her consent and the marriage took place on the 18th February 1843,[4] in the Palace Chapel at Hanover. Guests came from all over Germany and among those present were the bridegroom's cousins, the King of Prussia and the future Emperor William. For King Ernest Augustus and for Hanover, it was a great relief and the future seemed assured. He thought now only of his son, and after the wedding, when he betook himself out of his realms for recreation, he gave him full powers of state during his three months' absence so that he could accustom himself to the duties which would fall to him upon his death.

[1] Joseph, Duke of Saxe-Altenburg (1789–1868) was the King's nephew, his mother (1769–1818) being a sister of his wife.
[2] G.A. Crown Prince to King, 24th April 1842.
[3] *Ibid.* To Crown Prince, 26th April and 7th May 1842.
[4] See the account of the wedding, *Von Malortie*, Appendix VIII.

CHAPTER XXIII

VISIT TO ENGLAND

KING ERNEST AUGUSTUS did not cease to regard himself as an Englishman, though he had little enough association with the land of his birth after his removal to Hanover. Most of his old connections feared to have contact with him lest the Whigs should learn of it, and his unhappy ambassador in London, von Münchhausen,[1] reported that everyone was nervous of being seen in his company.[2] The King himself wrote to Croker hurt that he seemed to be dead to all his old political friends,[3] and Peel, who was visiting Germany in October 1837, refused his request to explain his case in England.[4]

Only the King's sisters did not waver in their admiration. " I was so very much delighted, my dear Ernest, with your reply to the states of Göttingen," wrote Princess Augusta,[5] " that I read it at least *twenty* times over. I positively fancy that I heard you speak it." The old ladies had precious little glory nowadays. The young Queen's natural jealousy and Whig sympathies created a gulf, even had she not been brought up by her mother to dislike

[1] During the Personal Union, there had been no Embassies, as the Hanoverian Chancellory was with the King's person in London. With the separation, diplomatic representation became necessary and in November 1837 the King announced that he would establish an Embassy in London under Borries von Münchhausen, with Charles Klingemann as Secretary of Legation. He had been represented by Count von Alten at the Coronation. In the latter part of the reign von Münchhausen was succeeded as Ambassador by Count von Kielmannsegg. The Queen appointed the Honourable John Duncan Bligh (1798–1872), son of the fourth Earl of Darnley, as her Ambassador in Hanover, where he took up his post on the 24th May 1838, with George Edgcumbe as his Secretary of Legation. Many diplomatic associations continued, especially in remote parts where the accrediting of a Hanoverian Minister was hardly necessary. The British representative in Lima, for example, asked if he were still to act for Hanover as before 1837, an offer which the Hanoverian Government accepted (F.O. 34/28, 4th June, 1838).
[2] H.A. Von Münchhausen's report, 31st October 1837.
[3] To Croker, 30th December 1838.
[4] H.A. Von Stralenheim's report ; Parker's *Peel*. The King learned that Peel was in Stuttgart and sent his envoy in Frankfurt, von Stralenheim, to answer any questions that he might have, as he was " most anxious that you, as the head of the Conservative Party, should be thoroughly acquainted with the true state of affairs here . . ." Von Stralenheim had a very long interview and answered all Peel's questions, but Peel declined to have anything to do with the matter, or to explain the King's case in Parliament if necessary.
[5] G.A. To King of Hanover, 13th December 1837.

her relations. William IV had once told the Duchess of Gloucester
" that he felt indignant at the Duchess of Kent's conduct and that
he should send her a message forbidding her lodging the young
Princes of Coburg at Kensington, for as she had upon pretext of
propriety kept Victoria from being permitted to see her *cousins of
England*, he thought the same was valid for her German cousins." [1]
With the coming of Prince Albert, the gulf widened and an act of
stupidity on the part of the Queen's advisers drove the King into
becoming the protector of the honour of his House.

Existing law made no provision for a Prince Consort, so the
Dukes of Sussex and Cambridge were approached with the suggestion that they might agree to give up their claims of precedence
before the Queen's husband. The King of Hanover was, of
course, in England still a Prince of the Blood, but nothing was
said to him, since it was thought better to let sleeping dogs lie (if
there were no malicious motive). The authors of the new ruling
thus placed themselves in the wrong and the King only learnt of
their doings by chance. If under other circumstances he might
have been only too willing to give way to this reasonable proposal,
under these, he instantly declared his refusal and stood up for the
honour of the family which had until so recently been reigning in
England. He described his actions to his brother-in-law.[2]

It was only by individual letters that I first learnt of this idea of giving
precedence to Prince Albert which my two brothers have unfortunately
ceded, one of them with certain conditions, the Duke of Cambridge
without thinking, without reflecting upon all the consequences. The
moment that I heard of it, I wrote to the Duke of Wellington and
several others of my old political friends *declaring* that, as Chief of the
House,[3] I protested against it openly and publicly, and I would never
renounce my rights, and that I was bound for the honour of my family

---

[1] G.A. Duke of Cumberland to Duchess, 11th May 1836.

[2] S.A. To Grand Duke of Strelitz, 20th February 1840.

[3] An extremely complicated dynastical situation had arisen, as, through the existence
of a female succession, no principle of *House* but of *Throne* applies in Britain. Thus
laws which in other lands would be enacted as binding upon members of the House
are enacted in England as binding upon persons related to the bearer, or a particular
bearer, of the Crown, e.g., the Royal Marriages Act. It is a point for discussion,
whether the Hanoverians ceased to reign in Great Britain in 1837 or with the death of
Queen Victoria. The other Guelphs still in Britain were subordinate to the King of
Hanover as head of the House and family and to the Queen as Sovereign of Great
Britain. The King tenaciously asserted his rights, giving his consent as head of the
House to the marriage of his niece in 1843, but he was equally aware of his duties
and his subordination to the Queen as an English Prince. The English Ambassador
always witnessed births in the family, and it has been seen how conscientious the King
was in complying with English law and requesting the Queen's consent to his son's
marriage.

living and for the memory of the deceased ; that even if my brothers
had yielded, I protested just as much against that, as they have no right
to do that alone, without previously consulting me.   And you will see
by the result that I was *right*.   I must at least do the Duke of Cambridge
the justice of saying that, after receiving my letter, he did all that he could,
for he went to see the Queen and Lord Melbourne, declaring to *them*
that after mature reflection he saw the impossibility of giving his consent
and that he was withdrawing it.   From letters that I have had since,
containing details of the wedding, it seems that the members of the *old*
Royal Family were treated in a manner to which I, had I been there,
would not have submitted ; for think, they *all* had to wait in the ante-
chamber with the Lords-in-Waiting and Officers of the Court while the
Duchess of Kent and the Coburgs were admitted into the Royal cabinet.
That is a bit too much, *it must be confessed*.   I have written at once to
the Duke of Cambridge, having heard that he wished to reply to Lord
Melbourne, if such a proposition were made to him, " that naturally
Her Majesty had the right to introduce what etiquette she judged proper
at her Court, but that that being so, although it would be very disagreeable
to him, he would not in this case be able to appear there."   It is vital,
believe me, not to cede a point, otherwise they are all lost and insulted.
What do you say to the fact that since the wedding, although the Queen
had given two grand dinners, no member of the old Royal Family was
invited, but the Coburgs daily ?   I am surprised that Madame Cambridge,
who knows so well what is proper, should not have spoken to the Duke
about it seriously, and he is more interested because of his *own son*.

Relations between the two Courts became strained and soon
other quarrels arose.   The King was asked to surrender his apartments at St. James's to the Duchess of Kent as she had conceived
a distaste for Kensington Palace.   This he declined to do.[1]   The
farther and longer his separation from England, the more these
places and memories meant to him and the more tenaciously he
clung to them.   The next dispute was more serious in its nature.
With the dissolution of the Personal Union, the question arose as
to which of the possessions and heirlooms in England had belonged
to the family as such, which would now return to Hanover, and
which of them belonged to the Sovereign of England as such.
Many of the family heirlooms of the Guelphs and the Hanoverian
Crown were, of course, in England, and the Queen was now
advised by her Whig Attorney-General and the Law Officers to
claim them as belonging to the British Crown.   The grounds
which they advanced for this claim were absurd even for a layman.
The King was incensed, especially when he heard that the Queen
had worn his jewels in public, " that she was loaded with my
diamonds, which made a very fine show." [2]   After much wrangling

---

[1] *Greville*, 29th March 1840, IV, pp. 289–90.   [2] To Strangford, June 1851.

and resistance on the part of the Government, a commission of three High Court judges was established. They were about to decide in the King's favour when one of them, Chief Justice Tindal, died, and the Lord Chancellor refused to renew the commission. So matters rested. The King, weary of the strife, said that he would let the Queen retain the jewels with the exception of a few which were very important to the Hanoverian Crown. Six years after his death the Government decided that the matter should finally be settled and appointed a new commission of three judges, who unhesitatingly pronounced in favour of the late King. " They had ample evidence," said one of them, " and they were all quite satisfied upon the point." So the King was posthumously vindicated and the jewels were handed over to his son.[1]

Despite the coolness between the two Courts, as the King became increasingly lonely, homesickness overcame him and he resolved to see once more the old scenes and those of his friends and relatives who survived. But it was a long time before he would make any precise plans. Not even the English Cabinet knew the date of his arrival, and Princess Alice, to whom he was to be godfather, had already been christened [2] when he suddenly appeared off the coast. A Royal Navy steamer had been waiting several days at Calais and he had arrived there on the 2nd June 1843. Since the King had announced his wish to land incognito,[3] there was no official reception for him at Woolwich, but his coming was betrayed from afar by the sight of the captain in full dress on the deck and a crowd had already gathered on the quay. Some of them doffed their hats and cheered, others hissed, as the police held a wide passage open for him to the Customs House. There the King and his suite [4] waited until a presentable coach was found in the neighbourhood and then set off at walking-pace " through a disgusting screeching mob." To the King, this was a sign that he was at home again, but attendants were not so impressed. " I would like to have taught the Britons how a German King is received," wrote von Slicher, " but I had to clench my fists in my pockets." The coachman turned into an empty side-street and they were soon clear of the mob running behind them.[5]

[1] *Greville*, 29th and 31st December 1857, VIII pp. 150–52.

[2] The Queen's third child, afterwards Grand Duchess of Hesse-Darmstadt, born on the 25th April and christened on the 6th June 1843.

[3] H.A. K.G. Hann. 9 Dom. 321.

[4] His suite consisted of von Falcke, von Malortie, von Hattorff, von Slicher, von Reitzenstein, Dr. Baring and, in England, Sir Frederick Beilby Watson, who acted as his chamberlain.

[5] The account of the arrival is from von Slicher's *Diary* and *The Times*.

The King lost no time in visiting his family and friends. From now on, for his visit, he was Duke of Cumberland again, and he issued all invitation cards in this name. All London society thronged to leave their cards at St. James's, even those who had formerly openly denounced the Duke of Cumberland in Parliament.[1] As Greville remarked,[2] " The King of Hanover must be rather astonished to find himself received as he has been here, and visited by all manner of men. Everybody seems to think it necessary to treat him with dinners and balls, and he is become the lion of the season with this foolish, inconsistent world," and he himself wrote of how happy he was,[3] " It is extraordinary how much better I feel in every respect since I am on my native shore, and I begin now to eat with appetite and delight. The measure in which I have been received by *all* persons, *high* and low, is most gratifying, *no* party feeling against me. What will you say, I have had *two* visits from Brougham. . . . My door is like a theatre and what files of carriages all day. . . ." He had, he said, no news but " the cordial and prepossessing attention constantly shown to me by all classes of people. They seem to vie with each other in inviting me to their houses and doing all in their power to prove their regard and esteem for me."

The villagers of Kew were making preparations to celebrate his return. On his birthday there were cricket and rural games and amusements on the Green during the day. At one o'clock there was a salute of twenty-one guns, in the afternoon the principal inhabitants dined together, and in the evening all the houses were illuminated and fireworks let off on the Green. The children of the Free School, in their classroom elaborately fitted up for the occasion, ate roast beef and plum pudding.[4]

On the 14th June the King was invited to a dinner and concert at Buckingham Palace. Queen Victoria wrote an account of it in her journal.[5]

. . . We dined at eight, the King of Hanover and four gentlemen . . . The King is much subdued to what he used to be, but he is a very strange, though by no means a stupid man, and very active. He amused me much by several observations he made, amongst others, one about the late King,

---

[1] Long lists of callers are given by *The Times* for every day of the King's visit.

[2] *Greville*, 14th June V, pp. 167–68. " He seems to have behaved very well, taking great pleasure in the attentions he has received, but giving no cause for complaint by any indecorous or imprudent language. In fact, he seems not to have meddled with politics in any way whatever."—6th August.

[3] G.A. To Crown Prince, 9th and 20th June 1843.

[4] *The Times*.   [5] W.A. The Queen's *Journal*.

which is certainly not untrue. Aunt Gloucester made some remark about the late King having done away with something, upon which he said : " Oh ! Poor dear William was an excellent good soul, but he gave away everything—he would have given away his coat at last ! " The King has instituted an Order, a new one, called St. George, of which the ribbon is red, and when I spoke about it, he said : " Why, the late King gave the Guelph Order away to ragtag and bobtail, so that I found it absolutely necessary to have another Order to give away." This one he gives very seldom. We had settled to have no other healths given out but the King's, and accordingtly this was done, the band playing a curious kind of hymn, after it, upon which he remarked laughingly : " That's a description of my character ' *tout craché* '—a gentle sort of song, I suppose because I am old now." After this he got up, and I felt hot and cold from nervousnesss, and from the recollection of the poor late King's unfortunate speeches. The King of Hanover began about as follows : " I have the honour to propose the health of Her Majesty Queen Victoria, and I beg to state distinctly that I do so as one of Her Majesty's subjects, and as I have frequently said in the House of Lords that she has not a more faithful subject than the individual who addresses you now and I am delighted to drink Her Majesty's health in her own palace. God bless you." [1] He then shook my hand, after which we ladies got up from dinner. Some more people came in afterwards and we had an excellent concert in the salon. The King sat between the Queen Dowager and me and Aunt Gloucester on my other side.

Every week-end the King went to Kew with a group of his friends, among whom Wetherell was usually to be found. Often they sat up reminiscing until dawn and the King frequently recited his parliamentary speeches. One of these was only broken by the guests' having fallen asleep, when the snoring moved him to retire. On another occasion the King played a joke on an old clergyman and gourmand, as von Slicher describes him in his account of it, who was particularly fond of turtle soup. He ordered water soup resembling it in appearance, and when he saw his guest taste it and then leave it untouched, he asked, " Hullo ! Don't you like my soup ? " " That's cursed dishwater ! " retorted the cleric to the King's amusement. [2]

In London the King went from one party to another, often returning when the sun was already high in the heavens. He was so happy and exuberant that Dr. Baring feared a reaction when he should return. Even his suite were finding the life which they were leading a great strain. [3]

---

[1] Von Kielmannsegg, in his report to von Schele, says that the King ended his speech with the words, " Kindly accept these wishes of your old uncle, and God bless you, my dear niece, with many years yet ! "—H.A. K.G. Hann. 9 Dom. 321.

[2] M.A. Von Slicher's *Memoirs*.   [3] Von Slicher's *Diary*.

The King's happiness was not destined to last, however. As has been seen, his relations with his niece, the Queen, had been strained, but so far their relations on his visit had been tolerably well maintained. It must have been conspicuous, however, that though seeing friends and relatives the whole time, the King had only twice been to Buckingham Palace. "The determination of the Queen and Prince not to go," wrote Greville of the poor showing of society at Ascot,[1] "is attributed by some to their dislike of all racing, and by others to the presence of the King of Hanover, who would have obliged her, if she had had the usual party at Windsor, to invite him there. . . . The King of Hanover has been the great lion of London, all the Tories feasting and entertaining him with extraordinary demonstrations of civility and regard, but not the Court, for the Queen has hardly taken any notice of him."

The great event of the King's visit was the wedding of his niece and nephew, Princess Augusta, the twenty-one-year-old daughter of the Duke of Cambridge, to Prince Frederick, the eldest son and Heir of the Grand Duke of Mecklenburg-Strelitz. With his brother, he was to give the bride away. The ceremony took place at Buckingham Palace on the 28th June. The King was to have driven there with Queen Adelaide, but when he called for her she was indisposed, so he went alone, in a richly-gilded coach, with an escort of his old regiment, the Royal Horse Guards. In the portico of the Palace the King was received by the gentlemen members of the Queen's Household, and escorted to where the procession was forming. The bride entered the Chapel between her father and the King, and the latter's suite followed. The Archbishops of Canterbury and York and the Bishops of Norwich and London performed the ceremony and the assembly then moved in reversed order back to the round salon in the middle of the long gallery for the signature of the certificates. This was to be done by all the Royal witnesses, the Bishops and Peel, the Prime Minister. First the Queen signed, then the King moved forward to add his signature, as next in rank. But Prince Albert stepped in between and signed first, whereupon the King indignantly refused to follow. But he had his revenge.

The procession began to move to the rooms above, where a large company of invited guests was waiting to offer congratulations. According to the programme, the Queen was to lead on the arm of her husband. But the King adroitly took her hand in time. Despite her attempts to free it, he held firm and when she

[1] *Greville*, 14th June 1843, V, p. 167.

said, " You're hurting me ! " he replied, " I am sorry, but I won't let go ; I know where I belong." So she yielded and led the procession with him. The King hurried away as soon as he could after the congratulations and, thoroughly disconcerted, he left immediately for Kew.[1] He did not wish to attend the Drawing Room the following day, and he sent his suite instead. A complete breach had resulted and the King withdrew to himself in low spirits, which were aggravated by a further *malheur*.

When he visited the Grand Duke and Duchess of Mecklenburg [2] the next day, he did not see the two steps at the door. He fell on his left arm and side and sprained his leg, which caused him great pain. But he dismissed his injury as nothing and went to dinner with Lord and Lady Ailesbury the same day. He returned to town on the morrow thoroughly off colour, complaining of aches and pains. However, he did not wish to miss a dinner given by Lady Salisbury, and cut short Baring's representations with " Rubbish ! " The result was that his pains increased, he spent a sleepless night and was for some days a thoroughly sick man. On the 5th July he felt better and the prospect of dining that evening with Sir Charles Wetherell at Inner Temple raised his spirits.

It was a hectic evening. As the King and von Slicher drove through the gateway of Temple Bar they were received by a noise which sounded like ravens, and this " goading, nauseating screech " continued the whole way, as the crowd was so thick that they could only proceed step by step. At places, von Slicher actually saw people putting out their tongues. He had never experienced anything like this before, but the King was almost happy at the familiar setting. " What do you think of that ? " he asked, grinning. " It is a disgusting scandal, a mob from Hell ! " replied von Slicher hotly. But the King remained quite calm. " My good friend," he said, " you are not used to it, but I am and do not trouble about it. I have experienced worse scandals than that, but it is a fine people and I love it ! " To his aide's relief, they turned into a side-street and it became quiet. They drove up King's Bench Walk to the entrance in Tanfield Court, where there was a crowd which *cheered*. At the doorway the King was greeted by Wetherell and other leading members of Bar and they went up to the library, where many old friends and Lord Brougham were waiting. After dinner in the Hall, Wetherell made a long speech, praising the King

---

[1] Von Slicher's *Diary* and (M.A.) *Memoirs*.
[2] They were staying at Cambridge Cottage, Kew, with the parents of their daughter-in-law.

for not forgetting his old friends in England. It was very late when the King and von Slicher drove home, but the streets were full and the same spectacle and din accompanied them to the City limits as on their arrival. The King, however, was in a gay mood and sang a song to himself as they drove.[1]

But the old antagonism between the King and the Court persisted and he left the next day for Kew to avoid a Drawing Room and parade. He sent his officers to represent him, but as he was not present, no horses were placed at their disposal and they had to stand among the spectators. He was in no good mood at his exile, for it prevented his dining the following day with Lord Kenyon. He was bored and irritable. Von Malortie and Baring sought to brighten him up, and succeeded somewhat on a long walk in the Gardens in the sunshine, but the next day (the 8th July) it poured in torrents " and our old master was as overcast as the sky." [2] On the 9th the weather cleared and the King drove out to visit the King of the Belgians,[3] also living in his old house at Claremont. The King did not return to London until the 10th, when he resumed his round of social visits.

The King also took a pleasure in revisiting the scene of his great parliamentary struggles. On the 9th June he took his seat in the House of Lords as Duke of Cumberland. " Lord Londonderry and Lord Kenyon," wrote the Queen in her journal,[4] " were urging him to take his seat in the House of Lords and he said to Aunt Gloucester : ' Old Wellington wishes me not to go,' but that he meant to do so. On Aunt expressing the hope that he would take no part in the debate, the King's characteristic reply was : ' No, I shall not, unless the Devil prompts me ! ' " and afterwards, " The Duke of Wellington thinks the King of Hanover (who took his seat in the House of Lords yesterday against everyone's wish but took no part in the debate) much pleased, and in very good humour." On the 19th June, Lord Strangford called on him at Kew and they rode up to Parliament. " I came up to town yesterday morning from Kew at eleven o'clock," the King wrote,[5] " to hear the judgment which was to be given upon the opinions respecting any alteration that might or could take place with respect to insane persons trying to take away the lives of others, and after sitting an hour and a half and listening with all

[1] *The Times* and von Slicher's *Diary* and (M.A.) *Memoirs*.
[2] Von Slicher's *Diary*.
[3] Formerly Prince Leopold, husband of Princess Charlotte, uncle of the Queen, now also on a visit to England.
[4] W.A. The Queen's *Journal*.   [5] G.A. To Crown Prince, 20th June 1843.

due attention, left the House as wise as I went into it. I attributed this to my ignorance and want of faculty of understanding, but was happy to find that many other Noble Lords were in the same situation as myself." On the 16th July he was again in his place and he found the debate so interesting that he did not leave until three in the morning. " It is to me most truly gratifying to hear *good* speaking and seeing how much better, clearer and more concisely all carry on a debate here," he wrote afterwards.[1] " I lost not a word, and my old parliamentary passion revived in me and I could have spoken myself. When I compare this to our way of debating in Germany, I feel the melancholy difference, for there they never stick to the subject, but always talk of a dozen others, which confuses all, at least me. Though I was *two* hours in the House and lost not a word, still I was not half so fatigued as at one of our meetings." On the 15th August he attended for the last time, when the Irish Arms Bill was being debated.

At the same time his presence had repercussions in the Commons, where there had already been some acrimonious discussion on the arrangements for the marriage of Princess Augusta. A Mr. Blewitt asked whether, as King of Hanover, Ernest Augustus could continue to discharge his constitutional duties in this country. As a foreign Sovereign, he said, he might conclude alliances against the Queen which would render him guilty of high treason as one of her subjects. Could he, then, continue to enjoy the privileges of a Peer ? he asked. The Speaker ruled that such a question was not to be considered and it was withdrawn. Of course, the position was now no different from what it had been for over a century, since the Crowns of England and Hanover had always, theoretically and constitutionally, been quite unassociated.

A more serious attack was made by the King's veteran antagonist, Hume, on the 30th June. He asked whether the King ought to continue to draw his income as Prince of Great Britain now that he had left the country. Peel replied that Parliament could not go back on its word. When sums had been voted for life, that was an end to it, and the House agreed. He might have added that none of the King's English income left the country, or was for his own use ; that it served for the upkeep of his two establishments, with their staffs, who had all been retained, and pensioners, and for charitable donations, the latest of which was a gift of five hundred pounds to the widow of Theodore Hook. But more interesting was the seconder of Hume's motion, Mr.

[1] G.A. To Crown Prince, 17th July 1843.

Wallace, as he brought an annihilating reply from Mr. Ferrand, who stated that he " was not ashamed to declare that he honoured and respected the King of Hanover [Laughter]. Yes, he [the King] had long stood the taunts and sneers of his enemies. Men had dared to slander him behind his back, but when he met them in the Courts of Law, before a jury of his fellow-countrymen, he had been acquitted and left the Court unstained [" Oh, oh ! " and laughter]. Who was the member that brought forward this charge against him ? A Member of that House who first obtained his seat within its walls under the influence and patronage of the King of Hanover [loud Ministerial cheers] and who afterwards applied to him to use his Royal influence that he might obtain a seat for the Borough of Weymouth.[1] He would not impute motives within these walls, but he left the Honourable Member to his own conscience, if he had one [Laughter]." The voting was 91–197, a majority of 106 against Hume's resolution.

The whirl of the King's social life did not abate but his stay was thoroughly soured by his feud with the Court. He was only remaining to press upon the Queen the necessity of bringing the affair of the Crown Jewels to a settlement. The Whigs with their personal antagonism were no longer her advisers ; Lord Aberdeen was more reasonable and it was agreed at last to settle the matter by arbitration, as the King had suggested six months before. He had only to wait for the appointment of the commissioners from the Government side and then he would name his own and leave. " Thus stands the business *now*, and more plague I never had in my life, and had I not taken it in hand myself, I doubt its ever coming to a close. . . . I am now longing to get away and see you all again. *Not one moment* longer than is absolutely necessary will I remain." [2]

It was therefore a welcome relief for the King when the Duke of Buckingham invited him to stay a few days at his country seat at Stowe, in Buckinghamshire. He left London on the afternoon of the 5th August, with his sister, the Duchess of Gloucester, and travelled to Wolverton by the London and Birmingham Railway. They arrived at six and were welcomed by the Yeomanry, with their band, for this was the week of their muster. There was a large house-party, everything was on a grand scale and the King called Stowe " one of the finest possessions in the country." On Sunday they attended service in the private chapel, with one of the guests, the Bishop of Rochester, officiating, and the next day a grand review of the Yeomanry was held in the Home Park. It

[1] In 1813. See Chapter IX.   [2] G.A. To Crown Prince, 13th and 21st August 1843.

was the last day of the muster, and the Duke himself, the Colonel-Commandant, in full dress, led them before the inspecting officer, Colonel Hall. On Tuesday, the 8th, the King and his sister left, taking the eleven o'clock train from Wolverton. There was a cloud-burst as they were leaving and the water rose up the steps into the hall so that fire-engines had to be brought up to pump it out of the house.[1]

At last the King received notification of the nomination of commissioners by the Government and decided to leave at once, for though everywhere else he had been enthusiastically received, " The Court pays not common civility to anyone except a Coburg or to what belongs to that family. . . . I have naught to complain for excepting the Court I have been fêted and honoured everywhere and by everyone, but certainly very miserably treated by the Court." [2] On the 2nd September he took leave of his staff and quitted Kew for the last time in his life. All the principal inhabitants were assembled on the Green and he recognised many as he stepped into his carriage. As he left, there was a loud farewell cheer. That evening he left St. James's for Woolwich, where H.M. steamer *Dover*, under Captain Lynn, R.N., was lying at Brunswick Wharf. Count von Kielmannsegg (his Ambassador in London), Charles Klingemann (Secretary of the Legation), Lord Strangford, Lord Bloomfield (Commandant at Woolwich) and Sir John Hall, the King's Consul-General (who had supervised arrangements for the embarkation), were waiting at the wharf to receive him and conduct him to the ship. At midnight she sailed for Antwerp.[3]

The King did not visit the land of his birth again. Its increasing industrialisation and the depression of the countryside, the difficulty with which the Factory Acts were passed, what he considered the treachery of Peel—all these things disgusted him ; he had struggled enough to preserve the Anglican supremacy but now, he said, with the admission of Jews and Freethinkers to Parliament, even the Christian supremacy was lost. " The more I consider how all is now unfortunately going to rack and ruin in England, the more I am determined not to put my foot there in a hurry," he wrote,[4] " as I could not disguise my sentiments and feelings on the occasion, and should probably quarrel with my old friends."

The final breach occurred when Palmerston became Foreign

[1] Details of the visit to Stowe are from G.A. To Crown Prince, 7th and 13th August 1843, and *The Times*.
[2] G.A. To Crown Prince, 27th August 1843.
[3] The description of the embarkation is from *The Times*.
[4] To Lord Strangford, 23rd June 1847.

Secretary. The King of Hanover saw for himself that he was encouraging revolutionary movements and attempting to subvert the existing order everywhere, and he found that Prince Albert, too, was furthering the work of the German nationalists and aggressive expansion of Prussia, as will be seen.[1] When the King observed the rôle which his country was now playing in European politics, he felt ashamed. " No one can lament this more than I do," he wrote,[2] " for my heart, soul and thoughts are British, and all that can raise its glory, fame and honour most sacredly dear to me." He had no wish to know the new Victorian England, with its characteristic smokestacks and rows of gloomy terrace-houses. When his nephew [3] announced that he had been invited to see the Great Exhibition, he replied,[4] " that even were I in England I would not put a foot in Hyde Park, as I disapproved of the whole thing and I feared it would bring all the ruffians and *canaille* from all parts of the world into the country, which might lead to very serious mischief, but that instead I would remove quietly and enjoy the fine weather and the sweet scents of my little cottage at Kew." Even this comfort was not preserved for him. The Sovereign had given Kew up and made it a public park. " Is this the march of intellect or the courtesy of popularity ? " he asked,[5] " both of which I am unfashionable enough to have no taste for. *Sic transit gloria mundi.*" [6]

To the last the King continued to take his old interest in the village of Kew and his contributions to its charities. To him, it was the symbol of the England which he had loved. When he died, there, at least, he was mourned. The inhabitants assembled to express their sorrow for a man " who will ever live in our grateful memory as a generous and constant benefactor to this parish during many years of favoured residence, and to which on all occasions he testified his attachment by acts of charity and benevolence." This would be perhaps a more reliable epitaph, from simple people who knew him personally, than that composed by axe-grinding politicians and historians with no acquaintance with him.

[1] The King pointed out to Palmerston, through his ambassador, how English interests would suffer if Prussia, in the years after 1848, were to absorb the other states of Germany. Palmerston promised to warn Prussia that England was interested in Hanover.—Bennigsen Archives.

[2] To Lord Strangford, 28th October 1843.

[3] Prince William of Prussia, afterwards Emperor.

[4] To Lord Strangford, 22nd February 1851.

[5] To the Rev. D. Delafosse, 4th September 1849.—*Van Thal*, p. 305.

[6] Ernest Augustus's original house is now a Grace and Favour residence of the Crown, that which he occupied after 1830 forms the Herbarium of the Royal Botanic Gardens.

CHAPTER XXIV

1843–48

THE pardons recently given to those convicted for offences
at the beginning of his reign and his sturdy resistance to
foreign pressure had established the King of Hanover's popularity
more firmly than ever. On his birthday in 1843 the citizens of
the capital dined together as customarily, but on this occasion,
the British Ambassador reported, in numbers three times as great
as usual. On the 5th September he returned to Hanover from his
English journey. Mounted citizens rode out to meet him and large
crowds round the Palace cheered him upon his arrival. In the
evening there was a torchlight procession and the City Councillors
waited upon him to present their congratulations.[1]

The King returned stimulated and in high spirits but the strain
had been great and now a reaction set in which was evident to all.
The Tenth Army Corps of the Confederation was assembled for
its annual manœuvres at Lüneburg and most of the Sovereigns had
accompanied their contingents (the cause of much headache to the
staffs on points of etiquette). This was an occasion which the
King of Hanover could not miss and he proceeded at once to
Lüneburg to act as host. He resided in the castle and invited the
other Sovereigns to brilliant dinners and theatre parties. But he
did not confine himself to his social duties, and ignoring the representations of his entourage he insisted upon going out with his
troops. As it rained incessantly he was often soaked to the skin
and at times he was in a state bordering upon unconsciousness.[2]

The King had suddenly become an ageing man. His features
showed increasing weakness, his hearing deteriorated and his
enormous correspondence was now dictated. There was also a
change in his habits of life. His journeys became rarer,[3] and even

[1] F.O. 34/39. 7th September 1843, and *Von Malortie*, p. 132. It is quite incomprehensible how Wilkinson could write that the King arrived unannounced and went to
his room without being noticed.
[2] M.A. *Von Slicher.*
[3] The King wished to spend the anniversary of the Queen's death in 1845 in Rotenkirchen and while there he suddenly announced his intention of visiting Göttingen.
The Prorector had requested such a visit for the summer so that he could describe to

E.A.—12   353

when he was mounted or hunting his earlier vitality failed him. He became increasingly aware of his weakness and often sighed, "Jch bin kaput und nichts mehr wert." What he could no longer enjoy himself he did not wish to hear spoken about by others and withdrew himself more and more from male company.

The King took great pleasure in the company of ladies. The loss of the Queen had left a great gap to be filled, for he really needed someone to look after him with tenderness and charm. On his way to the Göhrde in the summer of 1842 he called at Brese, the country seat of the late Count von Grote, and there he made the acquaintance of the forty-three-year-old widow, Countess Caroline von Grote (1799–1885). He was so much attracted by her conversation and her knowledge of the world—she had spent many years with her husband when he was ambassador in Paris and in Nice—and found her company so pleasant that in 1844 he asked her to come to Hanover as a Lady of Honour. Every day he spent two or three hours with her. She became the only person who could influence him, but she never used this influence for political or personal ends. There is no doubt, says von Slicher, that she lengthened the King's life; he would not otherwise have surrendered so readily to old age but would rather have sought distraction in travel and other exertions. She became indispensable. She did the honours at his private tea-parties and amused him with her conversation and finally, when the King was often weak and ill, she became his nurse, using her persuasion where no doctor could have succeeded. To her, the King showed the tender side of his nature which, since 1841, he had hidden to the world by stiffness and coldness.[1]

During 1845 the King suffered frequent indispositions and became weaker. He used to rise at eleven or twelve, dress and then

---

him the difficulties which the University was experiencing, mainly as a result of the conduct of the seditious professors in 1837. Great pains were taken to preserve the secrecy of the visit, rooms being prepared in a hotel for " a visiting Prince." Despite this, crowds gathered at the Weender Gate to greet the King, who, however, rode in on horseback accompanied by his aide by a path across the fields to another. He rode to the Library, where he received the academic staff and expressed his joy that the troubles and misunderstandings of 1837 were forgotten and forgiven and that professors occupied themselves again with studies instead of politics. He announced his intention of founding a hospital for the Academy of Medicine, and showed his attention to details by describing to the experts the advantages of iron beds, such as were used in London hospitals, over the wooden frames then in use there. He told the Mayor to let it be known how pleased he was with his loyal reception " and how happy I am to declare that the past has been *forgiven* and forgotten." (30th June–1st July 1845). See *Von Malortie*, pp. 137–42.

[1] M.A. *Von Slicher*; F.O. 34/45, 19th June 1845.

drive out for visits. For an hour before and after dinner his secretary read letters and papers to him and took down dictation. At half-past eight he joined the Countess and often the Intendant of the Court Opera, who kept him *au courant* with the social gossip of the town, and they sat together until midnight. It was striking that though at important moments the King was as collected and gave state affairs the same calm attention as he had always been wont, little things could now arouse his feverish excitement. His mind concerned itself increasingly with trivial affairs of Court and society. He wished to hear details of all social events, and he did not conceal his dissatisfaction if he had not been told of a dinner party or a visit to the country. There was no ball, no party, at which the old man was not a merry participant from start to finish. He was quite excited before such an event and could hardly wait for the departure to it ; he always completed his toilette too soon and could not understand that it was too early and the carriage was not yet there. By 1847 he was living only for balls and parties. Having lain in bed all day, he would often rise to go to one in the evening ; frequently the dancers were already tired when he asked for a ball to be prolonged, and on such occasions he could assure his host or hostess sufficiently how beautiful it had all been and how he had enjoyed it. But, his A.D.C. wrote, those who saw him in society, a regal figure in his Hussar uniform, could not have imagined that, only a few minutes before, he had been sitting sunken and exhausted.[1] Indeed, few could have guessed what went on within him.

"When it is said that time cures everything," he wrote to his brother-in-law,[2] "believe me, this is not true. Certainly it is possible when one is in society or has important business to transact, but when one retires and is alone, one feels one's grief thricefold. . . . I feel my loneliness and misery more and more every day. I try all that I can to distract myself and when in society I succeed, but when I come home to my loneliness, then I feel it doubly, and especially in the evenings, when I used always to go for a little while upstairs after completing my work and enjoy our talk, gay and happy. This is now gone ! . . . You know me, you know that I do not go in for poetry or such stuff, and yet I have if not more, still, as much feeling as other people and unfortunately I am very much inclined to melancholy and even hypochondria. Perhaps you will smile when I say this, but it is so. . . ."

[1] M.A. *Von Slicher.*
[2] S.A. To Grand Duke of Strelitz, 18th March, 29th March and 1st July 1844.

The King's loneliness increased yearly. In September 1844 he lost the only man in whom he had ever had full confidence, von Schele ; when he was informed of his death, he hardly spoke the whole day.[1] All the more, he held to his remaining relatives and old friends. When the Duke of Cambridge visited him in November 1845 they found it difficult to part and the visits of such old acquaintances as the Duke of Beaufort, Lord Westmorland, Lord Strangford, Sir Charles Wetherell and Lady Jersey were almost royal occasions.

One event brought light to this dreary scene. On the 20th September 1845 a son was born to the Crown Prince and Princess and this day the King called the happiest of his life. As soon as he learnt of the Crown Princess's safe delivery the King hurried to the Fürstenhof *on foot*, through the cheering crowds, accompanied only by his aide. He went straight up to the Princess's room and looked at the baby. " I thank you, my child," he said to the mother. " Now, with God's help, all danger is passed." The everyday life of the city ceased. Enthusiasm knew no bounds and in the evening Pastor Bödecker, one of the most popular clergymen of Hanover, addressed the King in the name of the crowds packed outside his windows on the Leinestrasse. The King received him and as many of the citizens as the room allowed. " You are all very dear to me and I only wish to make you happy," he told them. " I will have the boy brought up so that he also likes you and wishes to make you happy." In the evening almost every house was illuminated.[2] " Indeed," wrote Bligh,[3] " I had not imagined that so great a degree of loyal feeling existed here as has manifested itself among all classes upon this interesting occasion."

Now the old King could die reassured. The succession was secure, though the difficulties with which his son would have to contend caused him much anxiety. Would the Powers, contrary to assurances, seek to derive advantage from his succession, as they had done from Maria Theresa's, or would the same selfishness and lack of principle which had inspired Prussia then move her to a similar act now ? " Promise me sacredly," he wrote to his nephew, the King of Prussia,[4] " I beg you on bended knee, remain always his friend and help him with your wisdom when I am no more. Promise me this."

---

[1] The remarkable stability now achieved by the country is shown by the absence of political consequences of the death of von Schele and the historical insignificance of his successor, von Falcke.

[2] For the account of the birth of the Prince, see *Von Malortie*, pp. 142–45.

[3] F.O. 34/45, 11th September 1845.

[4] To King of Prussia, 3rd July 1841. See *Rosendahl*, p. 919.

In Ernest Augustus's time these considerations had not been important. Power lay with the monarchs and each of them saw that the interest of every other was his own. It has been seen what this unity meant in the years after his accession, when, through the firmness of Austria and Prussia, the conservative forces were enabled to present an impregnable front to the forces of destruction. The latter knew that as soon as they could breach this, they had triumphed. It was in Prussia that they succeeded in making the breach.

Ernest Augustus had always been a great lover and admirer of Prussia. As has been seen, the happiest days of his life were spent there and it was almost home to him. His nephews were his dearest relations, and throughout his reign the Courts of Hanover and Prussia had been on the most intimate footing. But Frederick William IV was a weak man and the power in his Kingdom quickly passed from his hands. His brother, too, who had been such a firm monarchist, had now been captured by nationalistic and anti-conservative intriguers. Ernest Augustus repeatedly warned them to be on their guard. He strenuously endeavoured to dissuade them from establishing Chambers there, which he called a " curse and cancer " for all governments. " Look at what has happened in England," he said,[1] " for there the Commons are all, the Peers very little and the Crown nothing. . . . Unfortunately, instead of observing and occupying themselves with the true welfare of the country, it seems to me that all their [2] efforts are devoted to frustrating the good intentions of the Government, and they quarrel among themselves for hours about single words and not the issue itself. For me, who have been occupied with these things for half a century, it awakes a sort of disgust, for most of them have not the slightest understanding of what they are talking about and so it is a waste of time to discuss it with him." But all in vain. Anti-conservatives had captured Prussia and made it the starting-point for conquering the rest of Germany as they were later to do with Piedmont in Italy.

In Germany they began with economic pressure. The 3ollverein or Customs Union was founded. By the integration of the economies of the other states with that of Prussia it was seen that they would come completely under her influence and eventually absorbed politically and socially. Prussia's smaller neighbours were easily bullied into this union through such measures as high transit tolls, but the north-west presented more of a problem. Those states had a seaboard and were thus invunerable to a Prussian blockade.

[1] S.A. To Grand Duke, 21st February 1846, and 12th January 1847.
[2] The Chambers'.

They had quite different interests, maritime and transcontinental; they consumed large quantities of wines, coffee, tea, sugar and tobacco which would be heavily taxed under the Zollverein tariff; they were not industrial lands and imported textiles and manufactured wares from England and other countries in considerable amounts. Their own customs tariff was very slight, yet produced surpluses. All this placed them in a position to resist intimidation and they had formed their own union, with a much lower tariff, the Steuerverein, consisting of Hanover, Oldenburg, Brunswick and Schaumburg-Lippe.[1] The Zollverein thus became a completely inland union and until the gates belonged to it, Prussia was not master in Germany. It was necessary for her to annex the Steuerverein. In the Prussian vocabulary, as in that of many other states, " necessary " was an ominous word.

The treaties establishing the Steuerverein were due to expire at the beginning of 1841 and its component states prepared a new agreement for its renewal. This had already been ratified when Brunswick suddenly proposed an impossible condition. Since the successful insurrection a decade before, the revolutionary party had naturally been very strong in that state and the Duke who had been called to displace his brother led a miserable life there. Power was in the hands of an upstart named Koch, who hated the King of Hanover and saw with apprehension the situation which would arise if the Duke had no heirs and the Duchy fell to Hanover. He therefore did all in his power to drive a wedge between the two cousins and sought to frustrate the agreement now reached between their states.

Hanover lay between Prussia proper and the western provinces which, by a fatal misjudgment, had been allotted to her in 1815 as a guarantee of the peace of Europe. Road (and later rail) communications were secured for her across Hanoverian territory and Hanover was obliged to build a road from Uelzen to Langwedel (in Prussia). Brunswick now claimed that this would diminish her importance and prosperity and proposed to the Hanoverian Government that it should request Prussia not to insist upon the fulfilment of this obligation. The Prussian Ambassador learnt of the Brunswick proposal and indignantly protested to the King of Hanover, who had heard nothing of it. The King was furious at the suggestion that he should ignore his obligations to Prussia and expressed his sentiments to the Court of Brunswick in no uncertain terms. Then the unexpected happened. Koch and the

---

[1] By agreement, enclaves of the two unions were left to that by which they were surrounded.

Ministers who had engineered the situation advised their Sovereign to free himself from Hanover and join the Zollverein.[1]

It might have been expected that Prussia, touched and gratified at Hanover's loyalty to her, would have stood by her in its consequences. But in that country the matter was seen in a different light. Here was the opportunity which had been awaited to explode the Steuerverein. The King was recommended to accept Brunswick's offer of accession to the union. In April 1841 the King of Hanover paid his usual visit to Brunswick for his cousin's birthday. The meeting was cordial, Bligh reported, but lacked the usual warmth, and the King was not able to alter Brunswick's policy.[2]

At least, von Schele wrote to Berlin, he hoped that the Prussian Government would see that Hanover were not injured by Brunswick's move, for the southern extremity of the Kingdom, containing Göttingen, was separated from the rest by the Harz and Weser districts of Brunswick. After much negotiation, it was eventually agreed to leave this district to the Steuerverein until the end of 1842, so that Hanover would have an opportunity to negotiate to join the Zollverein. Notwithstanding a visit of the King of Prussia to Hanover *en route* in April 1842, and King Ernest Augustus's prolonged visit to Berlin shortly afterwards, the situation did not improve. In any case, the King of Prussia was not his own master. All that was obtained was the renewal of the notice of the accession of the Weser district to the union for another year, until the end of 1843.

The King's resistance to the Zollverein was increasing, if that were possible, the loyalty and affection which his subjects displayed towards him. They saw the ruin of Brunswick and Lippe-Detmold (which had recently abandoned its complete economic independence to join the Zollverein);[3] business was ceasing and bankruptcy rife since their accession and the proud Duke was depressed and humiliated at what he had been led into by his evil advisers. "What an agreeable thing for the Duke of Brunswick," the King wrote,[4] "to have Prussian Custom Officers, to see the Prussian Eagle suspended at the *gate* of his city—this has enraged the inhabitants more than anything. One thing is *clear* as daylight, that from the moment you become a member of this, you are no longer independent master *chez vous* to make commercial arrangements."

It was then that a new form of blackmail was applied against the King—articles appeared in the Prussian Press questioning the Crown

---

[1] F.O. 34/43, 21st March 1843.   [2] *Ibid.* 34/34, 29th April 1841.
[3] *Ibid.* 34/39, 27th April 1843.   [4] S.A. To Grand Duke, 20th January 1842.

Prince's ability to succeed to the Throne on account of his blindness and also claiming that Prussia, not the King of Hanover, was the heir to the Crown of Brunswick. The King was so disgusted with this campaign that, for the first time, his relations with his nephew clouded—he always emphasised that he never allowed political differences to disturb personal friendships—and it was only very reluctantly that he was persuaded by him to visit Berlin when he was with his stepdaughter in Dessau in January 1843.

At the wedding Crown Prince George, his cousin, the King of Prussia,[1] once again became the affectionate relative, but immediately upon his return to Berlin he was faced with a recommendation from his Ministers that should Brunswick desire to include its Weser district in the Zollverein, no objection should be raised. The two Kings met again at the manœuvres at Lüneburg and hunting at Count von Asseburg's at Schloss Falkenstein in November 1843, but the persuasion and reproaches of Ernest Augustus were in vain. The Duke of Brunswick now lamented what was happening, but his Estates did not take his wishes into account. They voted for the inclusion of the whole land in the Zollverein, with no extension of the *status quo*, and at the end of 1843, the Weser district was separated from the Steuerverein and absorbed into the Zollverein.

A very critical situation had arisen. The southern extremity of Hanover was now completely isolated. Hanover took stern counter-measures. All her enclaves were withdrawn from the Zollverein and it was announced that all parts of Brunswick, including its enclaves, would be treated as foreign territory. This was a severe blow to Brunswick. One of her enclaves was Thedinghausen, far up in the north near Bremen, which lived through letting its pastures to herds from the Duchy itself and the steep and barren Harz; now, of course, it was stifled, and in April 1844 the business of another enclave, Bodenburg, near Hildesheim, was in such a state of stagnation that a despairing and unbalanced man set fire to the village and burnt down fifty-eight houses [2]; Hanover also levied heavy charges on a supply of rails from England for the Brunswick railways. At the same time the anti-smuggling treaty was to be applied no longer to Brunswick, nor the lower tariff for Zollverein states as granted by treaty in 1837. Towards Prussia, Hanover endeavoured to remain conciliatory and friendly,

---

[1] Proposing the toast, he said that it had rained in the bride's garland and that meant good fortune. Prince William was also present at the wedding.
[2] F.O. 34/43, 21st March 1834.

and the King was angry that Brunswick had so disturbed the relations between them. The King of Prussia, he was confident, would be shocked if he really knew what was going on in his Kingdom.[1] Nevertheless, Bligh reported that a visit which he had intended to pay to Berlin in January 1844 was given up and this was considered by the Hanoverians as at least one good result of the Zollverein.[2]

Brunswick had damaged herself much more severely than she had Hanover and she sought to make it as unpleasant for her neighbour as possible until she, too, was forced into the Zollverein. At the Brunswick customs houses in the Harz, Bligh reported.[3] " all sorts of proceedings unheard of in other countries are practised." He meant the interference with travellers' baggage— for in those days it was considered unheard of for customs to examine the baggage of private persons. The King learned of these incidents. Count von Hardenberg, his Grand Veneur, returning from the reserves of Solling, was held up from seven until nine in the evening while everything was unpacked and examined in the pouring rain. No traveller, no post coach was respected on the road between Einbeck and Alfeld. At first the King thought these incidents the result of clumsiness, but as the Brunswick officers became more and more arrogant and insulting, he realised that there was more behind their actions. By chance he learnt that because of lack of accommodation they lived in an inn situated upon his territory. Forthwith he had them ejected by the local gendarme and warned that if they returned they would be placed under arrest. At the same time he sent peremptory orders that at all places where convoys passed the yellow and white poles on his frontier, they were to be similarly treated.

Brunswick had ruined herself by becoming the tool of Prussia and Prussia herself had gained nothing. The King of Hanover was able to play a card against them—the support of the seafaring nations and, in particular, of Britain. He had long had a dispute with his homeland on the question of the tolls which were levied at Stade and Brunshausen on ships on the Elbe. This had been a grievance to Britain, but she was loath to take any steps ; she knew that this revenue was important to Hanover and that without it that country would be more exposed to the pressure of the Zollverein. For a long time an Anglo-Hanoverian commission sat in Hamburg upon the subject, and on the 22nd July 1844 a

---

[1] S.A. To Grand Duke, 5th February 1844.
[2] F.O. 34/43, 18th February 1844.   [3] Ibid. 34/43, 1st February 1844.

E.A.—12*

treaty was signed giving reciprocal privileges and lower tariffs to English and Hanoverian ships in each other's waters. This brought forth a storm of rage from the Zollverein.[1]

Now at last Prussia gave up the hopeless struggle. The old King of Hanover had caused the first setback. In October 1845 the two countries signed a treaty regulating frontier tariffs and providing for a give-and-take in the matter of enclaves. In September 1844 the King of Prussia went out of his way to flatter his uncle. During the manœuvres at Merseburg, he placed himself at the head of the 3rd Hussars [2] and handed to him, as Colonel-in-Chief, the regimental report; the old King was so touched by this attention that he embraced him. On the 29th July 1845 the Duke of Brunswick at last dined with the King of Hanover; he lamented all that was happening in Prussia, and his host gathered the impression that he regretted everything and wished only to retire.[3] In November 1847 the British Ambassador to Hanover was credited to Brunswick in addition, and before presenting his letters to the Duke he met him by chance on the railway station. When he told him of his mission, the Duke sighed; it was, he said, a pity that this had not taken place five years earlier The influence of Britain might have prevented his being forced into the arms of Prussia.[4]

But the relations between the three states which had at one time been so closely bound to one another were permanently disturbed and no change in policy followed these personal contacts of their rulers.[5] The King of Hanover was horrified by the thought of the hands into which his neighbour had fallen. " The more I reflect upon it," he wrote,[6] " the more I tremble, for if ever a catastrophe happens in Prussia, not only all Germany but all Europe will feel the consequences . . ." and " . . . there is every reason to look forward to horrible scenes in that unhappy country." [7]

[1] See the reports of the English Ambassador, etc., for the progress of these negotiations.

[2] The King, as Duke of Cumberland, had been appointed Honorary Colonel of the 3rd or Ziethen Hussars on the 18th May 1823. They were known for their red jackets with silver lacing.

[3] S.A. To Grand Duke, 9th August 1845.

[4] F.O. 34/50, 18th November 1847.

[5] Before a party, the King of Prussia once wrote to the Duke of Brunswick (M.A. 29th November 1844), " I do not conceal from Your Highness that I have been compelled through a coincidence of circumstances to invite the old hereditary enemy of our Customs Union, *King Ernest Augustus* [in English], as well. It would be very depressing for me if his appearance there were to deprive me of the pleasure of your company. I confess that, in the expectance of seeing *old King* there, I set even greater store, if that is possible, by your appearance, so please do not make me unhappy by declining."

[6] S.A. To Grand Duke, 21st February 1846.

[7] To Lord Strangford, 3rd December 1845.

More and more he inclined towards Austria, the Power whose
efforts were directed towards uniting and conserving rather than
narrow nationalistic objectives.   His son had even longer been
under Austrian influence, and Baron Kress, the Austrian Ambassador,
knew how to strengthen it.   The Emperor was aware of the King's
love for Hussars and when his uncle, the Archduke Palatine, died
in January 1847 he named him his successor as Colonel of the Second
Hussars, specially sending his own tailor from Vienna to make the
uniform for him.   All hussars have their origin in Hungary and
the King of Hanover did not conceal his satisfaction at this compliment.   Such things were, of course, only trivialities, but they
demonstrated Hanover's close relations with Austria which had
replaced those with Prussia of the beginning of the reign.[1]   The
far-sighted King of Hanover realised what would be the inevitable
result of this disunity—if the monarchs of Europe, instead of helping
each other, destroyed each other.   It was not the strength or
soundness of the revolutionary cause which frightened him, nor
was it those qualities which would bring it success, but stupidity
and unawareness on the part of the rulers.   " It seems to me," he
wrote,[2] " that the whole world is in a state which cannot remain
so for long, or the storm will soon break out, and we must all
hold ourselves in readiness to act together.   That is why it is so
necessary that the different Governments of Germany should
reach an understanding and not act each for himself."

"You can believe me," he told his brother-in-law,[3] " everywhere
clouds are appearing on the horizon and it calls for much prudence,
wisdom and harmony among all Governments to dissipate these
clouds and see that they do not become storms."   The outbreak
of civil war in Switzerland was the the first clap of thunder.   He
urged the Powers to take action.   " The old proverb is true," he
wrote,[4] " A stitch in time saves nine."   Thanks to Palmerston,
nothing was done.   The King was given over to the most melancholy reflections.   " The storm is gradually growing blacker and
blacker," he wrote early in 1848.[5]   " I hope that my fears may prove
unnecessary, but I cannot disguise the secret feeling within me
from you.   God grant that I may be wrong in thinking that the
storm will break out in the spring."

[1] F.O.   34/50, 18th June 1847.
[2] S.A.   To Grand Duke, 18th May 1847.
[3] Ibid.   To Grand Duke, 21st February 1846.
[4] To Lord Strangford, 24th November 1847.
[5] To Lord Strangford, 21st February 1848.

CHAPTER XXV

1848

ERNEST AUGUSTUS'S prophecy was fulfilled in all its exactitude. With devastating suddenness the storm broke out and swept over the whole of the Continent.

Disorders broke out in Paris, Louis Philippe's reign came to a close and a republic was proclaimed. It was the usual story of lack of firmness on the part of the Government. Ernest Augustus was enraged. " Why they should have permitted rebellious bands to parade the whole night when they had a garrison of regular troops to the number of 60,000 men seems to me unaccountable," he wrote. " Louis Philippe, or some of his sons, should have placed themselves at the head of the troops, and in various columns have crushed the rebellion in its infancy. . . . My blood boils when I consider what mischief this has already produced." [1] It seemed to him that the states in Germany would have to defend themselves against a militant and revolutionary France as in the days of his youth, and so he held his troops in readiness to march to the Rhine as soon as orders came from the Confederation. But it happened otherwise. Revolutionary emissaries from France spread themselves all over Germany and the news which they brought encouraged all the adventurers, the disaffected and the ambitious to attempt a like action if it could succeed so easily. The Governments of Germany, as the King of Hanover had observed since 1837, were in a ripe state for such an event. Years of attempting to please the Democrats and live in peace with them had so demoralised them that at the first news of the events in France they capitulated. The Governments of Württemberg, Saxony, Baden, Nassau and Darmstadt all handed the power to the revolutionaries. The respective envoys at the Diet thus came under the control of this party and had to move resolutions for a new Constitution for Germany and all the other items on the revolutionary programme. Life and property in these lands was no longer safe and complete anarchy reigned.

But Hanover under Ernest Augustus remained firm. His

[1] To Lord Strangford, 29th February and 9th March 1848.

364

policy of resistance rather than appeasement as the best way of
meeting revolution and rebellion had proved itself. In the eleven
years of his reign he had won the hearts of all his subjects, the
people were happy and the land prosperous. "Unless the people
are urged without," reported Bligh, "or are obliged to follow in
the stream which has overflowed south-western Germany with
hitherto unchecked strength, I do not anticipate any further demonstration in this country." [1] The King knew that, at least, he could
rely on his soldiers ; they had never wavered in their loyalty. He
also knew that the Prussian Army was staunch, and so it seemed
to him that these two Powers, forgetting in such a crisis old and
trivial differences, should act together to form a solid fortress
against the revolution in north Germany and then eventually to
reconquer the south.

But, of course, it was impossible that the events in the rest of
Europe should not have had their effects in Hanover. As soon as
the news of the French revolution reached the capital, all the
radicals and revolutionaries rushed to the station—thus vindicating
Ernest Augustus's misgivings with regard to railways—to meet
the train from Cologne with foreigners and newspapers, and the
revolutionary literature was eagerly passed from hand to hand.
If the "tyrannical" governments of 1848 had exercised the powers
which those of the twentieth century take for granted, all this
would never have happened. "Even in this country," reported
the British Ambassador, "pernicious example and foreign emissaries
have raised up a democratic spirit which threatens to dictate to the
Government and to upset all existing institutions which do not
harmonise with the spirit." [2] The King himself wrote, "These
damned railways bring in daily hundreds of Poles, French and other
canaille which, had it not been for the watchfulness of the citizens,
would have caused all sorts of rioting, and probably murder and
bloodshed, in the towns." [3]

The first sign of trouble was when a distiller in the Town
Council moved that a petition should be presented to the King
embodying the usual revolutionary demands. But the spirit there
was quite different from that of 1837. The members were hesitant,
none wished to offend the old King and none dared to present
such a petition to him. They therefore agreed upon one simply
praying for the summoning of the Estates, freedom of the press
and greater efforts for German unity. "In fact," wrote Bligh of

[1] F.O. 34/53, 10th March 1848.   [2] *Ibid.* 34/53, 13th April 1848.
[3] To Lord Strangford, 7th April 1848.

this proceeding, " I hardly believe that the step would have been taken at all except from fear lest a total abstinence from all movement at the present time might have exposed the inhabitants of this city to ridicule and animadversion from their more stirring countrymen in other parts of Germany. As it was, they made their petition as mild as possible ; and having heard, as I understand, from Baron Falcke that mooting the question of a Civic Guard would be very distasteful to the King they omitted all mention of it." [1]

That evening, the 3rd March, the petition was given to the officer on duty at the Palace and the King summoned a deputation to receive his answer the next afternoon. The Stadtdirektor and six others were shown into the King's presence. As he stepped towards them his majestic bearing made such an impression that the leader, whom he asked what they really wanted, could hardly find his voice. The King then observed sarcastically, seeing the members of the deputation, that he was very pleased that printers and masons thought themselves called upon to tell him how he should govern the Kingdom.

" I have been eleven years amongst you," he said, " and have those eleven years been devoted only to improving the institutions of the country, increasing the prosperity and expediting affairs in all departments of state. That my efforts have not been in vain the capital city itself is the best witness for you." He then said that their first request had no ground since the Estates had in any case to be called to approve the budget which was due. As to the second, the Press in fact enjoyed freedom (as even von Treitschke concedes), but to enact that formally would require some time for consultation with the other Governments and the Estates. As to German unity, he said, he was too dense to be able to understand what they meant. " The Germans believe that they can achieve unity on paper. If they want it, they can have it, but then they must wade through blood up to the breast." His efforts had always been to represent the land worthily both externally and internally, and the hour of danger would always find him, although no youngster (Jüngling) now, ready " to seal my loyalty to all my Hanoverians with the last drop of my blood." The deputation then left disarmed.

But in the assembly the report of the King's answer brought forth a storm of rage. The revolutionaries felt themselves humiliated before their fellows in other lands who achieved absolute

[1] F.O. 34/53, 10th March 1848.

power almost without effort. Seditious meetings were called and attempts made to stir up the people against the Government. Only in Göttingen did they meet with any success, as was to be expected, and even there the student-riots sprang rather from personal grievances against the Chief of Police than from the general revolutionary movement. " Our greatest plague," the King wrote, " are the advocates and hungry adventurers, who have nothing to lose, but hope to gain something for themselves through disorder. God be praised, the country is still loyal to me and the citizens have done all possible to maintain the peace." [1]

On the 14th March the King issued a proclamation to explain why he could not, as in normal times, see every petitioner individually, as he had to transact business from early morning until late at night and was often exhausted. " The majority of these petitions," he said, " prove to me still the love and confidence of my loyal subjects. When other wishes are expressed in them, they come, I am convinced, not from the Hanoverians themselves but are inspired by strangers, who are endeavouring to excite disorder and confusion everywhere. I am fully convinced of the loyalty and sound ideas of my subjects and that they will not destroy their own peace and prosperity which are the envy of every stranger who comes into the land. The foundation and maintenance of your happiness and prosperity, which have always been my unremitting care, are as much at my heart as ever. I endeavour to do all that is in my power to fulfil your wishes without destroying your real happiness. . . . Every Hanoverian will believe this assurance, for he knows that his King never says what he does not really mean and makes no promise which he does not intend honourably to discharge." Again, he said that he would shed the last drop of his blood for them.

For the revolutionaries such language was to pour oil on the flames. They felt that they must undertake some action against the only man who had dared to defy them, and two days later they fêted a revolutionary deputation from Cologne which was going to Berlin to threaten to proclaim a republic. Their final spur was provided by news of the outbreak of the revolution in Vienna.

On the 18th a mob filled the hall of the Rathaus to compel the Council to present its demands formally to the King. The Stadt= direktor agreed and in an hour had composed a petition which was read to the impatient crowd. Its principal demands were for the freedom of the press, a civic guard and German unity, and it

[1] S.A. To Grand Duke of Mecklenburg-Strelitz, 15th April 1848.

met with the applause of the mob. However, said Evers, the more moderate Stadtdirektor who attempted to brake the disorder a little, they could not take it to the King personally as he was ill. Several other more reputable persons present confirmed this. The Council would therefore present it at the proper time. But the mob was not to be influenced by such considerations. " No ! At once ! " it cried. " To the King ! If you won't take it, we will ! " Its demeanour was so threatening that the moderates yielded. So, as the result of sheer mob intimidation, the City Councillors headed the rabble as it swarmed out on to the street. It was joined by all manner of low society besides, of course, the merely curious, and made its way up the Leinestrasse to the Palais, to the accompaniment of a din of yelling and shouting.

Since the New Year the King had been confined most of the time to his room, and now he lay helpless in bed. He expected some sort of attempt at revolution, but when the shouts and cries of the mob were heard approaching in the street outside—for the King's bedroom was on the ground floor immediately against the pavement, protected from the curiosity of passers-by only by panes of blue-shaded glass in the lower portions of the windows— there were with him only the Counsellor von Münchhausen, who was reading a report, and in the ante-room Prince Bernard of Solms-Braunfels and the A.D.C.s. The King remained perfectly calm at a moment when his life might have been in danger. All present were astonished at his serenity, but afterwards he said to one of them, " My friend, you Germans are not used to such things and immediately see too black." [1]

The street outside was full as von Münchhausen went out to receive the petition from the City Councillors. He would take it to the King immediately, he said, and he did not doubt that His Majesty would accede to some of their wishes. But the mob was not to be sent away by such a general assurance. There were cries of " Answer ! Answer ! " and von Münchhausen convinced himself that it was in no ordinary mood. He therefore went back into the Palais to the King. The crowd grew tense. After an hour, von Münchhausen reappeared with some papers in his hand. Believing that all had been conceded, the mob broke into cheering and shouting as he took a chair in the doorway and, standing upon it, began to read. He could not, however, make himself heard. " Do you want to yell, or shall I speak ? " he demanded, and his tall, dignified person was such as to command respect.

[1] The description of the scene in the King's room is from M.A. *Von Slicher*.

The crowd became quiet and he began to read out his announcement. As the people seemed somewhat excited, he said, His Majesty had approved the publication of measures which it had already been intended to present to the Estates when they met in a fortnight. He then dealt with the demands in detail. Freedom of the Press, which in fact existed, would be formally enacted; that freedom of public assembly also existed, the meeting which formulated this petition proved; the formation of a civic guard would be expedient only when the army had to leave for the field, when it might indeed become indispensable; a congress to discuss German unity had already been called by the rulers of Germany. When he asked which persons convicted of political offences should be amnestied, as he was not aware that there were any, no one, to the universal sensation, could name any besides a doctor in Paris. This showed that the formulation of demands had been humbug and merely followed a pattern regardless of whether any such demands were to be met. As to the other points, von Münchhausen concluded, the time was not ripe and many had to be discussed by the Estates.

Only those of the crowd immediately in the proximity of the speaker could, of course, hear all these details, and the rest, thinking that everything had been conceded, began to move away. But those who had heard shouted, " No, stay ! " and the din was let loose again. " You can go home now ! " said von Münchhausen, but the crowd became more threatening and the Guard in the courtyard of the Palace opposite prepared to turn out to clear the street. Then the Stadtdirektor mounted the chair that von Münchhausen had just left and called out, " Who is a good citizen will follow me to the Rathaus ! " Only gradually, however, did the noise diminish and the crowd break up.

Furious that their demonstration had made no impression on the King, the most desperate of the revolutionaries gathered in groups after dark and paraded the streets, joined by hooligans and idlers. The windows of the houses of several of the Ministers were stoned and smashed, and the mob also sought to revenge itself upon the King's friend and nurse, the Countess von Grote, though she played no part whatsoever in political affairs. But as they did not know where she lived, they smashed instead the windows of one of her friends, Frau von Schulte, and so vented their spite on her by proxy. These were the people who were to bring Utopia to earth ! The King would not tolerate this sort of thing and ordered some seventy Garde du Corps and two companies of infantry to clear the Georgstrasse. Before the Minister of Justice's house the mob had found gendarmes drawn up, but their commander was apparently afraid to act. Grisly scenes might have resulted had not an A.D.C. of the King with six Guardsmen ridden up. The mob bolted without the soldiers' even having drawn sabres,[1] and in that little incident lay the whole moral of the revolution—weakness, not firmness, caused bloodshed. The King took energetic measures. The next day he ordered another squadron of the Garde du Corps into the town, strengthened each infantry company by thirty men and had all loose paving-stones and the chains round the gardens and grass verges removed in order to allow the cavalry freedom of movement.[2] After that there were no incidents. Citizens with arm-bands and sticks organised themselves to maintain order and military intervention was no more necessary. In Hanover the revolution was completely extinguished and King Ernest Augustus had remained firm and immovable. It was his greatest triumph.

Then, from outside, came the blow which shattered all his work. Revolution had broken out in Berlin and the weak King had given way without a struggle to a mob in the street. The garrison, thousands of the finest and staunchest guardsmen and soldiers who could have put down the riot in a matter of minutes, he ordered out of the city and they marched out to the jeers of the mob with their drums muffled to show how they felt their humiliation. Completely in the hands of the mob, the King conceded everything and appeared bare-headed at its demand, as revolutionaries who had met the fate which they would meet in all lands and all ages were carried by, while his loyal soldiers, murdered in fulfilling their duty, were buried without any mark of attention from him.

King Ernest Augustus could hardly credit the news. " What has become of the Hohenzollern blood ! " he cried. " What would Frederick the Great think of his successors, if he could look down from above ! " [3] His fortress against the revolution had collapsed— again through unnecessary weakness. He was quite alone. Wedged between two halves of Prussia, surrounded by anarchy and his own land traversed by agents and emissaries of the Prussian revolutionaries, he could not hope to hold his position as he had been doing. Von Falcke, whom he had appointed Minister upon von Schele's death, came to him on the same day, the 19th March, and asked

---

[1] *Wilkinson.*
[2] To King Frederick William IV. RB., 18th March 1848, and from *Wilkinson.*
[3] S.A. To Grand Duke, 29th June 1848.

for his release as his Ministry did not see how it would be possible
to continue now.   The King granted this request and so was completely alone, with chaos, anarchy, murder and pillage surrounding
and threatening to swamp his Kingdom.   " Though the country
was flourishing, and the highest to the lowest were able to live
comfortably at their ease," he wrote, " wc were overrun—after the
dreadful scenes at Berlin—by emissaries from that capital who were
in communication with the communists in Paris and the south of
Germany ; and so the storm broke out, and I had to consider
what I could do in twenty-four hours.   Finding that all the late
Ministers were, as it were, paralysed, having lost political courage
and resigned office, I was left totally to myself, and so took the
bull by the horns, and prior to any decision, considered what I
should do." [1]

The King decided that the only hope lay in organising all
moderate elements in the country against the revolution.   Now it
was seen in its true colours and many who had formerly opposed
him were shocked at what had happened.   It must be borne in
mind that the chief agitators at this time were the bourgeoisie, the
tradesmen and capitalists, with no idea of what it was that they
were unleashing until it turned upon *them*.   This did not begin
to happen until more than fifty or sixty years later, but a few of
the more far-sighted realised what was bound to follow and it
was they whom the King wished to win over to his side.

As the late Minister had recommended, the King appointed in
his place Count von Bennigsen, a man of the most aristocratic
nature and appearance, who had formerly often been among the
King's opponents.   But the Count considered the task of forming
a Ministry impossible in these times without the collaboration of
Stüve, from Osnabrück.   Stüve, however, had been the leader of
the opposition to the King at the beginning of the reign and had
even been tried for libel against him,[2] so it seemed to the Count
quite out of the question that the King would agree to his inclusion
in the Cabinet.   To his surprise, the King approved his proposals
and Stüve was summoned from Osnabrück.

So these two former antagonists joined hands to fight the
anarchy and bloodshed which threatened.   The former Liberal and
democrat had been undeceived and sought now to undo the damage

---

[1] To Lord Strangford, 15th May 1848.
[2] He had said that the King had threatened Count Münster that if he embraced the
cause of the 1833 Constitution, it was in his, the King's, power to cancel the award of
Derneburg Castle as his country seat, made by George IV.

done by the pernicious doctrines which he had represented. The King did not deceive himself, of course ; he knew that since the events in Berlin he would be obliged to make concessions, partly to win over more of those of the bourgeoisie who were disquieted at the revolution, but principally to secure peace and unity inside his own realm to fight the revolution which was being imposed from above, as will be seen later. " I have succeeded, under the blessing of God," he wrote, " not only in keeping all quiet in my country, but in bringing round some of the most violent radicals and opponents to become conservatives, which is no easy business." [1]

The difficulties which confronted the Cabinet and the lessons which its members had learnt soon became evident. Von Düring, the Minister of Justice, who had supported the 1833 party against the King, could not bring himself now to agree to the establishment of trial by jury, in which members of the public would have a say in the law, and Stüve also had grave misgivings. As to Ministerial (i.e. their) responsibility to the Chambers, which had been such an important feature of the 1833 Constitution, they also hesitated to work upon such a condition and eventually agreed only to resign if both Chambers demanded it. With such concessions, the Cabinet hoped to maintain peace in the country, but in the middle of their deliberations von Münchhausen arrived from the King with news of the deteriorating conditions in Berlin. There the King had ridden through the streets with the nationalistic cockade in his hat and announced that Prussia would head the movement for German unity. The new Ministers began to lose courage and wished to return their mandates to the King, but von Münchhausen persuaded them not to do so unless they wished to see a catastrophe overwhelm the country. At length they agreed to remain.

The experiment began to work. " I must say as an honest man that up to now I have no reason to complain," wrote the King. " I told them in my first conversation that I was fully aware that our principles up to now had widely differed, but that I trusted they would give me theirs, which I should listen to with the greatest attention, and they must expect—if I differed with them—to listen with equal attention to my remarks, upon which they one and all agreed, and thus we have gone on perfectly well." [2]

And Liberals are always more suitable for putting down rebellions and revolutions than other men, as they have not the same scruples. We hear repeatedly in modern history of monarchs

[1] To Lord Strangford, 7th April 1848.   [2] To Lord Strangford, 15th May 1848.

abdicating " to avoid bloodshed and civil war," but never has a democracy or a republic voluntarily abdicated in the face of such a threat. So now, when the only serious outbreak of violence in the whole of 1848 took place in the Kingdom, with Stüve as his Minister of the Interior, the King was able to adopt measures which the late Government would never have been able to carry out.

In all towns and villages revolutionary emissaries agitated and formed clubs to stir up hate and inspire fear. The life and property of their victims was not safe—in Celle, one Doctor Meyer offered a reward of fifty Thaler to anyone who could justify the suspicion that he was a Reactionary, " for if I had to choose between being a murderer and a Reactionary, I would prefer the former. Then I stand under the protection of the law and would be, at worst, beheaded, but as Reactionary I would be outlawed and unprotected and have to fear not only all men but the whole mineral kingdom." In Andreasberg the houses of some mine officials were burnt down; in Loccum, the ancient monastery buildings, now used by the Lutheran Church, shared the same fate, and the disorder reached its climax in Hildesheim.

One of those who went to Hanover with a petition on the 19th March was a bankrupt advocate from Hildesheim named Weinhagen. On his return he was greeted on the station by the revolutionaries of the city and they gathered in the streets in the evening. Soon he had established his complete mastery over them and they turned upon the City Council. They had some grievances against its members, although the Mayor had been one of the Liberals who opposed the King earlier on—another who was to learn in the hard school of experience. He agreed to distribute weapons to a civic guard, which, of course, immediately recognised Weinhagen as its leader. The city was now completely in his hands, all officials were afraid to act, citizens who had ever crossed the paths of the ex-convicts now in control had their houses demolished and the most important were taken as hostages, brutally manhandled and insulted. Such is the story of the Fight for Democracy. The local magistrates issued a warrant for Weinhagen's arrest. As he was at the moment in Hanover, the police there executed it and he was lodged in the gaol at the Klever Gate. When the mob back in Hildesheim learnt of this, of course, its wrath exploded. Trembling, the magistrates agreed by a majority of one to rescind the warrant and an official was forced to take the order to Hanover, accompanied by representatives of the mob.

After delivering it to the police at the gaol, however, he managed to escape and report what had happened to the Minister of the Interior, Stüve, who instantly hurried to the King.

The King was at dinner when Stüve and the official from Hildesheim arrived at the Palace. He agreed to the immediate re-arrest of the demagogue and ordered the military in Hildesheim to put down the revolution. Weinhagen was celebrating with his colleagues in the hotel opposite to the station while waiting for the next train to Hildesheim, when, to his surprise, he was taken into custody with his friends by members of the Citizen's Guard, which was here a force on the side of law and order.

When the news reached Hildesheim the enraged revolutionaries summoned all their bands, armed with scythes, pitchforks, knives and daggers, and erected barricades. The old general in charge of the garrison thought his force insufficient and was too paralysed to take any action, even to prevent the gathering in the city of revolutionary bands from the neighbourhood. When the King learned of this, he would not believe that an officer could possess such weakness and ordered his A.D.C., Lieutenant-Colonel Jacobi, to take his place. " A chastisement there will be very healthy and an example to *others*," he said.[1] Jacobi hurried in a special train to Hildesheim, reinforcements were sent and he declared that if the barricades were not demolished and all weapons piled on the square outside the barracks within half an hour, his troops would go into action ; if anyone met with an injury—this on account of the hostages—every other citizen would answer for it. The revolutionaries, who had not expected such a reply— which, indeed, they received nowhere else in 1848—could not obey quickly enough and the only serious trouble in Hanover was over. The King was satisfied, especially with Stüve's collaboration. " I must do justice to the Minister of the Interior, who acted not only with decision, but courage, and seconded all I told him to do. These are strange times and require much consideration and deliberation, but decision is the most important of all, and without it one is lost." [2]

So long as it was purely a question of fighting the revolution, the relations between the King and his Ministers were excellent. When it came to measures which would affect the normal structure of the state, other considerations prevailed, as will be seen. Unfortunately, the King was so ill throughout these times, added to the

---

[1] M.A. To Prince William of Prussia, 18th April 1848.
[2] To Lord Strangford, 19th April 1848.

" prostration " (as the English Ambassador called it) which overcame him after the events in Berlin and their repercussions in his
own land, that he could not devote all the attention to routine
measures as he had been wont.

Nevertheless, his iron will would not allow him to admit
defeat. In the worst days of the year he drove out regularly in an
open carriage, and at all crises his indomitable courage ruled.
During riots caused by new measures with regard to the guilds,
when there was a disorderly crowd in the Leinestrasse outside his
windows, his A.D.C. found him buckling on his sabre and about
to restore order himself if no one else would. The King's resolution also showed itself when a self-appointed assembly of revolutionaries gave itself the task of watching over the Estates. " We
have had an illegitimate meeting here of persons from different
provinces to control members of the Second Chamber," he wrote.
" They had the impudence to send a deputation to me, also to the
Ministry and Chambers, admonishing them to be quicker with
their deliberations, and demanding me not to adjourn the Chambers
during the holidays. I naturally refused to receive the deputation,
burnt their petition, and instantly adjourned the Chamber till the
8th of May. I think this was the best answer to such an outrageous
demand, and it had the desired effect, for the whole of the gang
disappeared quickly from the town. This will prove to the rest
of the country that I am not a person to be bullied." [1]

The King knew that he could always rely upon the loyalty and
affection of his soldiers. As soon as the trouble began, men on
leave rejoined their units of their own initiative,[2] and the King
was so impressed by such proofs of the army's fine spirit and
discipline that he decided that such punishments as flogging were
quite unnecessary and ordered their abolition. This General Order
(of the 18th and 22nd March 1848) was to be read out to all troops,
who were to be told expressly that they had moved him to this
command by their exemplary behaviour. Even the King's bitterest
detractor [3] has to confess, " As far as the author knows, this
abolition of flogging came about through the free will of the
Sovereign, for neither resolutions in the Chambers nor the innumerable petitions from the people mention this subject." Thus the
" brutal " Duke of Cumberland of 1810 did away with what was
not finally dispensed with in Britain for several decades.

[1] To Lord Strangford, 19th April 1848.
[2] To King Frederick William, RB., 18th March 1848.
[3] Geschichte des Königreichs Hannover (*Oppermann*), II, p. 61.

As far as Hanover was concerned the revolution of 1848 was over and the old King had triumphed, though everywhere else was chaos and disintegration. "At any rate," wrote Mr. Bligh, "it appears to me, Hanover has, to the best of its means, set an example of resistance to the revolutionary mania ; and had it been followed perhaps we should not now have to witness the farce intermingled with tragic scenes such as has lately been played at Frankfurt, nor be apprehending renewed outbreaks and anarchy in the principal capitals of Germany." [1]

The King knew that it did not depend upon him alone whether the revolution was to be victorious or not. So long as Prussia was in the hands of the revolutionaries, neither Hanover nor any other land of Germany was safe. "The influence of such a person," wrote Bligh of the appointment of a new Prussian Ambassador, "will not be necessary to drag this country in the course pursued by Prussia as, unfortunately, under the circumstances of the times, whither the latter leads Hanover must, I fear, follow." [2] The King of Hanover, therefore, devoted himself to strengthening and inspiring his weak-willed nephew to stamp out the anarchy in his Kingdom and appoint loyal and trustworthy Ministers instead of those whom he had at present about him.

"I beg of you," he wrote. "Pull yourself together [Ermanne Dich] and don't allow yourself to be led further by the destructive ideas of the day. . . . I cannot describe to you all that passes within me when I think of what Prussia was and how it is now. It is quite incomprehensible to me, for with such troops, such bravery, such loyalty, that Berlin is in such a state as it is now, I at least cannot grasp. . . . I confess, I would have surrounded the town and blockaded or bombarded it and so have restored order." [3] He also wrote to his more energetic nephew, William, in the hope that he might achieve something with his brother. "Alas ! Alas ! If only your brother possessed more resolution !" he sighed.[4] Repeatedly,[5] he urged the King to join his soldiers now gathered in great numbers in Potsdam and then besiege the city that was in the hands of the anarchists. Bloodshed then, or the threat of it, he said, would save it a hundredfold later, as he had often proved in his own land. What a comfort that Frederica had not lived to see Berlin and the Royal House in their present state ! "Everyone

[1] F.O. 34/53, 21st April 1848.
[2] Ibid. 34/53, 13th April 1848.
[3] RB. To King Frederick William, 13th April 1848.
[4] M.A. To Prince William of Prussia, 25th April 1848.
[5] Vide all the letters in Revolutionsbriefe and M.A.

sees the danger in which we all find ourselves," he wrote, " yet no
one will take measures, at least, to halt the evil. Why is this ?
My answer is : *cowardice* and lack of energy." [1] All along, the
chief danger lay not in his own land. He had also to fight the
revolution from above.

As has been seen, at the first sign of trouble most of the governments of Central Germany capitulated and their votes in the Diet
were thus at the disposal of the revolutionaries. Other member-
states were anxious to appease and conciliate them—the old weakness—and so the Diet declared itself in favour of establishing
German unity through a National Parliament, for which each
member-state would hold elections for it according to its own
electoral laws. This was not enough for the revolutionaries who—
gaol-sweepings, anarchists and a few romanticists and dreamers—
streamed to Frankfurt and formed themselves into their own
Parliament, utterly without mandate ; no one had elected them
and they represented nobody but themselves. Their meetings
were scenes of violence and hot-headed speeches by demagogues.
They addressed fantastic demands to the Diet, but this body was
so timid as to recognise their authority. The old ambassadors to
the Diet resigned and the assembly broke with the past. It now
ordered that the elections to the so-called Parliament, to meet on
the 1st May 1848, were to be annulled and held on a universal and
direct basis.

The King of Hanover and Stüve were of completely the same
mind in resisting these preposterous happenings. However, they
were in a difficult position as members of the Confederation. It
would be impossible to resist it alone, so the King sounded Prussia
as to adopting a common attitude. Prussia was, as in all things, a
broken reed. When the demand for new elections came, the King
and Stüve wished to refuse to obey, but when Prussia annulled
her elections Hanover, left in the lurch, had no alternative but to
follow her example. " Nevertheless," wrote Mr. Bligh, " I think
on the whole, there is a sort of reaction in the country. There is
nothing like eagerness shown to carry out the idea of a German
Parliament. It is rather looked upon as a necessity which must be
succumbed to." [2] Stüve declared that Hanover recognised the so-
called National Assembly only as a body to suggest and discuss
measures for national unity ; these measures would then have to be
approved and enacted by the various Governments in accordance

[1] RB. To King Frederick William, 6th June 1848.
[2] F.O. 34/53, 5th May 1848.

with their Constitutions. " That modifications were necessary to the Confederation, I am the first to admit," wrote the King. " But to upset and overturn everything I cannot give my consent, and, I am afraid, no Sovereigns apart from the minor ones will ever agree to give up their sovereignty and rights, so that they no longer rule in their own lands, but shall only be in them as prefects and governors. That unity might take place in some things in Germany is, I believe, not only possible, but desirable, such as weights, measures, money, the post. But when it comes to such things as internal changes, as taxes, laws, appointments, the troops, all this is hardly possible, for each land has its peculiarities and customs. . . . That this will come about in an assembly of nine hundred so heterogeneous as it will be, I believe to be impossible." [1]

So the Assembly met in Frankfurt on the 18th May, having postponed its opening on account of the new elections which had been ordered. It consisted of desperate revolutionaries and anarchists, ignorant and ambitious demagogues, advocates, dreamers, poets and writers. Of statesmen, men of responsibility, experience or moderation, none was to be seen, and from the start this motley crowd adopted an arrogant tone that showed its impossibility. It was, it said, the Sovereign Government of Germany, entrusted not only with legislative but executive powers. " I shudder at the thought of what we will see in Frankfurt," wrote the King. " I confess to you, I cannot swallow the idea of being tyrannised and commanded by professors, advocates, doctors and such stuff. I was ever an enemy of doctrinaires and I cannot alter myself." [2] And what followed showed how right he had been—brawls, disorder, shouting, invective. " The storm in Frankfurt seems to me to be growing daily and I believe that the time has come when we Sovereigns must decide firmly upon what we want to do. Is it possible that Prussia, Saxony, Bavaria and the Grand Dukes want to surrender and humiliate themselves, by becoming prefects, and that seems only too clearly to be the plan. Do you want to see your lands merely as provinces, the Sovereigns giving up all their rights and becoming merely Presidents, Governors, Landdroste and Prefects ? Do you believe that even the peoples themselves are inclined to be treated so dictatorially ? I confess I am not so inclined, but the time has come when we must reach an understanding between ourselves and act together." [3]

[1] RB. To King Frederick William, 8th–10th May 1848.
[2] Ibid. To King Frederick William, 14th April 1848.
[3] S.A. To Grand Duke of Mecklenburg-Strelitz, 9th June 1848.

An understanding with Prussia was most important. The King never ceased to urge upon his nephews the necessity of putting down the revolution which still raged in Berlin and then of joining him in resisting the pretensions of the assembly in Frankfurt. It happened that, on the 5th June, the King of Prussia's brother, Prince William, passed through Hanover on his way back from England where he had been advised to live during the riots in his capital, and his uncle utilised the opportunity to speak to him on the subject. He could not receive him officially as the Court was in mourning for the death of his sister, Princess Sophia, the month before (for which reason his birthday was not celebrated). The next morning, however, he visited him in the room which had been placed at his disposal in the smaller Palais at Herrenhausen. He told him of all that was going on in Berlin and the Prince expressed himself in full agreement with his views. The King warned him not to take part in the debates of the National Assembly in Berlin, as he would only expose himself to insult if he did. This the Prince promised—a promise which he broke and suffered precisely the punishment of which his uncle had warned him. As the King left the Palais, the Prince said to him, " Dear uncle, how can I ever repay you for all the love and friendship which you have always shown to me, particularly on this occasion ? " The King was moved and replied, " When I am no more, look after my blind son." His nephew extended both hands to him and promised that he would do so.[1] At a quarter-past eleven that morning he left with the train to Berlin.

A united front was soon proved to be necessary. The Frankfurt Assembly hurried on with its work of taking all power into its hands irrespective of any existing institutions or laws, and it wished to establish an executive at once. Though there were loud demands for a republic without further ado, the majority eventually decided to elect a provisional Vicar (as Verweſer is usually translated in this case) of the Empire, as provisional head of the executive, and their choice fell upon the insignificant but popular and well-meaning Archduke Johann,[2] " not because, but in spite of his being a Prince," the leaders explained. On the 29th June he was elected and the assembly had placed itself finally on the floor of the revolution, for the already existing executives, the Governments,

---

[1] Prince William had also passed through Hanover on the way to England. The above conversation was witnessed by A.D.C. von Reitzenstein, who related it to Baron A. von Hake, who, in turn, informed von Hassell, in whose history it is to be found.

[2] Brother of the Emperor Francis.

had not been consulted. There was thus no legal continuity and if the new office were to succeed it would be through might alone.

The King of Hanover and his Ministers were beside themselves at this sudden development. They had only recognised the assembly as a party in the negotiations towards German unity, not as an organ with sovereign powers, and if it elected an Archduke it could also elect the wildest anarchist. Now was the time for the Governments to act together. Counsellor Hoppenstedt was sent to the Courts of Berlin and Dresden to try to form a united front, while the King himself brought all his influence to bear upon his relatives. To King Frederick William he pointed out all that the late events implied—" By God, such a proposition clearly proves that the real intention of the Paulskirche [1] is : Republicanism. But they will still have to bite devilishly hard before they swallow me, and I do not think that the Prussian Eagle has lost its claws ! I have not lost my courage, and am convinced that if we all stand by one another faithfully and always understand one another clearly and firmly hold to our principles, we can save ourselves. Now God bless you, and do not lose spirit ; with calm and self-confidence we can come to our good destination." [2] The King spoke in a suitable voice to the more martial spirit of Prince William.

Dear William,
Now or Never !
These are grave words and will show to you my innermost thoughts and feelings, not taken in haste, but after I have had, since the events of the last three days, no other thought but what has been going on *chez vous* in Berlin.

He hoped that the Prince would not say that it was none of his concern ; if Prussia fell, all North Germany must follow, so he had a right to give him his opinion frankly on what happened there, even if not out of love and friendship. The letter closed with the same momentous three words. [3]

But although the King of Prussia asked for his uncle's advice, and the latter summoned his Ministers to prepare a detailed memorandum for him, [4] although the Prussian envoy in Frankfurt urged

[1] The Church of St. Paul, where the meetings were held in Frankfurt.
[2] RB. To King Frederick William, 2nd August 1848.
[3] M.A. To Prince William of Prussia, 12th September 1848.
[4] RB. To King Frederick William, 2nd August 1848.

his Government to act in the same sense, the Prussian Ministers now announced that they recognised the election of the Vicar. As so often in his life, Ernest Augustus stood alone and deserted. Hanover had now either to break with the assembly, in which case, war and civil war would break out all over Germany, or to recognise a purely revolutionary act and submit to a revolutionary authority. To the latter, the King would never give his consent. The Ministers did not know what to do and wished to resign. If they deserted him, he said, he would abdicate and leave the country. Through all the turmoil and trials of the last years, he had often longed for the peace and quiet of his Thames-side cottage and garden at Kew.[1] But whatever the outcome, he would not humiliate himself in submitting to revolutionary might. " So long as I can, I will stand firm," he said. " I will not, I can not, be a republican, better Death than that. . . . Remember, I am a true Guelph, who has never yet, thank God ! shown himself to be a coward or a Louis Philippe, whose infamous poltroonery has caused all this. . . ." [2]

On the 8th July the Government made a statement in the Lower Chamber, where the radicals and nationalists naturally were well represented. The King, it said, gave his consent to the election of the Archduke Johann in view of his fine personal qualities and capabilities. He also worked for German strength and unity, " but he has the irrevocable conviction that his princely honour would not allow him to give his consent to a constitution which did not adequately protect the independence of the states." In such a case, His Majesty would rather suffer the worst than offer his hand to measures which his duty and honour rejected. If, therefore, these negotiations did not have a favourable outcome, he would feel himself bound to remain in a position which would then, in his eyes, exclude any possibility of furthering the good of the land.

His warning had the effect which he had intended. Everywhere—in Hanover, among the Monarchs and at Frankfurt—this firm declaration caused a sensation. The Chambers were for some moments struck dumb after hearing it and all over the Kingdom the reality of the issue dawned on people. Whatever had been said

[1] Even in the hour of his great triumph in 1840, the King had written to Sir Henry Halford (8th August), " Oh ! How often do I sigh after dear Kew and my little cottage there. There is a great deal of glory but little enjoyment in a King's life, and as Duke of Cumberland I was much happier and more my own master than I now shall ever be again."

[2] RB. To King Frederick William, 18th March and 13th April 1848.

and done, Hanover without Ernest Augustus was unthinkable to its people; furthermore, civil war and Prussian domination would be the inevitable fruits. The people stood firm round their King, and when he appeared at the Marksmen's Fair (Schützenfeſt), immense crowds greeted him. " I still feel confident that this will be one of the last peoples in Germany to rise in open rebellion against their rulers," Mr. Bligh observed, and he commented upon the Vicar's election, " It is almost incredible that such an event should have created as little sensation here. . . . Of enthusiasm there is not the slightest symptom, although an annual fête now in progress [1] would have afforded the best possible opportunity for eliciting and manifesting anything of this sort. The fact is that (as I have reported ever since the commencement of the present universal agitation) this country, being contented with the enjoyment of prosperity and independence, required no material changes which might tend to lessen either the one or the other of these advantages." [2]

All Monarchs and Governments who had hitherto invariably capitulated to the demands of the revolutionaries were astonished and encouraged by the lone stand on the part of the old King of Hanover and a new spirit began to make itself felt among them. But in Frankfurt the declaration burst like a bombshell. One speaker after another rose to express his wrath at this defiance. Threats of deposition and mediatisation thundered across St. Paul's Church, taunts that this same King was proud to consider himself the subject of a foreign Queen and, finally, an official demand that Hanover should declare its unqualified submission to the Central Executive. These scenes naturally confirmed the King in his determination. " It must have been a hideous scene in the Pauls-Kirche last Monday," he wrote. " I have read a report of it to-day from an eye-witness and the scene was worthy of having taken place in a beer-house. Are these the people who should give *us* laws ? Are we supposed to be the *humilissimi servi* to such a base society ? For, I hear, they have not only used the most obscene words, but come to blows. My blood *boils* within me, and when this happens from written details, what would I feel if I saw it ? For myself, I like only the society of gentlemen and cavaliers, not that of professors and the mob." [3] To an English friend he wrote, " The National Assembly is a complete bear garden, and blackguardism wherever it appears meets with my resistance, and this

---

[1] The Schützenfeſt.   [2] F.O. 34/53, 6th July 1848.
[3] RB. To King Frederick William, 10th August 1848.

has given a little more spirit to other Governments, and even this assembly has become somewhat milder in their last sitting." [1]

On the 13th August the King of Prussia passed through Hanover on his way to Cologne for the celebrations of the Cathedral's sixth century. Ernest Augustus had been invited, but as the Vicar and most of the members of the Frankfurt Assembly were to be there, he declined and regretted that his nephew condescended to attend. With his nephew and suite he dined in fine weather in the Park at Herrenhausen. King Frederick William had previously said that he would like to discuss the line of conduct which they were to adopt,[2] so Ernest Augustus prepared himself. But the King of Prussia did not broach politics, so his uncle refrained as well.[3]

But the King of Prussia had, possibly inspired by his uncle, recovered a certain amount of energy ; he even reminded a deputation from the Frankfurt Assembly at Cologne that there were still Princes and he was one of them. King Ernest Augustus now suggested that the time was ripe for them, the Sovereigns, to concert their plans behind the scenes, and he recommended that each should appoint a confidential envoy to this purpose. The King of Prussia was in agreement. Towards the end of July von Wangenheim was sent to Berlin, and he found to his satisfaction that everyone there realised at last that the existence of Prussia was threatened. What had opened all eyes were the pretensions of the " War Ministry " of the Central Executive, which now demanded the allegiance of all German troops. That was too much even for the Prussian Government. Ernest Augustus had already given an example of resistance and now the tide of 1848 had definitely turned.

Hanover and Prussia were therefore united in refusing to hold parades and to announce ceremonially to the troops that they now owed allegiance to the so-called Central Executive in Frankfurt ; a non-committal order was merely read out *pro forma*. King Ernest Augustus was certain that if it were demanded of his troops that they should swear allegiance to the Frankfurt Assembly they would mutiny. As it was, all nominal acts emanating thence were ridiculed by them, including, for example, what was supposed to be the solemn attachment of black-red-and-gold to the regimental

---

[1] To Lord Strangford, 16th August 1848.

[2] The King of Prussia sent copies of his letters to the King of Hanover to the Duke of Brunswick, to whom he always referred to his uncle, in English, as " *Old King Ernestus* " or " *the Old King*."—M.A. King Frederick William to Duke of Brunswick.

[3] To Lord Strangford, 16th August 1848.

colours.[1] " I begin by declaring that I never can nor will bow
down to the sovereignty of the people, which the national assembly
at Frankfurt consider themselves," the King wrote to his cousin,
" and in my public declaration I stated clearly and unequivocally
to my own states that I only acknowledge the Reichsverweser as
agreed upon by the Sovereign Princes, as I do not acknowledge the
power or authority of the national assembly . . . and to prove
publicly this my decision, so that every stranger coming into my
country may be aware of this my decision, I have had all the sentry
boxes, railings, etc. freshly painted *white* and *yellow*, thus you see
clearly my opinion. . . ."[2] He hoped that this example would
encourage others. Later, the King received a letter from the
Central Executive asking him to send General Sir Hugh Freiherr
von Halkett, his English general, to Constantinople to announce to
the Sultan the Archduke Johann's election as Vicar. This was
intended to flatter the King, but he was indifferent to honours
from such a quarter. Angry at its presumption in dictating to him
what he should do with one of his officers, he replied that he could
not spare him.[3]

Ernest Augustus was also displeased with events in Schleswig-
Holstein. Throughout the 1840's he had always opposed the
Danish Government's attempts to make the provinces[4] into
Danish provinces, but when the Duchies declared a Provisional
Government and the Confederation resolved to assist them, he was
loath to place his troops at the disposal of rebels against their
Sovereign. For as long as possible he forbade his commander,
Halkett, to cross the Elbe, and when he did so it was only at the
behest of Prussia. On the 20th April Count von Bennigsen, the
Foreign Minister, asked him for such an order. For a long time
the King said nothing, then his aide asked if he should write to
Halkett as the Prussians desired. The King sprang fiercely from
his arm-chair. " You will write nothing at all ! " he cried angrily.
There was another long pause while he paced up and down in the
room ; then, as the Count pressed for a decision, he reluctantly
yielded, told Jacobi to send the order and dismissed them from his
presence ungraciously. Everything angered him. A Prussian,
General Wrangel, was put in command of the Federal force instead

[1] A very humorous description of one such ceremony is given in the Blätter aus
dem Tagebuch eines Hannoverschen Offiziers, which it is impossible to translate.
[2] M.A. To Duke of Brunswick, 23rd July 1848.
[3] F.O. 34/53, 6th November 1848.
[4] The Duchies of Schleswig and Holstein was attached to the Danish Crown in
the way in which Hanover had been to the English before 1837.

The King in the uniform of a Hanoverian General

(By Krüger)

The King in British uniform of a General of Hussars.

(Painted by William Owen, R.A., about 1818)

of Halkett, and he levied three million Thaler upon the Danish provinces. This led the King to declare to Berlin and Frankfurt " that I would not be a party to so infamous and outrageous an act. I never liked the whole Danish business from the outset. . . . I must say for the credit of all the troops in Schleswig-Holstein, that they dislike the manner in which General Wrangel has published this proclamation, and I trust that my disavowing to take a part in that horrible act of spoliation will make the Government in Prussia not ratify or countenance such a measure. I hope to God that the mediation of England will be accepted and that this business be settled. . . ." [1] Above all, it seemed to him significant that at a time when revolution was rife, troops should be sent out of the country by those in control at Frankfurt. His only comfort was that on the way back his troops were able to help to put down trouble in Hamburg and afterwards free Altenburg, where his son and daughter-in-law were staying, from the revolutionaries who completely dominated it. Through the threat of English, Swedish and Russian intervention, Frankfurt was obliged to conclude a not very glorious armistice at Malmö. This was a great relief to the King of Hanover, but Dahlmann, one of those whom he had dismissed from Göttingen in 1837, moved that the Assembly should reject the armistice and his resolution was carried by a majority. The Ministry of the Central Executive resigned but Dahlmann could not form another, as it would have had to fight England, Russia, Sweden and possibly France. Doubly humiliated, the Assembly had to ratify the armistice.[2] " How I was slandered when I threw seven professors out of Göttingen one day in 1838," wrote the King when he learnt of this, " and when one sees their behaviour in the Paulskirche and elsewhere, I am fully justified in the step I took." [3]

Chaos broke out in Frankfurt. The next day (the 18th September) there was riot and disorder and Prince Lichnowsky and General von Auerswald, who had been in no way concerned with the late events, were foully murdered. With that, all eyes were opened. The days of romanticism and dreaming were over and the Paulskirche Assembly seen for what it was, a brutal and

---

[1] To Lord Strangford, 24th May 1848.

[2] There is a curious idea to-day, abundantly contradicted by the above, that the Frankfurt Assembly and all that it stood for, together with the red-black-and-gold colours that were introduced after both World Wars, was a force for peace, while the Reactionary Courts represented aggressive nationalism and militarism. The real state of affairs was precisely the reverse and there can be few greater distortions in modern history than this.

[3] RB. To King Frederick William, 17th November 1848.

E.A.—13

barbaric rabble. Now events followed one another in quick succession. Ernest Augustus's stand had been the turning-point of the year; weakness and submission to blackmail were at last conquered. In October 1848 Prince Windischgrätz restored order in Prague, then he marched on Vienna and put down the revolution there. Ernest Augustus was overcome with admiration, especially as the Prince had accomplished this immediately after the murder of his own wife by revolutionaries. His only anxiety was that he might be too lenient to the murderers in Vienna.[1] He then sent Windischgrätz the Order of St. George, which he had created for Sovereigns only, and to General Jellačik, who had restored order in Croatia, the Grand Cross of the Guelphic Order, as signs of his deep admiration, and in the case of the former, sympathy.[2] On the 14th December Count Wengersky arrived in Hanover to announce to the King the accession of the young Emperor Francis Joseph. After some reflection he found this much to his satisfaction.[3]

Similarly, there was a new spirit in Berlin. The King of Prussia appointed Count von Brandenburg to be his Minister, a man who held the respect of Ernest Augustus, and he too acted with firmness and decision in restoring order there. Everywhere it became obvious that the revolution had only triumphed through weakness and surrender. Without any difficulty lost territory was won back from the mobs who ruled it. If only they had met with similar firmness at the beginning all the ruin and bloodshed and the terrible consequences for subsequent generations would have been saved. The Assembly in Frankfurt had, of course, sealed its own fate. "Though I am sure that the mess at Frankfurt must sooner or later crumble to pieces," wrote the King, "still I wish it could be prolonged a short time, in order that they may completely expose their consummate ignorance and total want of claim to the characters of statesmen and men of business. . . . If ever it was necessary to prove that doctrinaires are incapable of producing anything rational or practical, you have it here where philosophers, professors and attorneys are in abundance in the Assembly, with the addition of Jews and adventurers of every description, even sons of people who have been confined for robbing and stealing and every crime in the world, so that a more motley crew have

[1] NSJB. To Countess von Wallmoden, 14th January 1849.
[2] F O. 34/56, 8th March 1849.
[3] Ibid. 34/53. 18th December 1848, and to Lord Strangford, 16th December 1848. The King sent Prince Bernard of Solms to congratulate the Emperor and invest him with the order of St. George, on the 16th.

never before met together." As he told the King of Prussia, they must let it die of itself and of its own folly, and do nothing which might allow it to be said that they had brought it about.[1]

So, completely discredited and impotent, the Assembly drove its folly to a climax at the end of the year with its enactment of the " Fundamental Rights " which were to be put into effect by the different Governments of Germany. Prussia and Hanover agreed fully that such preposterous pretensions had to be resisted. Apart from the legal implications of recognising them, the laws which applied to one land would have been fatal applied to another and some were of a nature that no proper Government could accept, such as the unlimited right of a subject of one state to settle in any other if he pleased and the abolition of primogeniture. When Stüve declared this before the Chambers, a storm broke out from the opposition, who rejected his proposals. He then asked to be relieved of his post. But first, said the King, he would have to put his reasons in writing and then wait until a successor was found. None was, however, to be found, for the opposition was completely irresponsible and incapable of government. One of its spokesmen who had demanded the resignation of the Government declined forming one himself on the score of age. In the meantime a petition was organised to request the King to retain Stüve, and its bearers only reached the Palace after being attacked and beaten up by a mob. The Chambers were adjourned, then, as their members continued to agitate, dismissed. Stüve stayed and Frankfurt had sustained another defeat.

It only remained to receive the *coup de grâce*. Its delegates, who hurried to Berlin to offer an imperial crown to the King, as if it had one to offer, met with a firm rejection. Ernest Augustus had often pointed out to his nephew what a disgrace it would be if he were to accept, and it was largely through his persuasions that he refused.[2] On the 4th May 1849 the Assembly demanded that all Governments should recognise the Reich ; on the 10th it reprimanded Prussia for helping the King of Saxony against rebels in Dresden ; on the 14th Prussia called her delegates away, and on the 23rd the King of Hanover did likewise. These orders were declared void by the revolutionary majority. The more reputable members left the Assembly, which, a rump of disgruntled extremists, migrated to Stuttgart and faded away. Ernest Augustus had again been proved right.

[1] To Lord Strangford, 26th November 1848, and 15th January 1849.
[2] RB. To Frederick William, 4th April 1849.

"One thing I glory in, however," he wrote, "namely, that I was the first who positively refused obedience to their dictates and the impertinence assumed by the *soi-disant* ministry of the Reichs= verweſer . . . which naturally caused me to be proclaimed a rebel by the National Assembly at Frankfurt. . . . I have fought a most difficult and desperate battle, I may say, single-handed, abandoned by all other Sovereigns, and yet have maintained my ground." [1]

[1] To Lord Strangford, 18th December 1848.

CHAPTER XXVI

1849–51

IT was clear that the King was nearing the end of his days. The strain of 1848 had had its effects on his vitality and there was no doubt that it had shortened his life considerably. Half of the day he lay in bed, where he transacted official business. Only in the evening did his spirit recover its former freshness. He was loath to leave his room to entertain guests and even the larger Court functions were now held on the ground floor of the Palais where he lived ; formerly he had made a point of receiving in the Residence Palace. Only extremely rarely did he mount a horse now—for such occasions as the visit of his brother or the grand inspection on his birthday—and then not without difficulty. The horses were saddled, but no longer ridden ; the King liked to deceive himself as to his weakness and old age and he would often order the horses for a ride when the weather was bad and he knew that everyone would dissuade him from going out in it. His remaining joy was his grandson.[1] He was always a lover of children and the young Prince Ernest Augustus was his pride.

The King was also made happy in August 1849 by the visit of his brother, the Duke of Cambridge. Together they appeared at a grand review on the Waterloo Place, and throughout those days the King was very gay and lively. But the leave-taking was the more melancholy. The Duke was so overwhelmed that he did not take farewell of his brother, but gave von Malortie a farewell-letter as he stepped into his carriage outside the fürstenhof, saying, " We two brothers are old men ; one of us must go first—who knows whether we will see each other again ? " And, in fact, they did not.[2] Princess Sophia, Queen Adelaide, the Duke of Cambridge [3] and, what particularly grieved him, the King's step-daughter, Frederica, Duchess of Anhalt, all passed away in succession ; the King saw his circle of friends and relations narrow rapidly,

[1] Two daughters had also been born to the Crown Prince, the Princesses Frederica (1848) and Mary (1849). The former was so christened at the King's express wish.
[2] *Von Malortie*, p. 164.
[3] For an account of his death, see letter of the King of Hanover to Countess von Bennigsen, 11th July 1850 (Bennigsen-Banteln Archives).

and became accustomed to notifications of deaths. He spoke of his own death quite calmly, interested himself in the building of the mausoleum, and even lay on the sofa so that Rauch, the sculptor, could model his sarcophagus.[1]

He was almost continuously indisposed. But still, sick, tired and depressed as he was, there was no peace for him and he never let the reins go. Both inside and outside his Kingdom he was waging a desperate struggle for the principles which he had held his life long.

So long as it was a matter of fighting the revolution which endangered the works of both, the King and his Ministers had acted together. He was the first to recognise the qualities of his former opponents, their " uprightness, loyalty, integrity and courage. . . . This Ministry and myself are one. They have the fullest confidence in me, as I have in them." [2] But the revolution was over and now the problems were those of the permanent basis of peace and order in Hanover and Germany. Here their paths diverged. The King had called them to fight the revolution and had agreed to concessions to facilitate that task ; he demanded sacrifices from them also. But now, instead of confining themselves to their original purpose, they sought to put into effect innovations which even they themselves now viewed with misgiving. The First Chamber, elected on the law drafted by Stüve, disgusted its author. He had hoped that the Nobility, whom he had formerly fought, would be well represented in it, but this was not the case. There was no possibility of its being a moderating influence or a counterpoise to the hotheads of the lower Chamber ; it was every bit as irresponsible and Stüve missed its predecessor badly. He found it quite impossible to govern with the Estates at all, and eventually handed in his resignation (which, as has been seen, the King declined to accept). Here, then, was one democrat who had learnt his lesson.

As the King observed this, he began to feel that Stüve had exceeded the mandate which he had given him and had even deceived him as to the nature of the measures which he was bringing forward. Certainly Stüve had painted quite a different picture of what the result would be. The King felt that advantage had been taken of his sickness and his preoccupation with the revolution in its larger aspects to carry the long-cherished schemes of his former opponents.

Developments outside his realm were equally disturbing. The events of 1848 had left a lasting impression in Prussia's ambition. What had previously been a mild and slow infection now broke out

[1] *Von Malortie*, p. 153.   [2] NSJB. To Frederick William IV, 1st May 1849.

into an acute disease. A class of men had come into power in
Prussia bent upon seizing supreme power in all Germany. After
1848 the revolutionaries, democrats and nationalists had seen that
by direct action they would achieve nothing. They had rather to
work as they did in Italy, by achieving power in one state strong
enough to dominate the others, then nothing more was necessary.
And here it must be emphasised that the *nationalists* in Germany
were the *democrats*, not the forces of Reaction, as it is to-day taught.
A victory of the democrats in 1848 would have brought 1870 and
1914 appreciably nearer. Few events in modern history have
been more misunderstood, if not distorted. It was the Courts,
the Nobility and all the conservative forces which stood in the
way of the nationalists that year.[1] Eventually they did become the
tools of their destroyers, but that was the same development as in
England and everywhere else.

England was, indeed, responsible for much that happened, as
Ernest Augustus, with his experience, well knew. Palmerston,
Prince Albert and his brother, the Duke of Coburg (who had
ambitions of becoming King of Thuringia), Stockmar and Bunsen
(the Prussian Ambassador in London) formed a clique which worked
to weaken the conservative forces in Germany, and influence the
King of Prussia to unite Germany under his hegemony on radical
—almost republican—principles. Their *bête noir* was Austria,
that stronghold of Conservatism.[2] What was sown was later reaped,
though this British policy of supporting every revolutionary and
nationalistic movement abroad waited a century before punishing
its perpetrators. " What has Palmerston to answer for by his
conduct in throwing fire and flame throughout Europe ? "[3] wrote
Ernest Augustus when his conduct with regard to Switzerland let
forth all the hellish forces of 1848. As an Englishman he felt

[1] The King heard that Hofmann von Fallersleben, writer of the poem " Deutſchland
über Alles " which later, to a melody poached from Austria, became the German
national anthem, was in his Kingdom. He immediately gave instructions, " As there
is no doubt whatsoever that he is an archrogue and, after his conduct in Göttingen,
not to be tolerated, if it is true that he has taken up residence at Fallersleben, he must
never go out unless accompanied by a gendarme. This will soon become so irksome
to him that he will leave of his own accord. But if he can be deported from the land
without further ado, so much the better."—H.A. Cal. Br. 15 H438, 4th April 1843.

[2] For an exact account of this intrigue, see NSJB., King of Hanover to King
Frederick William, 20th April 1849. The King of Belgium had written very strong
letters of remonstrance to his nephew, Prince Albert, upon his conduct. Confirmation
of the Prince's rôle is to be found in his letters to the King of Prussia (RB., particularly
that of the 22nd February 1849), exhorting him to emulate the glorious deeds of his
ancestor, Frederick the Great, and ensure Prussia's supremacy in Germany to the
exclusion of Austria.

[3] To Lord Strangford, 21st February 1848.

ashamed, as " it is known that Palmerston, if not openly, has underhandedly supported and encouraged rebellion everywhere." [1] Now, of his incitement of Prussia towards self-aggrandisement, he wrote " One would think that Palmerston's whole object was to cause a European war." [2]

Of course, to attain its object, Prussia had to exclude Austria from Germany, where she had been the leading power for hundreds of years. Austrian statesmen were not concerned with narrow national policies, but conserving principles and order everywhere. The smaller states of Germany were under her protection and this was particularly important for Hanover. She was completely enclosed by the Prussian tongs, and on the Prussian theory of " necessity " she took the place which Silesia had occupied in the previous century ; only her connection with England had obliged Prussia to keep her hands away so long. Now that was gone. Hanover was in the position of any other of the smaller German states and only a powerful Austria could keep her from the tender mercies of Prussia. If Austria were excluded from Germany, nothing could keep Prussia in check.

This, then, the unity of Austria and Prussia, was the cardinal point of Ernest Augustus's policy. It would check the revolutionaries now in power in the latter. His other concern was for the smaller states which had proved themselves incapable of resisting the revolutionaries at home. To avoid this in the future, he proposed the formation of six curiae, each under one of the Kingdoms,[3] which would provide the forces for use in their smaller neighbours in times of crisis. His plans were not bound up with any national ambition, only with that unity against revolution and destruction which he had preached his life long.

That Ernest Augustus was not animated by party spirit towards Prussia was witnessed by his past. Since 1813 he had almost worshipped Prussia, he had spent the happiest years of his life there, only in Berlin did he ever feel at home and his two nephews were the relations who meant most to him. But the King of Prussia's was not Prussia's policy and his uncle's warnings against the men who surrounded him were of no avail. Ernest Augustus now looked to Austria, which he trusted and admired. " Never has an army proved itself so gallant, so loyal and so honest as our Austrian," he wrote, and he could not sufficiently express his pride in his

---

[1] To Lord Strangford, 27th July 1849.
[2] To Lord Strangford, 26th October 1849.
[3] Austria, Prussia, Bavaria, Saxony, Hanover and Württemberg.

regiment of Hussars. When one of the officers deserted to the rebels in Hungary, a Colonel Kiss, he demanded the sternest punishment for him, as he had caused the deaths of so many of his comrades by his treason. When he later heard of his flight, he gave an order that if he were to be found in Hanover he was to be arrested at once. As to the men who followed him, Ernest Augustus was indulgent, as good soldiers could be excused for following their officers.[1] This preoccupation in Hungary prevented Austria's paying much attention to German affairs. Ernest Augustus did not know what her intentions were, and in the meantime he had to answer Prussia's proposals for a meeting to discuss the future constitution of Germany.

Stüve and the Ministers were not such experienced men of the world as the King and they did not believe an accommodation with Prussia out of the question, so a second difference arose. The King warned them that the word of the Prussian Government was not to be trusted. However, as long as Austria could not act, he had somehow to reach an understanding and so he sent Stüve and von Wangenheim to Berlin. Prussia had invited all Governments to send trusted envoys to discuss their future course of action now that they had broken with the St. Paul's Church Assembly. The King instructed his representatives only to concert plans to fight the revolution if necessary, though he knew that Prussia had projects for a constitution.

Radowitz, the Prussian Prime Minister, immediately opened the discussions with plans for a constitution, and the King of Prussia issued a declaration " To my People," which was to have the effect, should the negotiations fail, of putting the blame on to the shoulders of the others. Austria left the conference when Prussia's plans for power became obvious, and there seemed to be a stalemate when Prussia suggested an alliance of herself, Hanover, Saxony and Bavaria " for the maintenance of the internal and external security of its members," which all members of the former Confederation could join. Recognising the impossibility of Austria's participating in German affairs at that moment, and therefore the necessity of seeking a *modus vivendi* with her great neighbour, Hanover agreed ; together with Saxony, she consented to join, though only with a reservation allowing freedom of action if circumstances should alter. This was a reference to the necessity of Austrian participation a soon as that should become possible. Bavaria declined to bind itself to the alliance, and so on the 26th May 1849 Prussia, Hanover

[1] NSJB. To Countess von Wallmoden, 2nd and 7th February 1849.

and Saxony signed the Three Kings' Alliance. " I have been forced, much against my will and wishes," wrote the King, " to concede to Prussia's proposals, owing to the unfortunate geographical position my country is placed in. However, I have done all in my power to prove my sincere attachment to our most true and faithful ally, Austria. Many a sleepless night have I passed in trying to bring the two contending powers to some understanding." [1] Now he felt the need for a Schele upon whom he could rely, especially now that he was senile and the Ministers had more independence than would have otherwise been the case.

His distrust of Prussia soon showed itself to have been justified. Radowitz had overruled Stüve's request that the Hanoverian and Saxon reservations should be incorporated in the protocol, and the official Prussian Gazette of the 31st May published an announcement of their acceptance of Prussia's constitutional proposals without any mention of it. Hanover and Saxony had been outwitted, for they could not now protest without seeming to be particularists opposed to German unity.

One evening shortly afterwards, various despatches, letters and newspapers were being read to King Ernest Augustus, as usual, and this issue was among them. The mention of a constitution struck him like a " clap of thunder." He had heard no word of it and when he concluded the alliance his only thoughts had been of defence and security. During the next few days inquiries reached him from all quarters, particularly England, as to what it meant, his having incorporated his Kingdom into that of Prussia. He now saw the significance of a report which he had previously ridiculed, one that the foreign Envoys in Hanover were about to be recalled and that Mr. Bligh, the English Ambassador, was making arrangements to sell his house.[2]   In all the other states of Europe, including Austria and Bavaria, the news caused indignation and the King saw how his Ministers had allowed themselves to be trapped. Prussia now proceeded in a high-handed manner to force other states into the alliance. She refused to help the Grand Duke of Baden against the revolutionaries unless he joined and a similar pressure was exerted unsuccessfully upon Bavaria. Finally, as there was now the possibility that Austria might make proposals for a German Constitution, Prussia considered it necessary to confront her with an accomplished fact and announced that a Reichstag,

---

[1] To Lord Strangford, 7th June 1849.
[2] M.A. To Prince William of Prussia, 10th January 1850; to Lord Strangford, 19th June 1849.

or German Parliament, would be elected and meet at Erfurt in March 1850.

This was going too far. Hanover had joined Prussia as a temporary alliance against the revolution and now Prussia had announced that this alliance would elect a Parliament and frame a Constitution, with neither Bavaria, Württemberg nor Austria, whose inclusion was the cardinal point of Hanover's policy.[1] The King sent von Wangenheim to Count von Brandenburg, " not as King of Hanover to the Prussian Minister-President, but as a staunch friend of Prussia and Prussian General to another Prussian General and patriot," but this was of no avail. It was made clear to him that the Prussian Government had to follow the Chambers and the democratic cliques. Ernest Augustus considered the King and Count von Brandenburg to be men of honour, but they were in the hands of two " whom I look upon as the most worthless unprincipled men that existed—I mean Major-General Radowitz and Bunsen." [2] As Prussia persisted in her course, there was nothing to do but to make use of Hanover's reservation in joining the alliance. On the 21st October 1849 von Wangenheim and von Zeschau (the Saxon plenipotentiary) announced that they could no longer attend the discussions. The next day von Wangenheim returned to Hanover. The language of his colleagues, he said, had been so violent as to remind him of St. Paul's Church the previous year.

Of course, a storm of wrath and anger against the Hanoverian " particularists " and " saboteurs of German unity " rose from the nationalists and democrats. The underhand scheme of the clique in Berlin and London had been foiled. The Prince Consort described the Hanoverians as guilty of " treason to the common fatherland " and their King as " indescribably base and dishonourable "—his excuse is that he probably did not understand what was going on, as he knew nothing of the Hanoverian reservation and saw all through the eyes of Bunsen and his brother.[3]

It was quite clear that Prussian duplicity had outwitted the Hanoverian Government. Prussia had succeeded in representing the temporary anti-revolutionary alliance to the world as one to establish German unity. Even the British Ambassador, usually so well-informed, thought this to be the case. In this way, were Hanover to make use of her reservation, whose publication Prussia

[1] M.A. To Prince William of Prussia, 10th January 1850.
[2] To Duke of Wellington, 7th/12th June 1850.
[3] To his brother, the Duke of Coburg, whose memoirs see.

had suppressed, she would appear to be opposing the first step towards that unity. Mr. Bligh was surprised at how disturbed the Ministers were at these events. They had not believed that Prussia would go so far as to cause a breach. But they had thought that they could back out of the alliance without danger, the reservation sufficing, " because Mr. Stüve, the principal Hanoverian negotiator, though a clever man, was unused to the transaction of business upon so large a theatre. . . ." [1]

The old unit of Lower Saxony and the old Steuerverein, Hanover's former sphere of influence, had been broken up. The diminutive Principality of Schaumburg-Lippe had, it was true, freed herself from Prussia, but the latter had made a gain in Oldenburg, which had formerly faithfully followed Hanover. A glance at the map will show the significance of this. In May 1850 the Grand Duke passed through Hanover on his way back from Berlin and the King went to his hotel to see him, though it was a hardship even for him to leave his own room. They had a long argument, but it was of no avail.[2]

It was the same story with Brunswick, to which the King stood in a special relationship as Prince and Heir. He read one day in a Hamburg newspaper that a military convention was being negotiated between Brunswick and Prussia, which would entail a sacrifice of the former's military sovereignty. Prussian troops would occupy her fortresses and Brunswick troops would join garrisons in Prussia. The King did not believe a report of such treachery, but he instantly sent his A.D.C., Major von Hedemann, to his neighbour to inquire if it had any foundation.[3] The Duke, who was himself averse to all that was going on in his realm, was embarrassed and evasive. He had to join, he said, as Hanover had not the forces to help him in time of need. Von Hedemann returned from the Duke's castle in Blankenburg on the morning of the 26th November 1849 and went to the King. With the latter were Count von Bennigsen, the Foreign Minister, and Count von Kielmannsegg (the Hanoverian Ambassador in London). The King told the officer to relate everything which he knew, and this he did. The King was so overcome by his account of the Duke's conversation that he burst into tears. Had he not been so old and confined to his room, he would himself have undertaken the journey to Blankenburg at once. What particularly upset him was that this should take place

[1] F.O. 34/57 and 61, 22nd October 1849 and 25th February 1850.
[2] Ibid. 34/57 and 61, 30th November 1849 and 31st May 1850.
[3] To Lord Strangford, 2nd December 1849.

inside the House of the Guelphs, and, with the agreement of the
Ministers, he decided to treat it as a family affair and write himself.
He hoped that his cousin would soon be restored to good health,
he said, and that they would then be able to go boar-hunting together
again ; he had to speak to him soon, as he had heard from his courier
that the report which he had read had not been a lie of the Press. " I
beg of you in the name of God, do not sign such a treaty without
first speaking with me personally, for such a measure must closely
touch us both and the honour of our Princely House." What would
the renowned Brunswicker soldiers feel, he asked, at having to
give way to foreign troops ? He could, he assured him, always
send eight to ten thousand men to his help immediately when there
was any need. He begged him to give his courier a definite answer.
Von Hedemann returned a second time but again with an evasive
answer ; no mention was made of the King's principal object, a
personal discussion.[1] The King could now only demand copies of
the projected treaty as Agnate of the House and Heir, and these
the Duke had to provide. Ernest Augustus was beside himself
with rage. The danger to Hanover of Prussian troops in Brunswick
was obvious ; furthermore, Prussia's act was in defiance of the
Federal Military constitution, in which Brunswick belonged to the
Tenth Corps with Hanover ; it was also in defiance of a Brunswick-
Hanoverian treaty of 1845, by which both armies were to use the
same calibre, a different one from the Prussian. A similar convention between Baden and Prussia was abortive as the King refused
to allow troops of the former to pass through Hanover.

" Everyone should be on guard regarding Prussia as her rapacity
and thirst for power and aggrandisement is too clearly proved," [2]
warned the King. Prussia was disturbed lest Austrian troops
should help the King of Saxony against rebels, as she had " private
£eḥn [3] for the possession of Saxony as well as for any neighbouring
country, her thirst to increase her territory being unsatiable." [4]
Her conduct " clearly shows that she is determined to place herself
at the head of the democratic party in Germany.[5]

This was especially painful to the King as he loved his nephews.
Prince William was his particular pride. He had always taken great
pains to show his affection for him. In 1848 he had done all in his

---

[1] M.A. Herr Wedemeyer to von Schleinitz, Minister of State of Brunswick,
27th November 1849 ; King of Hanover to Duke of Brunswick, 27th and 28th
November 1849.

[2] To Lord Strangford, 21st August 1849.   [3] Suzerainty.

[4] To Lord Strangford, 10th December 1849.

[5] To Lord Strangford, 28th September 1850.

power to " defend William against all the calumnies and prejudices that are now being made against this noble man." [1]   He was hurt beyond measure that his nephew should now lend himself to the schemes of the democrats and nationalists.   He heard, he said, that his wife Augusta cursed him (the King) for having become completely Austrian.   He was, he would reply, as Austrian as he was Prussian, for he was Hanoverian, and as such, German, " but, God forbid, not German in the new sense of the word, never that." [2] Whereas he had always passed through and visited his uncle, the Prince now avoided Hanover in his journeys.   The King was hurt at this ingratitude.   " This morning, soon after I awoke, they brought me your letter, instead of yourself," he wrote on one such occasion, " but I am honest enough to say that I did not expect that you would visit me.   Alas, alas, those good times are past and, notwithstanding all the friendly words and compliments which I receive, so it rests.   It is not my fault, for you cannot deny that I have always remained the same.   I cannot change my political principles and thoughts as one changes one's shirt." [3]   To the persuasions and reproaches of the Queen of Prussia,[4] he answered, " I will never give up the principles for which I have lived [5] from my youth on, and I warn you, it is better that you take farewell of me than that you attempt what I would never admit my whole life long, and what is now causing me such gall and anger." [6] For the first time, a grand Court function in Hanover was not attended by a Prussian Prince, the King's sixtieth military jubilee,[7] when a delegation of his Austrian regiment participated in the celebrations which animated the whole capital for several days with music and torchlight processions.   For a year correspondence ceased between the two Kings.

It need hardly be said that the King's confidence in his Ministry was shaken by the affair of the Three Kings' Alliance.   " Among all those whom I have at present," he wrote, " there is not one whom I recognise as a statesman.   Perhaps they could in time become so, if they are long with me, and I live long enough, but at present they are far from it.   Most of them have no experience and, worst of all, no knowledge of men, which is most necessary in this world " [8]

[1] RB.   To King Frederick William, 22nd February 1848.
[2] M.A.   To Prince William, 9th February 1849.
[3] Ibid.   To Prince William, 13th December 1849.
[4] Queen Elizabeth, daughter of King Maximilian I of Bavaria.
[5] Eingesogen, literally, sucked in.
[6] G.A.   To Queen of Prussia, 7th June 1850.
[7] Described in detail in Von Malortie, pp. 166–69.
[8] NSJB.   To King Frederick William, 6th August 1850.

. . . " I have not the slightest doubt of their honourable intentions, but they appear not to possess the power of mind to comprehend the real state of things, and are blinded by little paltry concerns " [1] —the truth of which has been seen.

What annoyed the King now was that the Ministers were still undecided and afraid to ally themselves openly with Austria, though they had irrevocably renounced and incurred the wrath of Prussia. " I have been living for the last six weeks in a sort of warfare with my own Ministry," he wrote, " and I am unable to say how it will end, except to say that I am determined not to give way and thus become isolated, which would inevitably be the case if I consented to their proposals." [2] At a Council on the 2nd February 1850, he told them, " If I do not ally myself with Austria, I will fall between two stools." It would be absurd, he said, to watch a union of Austria, Bavaria, Saxony and Württemberg while at the same time remaining alone and exposed to Prussia.[3] But Stüve knew no sense of proportion and wished to be independent of both. When the King invested Prince Windischgrätz and General Jellačik with his own Orders of Chivalry, the Ministers objected, as if they had a right to dictate to him to whom he should award a personal order instituted by himself.[4] When he was named arbitrator by the Grand Duke of Mecklenburg-Schwerin in a dispute with his Nobility, the Ministers also showed their annoyance that they had not been consulted, though it was a purely personal affair of his own and no concern of theirs.[5] The King saw whither this was leading. He had seen it in England.

The King alone displayed any wisdom or foresight. He saw what would be the result, not only to Hanover, but to Germany and Europe, of a difference between Prussia and Austria. He saw Prussia's endeavours to exclude Austrian influence and, finally, to subjugate her. That the land which had once ruled half of Europe and been a centre of its culture and civilisation should eventually become a mere province of Berlin, as it did a century later, was implicit in this formula—also, however, that Hohenzollern would share the fate of Habsburg and all the other ravished houses. But his attempts to convince his nephews of this truism were of no avail. Letter after letter he wrote to them to this purpose. A war between Prussia and Austria, he told Frederick William,

[1] To Lord Strangford, 31st March 1850.
[2] H.A. Council Records (destroyed 1943–45), quoted by B. Muehlen.
[3] To Lord Strangford, 31st March 1850.
[4] F.O. 34/56, 8th March 1849.   [5] Ibid. 34/61, 3rd April 1850.

"can only be of advantage to the democrats and radicals, who secretly incite one."[1] Prince William, he told, that "a difference or coldness between Austria and Prussia will be our ruin. . . . Unless Austria and Prussia hold firm together, we are all lost."[2] The Monarchs, he considered, should fight their enemies, not themselves. "I have been working, I may say, night and day, trying to bring Austria and Prussia together," he recorded, "but it is a Herculean labour."[3]

In September 1850 matters came to a crisis. Revolution had broken out in Cassel, and Austria and the other states proposed a Federal execution to restore order. No one thought that this would have any effect upon Austro-Prussian relations, for putting down rebellion was a common interest; Prussia herself had already done so once in Baden. But conservative or monarchist principles were of no interest to the men in power in Prussia. The exclusion of Austrian influence was their paramount consideration, and so it was declared that Prussian troops would bar the way to the Austrians and Bavarians marching towards Cassel. War seemed inevitable. Already the two armies faced each other near Fulda. The King of Hanover was in despair. "I beg you on bended knee to take care," he pleaded with his nephew. "Just think, if war breaks out between Prussia and Austria, a European war will result, which will destroy all."[4]

At last Prussia listened to reason, but the effects of the episode inside Hanover were lasting. The Hanoverian delegate at Frankfurt, Detmold, another of the King's former opponents (who had carried his opposition so far as to necessitate being placed under police surveillance) in whom he now had confidence for this task, had voted with Austria and the other states for the restoration of order in Cassel at a time when the Hanoverian Government was undecided in any policy. He was immediately recalled and rebuked, but the King received him with all possible favour, and invested him with the Guelphic Order.[5]

King Ernest Augustus was now convinced that the question of whether Prussia was to be master in Germany would be decided by the sword. Hanover's only protection would be its defences and so he set about putting these in suitable order. He conceived a plan whereby he would have an army of eighty thousand men in

[1] NSJB. To King Frederick William, 23rd November 1850.
[2] M.A. To Prince William, 9th February 1849.
[3] To Lord Strangford, 26th April 1849.
[4] NSJB. To King Frederick William, 8th November 1850.
[5] F.O. 34/61, 5th November 1850.

time of war, which was quite enough to make Prussia think twice before attempting to swallow the Kingdom. But the Ministers still held to their policy of having no policy. Not only did they refuse to carry out this plan, but they did not ask the Estates to prolong the extraordinary military budget approved at the time of the war in Schleswig-Holstein, although the Estates in Prussia had just voted fresh military expenditure of eighteen million Thaler. There was no doubt, either, that the Hanoverian Estates would have approved, so general was the feeling against Prussia, and the King's anger can well be imagined when he saw the Government request and receive extravagant sums for the building of court-houses and railways. He could tolerate them no longer. On the 26th June 1850 there was such a heated discussion that the Cabinet again threatened its resignation. That evening the King had to decide what he would do. Von Münchhausen, his most intimate adviser, bade him urgently give way to the ultimatum which it was certain the Ministers would present the next day, as a new Government, so long as the session lasted and the budget was not passed, was out of the question. It would be far better, he suggested, to wait and then bring matters to a head through withholding his consent to one of the new laws approved by the Government. The King reluctantly accepted this advice, but then arose the trouble in Hesse-Cassel.

The King supposed that the military reductions would now be postponed until the crisis was over. But again he was astonished by the conduct of his Ministers. He knew that the only argument which influenced Prussia was strength and that a weak and unarmed Hanover invited annexation. The Ministers, on the other hand, with their more restricted knowledge and experience, considered that the best course was to give Prussia no pretext for taking Hanover —not to disturb her, but to reassure her and pursue a course of peace and neutrality. History was to show who was right. The King could not dismiss his Ministers at such a time and upon such an issue without revealing everything to the world and endangering his position in Germany, so had again to give away; what course he would have adopted had this happened earlier in his reign, or when he was in better health, is an open question. The bungling of his Ministers had led him into a false position in which he was not his own master. So the ridiculous spectacle followed that while all Germany was in arms and bayonets all but crossed, in Hanover, the state most in danger, men were discharged or furloughed and horses sold. But the fate of the Ministry was sealed.

It has been seen how the King progressively lost faith in Stüve and his colleagues. Nothing could be farther from the truth than that reactionary influences now considered the time ripe for a change and so incited the King, as can be read in most accounts. The progress of the estrangement is to be followed quite clearly and it was only to be expected that it would eventually reach a climax. The British Minister, for example, reported that the new reactionary trend was illustrated by the grand celebrations of the King's birthday in 1850.[1] But this again was to be expected as soon as conditions had become normal again and, in any case, it was not politics but the King's indispositions and bereavements which had put a stop to Court functions since 1848. However, the King had seen no Minister but von Bennigsen for two months until his birthday, when he saw Stüve and, it was reported, they had an angry exchange.[1]

Stüve persisted blindly in the introduction of new laws and innovations, though he had been repelled by the results of those already in effect. Whether this was from pig-headedness, pride or fear, it is impossible to say, for he had now the support of no party. Since 1848 he had alienated democrats and reactionaries, artisans and aristocrats, Austrians and Prussians. Now he continued in the spirit of 1833, forgetting everything which he had learnt in 1848. His latest production was a new organisation for the administration which incorporated some of his political and social prejudices. This aroused some concern in the minds of all moderately-inclined people, and older officials, provoked at the Government's ingratitude, asked why it was proposed to alter just that which had stood firm and saved the country in 1848. The King, of course, was exasperated. In his opinion there was nothing to excel the old system—" Our class of officials was everything," he had once written. " They were the props of the state, families whose menfolk had been officials from father to son for 100 or 150 years, looking upon their charges almost as the breath of their lives, and brought up on the spot, they knew all their peasants, there was a spirit of father and confessor. . . ." [2] He also rejected Stüve's personal prejudices, especially that against the Nobility, which had given him an inferiority complex in state affairs and society. " Naturally, through this you can easily understand that I am more or less in a state of continual warfare with Mr. Stüve, who, in my opinion, if not an open enemy, is a private enemy of all that is

[1] F.O. 34/61, 7th June 1850.
[2] G.A. To the Queen, 16th May 1840.

aristocratic, and for that reason, I am always on my guard with him and watch him as a cat watches a mouse." [1]

Except when official business compelled him, the King rarely saw his Ministers now. In September 1850 he called their predecessor, von Falcke, from his retirement to Hanover to ask him for his advice as to the possibility of changing his Ministers, but no sooner had the veteran Minister arrived in the capital than he was taken ill and died. Members of the Government, not seeing the real reason for their loss of the King's confidence, dismissed it as the result of whisperings of Court society and ladies of rank. Count von Bennigsen, who had not forfeited the King's sympathies so much as the others, saw the King on the 6th October to sound him as to his intentions. He gathered the impression that a successor had still not been found and this increased his colleagues' confidence in their own power. They fancied themselves in a position to place before their King a number of demands as to how business should be transacted in the future; failing their acceptance they would not feel themselve sable to fulfil their duties towards King and land. These conditions were : the freeing of the War Minister, General Jacobi, from military obligations so that he would be in the same position as the other Ministers; the new reduced organisation of the Army to come into force by the end of the year at the latest; approval of the Government's German policy; replacement of the Ambassadors in Vienna and Berlin, Counts von Platen and Knyphausen—both "Reactionaries" —and that the Minister of the Interior discuss the appointment of officials with the King monthly.

Here again, the incompetence and ill-judgment of the Ministers showed itself. To address demands was the last way in which to achieve anything with Ernest Augustus. When Count von Bennigsen presented this " Immediate Representation " to him on the 19th October 1850, he could hardly credit his ears and the Count left without replying to him for fear (according to the English Ambassador) of failing in due respect or of being insulted in a way which no gentleman could tolerate. And he had deserved it. The King was enraged at the Ministers' impertinence. If he were to submit, he would no longer be their King but their servant. Without further ado, he dismissed them. One had to go, he said, and if he did not have a new Ministry, he would abdicate. That was a sufficient threat, and Edward von Schele, son of the deceased Minister, persuaded von Münchhausen to take office as the only

[1] NSJB. To Countess von Wallmoden, 9th June 1850.

man qualified to do so. At the same time, the King stressed, there was to be no radical change in the system of Government. What was needed was peace.

Peace seemed assured through the new policy of Prussia. At Olmütz an agreement was drawn up with Austria that the German Governments should confer at Dresden upon the future constitution of Germany. King Ernest Augustus emphasised there the necessity of fighting the revolution rather than one another. That seemed to him to be the object of a Confederation, and finally it was decided to go back to that obtaining before 1848 which had preserved the peace over a quarter of a century. The new Prussian Minister, von Manteuffel, had made a definite break with the revolution and the King of Hanover tried to convince himself that the future was assured. He saw that there could arise situations in which Austria would be in no position to protect Hanover. He knew that he was nearing the end of his days and doubted the ability of his son, at the very commencement of his reign, to maintain the extremely precarious balance which he had held between the two great Powers, especially if his succession were disputed. He therefore began to rely more and more upon the honour and affection of his nephews and their promise to stand up for his son. They had lived as an affectionate family since they first became acquainted in 1813, and with this thought the old King found peace of mind at last.

A family reconciliation followed. The King of Prussia was represented again at his birthday in 1850 by his uncle's own stepson, Prince Frederick, and there was also a deputation of the King of Hanover's Third Prussian Hussars. Gradually, correspondence and visits began again, including that of Prince William, in February 1851. The King, however, did not wish the discussion to come on to the painful subject of politics, and so he invited thirty people to meet him and arranged a magnificent State reception. It was then that his nephew told him of the Queen's invitation to the opening of the Grand Exhibition in May.

In 1851 the King seemed to be in better health than for a long time. The year opened with grand celebrations in accordance with his curious superstition that the year not so celebrated would be his last, and the winter abounded with brilliant Court functions. In March the Grand Duke of Mecklenburg-Schwerin had a son born to him and invited the King to its christening. The King accepted, and for the first time since 1846 undertook a considerable journey; during 1850 he had not even been able to leave the capital. Everywhere on the way crowds turned out at this unexpected pleasure and greeted him enthusiastically, as he had not been seen in the country for so long. In Lüneburg he inspected the Ninth Hussars, his old regiment, and arrived, thoroughly shaken up by the Mecklenburg railways, at Ludwislust, the Grand Ducal Palace, in the evening, on the 2nd May.[1] In Schwerin he fulfilled one of his principal objects in coming, in speaking to the Nobility upon their conduct towards their Grand Duke and in urging the unity of the two Mecklenburg Duchies. While there he received a pressing invitation from the Queen of Prussia to visit her so that they could see each other after all the catastrophes which had kept them apart. However, the old King had decided never to set foot in Berlin again, and he reflected for twenty-four hours upon how he could meet her wishes and at the same time make it clear that he was not going to Prussia for pleasure or curiosity. He therefore decided to go only to Charlottenburg.[2]

He took the train with the King of Prussia, who had also been at Ludwigslust, and everywhere elaborate arrangements were made to please and flatter him. On the festively-decorated station at Naum, the Third Hussars, of which he was Colonel, were drawn up to receive him. He remained two days seeing old friends and faces. The parting was hard for him and he would have remained longer were it not that he had to speak with von Münchhausen and von Schele before they left for Dresden. He had so exerted himself that the last day he could only revive his strength by a long sleep. To honour him, the King invested him with an Order, but although all this attention was shown to him in Prussia, on his way back through Brunswick, not even an A.D.C. was sent to receive him.[3] The jubilation in Hanover on his return on the 9th May defied all description. The square outside the station was packed with masses of people, and all the officers and officials of the capital were assembled to greet him. As he made his way through the crowds, it seemed as if the deafening cheering would have no end.

Similar demonstrations marked his birthday, when he entered his eighty-first year, and which occasion the King of Prussia honoured with his presence. Tattoos, processions and displays of

[1] G.A. To Crown Prince, 3rd May 1851.
[2] S.A. To Grand Duke of Mecklenburg-Strelitz, 14th May 1851. For this visit to Berlin, see also *Von Malortie*, pp. 176–78 and *von Slicher* (M.A.).
[3] F.O. 34/63.

fireworks followed each other throughout those days and the whole
town was decorated with flowers.[1]

The King often spoke of the necessity of revisiting Göttingen
and the scenes of his youth once more in his life, and so on the
4th August he gave orders, quite unexpectedly, for the journey.[2]
The official object was the presentation of the Clinic which he had
had built for the University.[3] Its establishment was solely due to
his initiative, for all sorts of obstacles and objections had been
raised, even from the University authorities themselves, and only
his insistence had brought it into being.

The King entered in the evening along the decorated Weender
Road; it was packed with people; there were three illuminated
triumphal arches and all the bells in the city pealed. On the 6th
August he spoke to the professors in the Aula from the same chair
upon which George II and George IV had sat. It was almost
exactly sixty-five years before that he had arrived in this city as a
boy straight from the quiet of Kew and he spoke of his studies
there now. He wished, he said, that he had learnt more there,
as he could have done, but, he added, smiling, " you know, gentlemen, youth does not know virtue. Now, at my age, it is too late
to make up for it." He would always do his best for his people,
he continued. The sciences, particularly political science, were
right good things and much could be learnt from them. But to be
a statesman required, above all, experience and knowledge of men.
Without such experience and knowledge of men, nothing reasonable
could be achieved. He concluded by adjuring them to teach always
loyalty and observance of the laws. The Rector then stepped
forward and put into his hands the matriculation book bearing his
own name and those of his brothers.

The King then inspected the hospital, accompanied by the
architect and doctors, and the document announcing its presentation
was read out. A banquet followed, the city was illuminated and
the students paraded in a torchlight procession. The following
day the King visited the Zoological Museum and the Riding-
School, where he himself had ridden, then he received all the
Royal and University officials as well as the clergy of the city in
the hall of the Library. Afterwards he spoke to the clergy alone
and told them that the great evil of the times was the deterioration
of religion; they should ensure that all the young received a truly

---

[1] For a full description, see Von Malortie, pp. 178–82.   [2] M.A. Von Slicher.
[3] The King had announced his intention of building a clinic during his visit to the
University in 1845. See p. 354 n.

religious education and were not affected by modern revolutionary teachings.[1] Then the King visited all the haunts of his youth and the day ended with similar celebrations as that before. The following morning he left on his return journey.

This last return to the scenes of his happy and peaceful youth refreshed the King. He arrived in Hanover in a gay mood and the members of his entourage were astonished at such liveliness and vigour after all the strain and excitement, but they saw from his features that it was the flicker of a dying ember. They were especially concerned by his tendency to sleep. Whereas before he had always been lively and talkative when driving out, now he fell asleep almost at once, and he had the expression of a dying man.[2]

On the 15th August the King of Prussia spent five hours in Hanover on his way to Hohenzollern. The King of Hanover, although he had been very unwell the day before, met him at the station and took him to the Park at Herrenhausen, where they dined. With all the guests, including Archduke Albrecht, and their suites, they saw the Palace, the fountains, the apartments of the Electress Sophia in the Orangery and the great palm in the palm-house. The King conquered his weakness and, ordering the rest of the company to wait for him in the gardens, himself accompanied his guest to the station, but there he yielded to the addresses of his entourage and drove straight home.

In September, great anxiety was caused by an indisposition, but once again he conquered it, heard reports, dictated long letters and was always fresh in the evenings.[2] On the 21st he had the joy of receiving his six-years-old grandson on his birthday and making him a present of his first watch. " Yes, dear Butt," [3] he wrote, " believe me, I have been really dangerously ill, it seems to be a similar attack to that that I had in Düsseldorf nine years ago, as to begin with my head was not clear." But that he knew that his

---

[1] On the 17th September 1851 the King received a deputation of the Teachers' Seminary, whom he reproached energetically for what he called the teachers' part in the corruption of the youth and the deterioration of religious feeling in Hanover during the last decades. He had, he said, even heard of seven-year-olds' being apprehended for theft and of teachers who told their charges that Christ was not the son of God. The principle of his government was and always would be that state and school should not be separated from the church. God did not intend that all men should be equal, otherwise he would not have made some tall and some short, but if he did his duty he had a right to expect that the teachers would do theirs. This they promised.

[2] M.A. *Von Slicher*.

[3] A type of plaice and, from his shape, the sobriquet in family circles of the King of Prussia. In letters to members of the family he sometimes signed himself with a sketch of the fish.

recovery was only a temporary victory was shown by his following remark. " However, let happen what God will, I have done my best to bring about peace and understanding between my colleagues." His increasing weakness and fast approaching end were to be seen most clearly in his political actions. For the first time in his long life he did not know what to do. Already in September 1850 he had written, " I begin to feel that the fatigue and the weight of business is becoming painful for me, particularly at the times when, instead of seeing the affairs become clearer, they become more and more complex and confused." [1]

It had cost him hard inward struggles to give his consent to many of the laws of Stüve's programme and also to Hanover's joining the 3ollverein, upon very favourable terms, which was one of the results of the partial reconciliation with Prussia. But he had always had a fear of breaking his word in not carrying out laws to which he had given his consent long ago, when their nature and consequences were not clear. Even after signing them he had hesitated months before permitting them to be published. With the law on the organisation of the administration, he considered that the limit had been reached. This was a dangerous measure, he said, and he determined not to put his signature to it. For six weeks he was " tortured and bombarded " by the Ministers to do so, but he put the document in the drawer of his desk, locked it and kept the key to himself.[2] Everyone agreed with him in the danger of putting the laws into effect, but did not see how it could be avoided ; when they were enacted, it was said, the necessary modifications could be made. " But," the King replied, " that seems to me to be easier before they are promulgated than after." So he kept the documents, hoping that something would " turn up." He realised that the present Ministry was bound to pass these measures as they were, and so he had to consider whether it was not his duty to call a new one to carry out the modifications which he proposed. He decided to ask the advice of one whom he could trust, his old Minister's son, von Schele, now his envoy at the Diet and the Dresden Conferences. He therefore called him to Hanover for a few days. On the 28th September von Schele left Frankfurt, but when he arrived in the capital his King was already ill in bed with a bad chill and could hardly transact official business.

---

[1] Bennigsen-Banteln Acrhives. To Countess von Bennigsen, 19th September 1850.

[2] To Edward von Schele, 22nd September 1851.—*Von Hassell*, Appendix. Von Hassell reproduces it as a facsimile of the King's handwriting. In fact, the King only dictated at this date, in this case to Count von Kielmannsegg, whose writing was similar to his master's, but considerably more legible.

Throughout September the King had always been somewhat weak and often indisposed, and towards the end of the month his condition deteriorated slowly but appreciably. On Sunday, the 28th September, he was so unwell that von Malortie tried to persuade him to keep to his room. He refused, however, and appeared at table, but very ill, unusually silent and restrained; the guests noticed this and it was clear that it would be—as it was—his last appearance at table. In the evening he had a few persons to tea, including the Austrian ambassador, and was quite lively. The next day he also felt a little better, but stayed in bed.

The whole of October the King kept to his room, rising at about five or six in the evening, when he received a few guests to tea. He always heard most of the reports as usual and gave audiences, feeling sometimes well, sometimes unwell, but his lack of appetite and his emaciation became more pronounced every day, and the latter worried him considerably. He always conducted his toilettes with great scrupulousness and pedantry, lasting from one and a half to two hours, and it was on these occasions that his great weakness began to make itself felt, for it was often such a strain upon him that he would collapse immediately afterwards, but nothing would induce him to shorten the procedure. On the 11th October the first official bulletin appeared, saying that the King had had to stay in bed due to a bad chill, but holding out hopes of a recovery within the next few days. On the 15th a second appeared, announcing still more favourable signs, but on that day the King was so weak that he could not leave his bed.[1]

Never did Ernest Augustus's iron will display itself more than in those last few days. For hours he dictated letters and on some days seemed so well as to justify hopes for his complete recovery. On the 21st October appeared another optimistic bulletin, and, of all the visitors who arrived in Hanover this month, the King received his nephew, the Duke of Cambridge, Lord Westmorland and Lady Jersey in his bedroom. To the 27th he was more or less unwell, and from then on the most disturbing symptoms and weakness increased continuously; the King inclined more and more to sleep, but up to the end of the month his mind was quite clear and he took an interest in politics and all that went on, so much so that when the notification of the death of the Countess of Maine arrived on the 1st November, he ordered Court mourning for three weeks, as she had been two hours Queen of France.[2] But a

---

[1] F.O. 34/63, 16th October 1851.
[2] After the abdication of King Charles X in 1830.

week later, on the morning of the 7th his weakness was so pronounced
that the doctors did not believe that he could survive the night.[1]
The Crown Prince and Princess arrived at eleven and remained in
the Palais. But again he rallied, and in the evening, papers were
read out to him. He also amused himself with his grandchildren,
taking his grandson on his knee and saying " God bless you, my
child." On the 8th his condition was so improved that he heard
routine reports again, but in the evening he became much weaker
and the bulletin announced that he had passed a disturbing night.
For a time on the 11th he again showed interest in his surroundings,
then lapsed into apathy. From the 12th to the 16th the bulletins
could only announce his ever-increasing weakness. Stubbornly
he fought death step by step. He was so wasted away that his
skin hung about him and the form of the bones was visible ; his
voice became weaker and weaker, soon it was difficult and then
almost impossible for him to speak a word, and his insensibility
to his surroundings increased. But his mind seemed to be working
and thinking all the time and opinions differed as to whether he
was conscious or not. Sometimes he said a few words, sometimes
he recognised someone, but he lay the day in a state of torpor.
Suddenly, however, he was overcome by fits of activity and sprang
out of bed as if in a dream-state, so that if he had not been supported
he would have collapsed. With much resistance he was put to bed
again and sank back into his former state. On the 17th fits of cramp
made their appearance and his condition was so grave that the Crown
Prince and Princess were again summoned to the Palais. In the
evening, however, the King became quieter and they returned
home at eleven o'clock. Within half an hour they were called back
as the stage had been reached where the King's dissolution was to
be apprehended every minute. From midnight into the 18th
he seemed to be sleeping, but his arms were in continuous movement, and so it went on until morning, the movements becoming
fainter as his weakness increased. The Crown Prince and Princess
with the former's suite, Prince Alexander of Solms, the Countess
von Grote, von Malortie, the A.D.C.s, doctors and the King's
valet stood round at his bed as, at a quarter to seven, as the sky
reddened for dawn, King Ernest Augustus of Hanover, Duke
of Cumberland, passed peacefully away. For half an hour all
remained still, then the two doctors approached the bed and
confirmed his passing. The new King and Queen knelt and prayed
for some time and, rising, kissed the deceased's forehead. The

[3] F.O. 34/63, 7th November 1851.

King's long life of eighty years five months and thirteen days was over.

The servants of the late King were allowed to pay their last honours to their master, and the Leinestrasse was barred to vehicles by barriers with black flags. It was a sad day for Hanover. For two days the late King lay in the Palais, then, on the 21st, his body was conducted through the street to the Leine Palace for the lying-in-state, for, in his will of the 9th December 1842, he had said that he had no objection to his subjects' being allowed to look upon him in death.[1]

At six o'clock in the morning the Royal remains were carried and escorted by the thirty-two senior N.C.O.s of the garrison of the city, by torchlight, to the Throne Room, where they were laid under the canopy of the Throne on the estrade covered with black silk. The way to the Throne Room, the corridors and staircases were all laid with black carpeting, and at all doors were posted double sentries of the Garde du Corps. The Throne Room itself was brilliantly lit by the candelabra, for the curtains were drawn. Beside the King lay, on silvern silk cushions, the Crown and Sceptre of Hanover, his busby and sabre, his English Field-Marshal's staff and the Chains of the Order of the Garter and of St. George. Round him was grouped the Guard of Honour composed of the Adjutant-General, two A.D.C.s, four Staff Officers, two pages and two body-gendarmes. Before the black silk-covered barrier stood the Head of the Domestic Staff, two valets and two of the King's personal rangers. On the morning and afternoon of the 21st and 22nd, thirty thousand persons, that is to say, the whole population of the capital, filed silently and in perfect order past their late King, whose expression was that which had characterised him in life, one of earnestness and resolution. The nine-year-old Crown Prince Ernest Augustus was also permitted by his parents to take farewell of his grandfather. In accordance with the deceased's exact instructions, on the evening of the 22nd, after Oesterley, the Court Artist, had sketched the scene, the valet dressed him in the English uniform in which he had walked to the altar at the side of his wife, and in which he wished to lie beside her in eternity, and a miniature of her portrait was placed over his heart, then, as he had ordered, Dr. Baring opened the vein at his neck and the coffin was sealed—a moment when von Malortie and the entourage could hardly master their feelings.

[1] *Von Malortie,* pp. 200–201. A translation is given in the *Dictionary of National Biography.*

The coffin lay two days in the Palace Chapel until midnight on the 25th–26th, when, together with that of the late Queen, which had lain in the crypt of the Chapel until now, it was conveyed to Herrenhausen for the funeral. The late King had expressed his desire to remain a week above the earth before finding a lasting place of rest in the Mausoleum, if it were ready, to which his remains were to be conducted together with those of the Queen.

It was an impressive scene. The two hearses were escorted by the Garde du Corps and five hundred citizens bearing torches. The whole population, still and silent, thronged the route as it had done on so many a happier occasion, out to the Stein Gate and up the Avenue to Herrenhausen, lined by two ranks of infantry. The crowds and the torches under the limes contrasting with the darkness beyond presented a solemn picture. The coffin of the Queen was conveyed straight to the Mausoleum, which was then consecrated, while that of the King was deposited in the Hall of the Palace, where officers of the Garde du Corps and Cuirassiers provided the Guard throughout the night.

The next morning, the 26th November 1851, the whole city was in mourning. All the church-bells tolled and every minute dull reports came from the batteries. A long procession of mourners, headed by the King of Prussia, leading his cousin, King George V on his left arm and Queen Marie with the little Crown Prince on his right, followed the hearse from the Palace to the Mausoleum opposite, already shaded by the old oaks which the late King had had planted round it. The coffin was then borne to before the altar, followed by the clergy and then as many of the mourners as the confined space of the edifice would allow. Pastor Niemann gave the funeral-address, and the English Domestic Chaplain, Mr. Wilkinson, read the liturgy of the Anglican Church. The clergy then led the way down the flight of steps to the vault and there the King's remains found their last resting-place beside those of the Queen. Their children, the King and Queen, knelt and prayed for some moments, then they left the Mausoleum, which was locked by the Lord Chamberlain, von Malortie, who gave the key to his master. With that the story of King Ernest Augustus comes to a close.[1]

---

[1] The account of the King's illness and death are from M.A. *Von Slicher* and *von Malortie*, pp. 193–98 ; of the obsequies, *von Malortie*, pp. 200–206 and Appendix IX.

EPILOGUE

" YOU know that my fate has always had something peculiar about it," the Duke of Cumberland once wrote and, indeed, few men's have been more extraordinary or more unhappy. Enough has been described in these pages of his thoughts and deeds to give an impression of the sort of man that he was. But how has he gone down in history ? As a great man or a good man ?

The Duke of Cumberland appears in the records of history as one of the blackest characters of modern times. There is no vice—not the most obscene—that has not been laid to his account. " The good that may be said of the Royal dead is little or none. In his pleasures he assorted the licence of an Orleans or a Stewart. . . . Rumour persisted in attaching to his excesses a certain criminal blackness below the standard dye of aristocratic debauchery. . . . The impartial historian will be likely to decide that there is little in the known character of Prince Ernest to exempt him from sore suspicions touching what remained concealed "—that obituary note [1] has also been the judgment of history upon him. But, unlike the foregoing assessment of his character, this judgment has not been based upon concrete evidence or derived from the study of original sources. The conclusion, then, is ominous but inescapable that the writing of history, in so far, at least, as it touches the periods and events with which Ernest Augustus was concerned, is, even if unintentionally or unconsciously, mercenary to politics, for only in politics can an explanation be found for the propagation of such a gross distortion in the guise of history.

Ernest Augustus was ever indifferent to calumny and no doubt the opinion of posterity would trouble him little, for the thing which earned his most unreserved contempt, and which he regarded as one of the most serious charges that could be brought against a man, was seeking popularity—the very thing which the word " democracy " demands and postulates in politics. The only consideration which guided him was his conviction of right and truth and with that he would suffer no compromise.

[1] *The Times.*

What, then, were the political ideals which have caused Ernest Augustus to be recorded in history as an ogre and a blackguard ?

His government was patriarchal and its object was to ensure to all his subjects justice, security and freedom from fear—just those things most desired and yet most conspicuously absent in modern political systems of all sorts.

Justice is represented as blindfold. It is something constant. How, then, can justice be claimed through the shifts and changes of parties and classes ? If a thing is morally wrong when done by one man, how can it be any less so when done by thousands—by, in fact, a majority ? Indeed, is not robbery by a thousand far graver than robbery by one ? And yet in this twentieth century a man need only win a majority for it, or interest a majority in it, to carry out any deed of spoliation, any crime. A man in the twentieth century cannot regard his rights, his property, or even his person, as safe. How can he know what party, what class or group will not gain the upper hand and administer its own version of justice with them ? This was just the fear and uncertainty against which Ernest Augustus's government was a safeguard. Under it, rights, properties and persons were guaranteed, and as long as it lasted, what a man had one day, he could be sure of having the next. Its principles were unchanging. Change, Ernest Augustus saw, brought with it—and must always bring with it—insecurity, and therefore he was *prima facie* opposed to it. His was no blind or negative determination to resist change from personal or family grounds, but the positive maintenance of what he considered to be those principles and ways of life most conducive to the happiness of his subjects and mankind in general.

So Ernest Augustus died, still trying to stem the flood which he had held back during his lifetime, and with his death one of the stoutest bulwarks against it was removed. Only a man of such a strong character could have mastered events so completely as he did, and in this mastery lies his uniqueness. He was not, like the majority of his fellow-monarchs and contemporaries, carried along with the stream which has brought us, for good or for evil, to where we are to-day, but placed himself four-square in its path and succeeded, for as long as he lived, in holding his ground. He thus demonstrated a fundamental truth which nowhere enjoys credence to-day—that *men* make history, and that it can take the course which *men* desire. They are not the helpless pawns of systems and patterns of fate as Hegel, Marx and all modern philosophers and economists teach us ; there are no such things as

" the times," to which it is futile to offer resistance. " The times " are only the sum of the doings of other men and changes are all brought about quite consciously by human agency.

One test of a great man is the gap which he leaves behind him, and when Ernest Augustus was gone, the future of Hanover became problematical, like that of the rest of Germany. We all know that his apprehensions of Prussian intentions justified themselves fifteen years after his death. Ignoring his wish to remain neutral, Prussian troops swamped his son's Kingdom and put an end to its existence. Ever since 1866 everything possible has been done to eradicate from the memory of the people the fact that it had ever existed. The Prussians, the republic, the Nazis, all alike showed their disapproval, yet the memory of old Hanover and, in particular, of its King Ernest Augustus has survived. During the war the Gauleiter wished to remove his memorial [1] for scrap, but feeling was so strong that he had to desist, saying, " Very well, the British bombs will move it for me ! " but, in the end, it was about the only thing which they did not. When the British troops arrived, the Guelphic Hanoverians breathed a sigh of relief. At last, after eighty years of resistance to Prussianism and nationalism, they could expect some sympathy from their former fellows-in-union. But they were mistaken. The very men who had been persecuted, often exiled, for their resistance to the Prussians, whose houses all boasted portraits of George III and George IV, were told that they were " junkers " and " militarists " and had to be rendered ineffective by confiscation of fortunes and other means, and the socialist government of Lower Saxony, set up under British patronage, has continued the traditional policy of forbidding or seeking to repress any trace of Hanoverian independence and of the old Hanoverian and Guelphic tradition.

When the Duke of Cumberland left England in 1837, it was confidently expected that he would be deposed in six months, yet his reign was far more peaceful, even including 1848, than the preceding fifteen years of riot and civil war in England. In Hanover, on the other hand, only one life was lost,[2] and that in the year of revolutions, and during the King's constitutional changes at the

---

[1] It was not an official act but a subscription among the people which led to the erection of a memorial to King Ernest Augustus on the square outside the station, in the centre of the city, in 1861—an equestrian figure in bronze, depicting him in Hussar uniform, with the legend " Dem Landesvater, sein treues Volf." There was not merely a military parade at its ceremonial unveiling but a procession of all the guilds, including those of the bricklayers, railwaymen, navvies and other manual workmen.

[2] At the village of Bovenden during a brawl between contending factions in 1848.

commencement of his reign, there had been only one demonstration, with no violence.[1]

True, in the comfortable and prosperous Victorian days, Ernest Augustus and his party seemed to be discredited old die-hards, frightening their opponents with bogeys. Even as late as 1920 Trevelyan could write of Grey's saving the country from revolution by Reform. " Ninety years have shown the substantial truth of this view, as contrasted with the Tory prophecy " that " all would be levelled to the plane of petty shopkeepers and farmers, this perhaps not without bloodshed, but certainly by confiscations and persecutions." Ninety years might have shown one thing, but Dr. Trevelyan had only to wait another couple of decades to see the prophecy vindicated—nay, more, the shopkeepers and bourgeoisie who were the Duke of Cumberland's principal persecutors and the red revolutionaries of 1848 are now reaping what they sowed, for, as Wellington had written, " Whatever the great may suffer, the middling and lower classes will bear their proportion and the ruin will be general." But Cumberland's and Wellington's opponents did not heed their warnings. The great Whig Houses which carried out these measures, where are they now ? Have they experienced any gratitude, or have they not been in effect expropriated and plundered together with their opposite numbers of the Tories ?

It is the same in Germany. In the great and prosperous Liberal post-1870 Empire, the warnings and lamentations of the reactionary and " particularist " old King of Hanover might well have seemed a trifle ridiculous. But now it is different. Where is their beautiful traditional Germany ? one may ask of Treitschke, the professors and poets who so bitterly fought King Ernest Augustus, of the nationalists and " patriots." That King always spoke as if the end of the order of society which he knew meant the end of the world, and when one looks at Germany it is indeed as if the Great Flood had passed over it. Little in Hanover survived those fearful nights of 1943-45 (apart from the almost untouched industrial

[1] It is a noteworthy fact that, however ardent his ecclesiastical partisanship in England, the King's reign over a country with a very large percentage of Roman Catholics, including the Bishopric of Hildesheim and the dormant Bishopric of Osnabrück (restored by his son), was one of religious peace and he endeavoured to behave towards both Lutheran and Catholic confessions with complete impartiality. The Pope even addressed a petition to him (H.A.) against the unfair treatment of Catholics under the 1833 Constitution. This is proof of the fact that the Duke of Cumberland's ecclesiastical standpoint in England sprang purely from the position of his House there and the Protestant succession which it had sworn and was obliged to maintain.

quarter), when the old mediæval centre went up in one blaze and not a stone, not a beam shows that it ever existed; the most beautiful works of art and architecture, Leibniz's house among them, turned to ashes and everything associated with King Ernest Augustus, wherever it lay, vanished. The Palace of Herrenhausen is, apart from a few steps which led up to the portal, level with the ground, the Leine Palace gutted; of the Altes Palais, where he lived and died, not a trace remains; the Mausoleum, where he had hoped to lie in eternal peace, was rent asunder, its roof blown off, its portal split and the marble sarcophagi, over which he had had such pains taken, blackened and broken. Osnabrück, a centre of opposition to him, was likewise visited with fire; Hildesheim, the mediæval Archbishop's city, was literally razed to the ground.

Everywhere are *millions* of persons driven from their home-lands, of bereaved and cripples. The Duke of Cumberland's house at Schönhausen is inhabited by the president of a communist terror régime. In Berlin, Asiatics march along the thoroughfares where he had ridden. Long after the end of the war the Royal Palace was levelled to the ground by the communists as a demon-stration-place. If only its inhabitants had listened to the King of Hanover!

Ernest Augustus's prophecy of the course of history has justi-fied itself. In both England and Germany, then, it is time to revalue this great but infamously libelled man, who, if heeded, might have played a decisive part in saving Europe from its Great Flood. The author modestly hopes that this work will have con-tributed in some measure to such a vindication.

APPENDIX

THE SCANDAL CAMPAIGNS AGAINST THE DUKE OF CUMBERLAND

IT has been found desirable to treat this subject by itself, as to relate the various episodes where they chronologically belong would be to hold up the flow of the narrative, for a biography, like a novel, has a "plot," and these incidents form a campaign which became a continuous background to the Duke of Cumberland's life in England. The first great series of slanders and libels against him began, as has been seen, with the Duke's attempted assassination in 1810. Before that, they had been of a rather trivial character, but then the tone was set for slanders and rumours of a more depraved nature. For ten years the Duke lived abroad in peace and quiet and there was there never a whisper or hint of scandal about him. This is, of course, an added disproof of its authenticity in England. He had only to set foot in the country to bring a hornet's nest of blackening slander and intrigue about his ears.

As soon as it was learnt that the Duke intended to return in 1829, a campaign of unparalleled viciousness was opened against him with, of course, the object of deterring him (though, as we know, it would have had exactly the opposite effect). Since this, at least, is not considered seriously by any historian, it need only be mentioned briefly, as its details are too distasteful to be dwelt upon. A certain Captain Garth, a man of thoroughly bad character, was the son of General Garth (an officer who had been about the Court in George III's time) and, it is generally believed, Princess Sophia (see *The Daughters of George III*; Garth is often mentioned in *The Letters of Princess Charlotte*). In 1829 it was claimed that he had deposited certain letters in Sir Herbert Taylor's hands against a payment of a large sum of money and that, wishing to increase this amount, he or his creditors were applying for an injunction against Taylor, as if blackmail were legally enforceable ; the letters were supposed to prove that Garth was the incestuous son of the Duke of Cumberland and his sister, Princess Sophia. This was whispered about in the enemy's camp and soon developed into a violent campaign against the Duke, though nowhere did it

appear in a tangible form that he could meet. It is doubtful, however, if any person not blinded by hate against the Duke believed
in it, and O'Connell himself, the Duke's principal opponent at this
time, denounced it at a public meeting. Lord Grey also showed
an understanding of the motives which lay behind the spreading
of these rumours. " This renewed attack on the subject of Garth,"
he wrote to Princess Lieven on the 18th November 1829, " looks
like a renewed apprehension of the effect of his [the Duke's]
influence."

The timing of these plots does, indeed, belie their object.
When it was learnt that the Duke was to stay and his wife was to
join him, the second one was touched off, which was of just such
a nature as to induce him to keep her out of the country. The
account which we have of it is from one source, and that a biassed
one, Greville. Even so, it is enough to exonerate the Duke.

It all began when, early in August or late in July 1829, a
scurrilous paper, *The Age*, printed a report that the Duke of
Cumberland had been turned out of the house of the Lord Chancellor after having assaulted his wife, Lady Lyndhurst. Sir Henry
Cooke drew the Duke's attention to this and so he sent a copy to
Lord Lyndhurst with a short note indicating the libellous paragraph and saying that he desired to contradict the report and
would like to have Lady Lyndhurst's authority for doing so. For
some reason, Lord Lyndhurst did not wish to oblige and evaded
the demand, one which was justified enough if the Duke were not
guilty of the charge. But were the Duke guilty of attempting
Lady Lyndhurst, her husband would have been bound to have
challenged him, yet Lord Lyndhurst did not do that either. Greville
pleaded that, as Lord Chancellor, he would have been obliged to
resign then and that he could not afford to give up his office—
hardly a very creditable excuse. Lord Lyndhurst therefore sent a
non-committal reply to the effect that he regarded the report with
indifference as one of a series of calumnies to which Lady Lyndhurst had for some time been exposed from the Press and would
prefer to let the matter drop. But the Duke was determined not
to let it rest, any more than any other man of honour so accused
would have done, so he wrote a second and more peremptory letter.
The Lord Chancellor, according to Greville, discussed the matter
with Wellington before sending another evasive reply—that he
did not " conceive it necessary to annoy Lady Lyndhurst by
troubling her upon the subject, and with what refers to Your
Royal Highness, the Lord Chancellor has no concern whatever,"

while adding that his regard for his Sovereign " made it impossible that any brother of that Sovereign should ever be turned out of his house." Now we quote Greville.

To this, the Duke wrote another letter, in a very sneering and impertinent tone in the third person, and alluding to the *loose reports* which had been current on the subject, and saying that " the Chancellor might have his own reasons for not choosing to speak to Lady Lyndhurst on the subject " ; to which the Chancellor replied that " he knew nothing of any loose reports, but if there were any, in whatever quarter they might have originated, which went to affect the conduct of Lady Lyndhurst in the matter in question, they were most false, foul and calumnious." So ended the correspondence ; all these latter expressions were intended to apply to the Duke himself, who is the person who spread the *loose reports* and told the lies about her.

But Greville did not say what lies the Duke of Cumberland was telling about her, and, from his tone, one would imagine that she and not the Duke was the victim of a slander-campaign. One cannot see what she would have had to lose by denying the allegation, for, as Lord Grey commented, " everybody who heard the story would at once conclude that no woman could be exposed to such an attack, as had been reported, without having in some degree brought it upon herself," unless Lord Lyndhurst had " his own reasons for not choosing to speak to Lady Lyndhurst upon the subject," and here one must think of Lady Lyndhurst's conversation with the Duke three months before, when she had sought to influence him with her charms and the Duke had been warned that the Government intended to " throw a handsome woman in his path to distract him from politics."

Actually, Greville did not seem sure of his story. On the 8th August he wrote that there was a story current that the Duke had called upon Lady Lyndhurst and insulted her and that after a scramble she had only saved herself by ringing the bell. On the 18th August he wrote that Lady Jersey " was very anxious to see the letters, for she had heard that the Duke had much the best of it, and that the Chancellor's letter was evasive and jesuitical." The next day, he said, he learnt the details of the affair, that the Duke had called upon Lady Lyndhurst ; " that his manner and his language had been equally brutal and offensive ; that he afterwards went off upon politics, and abused the whole Administration, and particularly the Chancellor, and after staying two or three hours, insulting her and offending her in every way, he took himself off. Soon after, he met her somewhere in the evening, when

he attacked her again. She treated him with all possible indignation, and would have nothing to say to him." There is, it will be
observed, a fundamental difference between the two stories. In
the second, there is no mention of a desperate struggle to summon
the servants and have the Duke ejected. On the contrary, the
attempted rape, as Creevey exultantly described it when he heard
the story from Greville, was followed by a three-hour political
harangue! Indeed, Greville does, in fact, agree that the story
which *The Age* had printed, and which he had believed on the
8th, is untrue. He goes on to say that

after the Duke's visit, Lady Lyndhurst told the Chancellor of his
abuse of him and the Government, but had suppressed the rest, thinking it
better not to tell him, as it would put him in a very embarrassing position,
and contented herself with saying she would never receive the Duke
again upon the other grounds, which were quiet sufficient ; but that some
time after reports reached her from various quarters (Lord Grey, Lord
Durham, Lord Dudley and several others) that the Duke went about
talking of her in the most gross and impertinent manner. Upon hearing
this, she thought it right to tell the Chancellor the other part of his
conduct which she had hitherto concealed, and this she did in general
terms—viz. that he had been very insolent and made an attack upon her.

In other words, *Lady Lyndhurst* had kept something back which
the Duke of Cumberland had not, *after and because of which* she
announced a version of her own. This certainly seems to show
the Duke as the innocent party and it is a great pity that what he
said of her in a " most gross and impertinent manner " is not
recorded. Greville, in fact, proves the Duke's innocence, for his
story unwittingly admits that *he* was the first to mention the matter
and that, had *he* not done so, it would have remained unknown to
the outside world. The talk of both Lord and Lady Lyndhurst's
sparing of " annoyance " and " embarrassment " to each other is
somewhat unconvincing in view of what was involved, an attempted
attack upon the lady in her own house. Apparently, everyone
realised the Duke's innocence except Greville, who was spreading
his version of the matter broadcast. Again, the Duke did what
we would expect him to do, and Greville unconsciously condemns
himself ; certainly he did not act as if with clear conscience and
conviction. On the 20th August the Duke sent Sir Henry Cooke
to him with the request that, as, he had heard, he had seen the
correspondence and given an account of it unfavourable to the
Duke, he would call upon the Duke and hear his statement of the
facts. The cowardly diarist, however, after having told his version

to all and sundry and recorded it for posterity, had not the courage to face the Duke, and declined the invitation.

Lord Lyndhurst was meanwhile showing the correspondence, thinking that it would create a favourable impression, but, as Lady Jersey had said, it did the contrary, proving the Duke's side of the matter and, Princess Lieven told Lord Grey, " I could not have imagined that any creature existed so vile and so mean as the Chancellor has shown himself to be. One of his letters is a perfect model of infamy. . . . I think in the present instance he [the Duke] has a clear case in his favour. If all the Chancellor's wife has said were true, the Duke would certainly not have begun this correspondence, and would not have taken up the tone he does. . . . To my mind, the mere fact that the Duke of Cumberland began this correspondence proves him to be innocent of the charge laid to his account. His first two letters are perfect ; the answers from the Chancellor are miserable productions—trying to evade the question and failing therein." However, Greville's being the only account written, he spread his revenge over the next hundred and more years like most of these Whigs, who wrote in secret for posterity what they dared not say in their own day.

The Duke remained in England and, by his undaunted political activity, was, in so doing, laying himself open to another dastardly plot. Sure enough, this was timed to secure his removal before the opening of the parliamentary session for 1830.

He and the Duchess lay ill at Kew and the snows covered the Green outside as the campaign began. From somewhere appeared the report that the Duke had been found with Lady Graves at Hampton Court ; on the 19th January 1830 Neumann wrote that everybody was talking of it ; by the end of the month it was depicted in caricatures in the papers and the streets—a perfect example of *La Calunnia* in practice.

The story was, of course, absurd. Lady Graves, the first woman in London to dance the waltz, was now in her fifties, the mother of thirteen children, and wore spectacles, so was hardly likely to have attracted a man like the Duke of Cumberland. It had, therefore, not even the plausibility of the Lady Lyndhurst story, for *she* was beautiful. Lady Graves was living apart from her husband, but, to show that he was quite convinced of the falsity of the rumours, he saw her and they arranged to go about together again in public.

But Lord Graves was not the Duke of Cumberland. Suddenly to become the centre of such a campaign as this was too much for him. For many days his servants noticed that he was very depressed ; he saw a caricature in a shop-window, or in the street, then, on the 6th January, he received an anonymous letter with cuttings from all the newspapers, saying that he had been paid to live with his wife again. It was the limit. As he sat there, alone in his dressing-room, borne down by despair and melancholy, he took hold of his razor and cut his throat.

Seen close-up, the struggle for Democracy does not look so pleasant—for these were the things that broke the " Reactionaries " in England, whatever may be the case elsewhere. The Duke of Cumberland may have been able to withstand calumnies, hoots, jeers, threats, stonings and manhandlings by mobs, but more average men could not, any more than poor Lord Graves. By this means the opposition to the mob was paralysed. Men who would proudly have gone to the guillotine found the endurance of such warfare over a protracted period beyond them. After only a fortnight of it Lord Graves had cut his throat.

The theory was, of course, that it was his belief in the Duke's guilt which led to the Peer's suicide. " The town was in an uproar," wrote Knighton, and " it was enough for the Duke of Cumberland's name to get mixed-up in it—he is the most widely hated man in England—for the public to take far more interest in the matter than there was any occasion for," Princess Lieven wrote. " For him the consequences must be most serious, and his friends have advised him not to attempt to face the storm, as they believe that he would be stoned by the populace if he were to show himself. Luckily he is just now laid up at Kew, but that cannot last long." To the Government these events were very opportune, as is shown by the entry in Lord Ellenborough's diary the day after the suicide— " The suicide of . . . on account of his wife's seduction by the Duke of Cumberland will drive the Duke of Cumberland out of the field."

With an ordinary man, it might have succeeded in doing so. Even those who knew the Duke thought that he could not with-stand it. " I understand," wrote the Duke of Rutland to Lady Shelley, " the Duke of Cumberland will leave this country as soon as he can do so without *appearing* to have been driven out of it by implication in the late melancholy catastrophe." The Duke of Cumberland himself, however, was writing to Lord Eldon that " they may as well move St. Paul's to this place, as get me to *flinch*."

The Duke thought of prosecuting the authors of the calumny, whose names, he said, he could guess, but that would mean throwing himself on to the protection of the Government; he also considered making a statement in the House of Lords. That, however, he rejected as being beneath his dignity and seeming to imply that there was *something* embarrassing in the affair. He had the fullest proofs of Lord Graves's confidence in him, how up to the very last they were friends—they had spent the evening of the 5th together and the nex day, Lord Graves had called upon him when he was not at home.

"It is disgusting to live in a country where every man's character is at the mercy of hirelings who, to carry out any purpose or gratify any party motive, can insinuate the greatest lies against anyone," the Duke wrote to Lord Eldon. "*This* is in fact but a second volume of all that took place *last year*, and at the self-*same moment*, just as the meeting of Parliament took place. . . ." The Government had hoped to induce him to leave the country, "but, by God, *nothing shall*." He would answer, "If you think me to be such a d——d coward as to run away, by God, I am *not*, and will face that and every other false and infamous libel and cabal." Threats and anonymous letters he received daily but threw them straight into the fire.

As a matter of fact the Duke's enemies defeated their own object, for, as Lord Grey wrote to Princess Lieven, "His best chance is the violence of those who are endeavouring to excite the popular feeling against him," and so it actually happened. On the 13th, Princess Lieven said that scurrilous comments by *The Times* had brought about a favourable reaction and "People are beginning even to doubt whether there was, after all, any real intrigue between the Duke of Cumberland and Lady Graves," though "Whatever may be the truth of it, the greater part of the world will always remain prejudiced against the Duke."

The Duke of Cumberland, who thus knew what it was to be the victim of such attacks, would not countenance them upon his opponents. In September an article attacking Wellington appeared in the *Morning Herald* and, writes Princess Lieven, "I asked the Duke of Cumberland if it were true that the writer of the libels was a person of his Household. He answered that he had dismissed him from his service the same day the letter had appeared, because, though he, the Duke, was, and ever would be, the Duke of Wellington's personal and political adversary, yet he did not wish to pass for the protector of those who wrote defamatory libels against him."

The next of the great libels occurred at one of the most tragic junctures of the Duke of Cumberland's whole life, within a few days of his son's becoming blind. On the 16th September 1832 he had ridden up to Kensington to give his sister an account of the latest developments with regard to his son's state when, on the way back through Hammersmith, he was greeted by a mob which hooted and shouted at him. He was at a loss to account for this, as such scenes had not taken place of late, especially in such a locality. But then he learnt of the latest libel that had appeared against him.

On the 18th September a letter had been published in the *Globe* from an anonymous "Friend of the Ladies," describing an incident alleged to have taken place on the 15th. Four young ladies were crossing the bridge between Barnes and Hammersmith when a rider answering to the description of the Duke of Cumberland had overtaken them and ridden his horse up to them so closely that they were forced against the rails and their skirts disarranged. He had turned and laughed, then galloped on. The name of his unfortunate victims was the Misses Perfect. The next day *The Times* took the matter up in its leading article, denouncing the Duke of Cumberland in the usual terms, and soon all the camp following of lampooners and caricaturists was at work on the theme.

The Duke first learnt of all this on the 21st, when he discussed it with Jelf. He had not the least recollection of such an incident, nor even of having left the house on the 15th, when Waller, Alexander and Cooper were there for a consultation about Prince George. Now, however, he could account for the mob next day. He therefore charged Jelf and his lawyer brother to go to the Misses Perfect, who lived near the bridge, and inquire into all the circumstances of the case, explaining that if he had alarmed them, he had no recollection of it. This Jelf did, and the young ladies were quite content, one of them assuring him often that " if he [the rider] had taken off his hat to me, I should have thought it a compliment." Mr. Perfect also agreed to write to *The Times* disavowing any connection with the correspondent, who was, he knew, a Radical who had been importuning his daughters lately. When Jelf returned, he was summoned by the Duke and found him with Sir Julius Quentin, one of his officers. The mystery was solved, said the Duke. Quentin, who had, as often, been riding his horse, recollected unintentionally alarming some ladies on the bridge that day. The next morning, therefore, Quentin and Jelf rode over to the Perfects again and the former asked if it was not he who had been the mysterious rider.

On the 26th *The Times* brought a distorted version of these happenings. Jelf and his brother had been to the Perfects, it said, to apologise on behalf of the Duke, who excused himself on the grounds of his poor sight and the worry about his son. It then related the seemingly contradictory incident with Quentin, and how the Jelfs had brought pressure to bear upon the girls to declare that they recognised in him the rider on the bridge. Jelf immediately wrote to the paper contradicting these falsehoods, and affidavits were taken from several persons, including the keepers and a passer-by, who volunteered his testimony, that the Duke had been shooting in the grounds behind his house (which could be seen from the road and the river-bank) at the time when the incident was alleged to have taken place.

The Times became very impertinent, saying that not it but the Duke's friends were responsible for prolonging the matter ; " Grim and dreary takes the field once more," its leading article began, when the affidavits were presented. The embarrassed journal became so sarcastic at the Duke's pains to prove his innocence—as if that were an indifferent matter to a man—that the Duke considered prosecuting. He was, indeed, nearing the end of his patience with these libels and when the next appeared, he had had enough.

But before coming to this, it is pleasing to note, at last, a pamphlet written in the Duke's defence by a Mr. Thomas Norton, in 1832. It is so much to the point that some extracts must be given here.

The man who, by his writings or his conduct, if a man of importance, displays a just contempt for *cant* and hypocrisy, arouses not the *lion* indeed, but the *wolf* and the fox—*cruelty* and *subtlety* in the breasts of an immense majority of mankind, who mark him for their vengeance, and by the aid of these amiable auxiliaries, generally come off victorious from the ungenerous and unequal conflict. . . . But there is a peculiar straight-forwardness and manliness in his [the Duke's] reported speeches on many occasions, a freedom from all *cant*, which, among other things, induces me to be satisfied that my conclusion is correct. . . . Yet because *this man*, fairly and openly, in a great national assembly, does what *he* conceives to be his duty by his Sovereign, his country and his kind, a thousand pens are dipped in gall to blast his fame. . . . If he had, from timidity, sacrificed his integrity at the shrine of popularity, by the expression of sentiments foreign to his conception of right, *then*, like Caesar, he might have been doomed to listen to the utterance of " such a deal of stinking breath " in his acclaim, as absolutely " to swoon " and " fall down in the market place." . . . It has long been the *fashion* to decry the Duke of Cumberland, and to such an extent has it been carried that there is scarcely a cur in the human shape, from Hyde Park Corner to Aldgate Pump, that has not joined in his contemptible yelp to swell the universal clamour. . . . [After his attempted murder in 1810]. When at last he is enabled to quit his room, and walk abroad to inhale the blessed air, what does it carry on its wing? Congratulations upon his safe recovery? No, no, no; an infamous insinuation that *he himself* had been the murderer ! "

This latter sentence had reference to the following and last of the great libels against the Duke, a pamphlet published in the same year entitled *The Authentic Records of the Court of England during the Last Seventy Years*, by a certain Josiah Philips and priced at one guinea. Its attack opened thus :

We hope our efforts in the best of causes, truth, will be crowned with success, and trust, though we may pay the price of liberty, that our testimony will not only enrich mankind, but prove an undefinable legacy to every child of humanity. . . . We will now recur to a Prince, whose very name has proved a stain upon the Kingdom in which he was born. Sensibility and virtue were strangers to his breast, while cruelty and the baser passions had perfect control over his imagination and actions. His countenance was indeed an index to his mind, as it is scarcely possible that more horrible features could be associated in one human being.

The libel upon the Duke was built upon that fruitful episode, his attempted murder by the valet Sellis twenty-two years ago. It described the Duke and Neale as accomplices in the grossest and most unnatural immorality, whose guilt was discovered by Sellis. The latter was therefore murdered by Neale upon the Duke's orders. The Duke's wounds and Halford's visit were arranged ; important witnesses, including a man named Jew, had not been called and an amenable second jury selected by Lord Chief Justice Ellenborough.

The Duke decided that with this, the slanders and libels which he had suffered in silence for so many years had gone far enough ; whatever the explanation of the Sellis affair, queer things had taken place that night and it was now so remote that spurious accounts could easily circulate which would have nowhere gained credence in the decade following it. As time had passed, such stories, vague and untraceable, had been in the air and now that they appeared in a convenient and tangible form in this book an excellent opportunity was presented for scotching them once and for all. The Duke therefore consulted Sir Charles Wetherell, whom he entrusted with the prosecution of the libeller. The case opened in the King's Bench on the 1st May 1883. Defending counsel, a Mr. Wakefield, who had undertaken the cause without a fee *solely for the good cause*, immediately showed the peculiar position of the litigant and the means by which, it was hoped, he would be induced not to proceed with the action. Wakefield said that it was undignified for the Duke to order a prosecution and that he was ill-advised, for this, instead of deterring calumny, would cause even more. In other words, the Duke was not to prosecute a libeller under the threat that an even greater campaign would be opened against him. Sir Charles immediately seized upon this. The defence, he said, was saying " that if he dares, as a Prince of the House of Brunswick, to come into this Court and claim at Your Lordship's hands that which the lowest of the King's subjects has the right to claim, namely, that his case should be fairly and impartially heard, then—that his dignity as a Prince will be let down, and that he will merit, and consistently with his merit, obtain, an accumulated load of calumny, insult and reproach. . . . My learned friend has attempted to avert this prosecution and the course of justice by insinuating a threat against the Duke of Cumberland."

Sir Benjamin Bloomfield and Sir Wathen Waller described their visits to the Duke the morning following the attempt on his life, and Adams and Place carefully described the procedure followed at the inquest, then the Duke himself went into the witness-box and answered Sir Charles's questions. He gave an account of the attack on himself and pointed to the places where he had been wounded, the scars still to be seen.

Philips and his counsel had believed Jew, whose real name was Joseph Joux, and who was the alleged source of the story, to be either dead or untraceable after all these years. He had apparently gone to Belgium in the service of Prince Leopold and was considered quite out of the way. Now the prosecution announced that he was waiting to give evidence. He denied any connection with the publication whatsoever. His only part in the Sellis affair had been that of the footman who had called Sir Henry Halford to the scene.

Of course, the defence could only plead for mercy and that the pamphlet was a piece of folly. What a change from that bold sentence, " The brutality of this Prince is best proved by the apparent ease and indifference he manifested when he knew himself to be universally hated," written when the miserable author felt himself safe in following the fashion of libelling the Duke of Cumberland ! Now he was called to render an account. " I have thought," said Wakefield, " that magnanimity was a large, noble quality—that it was one which enabled the possessor of it to overlook all petty injuries—all minor insults—all attacks upon his character which could not be believed." Was it to be believed " that His Royal Highness has suffered one tittle of injury whatever, from the publication in question ? I own that I cannot understand how a person of his exalted rank can suffer by the attack of a man who is almost anonymous." He also whimpered that he was a poor lawyer compared with the illustrious counsel who represented the plaintiff.

Without retiring, the jury found the defendant guilty, and Lord Denman sentenced him to six months' imprisonment. This was the height of lenity in view of the monstrous nature of the libel ; a lesser one had been punished much more severely in 1813, and the moderation in this case can only be ascribed to the fact that the judge had been one of the Duke's worst political enemies—he had spoken against him in the debates upon his income in Parliament—and was allowing his politics to influence his judicial actions. In any case, Philips broke his bail and fled the country. The fact, however, that both in 1810 and 1833 bitter enemies of the Duke found themselves engaged in clearing his reputation is not without significance.

This prosecution had a very salutary effect. So much had been said and written about the Duke with impunity that it had become taken for granted that it was done in perfect safety. Now it was shown that he was protected by the Law as much as anyone else. The libels which had followed upon one another as a matter of course for the last seven years suddenly ceased. Indeed, the effects of the trial became immediately apparent through an unfortunate incident which took place just before the Duke left the country in 1833. One of his servants, a table-decker named Hampfeldt, dreaded for some reason of his own returning to Germany and drowned himself in the Thames, leaving a note attacking his master and the pantry-man, Ball. In this jealousy there was a strange echo of the Sellis affair. Ball had found him drunk and forbidden him the pantry. When the Duke's plate had been sent to London for the journey, Hampfeldt remained at Kew, as the Duke needed him there, but he thought it to be a sign of distrust resulting from the incident. The inquest was held at Mortlake on the 24th September and the Duke went to it. Anxious that no stories should arise from this, he announced that he would give every possible assistance and he and Jelf frequently questioned the witnesses, all of whom spoke highly for their master. How was it that this event, with all its possibilities for exploitation, was not the signal for another great campaign against the Duke? The recent trial of Philips provides the answer.

There remains to be recorded only a trivial and almost imbecile attempt to defame the Duke of Cumberland, which was, however, foiled in advance. A man named Ashe had written a book of the usual pattern and the manuscript had come into the Duke's hands. Thereupon, the author threatened that he would assassinate him if he did not surrender it. It seemed as if he were in earnest, for he walked all the way from Carlisle to London and was seen loitering about Kew. The Duke's friends, including Lord Kenyon (whose letter is preserved in the Add. MSS.), warned him to take care, but the Duke was ever indifferent to such dangers. The suspect was eventually taken into custody and the Chief of the Bow Police called on the Duke to announce this. Formerly, the Duke explained, he had not bothered about his threats as he did not know who he was, " and he styling himself a *captain*, I could not say that I was in bodily fear of any man, but that *now* I looked upon him not as a gentleman and therefore could only consider him as a coalheaver or a blackguard in the street and not put myself on a par with him." On the 11th March 1835 the Duke, accompanied (as nearly everywhere) by Holmes, went to the Magistrate's office, where the " miserable " culprit was brought in between two Peelers, completely broken down. " My Lord," he pleaded, " I am the greatest miscreant that exists. Bred and born a gentleman, having been an officer, too, in the army, I have *forfeited* the character of a gentleman. My whole excuse is that I have aberrations of mind, and having been wounded in the head am at times deranged and know not what I say, write or do, and thus I have calumniated a Prince whom I ought to have venerated. I throw myself to your mercy." (G.A., Duke to Duchess, 6th and 11th March 1835). As a harmless case, the man was merely bound over to keep the peace for two years.

In the campaigns of calumny against him, the life of the Duke of Cumberland must be a historical curiosity, though, as has been seen, such were to a certain extent the accepted weapons of the " progressives," and all those who stood in their way, particularly the family of George III, have suffered in varying degrees from them. With none, however, did they approach the viciousness of those against the Duke of Cumberland, and many will consider his scornful defiance of his tormentors, who goaded him at his every move and turn throughout all the years of his life, the greatest proof of his moral courage and conviction.

SOURCES

THE Duke of Cumberland's letters are a chaotic jumble of languages —English, French and German—which sometimes relieve each other in the middle of a sentence. His script is all but illegible, possibly as a result of his poor eyesight, though from 1843 onwards the letters are nearly all dictated, and as his thoughts raced ahead of his pen, one sentence frequently gives way to another before it is completed. The letters to his wife are mostly in French, those to his Prussian relatives in German, to his Mecklenburg relatives in French and German, to his son and the Duke of Brunswick in English and to his other friends and acquaintances according to their own language. The abbreviations below are the signatures used in the footnotes.

W.A.   The Queen's archives at Windsor. Those marked with an asterisk are published in *The Letters of George IV*.
G.A.   The Prince of Hanover's archives at Gmunden, in Upper Austria.
M.A.   The Prince of Hanover's archives at Schloss Marienburg, near Hanover.
S.A.   The Archives of the Grand Duke of Mecklenburg.
H.A.   The State Archives in Hanover.
F.O.   The Foreign Office Papers in the Public Record Office.
W.O.   The War Office Papers in the Public Record Office.

The Liverpool, Place and miscellaneous Add. MSS in the British Museum. The papers of the Earl of Eldon, Baron von Linsingen, Count von Grote, the Vaterländisches Museum in Celle and the Counts von Bennigsen in Banteln.

PRINTED WORKS

Almost any memoir of the first half of the nineteenth century will contain references to the Duke of Cumberland, but they rarely reveal anything which is not better covered by research from original sources. Only those that do so are listed here. Various pamphlets, manifestos and similar publications of the time of his reign are not included.

ANONYMOUS. *A Minute Detail of the Attempt to Assassinate the Duke of Cumberland.* London, 1810.
—— *The Trial of Joseph Philips for a Libel on the Duke of Cumberland.* London, 1833.
—— Königin Luise. Berlin, 1849.
ARTHUR, SIR GEORGE. *The Story of the Household Cavalry.* London, 1909.
BURNEY, FRANCES, afterwards D'ARBLAY. *Diary and Journals*, 1778–1840. Edited by her niece, Charlotte Barrett, 1842–46.

BUCKINGHAM, DUKE OF. *Memoirs of the Regency.*

BROUGHAM, LORD. *The Life and Times of Lord Brougham.* London, 1871.

CASTLEREAGH, LORD. *Memoirs and Correspondence,* edited by Lord Londonderry. London, 1848–53.

CHARLOTTE, PRINCESS. *Letters of Princess Charlotte,* edited by A. Aspinall. London, 1949.

COKE, LADY MARY. *Letters and Journals.* Edinburgh, 1889–96.

COTTON, SERGEANT-MAJOR EDWARD. *A Voice from Waterloo.* Brussels, 1849.

CREEVEY, THOMAS. *The Creevey Papers,* edited by Sir Herbert Maxwell. London, 1904.

—— *More Creevey Papers,* edited by John Gore. London, 1934.

CROKER, JOHN WILSON. *The Croker Papers,* edited by L. Jennings. London, 1885.

ELIZABETH, PRINCESS. *Letters to Miss Swinburne,* edited by P. Yorke. 1898.

ELLENBOROUGH, LORD. *Diary.* London, 1881.

ERNEST AUGUSTUS, KING. *Letters of the King of Hanover to Viscount Strangford.* London, 1925.

—— Revolutionsbriefe (containing letters to King Frederick William IV of Prussia, 1848–49). Edited by Karl Haenchen. Leipzig, 1930. This is denoted in the footnotes by the letters RB.

—— Letters to same, 1849–51, edited by Karl Haenchen. Niedersächsisches Jahrbuch für Landesgeschichte, 1934. This is denoted in the footnotes by the letters NSJB.

—— Letters to General Count von Wallmoden and his wife, 1848–51. *Ibidem,* 1952.

—— *Answer of His Royal Highness the Duke of Cumberland to the Address of the Grand Orange Lodge of Longford,* 1835.

—— Ernst August Album. A description of the unveiling of the memorial to the King in 1861. Hanover, 1862.

—— Sammelband in the Landesbibliothek, Hanover, i.e. poems, sermons, dedications, accounts of ceremonies, etc., bound into a volume.

FARINGTON, JOSEPH. *The Farington Diary,* edited by J. Greig. London, 1922–28.

FITZGERALD, PERCY. *Dukes and Princesses of the Family of George III.* London, 1882.

—— *William IV and his Times.* London, 1884.

FONBLANQUE, EDWARD DE. *Lives of the Lords Strangford.* London, 1877.

FORD, GUY STANTON. *Hanover and Prussia,* 1795–1803, *a Study in Neutrality.* Columbia University series. New York, 1903.

FORTESQUE, THE HON. SIR JOHN. *A History of the British Army.* 1899–1930.

FRENSDORFF, FERDINAND. Article on King Ernest Augustus in Allgemeine Deutsche Biographie. 1884.

—— Die englischen Prinzen in Göttingen. Zeitschrift des historischen Vereins für Niedersachsen. 1905.

GEORGE III, KING. *Letters of George III,* edited by Fortesque. 1927.

GEORGE IV, KING. *Letters of George IV,* edited by A. Aspinall. Cambridge, 1938.

GIBBS, THE HON. VICARY. *The Complete Peerage.* 1910.

GOETHE, JOHANN WOLFGANG VON. Briefe an Großherzog Carl August. 1863.

—— Die Campagne in Frankreich. 1792. 1868.

—— Briefwechsel zwischen Goethe und Zelter. Berlin, 1834.

GREVILLE, CHARLES. *Memoirs.* London, 1888.

GREY, EARL. *Correspondence of King William IV and Earl Grey, 1830–32.* London, 1867.

HALL, SIR JOHN. *The Bravo Mystery and other Cases.* London, 1932.

HARCOURT. *The Harcourt Papers.* Privately printed.

HARTMANN, R. Geschichte Hannovers von den ältesten Zeiten bis auf die Gegenwart. Hanover, 1886.

HASSELL, W. VON. Geschichte des Königreichs Hannover. Bremen, 1898.

JESSE, J. H. *The Life and Reign of George III.* London, 1867.

JACKSON, SIR GEORGE. *The Bath Archives,* edited by Lady Jackson. London, 1873.

JORDAN, MRS. *Mrs. Jordan and her Family,* edited by A. Aspinall. London, 1951.

KNIGHT, CORNELIA. *Autobiography,* edited by Sir J. W. Kaye. London, 1861.

KNIGHTON, SIR WILLIAM. *Memoirs,* edited by Lady Knighton. London, 1838.

KNIGGE, FREIHERR. Tagebuch eines Hannoverschen Offiziers, 1848–49. (Author's name not given in book.)

KOBBE. Memoiren eines Hannoverschen Landgendarmen.

LANDMANN, COLONEL, R. E. *Adventures and Recollections.* London, 1852.

LIEVEN, PRINCESS. *Letters,* edited by Robinson. 1902.

—— *Diary,* edited by Temperley. 1925.

—— *Correspondence with Lady Cowper,* edited by Lord Sudley. 1943.

—— *Correspondence with Earl Grey,* edited by C. le Strange. 1890.

LEVENSON-GOWER, LORD GRANVILLE. *Private Correspondence,* edited by the Countess Granville. 1916.

LINSINGEN, VON. Aus Hannovers militärischer Vergangenheit. (Author's name not given in book.)

LONDONDERRY, MARQUESS OF. *Narrative of the War in France and Germany, 1813–14.*

MALORTIE, C. E. VON. König Ernst August. Hanover, 1861.

—— FAMILY VON. Nachrichten der Familie von Malortie.

—— BARON C. VON. *'Twixt Old Times and New.* London, 1898.

MUEHLHEN, BERNHARD. Hannover und sein Ministerium, 1849–50. Niedersächsisches Jahrbuch für Landesgeschichte, 1950.

MUNK, H. *The Life of Sir Henry Halford.*

NEUMANN, PHILIP VON. *Diary.* London.

NORTON, T. *The Duke of Cumberland, and a Word, by the Way, of Cant and Slander.* 1832.

OPPERMANN, HEINRICH. Zur Geschichte des Königreichs Hannover. Leipzig, 1860–62.

PAPENDIEK, MRS. *The Journals of Mrs. Papendiek.* London, 1887.

PARKER, CHARLES S. *Sir Robert Peel.* London, 1891–99.

PLOWDEN, FRANCIS. *History of Ireland,* 1801–10. Dublin, 1811.

POCKWITZ, L. Einzug Seiner Königlichen Hoheit des Herzogs von Cumberland in Hannover. Hanover, 1814.

ROMILLY, SIR SAMUEL. *Memoirs.* London, 1840.

ROSENDAHL, ERICH. Geschichte Niedersachsens. Hanover, 1927.

ROTHERT, WILHELM. Allgemeine Hannoversche Biographie. Hanover, 1912.

RUTTON, WILLIAM. *The Royal Residences of Kew.* 1905.

SHELLEY, LADY. *The Diary of Frances, Lady Shelley,* edited by R. Edgecumbe.

SICHART, L. VON. Geschichte der Königlich Hannoverschen Armee. Hanover, 1866–98.

SLICHER, MAJOR-GENERAL VON. Tagebücher der Reise nach England, 1843. From Hannoversche Geschichtsblätter, 1898.

STANHOPE, GILBERT. *A Mystic on the Prussian Throne.* London, 1912.

STANHOPE, LADY HESTER. *Memoirs, as Related by Herself in Conversations with her Physician.* 1845.

STUART, DOROTHY M. *The Daughters of George III.* 1939.

TAYLOR, SIR HERBERT. *The Taylor Papers.* London, 1913.

TREITSCHKE, N. VON. Deutsche Geschichte im neunzehnten Jahrhundert. Leipzig, 1889.

TREVELYAN, G. M. *Lord Grey of the Reform Bill.* London, 1920.

TWISS, HORACE. *The Public and Private Life of Lord Eldon.* London, 1844.

VAN THAL, HERBERT. *Ernest Augustus, A Brief Survey of the Man and His Times.* London, 1936.

VICTORIA, QUEEN. *The Girlhood of Queen Victoria,* edited by Lord Esher. 1912.

—— *The Letters of Queen Victoria,* 1837–61, edited by Lord Esher. 1908.

WALPOLE, SIR SPENCER. *Life of the Right Hon. Spencer Perceval.* 1874.

WELLINGTON, DUKE OF. *Correspondence and Memoranda,* 1819–32. London, 1867–80.

WILKINSON, REVEREND C. A. *Reminiscences of the Court and Times of King Ernest of Hanover.* London, 1886.

WILLIS, G. M. König Ernst August von Hannover im Licht neuer Forschungen. Hanover, 1951.

—— with HOWES, F. N. *Notes on Kew and the King of Hanover.* Kew Bulletin, 1950.

WYLLY, COLONEL H. C. *The 15th King's Hussars,* 1759–1913. London, 1914.

YONGE, C. *Life of Lord Liverpool.* London, 1868.

PERIODICALS, ETC.

Times, Gentlemen's Magazine, Annual Register, Morning Herald, Public Advertiser, St. James's Chronicle, Globe, Hansard, Heimatkalender, Deutsch-Hannoversches Taschenkalender, Hannoversche Zeitung; various local journals.

INDEX